Soviet and Post-Soviet Politi
ISSN 1614-3515

General Editor: Andreas Umland,
Stockholm Centre for Eastern European Studies, andreas.uml

EDITORIAL COMMITTEE*

DOMESTIC & COMPARATIVE POLITICS
Prof. **Ellen Bos**, *Andrássy University of Budapest*
Dr. **Gergana Dimova**, *University of Winchester*
Dr. **Andrey Kazantsev**, *MGIMO (U) MID RF, Moscow*
Prof. **Heiko Pleines**, *University of Bremen*
Prof. **Richard Sakwa**, *University of Kent at Canterbury*
Dr. **Sarah Whitmore**, *Oxford Brookes University*
Dr. **Harald Wydra**, *University of Cambridge*

SOCIETY, CLASS & ETHNICITY
Col. **David Glantz**, *"Journal of Slavic Military Studies"*
Dr. **Marlène Laruelle**, *George Washington University*
Dr. **Stephen Shulman**, *Southern Illinois University*
Prof. **Stefan Troebst**, *University of Leipzig*

POLITICAL ECONOMY & PUBLIC POLICY
Dr. **Andreas Goldthau**, *Central European University*
Dr. **Robert Kravchuk**, *University of North Carolina*
Dr. **David Lane**, *University of Cambridge*
Dr. **Carol Leonard**, *Higher School of Economics, Moscow*
Dr. **Maria Popova**, *McGill University, Montreal*

FOREIGN POLICY & INTERNATIONAL AFFAIRS
Dr. **Peter Duncan**, *University College London*
Prof. **Andreas Heinemann-Grüder**, *University of Bonn*
Prof. **Gerhard Mangott**, *University of Innsbruck*
Dr. **Diana Schmidt-Pfister**, *University of Konstanz*
Dr. **Lisbeth Tarlow**, *Harvard University, Cambridge*
Dr. **Christian Wipperfürth**, *N-Ost Network, Berlin*
Dr. **William Zimmerman**, *University of Michigan*

HISTORY, CULTURE & THOUGHT
Dr. **Catherine Andreyev**, *University of Oxford*
Prof. **Mark Bassin**, *Södertörn University*
Prof. **Karsten Brüggemann**, *Tallinn University*
Dr. **Alexander Etkind**, *University of Cambridge*
Dr. **Gasan Gusejnov**, *Moscow State University*
Prof. **Leonid Luks**, *Catholic University of Eichstaett*
Dr. **Olga Malinova**, *Russian Academy of Sciences*
Dr. **Richard Mole**, *University College London*
Prof. **Andrei Rogatchevski**, *University of Tromsø*
Dr. **Mark Tauger**, *West Virginia University*

ADVISORY BOARD*

Prof. **Dominique Arel**, *University of Ottawa*
Prof. **Jörg Baberowski**, *Humboldt University of Berlin*
Prof. **Margarita Balmaceda**, *Seton Hall University*
Dr. **John Barber**, *University of Cambridge*
Prof. **Timm Beichelt**, *European University Viadrina*
Dr. **Katrin Boeckh**, *University of Munich*
Prof. em. **Archie Brown**, *University of Oxford*
Dr. **Vyacheslav Bryukhovetsky**, *Kyiv-Mohyla Academy*
Prof. **Timothy Colton**, *Harvard University, Cambridge*
Prof. **Paul D'Anieri**, *University of Florida*
Dr. **Heike Dörrenbächer**, *Friedrich Naumann Foundation*
Dr. **John Dunlop**, *Hoover Institution, Stanford, California*
Dr. **Sabine Fischer**, *SWP, Berlin*
Dr. **Geir Flikke**, *NUPI, Oslo*
Prof. **David Galbreath**, *University of Aberdeen*
Prof. **Alexander Galkin**, *Russian Academy of Sciences*
Prof. **Frank Golczewski**, *University of Hamburg*
Dr. **Nikolas Gvosdev**, *Naval War College, Newport, RI*
Prof. **Mark von Hagen**, *Arizona State University*
Dr. **Guido Hausmann**, *University of Munich*
Prof. **Dale Herspring**, *Kansas State University*
Dr. **Stefani Hoffman**, *Hebrew University of Jerusalem*
Prof. **Mikhail Ilyin**, *MGIMO (U) MID RF, Moscow*
Prof. **Vladimir Kantor**, *Higher School of Economics*
Dr. **Ivan Katchanovski**, *University of Ottawa*
Prof. em. **Andrzej Korbonski**, *University of California*
Dr. **Iris Kempe**, *"Caucasus Analytical Digest"*
Prof. **Herbert Küpper**, *Institut für Ostrecht Regensburg*
Dr. **Rainer Lindner**, *CEEER, Berlin*
Dr. **Vladimir Malakhov**, *Russian Academy of Sciences*

Dr. **Luke March**, *University of Edinburgh*
Prof. **Michael McFaul**, *Stanford University, Palo Alto*
Prof. **Birgit Menzel**, *University of Mainz-Germersheim*
Prof. **Valery Mikhailenko**, *The Urals State University*
Prof. **Emil Pain**, *Higher School of Economics, Moscow*
Dr. **Oleg Podvintsev**, *Russian Academy of Sciences*
Prof. **Olga Popova**, *St. Petersburg State University*
Dr. **Alex Pravda**, *University of Oxford*
Dr. **Erik van Ree**, *University of Amsterdam*
Dr. **Joachim Rogall**, *Robert Bosch Foundation Stuttgart*
Prof. **Peter Rutland**, *Wesleyan University, Middletown*
Prof. **Marat Salikov**, *The Urals State Law Academy*
Dr. **Gwendolyn Sasse**, *University of Oxford*
Prof. **Jutta Scherrer**, *EHESS, Paris*
Prof. **Robert Service**, *University of Oxford*
Mr. **James Sherr**, *RIIA Chatham House London*
Dr. **Oxana Shevel**, *Tufts University, Medford*
Prof. **Eberhard Schneider**, *University of Siegen*
Prof. **Olexander Shnyrkov**, *Shevchenko University, Kyiv*
Prof. **Hans-Henning Schröder**, *SWP, Berlin*
Prof. **Yuri Shapoval**, *Ukrainian Academy of Sciences*
Prof. **Viktor Shnirelman**, *Russian Academy of Sciences*
Dr. **Lisa Sundstrom**, *University of British Columbia*
Dr. **Philip Walters**, *"Religion, State and Society"*, *Oxford*
Prof. **Zenon Wasyliw**, *Ithaca College, New York State*
Dr. **Lucan Way**, *University of Toronto*
Dr. **Markus Wehner**, *"Frankfurter Allgemeine Zeitung"*
Dr. **Andrew Wilson**, *University College London*
Prof. **Jan Zielonka**, *University of Oxford*
Prof. **Andrei Zorin**, *University of Oxford*

* While the Editorial Committee and Advisory Board support the General Editor in the choice and improvement of manuscripts for publication, responsibility for remaining errors and misinterpretations in the series' volumes lies with the books' authors.

Soviet and Post-Soviet Politics and Society (SPPS)
ISSN 1614-3515

Founded in 2004 and refereed since 2007, SPPS makes available affordable English-, German-, and Russian-language studies on the history of the countries of the former Soviet bloc from the late Tsarist period to today. It publishes between 5 and 20 volumes per year and focuses on issues in transitions to and from democracy such as economic crisis, identity formation, civil society development, and constitutional reform in CEE and the NIS. SPPS also aims to highlight so far understudied themes in East European studies such as right-wing radicalism, religious life, higher education, or human rights protection. The authors and titles of all previously published volumes are listed at the end of this book. For a full description of the series and reviews of its books, see www.ibidem-verlag.de/red/spps.

Editorial correspondence & manuscripts should be sent to: Dr. Andreas Umland, Department of Political Science, Kyiv-Mohyla Academy, vul. Voloska 8/5, UA-04070 Kyiv, UKRAINE; andreas.umland@cantab.net

Business correspondence & review copy requests should be sent to: *ibidem* Press, Leuschnerstr. 40, 30457 Hannover, Germany; tel.: +49 511 2622200; fax: +49 511 2622201; spps@ibidem.eu.

Authors, reviewers, referees, and editors for (as well as all other persons sympathetic to) SPPS are invited to join its networks at www.facebook.com/group.php?gid=52638198614
www.linkedin.com/groups?about=&gid=103012
www.xing.com/net/spps-ibidem-verlag/

Recent Volumes

230   *Christopher Ford*
UKAPISME–Une Gauche Perdue
Le marxisme anti-colonial dans la révolution ukrainienne 1917 - 1925
Avec une préface de Vincent Présumey
ISBN 978-3-8382-0899-2

231   *Anna Kutkina*
Between Lenin and Bandera
Decommunization and Multivocality in Post-Euromaidan Ukraine
With a foreword by Juri Mykkänen
ISBN 978-3-8382-1506-8

232   *Lincoln E. Flake*
Defending the Faith
The Russian Orthodox Church and the Demise of Religious Pluralism
With a foreword by Peter Martland
ISBN 978-3-8382-1378-1

233   *Nikoloz Samkharadze*
Russia's Recognition of the Independence of Abkhazia and South Ossetia
Analysis of a Deviant Case in Moscow's Foreign Policy Behavior
With a foreword by Neil MacFarlane
ISBN 978-3-8382-1414-6

234   *Arve Hansen*
Urban Protest
A Spatial Perspective on Kyiv, Minsk, and Moscow
With a foreword by Julie Wilhelmsen
ISBN 978-3-8382-1495-5

235   *Eleonora Narvselius, Julie Fedor (Eds.)*
Diversity in the East-Central European Borderlands
Memories, Cityscapes, People
ISBN 978-3-8382-1523-5

236   *Regina Elsner*
The Russian Orthodox Church and Modernity
A Historical and Theological Investigation into Eastern Christianity between Unity and Plurality
With a foreword by Mikhail Suslov
ISBN 978-3-8382-1568-6

237   *Bo Petersson*
The Putin Predicament
Problems of Legitimacy and Succession in Russia
With a foreword by J. Paul Goode
ISBN 978-3-8382-1050-6

238   *Jonathan Otto Pohl*
The Years of Great Silence
The Deportation, Special Settlement, and Mobilization into the Labor Army of Ethnic Germans in the USSR, 1941–1955
ISBN 978-3-8382-1630-0

Mikhail Minakov (Ed.)

INVENTING MAJORITIES

Ideological Creativity in Post-Soviet Societies

Bibliographic information published by the Deutsche Nationalbibliothek
Die Deutsche Nationalbibliothek lists this publication in the Deutsche Nationalbibliografie; detailed bibliographic data are available in the Internet at http://dnb.d-nb.de.

Bibliografische Information der Deutschen Nationalbibliothek
Die Deutsche Nationalbibliothek verzeichnet diese Publikation in der Deutschen Nationalbibliografie; detaillierte bibliografische Daten sind im Internet über http://dnb.d-nb.de abrufbar.

ISBN-13: 978-3-8382-1641-6
© *ibidem*-Verlag, Stuttgart 2022
All rights reserved.

No part of this publication may be reproduced, stored in or introduced into a retrieval system, or transmitted, in any form, or by any means (electronic, mechanical, photocopying, recording or otherwise) without the prior written permission of the publisher. Any person who does any unauthorized act in relation to this publication may be liable to criminal prosecution and civil claims for damages.

Alle Rechte vorbehalten. Das Werk einschließlich aller seiner Teile ist urheberrechtlich geschützt. Jede Verwertung außerhalb der engen Grenzen des Urheberrechtsgesetzes ist ohne Zustimmung des Verlages unzulässig und strafbar. Dies gilt insbesondere für Vervielfältigungen, Übersetzungen, Mikroverfilmungen und elektronische Speicherformen sowie die Einspeicherung und Verarbeitung in elektronischen Systemen.

Printed in the United States of America

Contents

Mikhail Minakov
Ideological Creativity. Introduction to Post-Soviet
Ideologies 7

I Self, Otherness, and Ideology

Natalia Kudriavtseva
1 Reconfiguring Identities within the Cityscape: Ideologies
of Ukraine's Decommunization Renaming 27

Petra Colmorgen
2 The Friends So Far, the Foes So Near? Ambiguities of
Georgia's Othering 55

Nadiia Koval and Ivan Gomza
3 The Splendid School Assembled: Studying and Practicing
International Relations in Independent Ukraine 85

Augusto Dala Costa
4 Toponymy and the Issues of Memory and Identity on the
Post-soviet Tbilisi Cityscape 141

Roman Horbyk, Yana Prymachenko and Yuliya Yurchuk
5 Mediatization of History: Introducing the Concept and
Key Cases from Eastern Europe 177

II Post-Soviet Sovereigntism in Comparative Perspective

Oleksandr Fisun and Nataliya Vinnykova
6 The Rise of Precarious States: A Shadow Side of
Sovereignity Loss 205

Ruslan Zaporozhchenko
7   Sovereigntism as a Vocation and Profession: Imperial Roots,
    Current State, Possible Prospects 231

Mikhail Minakov
8   Sovereignty as a Contested Concept: The Cases of
    Trumpism and Putinism 281

Gulnara Shaikhutdinova
9   Implementing International Human Rights Law: Recent
    Sovereigntist and Nationalist Trends 321

Yurii Mielkov
10 The Evolution of Sovereignty: From Nation State to
    Human Person 343

    On the Authors 363

    Index 369

Ideological Creativity
Introduction to Post-Soviet Ideologies

Mikhail Minakov

The Ontological Foundations of Human Creativity

Human being is an existence with a capacity for creative self-realization in the world. "To be" means to participate in the world's continual change, to re-interpret it and to launch new beginnings within it. Each human presence in the world is limited by the time span of individual existence, from birth to death. Yet human presence transcends these limits due to the intersubjectivity of individual existence and to the interobjectivity of the material change resulting from humans' creative presence in the world. As human beings we are born into the world created before us (by human and non-human existences), and we leave it with our addition to it. Human beings are a part of the many forces participating in a creative interplay of the world's creation and re-creation.

This philosophical proposition also translates into the ontology of politics. Politics is one of several spheres in which human creative existence—individual and collective—is dominant. To study politics and its many phenomena means to add to the understanding of what human being/s is/are in his/her/their individual-collective ontological interwovenness of (co)presence.

Authority and subjection, conflict and agreement, freedom and serfdom, justice and crime, citizenship and statelessness, individual and common good—these and many other political phenomena stem from our transpersonal copresence. In this copresence humans are doomed to communicate, to reach for conclusions and to implement them together. Such communication is a rich process, one that allows human individuals to convey their conditions: formulated as equality or inequality, an active or passive position, a central or marginal role, acceptance or resistance vis-à-vis the results of yet another communicative act. And each act is an act of creation, a decision that alters a human's behavior and the material conditions of their life, their social reality.

Imagery is an important part of social reality. Human imagination is a complex cognitive act which unites various other human cognitive faculties in reaching out toward stable cognitive posits—ideas, conclusions, beliefs—that translate into action and change of reality. Basically, by creating imagery and causing a change in reality, the human imagination can be understood as one of human creativity's key elements.

Creativity and Imagination

The imagination is an object of study from many perspectives, including philosophy, psychology, sociology and political science.

In *philosophy*, imagination is interpreted as a cognitive operation with a thing or situation, whereby all rational categories are applied to the possible object of sensation that is not given at the time (Plato 1989; Aristotle 1964; Vico 1956; Kant 2013; Heidegger 1997; Ricoeur 1994; Cocking 2005; Bottici 2014). For over two thousand years, imagination was considered a faculty joining fantasy (Plato, Aristotle) and productivity (Kant), and enabling an understanding of other humans and/or being itself (Heidegger, Ricoeur). A concise resume to this line of philosophical argumentation was offered by Paul Ricoeur, who famously defined the imagination as a cognitive act that can simultaneously be used:

> to think of things, which are not present in the current perception, but which can exist,
> to create in the mind images of things that do not and cannot exist, and
> to bring about images representing things, persons, and/or ideas. (Ricoeur 1994: 120ff)

Which means that imagination unites aspects of fantasy, virtuality and possibility in cognition.

Another cognitive aspect of imagination is problem-solving. The pragmatists have interpreted the imagination as a key human faculty for managing situations of uncertainty by merging work with the past (memory), work with the future (fantasy), and work with the current situation (intelligence). In doing so, imagination creates a list of possible solutions (Dewey 1998: 32, 87ff, 189ff; Rorty 1998: 167ff).

However, the imagination has other, non-cognitive dimensions that are critical for understanding individual and collective human life. Those dimensions actually include emotional, social, political, cultural and other aspects. From the existential point of view, human life consists of many acts, which also involve projections and existential acts of fulfilling the projected, allowing the projected to be (Husserl 1980; Heidegger 1996, 1997; Sartre 2001). Here the imagination plays the huge role of making these acts meaningful, possible, and creative.

Philosophers also see imagination as a critical human faculty for constructing social reality and selves in correlation with collective identities. This social dimension of imagination is equally studied in social phenomenology (Berger & Luckman 1956; Schutz & Luckman 1960), philosophical critique (Castoriadis 1987, 1997a, 1997b; Marcuse 1991; Fadieiev 2021), and political philosophy (Taylor 1989, 2004; Honnet 1995). The common ground here is the understanding of imagination as the main source of meaning in social life, providing human individuals and collectives with a framework for the interpretation and practical change of reality.

Contemporary psychology tests many ideas discussed by philosophers. However, psychology's major focus has been on the imagination's ability to connect ideal and material spheres in human feeling and action. From this point of view, imagination is a higher psychological function, aiming to "build things acting as if they were abstractions, and build abstractions acting as if they were real things," and thus to transcend the dichotomy of ideal and material (Tateo 2015a: 146, 2015b: 4ff).

The synthetic and productive force of imagination also transcends the individual–collective dichotomy. For example, in her empirical psychology studies, Jacqueline Adams found that "the imagination permeates our decision-making, routinely enters our thoughts, is a domain in which individuals immerse themselves regularly, and, in the form of collective imaginings, can inspire social change" (Adams 2004: 277). This and many other studies (Newman 1993; Pileggi et al. 2000; Kane et al. 2007; Zittoun and Cerchia

2013; Oklopcic 2018) show that imagination is a central function of mind, which constantly brings the individual psyche out of a now-reality into some other "space," and this "space" is of a transpersonal or intersubjective nature (Killingsworth and Gilbert 2010; Schooler et al. 2011; Mooneyham and Schooler 2013; Smallwood 2013). These "mind travels" seem to be another way of describing the imagination's power to offer alternative situations as problem-solving or adaptational practices.

Psychologists also show the imagination's rootedness in collective human presence. For example, Adams (2004) concludes from her studies of decision-making in cross-cultural families:

> Finally, class and nationality may be among the shapers of the imagination. Of those in the middle class, dreams might be different from those of the working class... Many people from the same nation have shared imaginings, or collective fantasies, and different cultures have different imaginative traditions or themes. The shared imaginings can be about other people... (Adams 2004: 294–5)

These social and political roots link contemporary psychology and political sciences with respect to their interest in imagination.

Political science studies imagination as an important aspect of human participation in political life. One example can be a vision of the past, present and future shared by a political community or society. In a recent study of political imagination, researchers found that the "process of imagination extends not only to how we anticipate the development of our personal lives, but also how we envision the future of our social groups, be they micro-groups such as families, or macro-groups such as nations or even the fate of humanity itself" (De Saint-Laurent et al. 2018: 4). Imagination turns individuals into participants and co-authors of transpersonal, imaginary — and thus, socially real and affectively perceived — worlds.

Special attention is paid to the political creativity that merges the "unreal" projections (fantasies) with "real" political consequences through an interplay of present, future and past. Tania Zittoun and Alex Gillespie (2018) studied several cases in which the political imagination of the future was applied for the same situation as our study: the quest to remedy collective traumas. In their study they show that:

> Imagination [of collective future] involves a three-step sequence. First, there is a trigger—usually, disruptions of some kind questioning a person's involvement in a current conduct that initiate the person's uncoupling from the proximal sphere of experience... Second, the burgeoning loop of imagination utilizes resources—drawn from a wide range of semiotic and material elements previously internalized by the person along the life course, or present in the immediate environment, through the presence of others, the affordances of the setting, or the power of guidance of complex artefacts... Third, the sequence ends with a return—when the person loops out of imagining, and recouples with her proximal circumstances, a few seconds or hours older. (Zittoun & Gillespie 2018: 17)

Such processes took place when dissidents, or the politicians who brought down the Berlin Wall, or started Perestroika in USSR, imagined a free post-communist world (ibid., 19–20).

The use of time in political imagination preconditions the understanding of common good, of who belongs to the groups deemed to be legitimate participants, and of the rules of political actions. In these terms, the imagination of the past, in terms of collective memories, is one of the constant factors predefining political action. For example, Constance de Saint-Laurent (2018) analyzed the political imagination of the past in terms of "collective memories." Her studies show three main models of the political use of the past (collective memory, history):

> history as a "frame of reference, determining the main actors and the roles they should play in the future"; history as "a source of experiences and examples" of what is "likely, possible, or desirable"; and history as "generalizable experience from which global representations of the world can be built, which in turn, inform the imagination of collective futures" (de Saint-Laurent 2018: 64).

So imagination of the past represents a faculty of specific conservative creativity that deals with phenomena from academic historical imagination to radical nostalgia with political consequences.

The political imagination of the future is vested in the understanding of purposes, of possible and impossible plans, of virtual problems and disasters. The radical imagination deals with utopian visions. The functionality of such imagination aims at "keeping us from becoming complacent with the present" (McBride 10), at looking for "new beginnings" (Arendt 1963: 12ff) in spheres of equality, justice and common good.

Ideological Creativity

Keeping the above ontological, theoretical, and empirical arguments in mind, it is important to stress that political ideologies are specific phenomena rooted in human creativity. The imagery that forms, makes sense, and motivates human individuals to participate in political communication and action reveals ideology as a creative force that cannot be separated from humanness itself. This creativity stems from the specificity of the human presence in the world. It is simultaneously a cognitive and practical act in which human life—individual and collective—vests itself. And this ideological creativity makes human participation in politics ontologically, cognitively, and psychologically meaningful.

Creativity and imagination go hand in hand with political processes, power distribution, wealth of choice, and political inclusivity. By continuing Hanna Arendt's intuition in looking at politics as a sphere of human self-realization and creativity (Arendt 1960, 1963), Vlad Glaveanu, a researcher of political imagination, offered a widely accepted definition:

> Creativity is best understood as a form of action in and on the world, performed in relation to others, and leading to the continuous renewal of culture... Creativity and imagination designate the human capacity to generate meaningful novelty in thought and in action. Both processes express our agency and help us expand our range of mental and cultural resources (e.g., ideas, schemas, images, objects, norms, and so on). (Glaveanu 2018: 84–85)

Thus, the political study of imagination proves certain philosophical intuitions, which in turn have inspired political scholars in recognizing creativity as the foundation of political action.

This creativity can manifest itself in the production of ideological positions and beliefs. George Kateb has famously defined this connection as imagery of two kinds: seeing-non-existent and not-seeing-existent, which can also be another definition of ideology (Kateb 2002: 485ff). Kateb, and later Oklopcic, also link political imagination with specific political emotionality. Both researchers prove that different ideologies lead to emotions of different force and kind: ethnonationalism and antiliberal ideologies provoke stronger emotional reactions and more active political imagination than the liberal ideologies (ibid. 500; Oklopcic 2018: 8ff). Thus political imagination, by provoking emotions, leads to collective actions. However, the more rational ideologies have weaker motivations for collective solidarity than less rational ones.

Ideological creativity's conceptualization is based on four elements. First, by merging cognitive, aesthetic and emotional acts with behavioral consequences, imagination has its own ideological materiality. Second, this materiality is connected with human creativity as a faculty to begin anew, to use the past for projecting the future, and to solve present problems by elaborating past experience (personal and collective) and a fantasy of the future. Third, imagination transcends ideal and material, as well as individual and collective, and preconditions political actions in changing the current state of affairs. And finally, the production of imaginary meanings leads to collective/political, materially manifested results. Altogether, ideological creativity can be seen as the existential and functional unity of three aspects of social imagination:

> real aspect: imagination is embodied in the social reality, and it participates in its reproduction; intersubjective aspect: imagination refers to the experience of individuals and groups simultaneously; ideal aspect: imagination focuses on alternatives to the state of affairs, offers a utopia or nostalgia as possible solutions.

Ideological creativity as a concept manifests the ability of human existence to cast projections into nothing and fill this nothing with its own presence, thus bringing the project into being. At this level, there is no rationalized division of human existence into categories of individual, collective or humankind; all these divisions are actually the result of ideological creativity, not its foundations.

Ideological creativity as a concept refers to cognitive operations with real and not-yet-real things, processes, ideas, and persons. These operations work with images and imageries, as practice, cognitively projecting a spatio-temporal real and unreal toward specific ends. The ends of these ideological cognitive processes unite aspects of fantasy, virtuality, and possibility, making possible a change of reality through human action.

Ideological creativity as a concept refers to social practice based on the merger of the collective past (collective memory), collective future (social fantasy), and work on the current situation (transpersonal intelligence). Due to social imagination, ideological creativity translates into the construction of social reality and political selves in correlation with collective identities. This concept reveals Aristotle's definition of politics (as communication about the highest common good) as a complex interpersonal process in which there is simultaneously:

> exchange with politically important information; decision-making where real needs and possible solutions meet each other in the conflict and agreement of imageries; distribution, confirmation, and/or change of power position of persons and groups participating in the communication and support of imageries; implementation of and/or resistance to the decisions; (re)production of the political community as living collective of involved political subjects.

Ideological creativity, by merging projections with real political consequences, is the source of meaning in political life that provides human individuals and groups with a framework for the interpretation and practical change of social reality. It is a human faculty allowing us to engage with the world and re-create it toward certain common ends. As such it opens a space for authority and subjection, conflict and agreement, freedom and serfdom, justice and crime, citizenship and statelessness, individual and common good.

Post-Soviet Ideological Creativity

The combination of a future-oriented critique of reality, a problem-solving approach, and the planning of a future state of affairs on one side, with history, memory and nostalgia on the other side, establishes the limits of the ideological imagination in specific historical, cultural, and geographic situations. One such situation is connected with the experience of people living in Eastern Europe and Northern Eurasia in the late 20th and early 21st centuries.

Soviet and post-Soviet epochs differentiate and interconnect in many ways, and one of them is the ideological specificity of these epochs. Svetlana Boym has meaningfully expressed the Soviet and post-Soviet ideological continuity in the following way:

> The twentieth century began with a futuristic utopia and ended with nostalgia. (Boym 2001: 11)

However, utopia and nostalgia are both grounded in real, current problems, and offer common solutions. Thus, ideological creativity always deals with current groups, communities and other types of collectivities that affectively and existentially involve individuals in a life that transcends their own personalities through politics or social action.

In our past study of the post-Soviet ideologies, Alexander Etkind and I (Etkind & Minakov 2020) described the politically driven reimagination of the future and past of the newly established societies. The unpredictable future was wide open and seen as a source of danger. Yet the past, as it was reinvented in the times of Perestroika, was full of threatening imagery as well. For this reason:

> The new societies of Eastern Europe and Northern Eurasia faced tectonic transformations, which led to a flourishing of different phenomena related to ideology. But the social structure adapted slowly. The new social reality had to normalize political competition, multiparty systems, private property, the significance of money, the coexistence of consumerist lifestyle and totalitarian traditions, and the contradictions between democratic politics and oligarchic economies, between atheism and religious renaissance, and so on. Events throughout the late 20th and early 21st centuries inspired new ideological frameworks, which allowed individuals, institutions and social groups to accept and interpret the new political and socioeconomic reality in a way that was eclectic, relativistic or — the most popular ideological term of the epoch — post-modern. Though philosophical genealogies of the post-modern and post-Soviet conditions were vastly different — if not opposite — these concepts often merged or conflated in their popular usage. (Etkind & Minakov 2020: 9-10)

In this current collection of research, scholars indicate and analyze specific cases of post-Soviet ideological creativity.

Aims and Structure of This Book

One of the major results of the post-Soviet ideological creativity has been the creation of majorities. In various national contexts the quest for a majority took place over several years (Azerbaijan, the Baltic countries, Kazakhstan, and Uzbekistan) or several decades (Armenia, Kyrgyzstan, and Ukraine). When the ideological and demographic construction of the majority is finished, power elites have an opportunity to legitimize their rule through elections. In cases like the Baltic countries, these elections have a democratic character (though it may not save them from an illiberal turn). In cases like Russia or Kazakhstan, these elections lose their democratic meaning but remain as a provider of legitimacy to the ruling group that "defends the people" (that is, the majority). The ideological construction of majorities was crucial for establishing a government-controlled political order after the Soviet Union's dissolution.

This book consists of ten research papers dedicated to the ideological construction of new majorities, which have both universal meaning and post-Soviet specificity. Each paper, after a double blind peer-review process, was previously published in the *Ideology and Politics Journal* issues of 2019-2021. Later, these chapters were additionally reviewed and updated by their authors for this publication.

Our book's chapters are divided into two parts. The first part studies how the new post-Soviet majorities create their own symbolic reality, give names to the significant *topoi* of their collective space, regulate the knowledge of the past in collective time, and prescribe major features that differentiate and link collective selves and others. The intensive instrumental (mis)use of the images of the self and the other has been based on a set of intertwined cultural, ethnic, gender, social and religious stereotypes born in the 18th and 19th centuries, and redefined by the post-Soviet national revivals, civil and world wars, as well as ethnic and religious conflicts aiming to reestablish "historical justice." The construction of the self and the other in their own country facilitates re-energized identity politics, sometimes in its most extreme forms.

The first part opens with a chapter on the decommunization of place names in the southeastern Ukrainian city of Kryvyi Rih. Natalia Kudriavtseva explores attitudes towards the ongoing renaming among an expert community of researchers from different fields. The working group, organized by the researchers with the aim of developing their own toponymic suggestions to be then publicly discussed, stands here as a separate aspect of the symbolic changes. Employing the sociolinguistic concept of language ideology, the author transforms it from a belief about language into a belief about place name in order to analyze the working group, naming motives and toponymic choices. In a similar way to the ideology which links ethnic identity to language, the toponymic ideologies of the renaming group members are governed by the view that the toponym is an expression of national identity, where a specific historical interpretation functions as a structural piece. The processes structuring these ideologies—iconization, fractal recursivity and erasure—necessarily lead to a selective commemoration of events and historical figures, which are defined by their belonging to the place. As foreseen by the national agenda, "decommunizational" renaming in this local context is also perceived as a reconstruction of identity.

In the second chapter, Petra Colmorgen analyzes the case of Georgia building its post-Soviet national self through the othering of its two most powerful neighbors. Russia and Turkey are constructed to be the other in relation to Westernness and Orthodoxy, two key Georgian identity markers. But perceptions of us versus them are not always led by exclusively negative perceptions, nor are they directed only outwards. On the one hand, Georgia's othering of Russia and Turkey remains incomplete, because the neighbors also represent characteristics close to aspects of the Georgian majority's self. On the other hand, a "spillover effect" of othering takes place within the Georgian state border in Adjara as well as in South Ossetia and Abkhazia, since the Georgian identity parameters of Orthodoxy and Westernness are challenged in those territories. Analyzing these complex links, the author discusses how Russia and Turkey can contain elements of identification with and differentiation from Georgianness simultaneously. Furthermore,

Colmorgen explores how othering is transmitted to objects within the internationally recognized Georgian territory, when, for example, Adjara, South Ossetia, and Abkhazia, are perceived to be insufficiently Orthodox or Western. The author explains how such complex othering patterns in Georgia might be found in conflicts within the Georgian self. Discussing how Georgia's identity is formed between the extreme poles of Westernness and Orthodoxy, questions of how much Westernness is tolerable for Georgian Orthodoxy and to what degree Orthodoxy can be part of a Westernized Georgian society are not only key to understanding the current Georgian self, but to contextualizing relations to Russia, Turkey, South Ossetia, Abkhazia and Adjara respectively.

In the next chapter, Nadiia Koval and Ivan Gomza analyze the development of Ukrainian IR (International Relations) sociology and its theoretical and ideological limitations. In particular, the authors look at the degree of Ukrainian scholars' integration in the global IR community, their favorite theories and methods, and their lack of influence on policymakers. Based on the TRIP-2017 survey data analysis, the authors discovered that, due to Soviet tradition and partial Westernization, Ukrainian IR scholars tend to espouse realism and constructivism as their preferred IR paradigms; they prefer to use descriptive methods, and their area studies focus is primarily on the CEE region and Western Europe. Their policy and political influence are minimal, and their involvement with the global community of IR scholars is limited. On the whole, Ukrainian IR scholars enjoy little prestige domestically and cannot effectively prevent the "double peripheralization" of Ukrainian IR studies.

Augusto Dala Costa narrates a massive renaming in Tbilisi, which took place from 1988 to 2007. The author emphasizes that the toponymic changes in Georgia's capital reflect the political transformations of the time and accord with the post-Soviet national discourse of Georgia. Drawing upon the data previously not translated from the Georgian language, Costa detects the points where the national discourse meets Tbilisi's local history and highlights a selective nature of commemoration of early independence. Replacing ninety percent of Soviet personal names with the same number of place names memorializing Georgian historical figures, the authorities performed a "Georgianization" of the capital, incorporating not only cultural but also religious and ethnic elements into its cityscape. Deprived of local peculiar traits, the toponymic portrait of Tbilisi depicts the whole of Georgia as a homogeneous monoethnic nation whose unity is secured by the commemoration of national historical events and figures, which its capital readily illustrates. This national discourse characterizes the Menshevik nature of the First Republic, the local minorities of the Armenians and Azeris, and even the shared Transcaucasian history erased from the post-Soviet Tbilisi cityscape. Reconfigured in such a way, the symbolic landscape of Georgia's capital reflects the politics of the then Georgian leaders—Zviad Gamsakhurdia and Mikheil Saakashvili—and brings about "the democratic expression of power from the Georgian nation," while also cultivating its self-perception as it shapes Georgian national identity defined by the political agenda of the time.

Finally, a chapter authored by Roman Horbyk, Yana Prymachenko and Yuliya Yurchuk analyzes the mediatization of the sphere of public history, which has become a mainstream trend in Central and Eastern Europe. To some extent, this was provoked by the policies of the Russian government, which actively used historical arguments to justify aggressive foreign policy. Based on the theory of mediatization and collective memory studies, the authors consider relevant processes throughout the region and then consider the case of Likbez, a public initiative of Ukrainian historians aimed at refuting historical myths both in and around Ukraine. The authors highlight the general trend of the government losing its exclusive role in interpreting and representing the historical past. They also note that the use of media technologies affects the status of professional historians. On the one hand, it leads to a blurring of professional standards; on the other hand, it promotes giving the "meaning-producers" direct access to the target audience, where they enter into competition with other actors, including the political class and government bureaucracy.

The second part of this book is dedicated to sovereigntism and the comparison of its manifestations in post-Soviet and Western societies. The international order has recently entered a period in which national elites and popular movements have risen up against universalism and advocated for the supremacy of their government and individual state's interests—a phenomenon referred to as sovereigntism. If in earlier years, the global order was challenged mainly by radical left and right groups that had little impact on the norms and principles of the global agenda, the primary challenge to universal norms of justice and human rights today comes from the ruling groups of some of the world's largest powers and economies.

The chapters of this part focus on a number of questions stemming from the ideological divide between universalism and sovereigntism. How did sovereigntists become so influential on the national and international stage? Can international peace and human rights norms survive in a world-system of national exceptionalism? What are the potential implications of continuing down the current path of divisions between universalism and sovereigntism?

In their opening chapter, Oleksandr Fisun and Nataliya Vinnykova look at the controversy over universalism and sovereigntism as part of a wider theoretical debate over the fate of state sovereignty and democracy. The authors argue that sovereignty is going through a period of de-etatization: real policymaking is now being done in network formats, where the role of non-state stakeholders causes the state to lose its sovereign monopoly on decision-making and undermines state legitimacy. They also show how post-Soviet—Ukrainian—ideological creativity became influential for understanding contemporary politics in more distant countries.

Ruslan Zaporozhchenko continues the discussion by stating that in times of globalism, sovereigntism consolidates the instruments and practices of populism, particularism, nationalism, or separatism, in varying combinations, to deconstruct the existing sovereign system of power nationally and internationally. Such a deconstruction may catalyze protest movements, revolutions, civil wars, or mass rallies, which in turn may lead to a further (re)production of divisions within the political systems and regional orders.

In the following chapter, I offer an analysis of the concept of sovereignty as promoted by contemporary sovereigntists. I argue that although the sovereigntist ideology varies from country to country, it is consolidated around a specific interpretation of the concept of sovereignty. Taking as examples Trumpism and Putinism, the sovereigntist ideologies in an old democracy and a new post-Soviet autocracy, I show that sovereigntists define sovereignty as the supremacy of the people as an imagined majority, a perspective that denies the sovereignty of the human person and the legitimacy of cosmopolitan norms of justice.

Gulnara Shaikhutdinova examines how international human rights law is experiencing a sovereigntist and nationalist turn in domestic legal systems, adducing the legal systems of the EU, Germany, Italy, the UK, and Russia as examples. The author argues that the sovereigntist trend in implementing international human rights law leads to the fragmentation of contemporary international law and the emergence of multiple legal values and practices that contradict each other and the international legal order.

In the concluding chapter, Yurii Mielkov contends that universal norms take precedence over a particularist ethos and provides a framework for any moral particularity that could serve to achieve more peaceful and just universal goals for the world. Using arguments from post-Soviet experience, the author argues that moral particularism can only lead to a world of closed societies, with little space in the national and international public sphere.

On the whole, the selected research provides our readers with many specific cases of post-Soviet majority construction, with their attendant insights, as well as a general account of ideological creativity.

Bibliography

Adams, Jacqueline (2004). The Imagination and Social Life. *Qualitative Sociology* 27(3): 277–297.

Arendt, Hannah (1960). *Vita activa oder Vom tätigen Leben.* Bonn: Paul.

Arendt, Hannah (1963). *On Revolution.* New York: Penguin.

Aristotle. (1964). *On the Soul. Parva Naturalia. On Breath.* Cambridge: Harvard University Press.

Berger, Peter and Luckman, Thomas (1956). *The Social Construction of Knowledge*. New York: Doubleday.

Bottici, Chiara (2014). *Imaginal Politics: Images Beyond Imagination and the Imaginary*. New York: Columbia University Press.

Boym, Svetlana (2001). *The Future of Nostalgia*. New York: Basic Books.

Castoriadis, Cornelius (1987). *The Imaginary Institution of Society*. Cambridge, MA: Polity.

Castoriadis, Cornelius (1997a). "Radical Imagination and the Social Instituting Imaginary," in Curtis, D.A. (ed.). *The Castoriadis Reader*. Oxford: Blackwell, 321–337.

Castoriadis, Cornelius (1997b). "The Discovery of the Imagination." In Curtis, D.A. (ed.). *World in Fragments: Writings on Politics, Society, Psychoanalysis, and the Imagination*. Stanford: Stanford University Press, 246–272.

Cocking, John (2005). *Imagination: A Study in the History of Ideas*. London: Routledge.

De Saint-Laurent, Constance (2018). "Thinking Through Time: From Collective Memories to Collective Futures," in De Saint-Laurent, Constance, Obradovic, Sandra and Carriere, Kevin R. (eds.). *Imagining Collective Futures: Perspectives from Social, Cultural and Political Psychology*. London: Palgrave Macmillan, 59–82.

De Saint-Laurent, Constance, Obradovic, Sandra and Carriere, Kevin R. (eds.) (2018). *Imagining Collective Futures: Perspectives from Social, Cultural and Political Psychology*. London: Palgrave Macmillan.

Dewey, John (1998). *The Essential Dewey: Pragmatism, Education, Democracy* (Vol. 1). Indiana University Press.

Etkind, Alexander and Minakov, Mikhail (2020). Post-Soviet Ideological Creativity. In Etkind A., Minakov M. (eds.). *Ideology after Union: Political Doctrines, Discourses, and Debates in Post-Soviet Societies*, Stuttgart: ibidem, 9–18.

Fadieiev, Volodymyr (2021). *Poza mezhi natsionalnoho: Sotsialne uiavne i kosmopolityzm* [in Ukrainian: Beyond the National: The Social Imaginary and Cosmopolitanism]. *Ideology and Politics Journal* 1(17): 131–167.

Glaveanu, Vlad Petre (2018). "Perspectival Collective Futures: Creativity and Imagination in Society," in De Saint-Laurent, Constance, Obradovic, Sandra and Carriere, Kevin R. (eds.). *Imagining Collective Futures: Perspectives from Social, Cultural and Political Psychology*. London: Palgrave Macmillan, 83–106.

Heidegger, Martin (1996). *Being and Time*. New York: SUNY press.

Heidegger, Martin (1997). *Kant and the Problem of Metaphysics*. Bloomington: Indiana University Press.

Honneth, Axel (1995). *The Struggle for Recognition: The Moral Grammar of Social Conflict*. Cambridge: Polity.

Husserl, Edmund (1980). *Phantasie, Bildbewusstsein, Erinnerung. Zur Phänomenologie der anschaulichen Vergegenwärtigungen. Texte aus dem Nachlass (1898-1925)*. In Husserliana, vol. 23. The Hague: Nijhoff.

Kane, Michael J., Brown, Leslie H., McVay, Jennifer C., Silvia, Paul J., Myin-Germeys, Inez and Kwapil, Thomas R. (2007). For Whom the Mind Wanders, and When: An Experience-Sampling Study of Working Memory and Executive Control in Daily Life. *Psychological Science* 18(7): 614-621.

Kant, Immanuel (2013). *Critique of Pure Reason*. London: Read Books Ltd.

Kateb, George (2002). "On the Adequacy of the Canon." *Political Theory* 30(4):482-505.

Killingsworth, Matthew A., and Gilbert, Daniel T. (2010). "A Wandering Mind Is an Unhappy Mind." *Science* 330(6006): 932-932.

Marcuse, Herbert (1991). *One-Dimensional Man: Studies in the Ideology of Advanced Industrial Society*. Boston: Beacon

McBride, Keally D. (2005). *Collective Dreams: Political Imagination and Community*. University Park, Pennsylvania: The Pennsylvania State University Press.

Mooneyham, Benjamin W. and Schooler, Jonathan W. (2013). "The Costs and Benefits of Mind-Wandering: A Review. *Canadian Journal of Experimental Psychology/Revue canadienne de psychologie expérimentale* 67(1): 11.

Newman, Katherine S. (1993). *Declining Fortunes: The Withering of the American Dream*. New York: Basic Books.

Oklopcic, Zoran (2018). *Beyond the People. Social Imaginary and Constituent Imagination*. Oxford: Oxford University Press.

Pileggi, Mary S.; Grabe, Maria Elizabeth; Holderman, Lisa B; and de Montigny, Michelle (2000). "Business as Usual: The American Dream in Hollywood Business Films." *Mass Communication and Society* 3: 207-228.

Plato. (1989). *The Collected Dialogues*. Princeton: Princeton University Press.

Ricoeur, Paul (1994). "Imagination in Discourse and in Action," in Robinson, John F. and Robinson, Gillian (eds.). *Rethinking Imagination: Culture and Creativity*. London: Routledge, 118-135.

Rorty, Richard (1998). *Truth and Progress: Philosophical Papers* (Vol. 3). Cambridge: Cambridge University Press.

Sartre, Jean Paul (2001). *Being and Nothingness: An Essay in Phenomenological Ontology*. Boston: Citadel Press.

Schooler, Jonathan W.; Smallwood, Jonathan; Christoff, Kalina; Handy, Todd C.; Reichle, Erik D.; and Sayette, Michael A. (2011). "Meta-awareness, perceptual decoupling and the wandering mind." *Trends in Cognitive Sciences* 15(7): 319–326.

Schutz, Alfred and Luckman, Tomas (1960). *The Structures of the Life World*. London: Heinemann.

Smallwood, Jonathan (2013). Distinguishing how from why the mind wanders: A process–occurrence framework for self-generated mental activity. *Psychological Bulletin* 139(3): 519–535.

Tateo, Luca (2015a). Giambattista Vico and the psychological imagination. *Culture and Psychology* 21: 145–161.

Tateo, Luca (2015b). Just an Illusion? Imagination as Higher Mental Function. *Journal of Psychology and Psychotherapy* 5-6: 1–6.

Taylor, Charles (2004). *Modern Social Imaginaries*. Durham: Duke University Press.

Vico, Giambattista (1730 [1956]). *Principii d'una scienza nuova* (secondo ed.). Naples: Felice Mosca.

Zittoun, Tania and Cerchia, Frédéric (2013). Imagination as Expansion of Experience. *Integrative Psychology and Behavioral Sciences* 47: 305–324.

Zittoun, Tania and Gillespie, Alex (2018). "Imagining the Collective Future: A Sociocultural Perspective." In De Saint-Laurent; Constance, Obradovic; Sandra and Carriere; Kevin R. (eds.). *Imagining Collective Futures: Perspectives from Social, Cultural and Political Psychology*. London: Palgrave Macmillan, 15–38.

I
Self, Otherness, and Ideology

1
Self, Otherness, and Ideology

1 Reconfiguring Identities within the Cityscape
Ideologies of Ukraine's Decommunization Renaming[1]

Natalia Kudriavtseva

Recent research into the symbolic transformation of urban spaces in post-communist countries have analyzed the political significance of place names as vehicles of commemoration (Azaryahu 1997; Light 2004; Gil 2005; Palonen 2008; David 2013). This focus, partially intersecting with the linguistic landscape perspective (see e.g. Berezkina 2016; Pipitone 2019), allows us to go beyond the descriptive approaches to place-naming traditionally taken in sociolinguistics, and to adopt a critical standpoint on place names as means of re-constructing history. In landscape approaches, this view has been known as "place-making" – understood as "a way of constructing the past [...] and, in the process, personal and social identities" where place names are by all means involved in this "place" production (Basso 1996, cited in Pipitone 2019: 16–17; see also Azaryahu 2011: 32). In the field of cultural geography (see e.g. Berg & Vuolteenaho 2009), where the influence of linguistic theory has been recognized (Bucher et al. 2013: 25), place names, in their commemorative capacity, are considered to make up a "city-text" which reproduces a particular version of history and contributes to shaping a local and national sense of belonging (Azaryahu 2009).

Studies of urban toponymy, as a reflection of social memory and of renaming as a promotion of the ruling elite's ideology in the context of Central and Eastern Europe (Stipersky et al. 2011; Bucher et al. 2013), point out an iconic link between street names and

---

1 I am grateful to Prof. Yaroslav Shramko for his support and help with this research, as well as his insightful and constructive comments on earlier versions of this paper. I am also indebted to Sarah Rosenthal for her help with editing and proofreading the paper.

official versions of history, which works as a structural component of the group identity authorities try to design. These studies draw on Duncan Light's notion of "iconographic landscapes", as suggested in his research of renaming in post-socialist Bucharest (Light 2004). Light argues that iconographic landscapes arising as a consequence of renaming in post-socialist states are necessarily in accord with the ideals of new regimes, and that the examination of these toponymic changes can offer important insights into the ways in which these states are redefining their national identities and national pasts (Light 2004: 154). Light also notes that in this post-socialist identity-building, there are two processes that complement each other: that of commemorating certain historical facts and that of forgetting others (Light 2004: 156). Therefore, the city-text which results is doomed to highlight certain things and erase others as "the gesture of street naming constitutes an attempt to constitute and represent imagined communities" (Palonen 2008: 220). In this respect, the differentiation between city-related, regional, national, and international "identity levels" (Stipersky et al. 2011: 186) seems to be an effective methodological tool, as it allows us to check the intensity of each of these levels in a particular cityscape, as well as to examine whether the processes of commemorating and forgetting the past unfold similarly at different identity levels.

In Ukraine, as in other countries of Eastern Europe, the rejection of communist past has been accompanied by the search for a new consolidating element that all Ukrainians might possibly share. Decommunization—which intensified after the Euromaidan Revolution, including two laws on the censure of the communist and Nazi regimes and on the commemoration of strugglers for Ukraine's independence (Law 2015a; Law 2015b)—triggered a large-scale toponymic renaming targeting primarily the south-east of Ukraine. In these regions, unlike in Western Ukraine, where a massive renaming already occurred as early as 1991, the bulk of toponymy[2] was still of the Soviet origin; thus, the decommunization process has been most evident there. Though the renaming strategy

---

2 In this paper, I use the terms "place name" and "toponym" interchangeably with no difference in meaning.

pursued by authorities in this part of the country was to maximally avoid commemoration, as explained by the need to deideologize and depoliticize urban place names, it is possible to identify three memorialized historical strata in the officially sanctioned toponymy seen by the local authorities as readily accepted by all. These are the Kievan Rus and Cossack epochs, the 20th century national liberation movements, and certain military events and figures of the Soviet period (Gnatiuk 2018: 128; see also Gomaniuk 2017; Pavlenko 2018). Among the commemorative names, which were not directly related to either the military sphere or politics, the most drew on pre-Soviet era heritage, specifically the Austro-Hungarian and Russian empires (Gnatiuk 2018: 129). Overall, these trends in the toponymic renaming, as brought about by the 2015 decommunization, coincide with those exhibited by other post-socialist countries, specifically in their appeal to the pre-socialist era as an object of commemoration, a decrease of political and military place names, and an increase in local toponymy (Gnatiuk 2018: 134).

Reviewing officially endorsed renamings, however, it is possible to detect only officially expressed or imposed identities articulated by political elites. Those are not necessarily similar to the identities embraced by actual communities who inhabit cities and towns (Stipersky et al. 2011: 184). Maoz Azaryahu has stressed the necessity to refine our understanding of renaming by examining "the operation of naming commissions as municipal agencies that 'author' the landscape-as-text," and thus explore the relation between the "input" (i.e. names offered for commemoration) and the "output" (i.e. the actual names approved by the officials) (Azaryahu 2011: 29–30). It is only in the case of looking into these suggestions on renaming (i.e. in the case of input) that place names can be seen as "mirrors" of those identities that people tend to manifest. So far, such cases have rarely been subject to academic scrutiny, and even when studied, those surveyed were namely capital cities (see e.g. Azaryahu 1997). Similarly rewarding appears to be an exploration of renaming suggestions in provincial cities and towns, both in terms of additional empirical data (Azaryahu 2011: 29), and the specifics of the input that is analyzed.

It is such a study of toponymic suggestions that I describe in this chapter. The case is Ukraine's south-eastern provincial city of Kryvyi Rih. I set out to establish whether the suggested place names are in any way different from those authorized by the local officials. Do the authors of the suggestions and the authorities work on a similar range of objects which should be renamed under the law? Do the suggested toponyms relate to the same historical periods as those identified as common for the south-east of the country? How do any historical strata, expressed in the suggested toponymy, come to be realized at different identity levels? And which of these levels — local, regional, or national — is preferred?

I will not only review the full list of toponyms offered by a naming commission, but also survey the attitudes of its members towards the decommunization renaming as such. From a methodological point of view, I will thus follow a socio-onomastic approach, which allows for a discussion of the members' naming motives behind their choices, as well as their perceptions of the various roles that toponyms play. My main objective is to reveal what can be called the commission members' ideologies of place names, or their *toponymic ideologies*, as expressed in their associations, evaluations, and practices, connected to place names. In line with the abovementioned critical toponymy studies, where the focus moves from a mere description of toponymy to the processes involved in naming places and creating names, I aim to show the kind of processes that structure these toponymic ideologies and motivate the concrete choices that the commission members make.

Theoretical Framework

In this study, I will not refer to "ideologies" in the sense often used in studies of socialist and post-socialist renaming, where it means an official state ideology legitimized in the symbols of urban space (e.g. Light, Nicolae & Suditu 2002; Gnatiuk 2018). Here, I draw on the sociolinguistic concept of *language ideologies*, broadly defined as "beliefs and feelings about language" (Field & Kroskrity 2009: 4). The notion of an ideology as a belief about something might readily lend itself to critical linguistic research on toponymy, as it can be extrapolated to denote people's attitudes to place names and their beliefs of the influence that place names have. Research on attitudes towards toponyms, including the issue of renaming, has been conducted in the field of cultural geography (see Kostanski 2009) as well as in the field of sociolinguistics (see Berezkina 2016). The concept of language ideologies was first used within the context of attitudes towards American indigenous place names (see Pipitone 2019). As I will show here, this framework can also be usefully extended to the discussions of decommunization renaming in Ukraine.

Defined as "the cultural (or subcultural) systems of ideas about social and linguistic relationships, together with their loading of moral and political interests" (Irvine 1989: 255), *language ideologies* are otherwise described as accustomed cultural stereotypes about language in general, particular languages, linguistic structure, or language use. On a large scale, these ideologies always concern more than just language, since they "envision and enact links of language to group and personal identity" (Woolard & Schieffelin 1994: 56).

The associations between languages and identities are formed through the three semiotic processes, identified by Judith T. Irvine and Susan Gal (2000) as iconization, fractal recursivity, and erasure. *Iconization* means that certain linguistic features are perceived as iconic representations of particular groups of people—as if "a linguistic feature somehow depicted or displayed a social group's inherent nature or essence" (Irvine & Gal 2000: 37). The notion of *fractal recursivity*, reminiscent of geometric fractals, suggests that intergroup oppositions between linguistic varieties or groups are projected onto intragroup relations, or vice versa: "[…] the myriad oppositions that can create identity may be reproduced repeatedly, either within each side of a dichotomy or outside of it" (p. 38). The process of *erasure* renders certain phenomena invisible, since language ideology is "a totalizing vision, elements that do not fit its interpretive structure […] must be either ignored or transformed" (p. 38). For example, Aneta Pavlenko (2011: 49) uses this scheme to illustrate associations between languages and identities in Latvian and Ukrainian postcolonial narratives:

In the process of *fractal recursivity*, a political opposition between Russia and the new nation-states is projected inward, onto the relationship between Russian speakers and the titulars and between Russian and the titular language. In the process of *iconization*, Latvian and Ukrainian are symbolically linked to morally superior ethnic and national identities and a European or Western identity, and Russian to an inferior 'colonizer' identity. Its linguistic features, such as swearwords, become an iconic representation of the moral inferiority of its speakers. And because linguistic ideology is a totalizing vision, elements that do not fit its interpretive structure, such as variation within both groups, are rendered invisible through the process of *erasure*.

Since a toponym is, in the first place, a linguistic form (and therefore a sign), the three processes that construct language ideologies can also be seen as structuring the ideologies of place names. These processes can be employed in the analysis of associations between identities and place names. Under this framework, the use of a certain place name can be considered as symbolizing and indexing a particular identity, as this place name refers to a specific historical vision iconically represented by certain figures and events. Applied to the previous research on post-socialist renaming, this scheme explains the link that brings about "iconographic landscapes," where commemorating and forgetting are grounded by the processes of iconization and erasure.

Methodology

Toponymic Classification

In this study, I have adhered to the methodology used in previous works on urbanonymy, seen as reflecting identity in some central and regional European cities (Stipersky et al. 2011; Bucher et al. 2013) and thirty-six of the largest cities in Ukraine (Gnatiuk 2018). This included the quantification and classification of toponyms according to *themes* and *scales*, or identity levels. In order to enable comparisons of the "input" names with the "output" names approved by the officials, I used the following thematic classification, based on (Stipersky et al. 2011 and Gnatiuk 2018). First, I distinguished between (I) restored historic toponyms, and (II) non-historic, or newly given, place names. Then, I classified the non-historic names into (1) commemorative, (2) topographic, (3) poetic, (4) denoting crafts and trades, and (5) others. Of these five groups, only topographic and commemorative names were further subdivided into classes. Topographic names were classified into geographic (various geographic designations, such as rivers, towns, mountains, etc.), localities (vicinity to some significant locality, such as a hospital, railway station, etc.), and appearance (physical nature of a street, such as wide, narrow, etc.). Commemorative names, including personal and collective names, were grouped into names referring to political and military spheres, and into other names.

The political and military group of the commemorative names was additionally categorized according to historical periods, such as those identified by Oleksiy Gnatiuk (2018: 124): Kievan Rus; Polish-Lithuanian Commonwealth; the Cossack State between the middle of the 17th and 18th centuries; Russian and Austro-Hungarian empires; the Ukrainian Struggle for Independence 1917–1921; the Soviet Union; the Ukrainian Insurgent Army and related liberation movements; Independent Ukraine (including the Euromaidan Revolution and the Donbass military conflict). The group of other names includes commemorative names related to spheres other than war and politics, such as science, culture, religion, industry or business. These names were also specifically arranged into historical categories of pre-Soviet, "Soviet-persecuted" and "Soviet-favored" (i.e. people having no obvious problems with the Soviet regime), ex-Soviet, and post-Soviet people.

In terms of scales, which is another criterion used in the classification, all commemorative names were related to the kind of historical context that a certain figure is perceived to represent—local, regional, national—which, in its turn, symbolizes a particular dimension (or level) of identity. Thus, names of persons commemorated for their contribution or relation to the city's history are thought to be local-specific. Names of persons having somehow influenced a wider region where the city is located belong to the regional level. Names of persons who have historical significance for the whole of Ukraine are seen as embodying the national identity dimension.

Socio-onomastic Attitudinal Survey

To allow a deeper insight into the ideologies embraced by the authors of the toponymic suggestions that I examine, I have surveyed their attitudes towards renaming, as well as place names themselves, to find out more about the reasons for toponymic preferences and the associations related to them. I used both a questionnaire and in-depth interviews for this study, as outlined in previous research (Kostanski 2009; Berezkina 2016).

Besides traditional questions of age, gender, and nationality, the questionnaire was comprised of three parts, including thirteen different questions. Two of these parts included multiple-choice questions, and the other part contained two open-ended questions. The three questions in the first part identified beliefs about the nature and significant characteristics of the toponym, as well as the kinds of toponyms to which the respondents paid most of their attention. The second part listed eight different place names in the city which had to be renamed under the decommunization legislation, and asked the respondent to choose the most suitable variant for the renaming. The final part with the open-ended questions asked about the respondents' opinion on the officially approved list of renamed toponyms in Kryvyi Rih, and also about their ideas of why / whether this renaming is altogether important.

As for the interviews, I followed a conversational-style interview — also known as the "open" semi-structured interview question routine (Kostanski 2009: 113). It is a method of open-ended questions, which allows the interviewer to build upon new information gleaned in the process of an interview, as it arises. While the list of questions asked was therefore not identical for each participant, basic themes were eventually covered by all of them. These themes concerned the interviewees' associations with the city, their reflections on the work of the naming commission, as well as their perceptions of the functions of place names and of the impact of the decommunization renaming as a whole. As such, my methodological approach has been fundamentally qualitative in nature, with occasional uses of quantitative methods, the latter applied in the toponymic classification part.

Data and Analysis

The city of Kryvyi Rih lies on the junction of the Inhulets and Saksahan rivers in the south-western part of the Dnipropetrovsk region, a central-eastern region of Ukraine. The region borders the Donetsk region in the east and the Zaporizhzhia and Kherson regions to the south. Kryvyi Rih is its second largest city, itself being located close to the central Kyrovohrad region and to the southern regions of Kherson and Mykolaiv. Founded in 1775 by Zaporizhzhia Cossacks as a post station, Kryvyi Rih first evolved into a town and then a city, largely due to the extraction of rich iron ore deposits. The discovery of Ukraine's largest iron ore field was made by Ukrainian-German archaeologist and landowner Oleksandr Pol in 1866. This kicked off the first mine and a railway connection in Kryvyi Rih, bringing the city into the industrial conglomerate of Prydniprov'ia and Donbas.

In 1918, this industrial cohesion was even seen as sufficient grounds for creating a separate Soviet quasi-state — the Donetsk-Kryvyi Rih Soviet Republic, which existed for hardly a month before it was joined with the Ukrainian Soviet Socialist Republic, where it became completely dissolved as an independent territory by 1919. The city's iron ore potential was most exploited during the Soviet period, which brought its push for heavy industry. This included the construction of Ukraine's biggest mining and smelting complex "Kryvorizhstal" (1931). During World War II, Kryvyi Rih was occupied by German troops for almost three years (1941–1944), and the city's industrial equipment was either evacuated to Russia or blown up. The post-war period, however, saw even greater industrial expansion, as well as housing and infrastructure growth. Today Kryvyi Rih is one of the country's largest industrial centers — home to more than 600,000 people.

The naming commission — whose particular toponymic suggestions and ideologies I have examined — was independently organized in one of the city-based universities in Kryvyi Rih. It involved eight members, including the rector of the university (Korotaiev 2017: 136). This commission was not affiliated with an official municipal agency, but was rather a citizens' grassroots initiative (working group). However, it was their activity that triggered a massive public discussion and encouraged the city officials to attend to decommunization renaming foreseen by the law. The city council and mayor were supposed to facilitate and administer the process from the very beginning, but they did not end up making any decisions regarding the renaming of city places within the specified time of nine months. The working group, however, did prepare renaming suggestions and initiated their own discussion long before the decision was to be made on the subject by the regional self-government. Two representatives of the working group were then invited to work on a special naming commission created at this official level, where the final decision on the renaming process in the city of Kryvyi Rih was to be made and endorsed.

I have concentrated my research on seven of the nine members who made up the core of the group and also authored the list of toponyms submitted to the officials. Of the seven scholars, there were two historians, two geographers, two Ukrainian language experts, and one scholar specializing in philosophy and logic. It is important to note that in the group's work on toponymic suggestions, it was on their own that they identified objects that had to be renamed under the decommunization legislation. As a result, they actually ended up with even more decommunized place names than was originally recommended by the Ukrainian Institute for National Memory (Viatrovych et al. 2015). Out of the 239 streets, squares, parks, ponds, city districts, and metro stations that the working group saw as bearing communism-related labels, 231 objects were recommended new names, and 8 streets were suggested to reorganize. The group's most intensive work on the renaming suggestions took place in January 2016; of course, much historical and geographic research preceded these January discussions.

Toponymic Classification

The list of toponymic suggestions, which I have classified according to the abovementioned themes and identity levels, was given to me by the university rector. Table 1 shows quantities in the designated categories of commemorative names, such as *vulytsia Kostia*

Hordiienka (Kost Hordiienko Street), *park Mershavtseva* (Mershavtsev Park), and *vulytsia Ukrainskykh voiniv* (Ukrainian Warriors Street); topographic names, such as *vulytsia Umanska* (Uman Street), *vulytsia Hoverlivska* (Hoverla Street), and *vulytsia Staroinhuletska* (Old Inhulets Street); denominations of crafts and trades, such as *vulytsia Hirnykiv* (Miners Street) or *vulytsia Kobzarska* (Kobzar Street); poetic names, such as *vulytsia Chervneva* (June Street) and *maidan Svobody* (Freedom Square); restored historic names, such as *vulytsia Tserkovna* (Church Street) or *vulytsia Poshtova* (Post Street); and other names, which include at least one habitual name of popular origin — *maidan 95 kvartal* (95th Kvartal Square) and one name homonymous with the previous toponym *park Pravdy* (Truth Park), which was formerly known as the park named after the communist newspaper *Pravda* (Truth).

The table also indicates the numbers of commemorative names with reference to the identity scales (local, regional, and national), and with respect to particular historical periods. One of the main problems that arose during this classification was deciding which of the identified historical periods should this or that figure be assigned to. For example, Volodymyr Byzov and Pavlo Shevchenko, both former rectors of two of the city's universities, were suggested to be commemorated in the names of the streets where the universities are located. They served as rectors and contributed to the development of their respective universities during both the Soviet and post-Soviet times. Another instance is Eduard Fuks, a geologist and photographer known to have been the most qualified explorer of iron ore deposits in Kryvyi Rih during both the pre-Soviet and early Soviet period. He was later persecuted by the Soviets and died of a self-imposed hunger strike in 1938. Further, such collective names as "Ukrainian warriors" and "Heroes of Ukraine" might have associations with various historical periods.

Table 1. Classification of toponyms suggested for places in the city of Kryvyi Rih (quantities in dubious categories marked by means of ±)

Category	Group	Subgroup
COMMEMORATIVE NAMES (83)	**persons (77):** local (62) regional (4) national (11)	*political and military* **(15):**
		<u>local (9)</u>: Cossack State (3) 1917-1921 (1) Russian Empire (1) Soviet Union (2) Independent Ukraine (2)
		<u>regional (2)</u>: Cossack State (2)
		<u>national (4)</u>: 1917-1921 (2) Soviet Union (persecuted) (2)
		other **(62):**
		<u>local (53)</u>: pre-Soviet (17±1) Soviet-persecuted (6±1) Soviet (23±4) post-Soviet (2±4)
		<u>regional (2)</u>: pre-Soviet (2)
		<u>national (7)</u>: pre-Soviet (2) Soviet-persecuted (4) ex-Soviet (1)
	collective names (6): local (1) national (5)	***political and military* (5):** <u>local (1)</u> Soviet
		<u>national (4)</u> Independent Ukraine (1) all times (3)
		***other* (1):**
		<u>national (1)</u> Independent Ukraine
TOPOGRAPHIC NAMES (105)	**geographic names** (72)	
	localities (32)	
	appearance (1)	

CRAFTS & TRADES (14)		
POETIC (4)		
RESTORED HISTORIC (23)		
OTHER (2)		
TOTAL (231)		

Out of these 231 suggested place names, there were 122 toponyms accepted by the regional authorities, and which were approved by their order, issued in May 2016 (Order 2016). Ninety of the recommended names were used on the same objects, while thirty-two names were used to rename streets, squares, and parks, other than those suggested by the working group. Besides, seventeen of the accepted 122 toponyms were taken in a slightly different form. For example, *vulytsia Osvity* (Education Street) was adapted as *vulytsia Osvitianska* (Educational Street), and *vulytsia Rybalok* (Fishermen Street) as *vulytsia Rybalska* (Fishing Street).

In terms of the designated categories, the most frequently used category was that of topographic names, followed by commemorative toponymy. These two types of toponymy also prevailed through the officially endorsed process of renaming, except that the biggest group was instead commemorative names (see Gnatiuk 2018: 125).[3] The most pronounced historical context "named" in the subgroup of political and military commemorative toponymy was the Cossack period (17th–18th centuries), in both the input and output. Such historical periods as Kievan Rus and the Polish-Lithuanian Commonwealth were altogether absent from the renaming recommendations, though they figured in the list of place names officially approved. Among other commemorative toponyms (e.g. science, culture, religion, industry, and business) preference among the recommendations was given to the so called "Soviet-favored" personalities, this category closely followed in preference by names of other representatives of the pre-Soviet time. In the approved list,

---

3   Since there are no exact quantities for each category given in Gnatiuk's study of official renamings, I do not provide any numerical comparisons between input and output toponyms.

however, the order was just the opposite: pre-Soviet commemorative names ranked first, while Soviet names came in second.

As for the identity dimensions, there were no discrepancies between the input, suggested by the working group, and the output toponymy, produced by the officials. Local history is expressed most vividly in both the renaming suggestions of the commission and in the list of officially authorized place names. When juxtaposed with the identified historical contexts, the identity levels in these toponymic suggestions exhibit an interesting pattern: while the most frequent appeared to be Soviet-related toponymy, including names of non-persecuted political and military figures from the Soviet Union, and "Soviet-favored" personalities, representing other spheres of life, these were only found in the local identity dimension, which means that the commemorated people have significance exclusively at the local level in the city of Kryvyi Rih. At the regional and national levels of identity, there are either names of Soviet-persecuted persons, or names of those who do not have any relation to the Soviet Union as such.

In the political and military group under the national identity dimension, there are such figures as Mykhailo Hrushevskyi, a leader of the 1917–1921 Ukrainian struggle for independence and an outstanding scholar; Ivan Ohiienko, a political and public figure of the same historical period; Oleksa Hirnyk, a Ukrainian dissident and Soviet political prisoner known for his self-immolation to protest again the Soviet russification of Ukraine; and Viacheslav Chornovil, a Soviet political prisoner and initiator of Ukraine's independence in 1991. At the regional identity level, there are two Cossacks — Sydir Bilyi and Kost Hordiienko — who are both commemorated as eighteenth-century atamans of the Zaporizhzhia Sich. Among those personalities representing spheres of life other than war and politics, there are four authors suggested to be commemorated for their national significance: Mykola Hvyliovyi, Vasyl Symonenko, Vasyl Stus, and Oleksandr Oles — their prose and poetry having been either forbidden or neglected during Soviet times. The Georgian-born film director Serhii Paradzhanov is also remembered as a national figure who was persecuted by the Soviets and exiled from Ukraine. Two additional personalities from the pre-

Soviet period, who are memorialized in the national identity dimension, are the author of Ukraine's anthem lyrics, Pavlo Chubynskyi, and the Ukrainian culture and education leader Mykola Arkas. Both of them contributed to the Ukrainian history and culture in the second half of the nineteenth century. At the regional identity level, there is also a natural science scholar and local flora researcher, Yosyp Pachoskyi, and the theatre playwright and director, Pavlo Saksahanskyi. They both worked in the pre-Soviet and early Soviet times.

The pattern in the toponymic suggestions—whereby there is no commemoration of "Soviet-favored" personalities in the national identity dimension, but instead an abundance of them at the local level—can be explained with data from the questionnaire and in-depth interviews, and their analyses below.

Toponymic Ideologies

The socio-onomastic survey, I will focus on in this part of the chapter, was carried out in the autumn of 2019. The questionnaire, preceding the in-depth interviews with the naming commission members, was an anonymous online questionnaire to which I received answers from the seven members of the group. A month later I recorded interviews with six of the seven experts on the commission, one of the geographers being unavailable at the time. I will analyze these data using Irvine and Gal's (2000) language ideology theoretical framework, as outlined earlier in section two.

Iconization. As much as certain linguistic features, or even whole languages, can represent individuals, groups, or cultures, certain place names can become indexes of personal and group identities, defining identity through reference, or rather adherence, to a particular historical interpretation. The view of toponym as a reference to history (as opposed to, for example, a spatial reference, or a description of the designated object) is itself an ideological vision characteristic of many post-socialist societies, but absent from some other cultures of the world: for example, see (Pipitone 2019) for ideologies and processes of indigenous place naming in North America. This approach to toponymy, where it functions primarily as a means of commemorating things by applying their proper names to physical objects (rather than producing a name by describing the nature of the object itself), ensures that certain names will become iconic representations of certain historical periods, and the choice of these names in the process of toponymic renaming will be perceived with positive appreciation along with related historical events and figures, thus augmenting desires to identify with them.

This is the attitude towards place names that prevailed among the members of the naming commission that I worked with. In the questionnaire, six of the seven respondents chose to characterize the toponym as an "element of history," and five agreed that the best kind of toponym is the one that has some "historical association." Five of the seven experts answered that during their work on the renaming suggestions, they paid most of their attention to commemorative names, while the other two focused on the restoration of historic names. "We can take off strata of history by exploring how renaming occurred at this or that period of time," one of the historians said.[4] Describing the process of renaming and discussions among the group, another commission member said, "[first], we considered a historic name, then we looked at which historical part of the city a street was located in, and then [looked] at a possible commemorative name for it."

"The most important thing is to rename [places] in such a way as not to offend the memory of the people," remarked one of the Ukrainian language experts. "Today the function of the toponym is to preserve history and culture," the other philologist said. "To me it was important to bring back all the historic names," explained the philosopher. This confirms the shared view of toponymy as symbolizing history where even some of the suggested geographic names were viewed through a historical prism. For instance, the street name *vulytsia Karachunivska* signals that the street is located

---

[4] The interviews were originally conducted in Ukrainian and Russian, transcribed and translated into English by myself. The interviewees were then familiarized with the translation, and their approval to publish them was received.

in the neighborhood called *Karachuny*, and derives its name from this historical toponym. There is presumed to have been a village there which dated back to the end of the 18th century, and was named *Karachunivka* after the family name of its founder — Captain Karachunov (Melnyk 2015: 27).

The name of another street, *vulytsia Dekonska*, also refers to the location in the area of the former estate called *Dekonka*, which derives its name from the family name *Dekonska*. Kateryna Dekonska was the lady who once owned the land. This suggested street name, *vulytsia Dekonska*, repeatedly described in my interviews with the naming commission members, arises as an icon of the pre-Soviet period in the city's history. Before the 1917 revolution, the major part of today's Kryvyi Rih and some neighboring villages existed as a number of estates owned by landed gentry, and this memory is still alive among many of the city inhabitants. "I want to say Dekonka instead of Artem Square," said one of the Ukrainian philologists in the interview.[5] "Dekonka is the old name ousted by the Soviet renaming," the philosophy expert said.

Another iconic name representing this pre-Soviet period is Oleksandr Pol — the pioneer of the Kryvyi Rih iron ore mining, who initiated the industrial extraction of the deposits beginning in 1881. The group suggested to commemorate him at four different places in the city: an avenue, a park, a square, and one of the city's districts. His name was the most frequent personal name on the commission's list. The square, which had been known as *maidan Artema* was renamed after Oleksandr Pol by the authorities in 2016. However, two years later, in October 2018, the name was changed again to *ploshcha Volodymyra Velykoho* (Volodymyr the Great Square) to commemorate the iconic figure of Kievan Rus, whose monument was erected there in the same year. "[...] Oleksandr Pol Square. It was there that the industrial extraction of the iron ore began in 1881. Now that it's Volodymyr the Great Square, this is not quite logical,"

---

5   *Maidan Artema* "Artem Square" used to be the name borne by one of the city's squares which memorialized "comrade Artem" — the head of the Donetsk-Kryvyi Rih Soviet Republic. Artem was a Soviet political and party figure, and used to be widely commemorated on various objects throughout the city of Kryvyi Rih.

remarked one of the historians of the commission, emphasizing that their renaming suggestions were not random. He went on to add that, "[my] attitude to Kievan Rus commemorative names is positive, since it means that we link our [local] history to Kievan Rus too."[6] However, "the main question about commemorative names is 'what do these people have to do with Kryvyi Rih?'" said another.

This idea of needing to have a direct relation to the city was most recurrent in the interviews. It was accurately summarized by a geography expert:

> Renaming is shaping a personalistic image of the native land. When we picked up local place names, we exposed what is *individual* about it [this land].

This belief of individualizing a toponymic landscape was also expressed by the other experts, as they contrasted it with the previous practice of universalizing place naming and its pervasive Lenin and Karl Marx Streets. This belief also explains the abundance of Soviet period commemorative names at the local identity level. However, these local figures are not perceived as "Soviet-favored" and not at all associated with the Soviet era, but are commemorated for what they did for their native city, for their contribution into its industrial development and social life. An iconic figure of the Soviet time in this local dimension is Hryhorii Hutovskyi, who was the head of the Kryvyi Rih city council between 1979 and 1992. Hutovskyi had been commemorated in the names of several places in Kryvyi Rih, but came within the purview of the decommunization laws in 2016. "Our idea was not to rename Hytovskyi Street because he contributed a lot into the development of the city," said one of the historians." A lot was built in the city during Hutovskyi's time," further argued one of the Ukrainian language experts.

The Soviet communist past is linked to a range of quite different personalities, the icons here being Lenin and Marx. Once a necessary attribute of any Soviet city, these toponyms have been the

---

6 The territory of Kryvyi Rih was never a part of the Kievan Rus medieval state. This area was known as *Dyke pole* 'Wild Field' where various nomadic tribes travelled at the time.

first to be wiped out. "We also wanted to remove place names commemorating [Soviet] poets and writers. But those are outside the scope of the decommunization laws," said one of the historians. "Mayakovsky Street and Gorky Square should have been removed in the first place. Gorky is a [Soviet] emblem, an idol. These should have been removed," explained the geography expert. He added that "they [the authorities] should have renamed much more places because those names are foreign to this country, they are foreign to this city. We consulted with the Ukrainian Institute for National Memory, but the answer was—'leave them.'" This opposition of "our own versus foreign" ran through all the interviews. "This practice [of naming places] has to label the space, make it more comprehensible, make it one's own," the historian went on. Renaming is "stating the city's identity. For this city to be *our city*," said one of the Ukrainian language experts.

When asked about associations they have with Kryvyi Rih, a question aimed at revealing the imagined nature of "the city's identity", the commission members named various historical periods ranging from the times of nomads and Cossacks, to the industrialization of the Soviet times. The mention of nomadic tribes, such as Scythians and Sarmatians, was quite frequent in the interviews. This was a reflection of the multi-ethnic identity of Kryvyi Rih. One of the historians said about his associations:

> As for me, I cannot definitely prioritize something... in our suggestions, we defined those separate [ethnic] groups, communities who used to inhabit the Kryvyi Rih area, but were not represented [in its place names]. I mean the nomads: Polovtsians, Scythians, Sarmatians...

He went on to explain that their idea was to designate in the suggested place names those ethnic groups that used to live, and in some cases still do live, on this territory today. An iconic representation of this ethnic variety has become the Roma community, memorialized in the name of Romany Street (*vulytsia Romska*) (also officially endorsed). This is where most of the Roma live in Kryvyi Rih today. "I think it is the only street in Ukraine bearing the Roma name. [In Kryvyi Rih] the Roma people live in Romany Street", said the other historian, adding that, by suggesting this place name, they undertook a reconstruction of the local and national identity, as well as designated in place names all those people who historically inhabited the area notwithstanding their ethnic identity and native language. This belief of a multi-ethnic nature of Ukrainian identity realized in the practice of commemorating a rather marginal social group is again constrained by the "own versus foreign" dichotomy, which is evident in the emphasis on commemorating those groups who "historically inhabited this area". As such, they are considered to belong to the city and country — and consequently, are seen as "our own".

Fractal recursivity. Under this view, communist place names are iconically linked to foreignness and are thus opposed to those which explicate the local topography, and commemorate people who have a relation to the city, the region, and Ukraine as a whole. As seen in Table 1, there is no commemoration of "Soviet-favored" personalities at the regional and national identity levels, which testifies to the perceived foreignness of this period of time. Yet, this is not the only point of opposition in the "toponymy-as-identity" ideological framework. The dichotomizing process that was involved in the intergroup opposition (i.e. communist vs non-communist place names) is projected inward onto intragroup relations, thereby creating subcategories within the group of non-communist place names. The basis for further partitioning is a similar iconization of certain toponyms as foreign — which, in their turn, are contrasted with those seen as belonging to the place.

Among the identified historical strata expressed in the officially approved toponymy (Gnatiuk 2018: 124), there are two periods not articulated in the toponymic recommendations I examined. These are Kievan Rus and Polish-Lithuanian Commonwealth, and the Ukrainian Insurgent Army. Though absent from the list produced by the working group, these respective toponyms were included in my questionnaire as variants of renaming that the group members could choose from. For each of the eight decommunized place names, there were given eight different naming suggestions. Of these, the only case in which commemoration of Kievan Rus was chosen was the name *ploshcha Volodymyra Velykoho*, selected for the abovementioned Artem Square. There was not a single mention of variants relating to the Ukrainian Insurgent Army, or the Organization of Ukrainian Nationalists.

Although positively appreciated by the history experts, Kievan Rus and its iconic figures were not mentioned in any answers to my question about historical associations that the working group members had with Kryvyi Rih. The various periods referred to were nomadic tribes, Cossacks, pre-Soviet industrial history, and Soviet-era industrialization. Commemorating the historical period of Kievan Rus, a trend popular among the city's officials, was not accepted eagerly by the group experts, since respective toponymy was seen as "abstract," "trivial and banal," and not related to the city of Kryvyi Rih. "What does Volodymyr the Great have to do with Kryvyi Rih?" asked one of the Ukrainian philologists. Emphasizing the individualization belief again, the philosophy expert explained the attitude:

> To use similar names in all [Ukrainian] cities, like those of Kievan Rus personalities, means they [those names] will be devoid of local specifics, and will soon become worn, as it's used to be with Karl Marx Street before. What does Karl Marx have to do with Kryvyi Rih?

The same attitude was expressed towards commemoration of Ukrainian Insurgent Army and the Organization of Ukrainian Nationalists, iconized in such figures as Stepan Bandera and Roman Shukhevych. It was neatly articulated by the geography expert in the following statement:

> We agreed upon one thing from the very start—no disputable issues... moreover, Stepan Bandera has nothing to do with the development of our region.

This attitude was reiterated in other interviews. "We didn't suggest Bandera Street, since we knew it might not be accepted," said one of the linguists. These arguments, given by the working group members, suggest that the intergroup opposition of "our own vs foreign" is reproduced within the category of non-communist place names, which are also divided into "foreign" and "our own."

Erasure. In case of toponymic ideology, erasure is the process in which some historical periods are rendered invisible. "Awkward" historical facts, and those inconsistent with a particular identity, will either be unobserved or erased from the toponymic landscape. This is a common goal of the process of renaming. By remembering certain events and figures, and simultaneously forgetting others, it is possible to concentrate on those features of identity formation that shape our particular definition of the self, as contrasted with some imagined "Other." As in the case of language ideologies, the Other is often imagined as homogeneous, essentialized, and simplified (Irvine & Gal 2000: 39).

The process of erasure can be identified in the following explanation of the purpose of the decommunization renaming. An explanation is offered by the expert in philosophy and logic:

> It is necessary to eradicate all the remains of the Soviet past from Ukraine. Otherwise, it will hang as dead weight. [...] Our young people should forget about this Lenin and never ask who he was. In such a case, Ukraine has good prospects. This [nostalgia] is what hampers our progress. It means that we are not oriented at Europe, but at some kind of obsolete social structure. This is particularly important for Ukraine, for these post-Soviet countries. We see that it [eradication of the Soviet past] has not occurred in Russia. Not only has it not occurred in Russia, but, on the contrary, it [the Soviet past] is being cherished, extended there. And we see that this is a dead end. [...] If we continued to strive for Europe with the old names and the old monuments, they would have dragged us back. While today's situation [after the renaming] is already taken as natural.

This thesis on forgetting the Soviet past was reiterated in responses to the questionnaire, especially when asked about the general importance of the renaming: "communism must be relegated to oblivion," "the city has to acquire a new identity, so that the place names could be associated with this particular city," "former names are either too abstract or do not accord with Ukrainian reality." The idea also surfaced in the interviews. This is what one of the historians said:

> The purpose of the renaming was to change the city's identity. [...] We had to change this communist city, which, judging by its street names, dated back to 1934, into an ancient city that arose on the spot of a Cossack settlement in the 17th century... we wanted to connect with a great history, with

a Ukrainian history, with Cossacks, with the history of Ukraine as a whole. [...] Renaming is a symbolic parting with our past for good.

"Very often opponents of the renaming would put forward an argument: 'This is history.' But we used to have Hitler Street, Hitler Strasse. And it was renamed," said another historian. "People have inhabited this place since very early times. It was not just Wild Field. There were some settlements here..." one of the linguists suggested, adding that the city's history could be drawn even to pre-Cossack times.

An important point in this narrative is that this "great Ukrainian history" is not imagined to be overly political and military. Out of seventy-seven commemorative toponyms, only fifteen memorialize people who were somehow concerned with political and military activities at various periods of time. These include Cossacks, such as Petro Kalnyshevskyi, who initiated the construction of the post road passing via the territory of today's Kryvyi Rih; political figures involved in the 1917–1921 Ukrainian struggle for independence, such as Mykhailo Hrushevskyi and Panas Fedenko; military men defending the city during occupation in World War II, such as Ivan Bedianko, the commander of a local partisan group; as well as those who died in the current Russian-Ukrainian armed conflict, such as General Radiievskyi, whose former regiment is located in Kryvyi Rih. Notwithstanding the little attention paid to such aspects as war and politics, this constructed Ukrainian history is, nevertheless, explicitly masculine. In the group of commemorative toponymies, there are only two names belonging to women remembered for their significance at the city's local scale. The names are of musician and author of the city's anthem, Iryna Shevchenko, and local newspaper journalist and World War II veteran, Tetiana Voronova.

This gendered aspect was explained by the commission members in quantitative terms of commemorating people's direct contributions to the city's and country's histories: "It was namely their contribution, rather than gender, that was accounted for." The paucity of political place names is caused by the perceived instability of an official state ideology and memory politics. "By contrast to science and art, political values are changeable," explained the philosophy expert, who also expressed hope that a small number of political toponyms would help to prevent the chance of future renaming. "There should be more local place names, and then the chance of a new renaming is smaller," said the geography expert, who insisted on including more topographical names in the suggested list. "This must be the final renaming. These place names should be of such a kind as not to ever be changed," emphasized one of the experts in history. He also accounted for the very little number of commemorative names referring to contemporary Ukrainian history. "As in the case with the ongoing Russian-Ukrainian conflict, let's wait for some years and then figure out exactly whose names we should commemorate," he said. This perceived changeability of Ukraine's present, and particularly its ideological doctrine, is the reason why political place names so rarely show up in the new toponymic landscape, and that political history is thus largely unobserved and unattended to in this way.

Conclusion

This study presents an original approach to capturing a "snapshot" of the decommunization process, embodied in the renaming of toponymic cityscape. While previous research concentrated on the officially approved lists of toponyms, this study examines a preceding stage in the process—the renaming recommendations authored by a local initiative group. Besides reviewing and comparing them with the officially endorsed place names, this research offers a deeply contextualized examination of the motives behind the group's renaming suggestions. From a methodological point of view, the study combines results from a questionnaire and in-depth interviews, while also taking a socio-onomastic approach to the problem of revealing the general tendencies for naming motives, which allows us to gain an insight into how certain place names are perceived. The framework of toponymic ideologies applied in the interpretation of these motives makes it possible to go beyond defining main regional strategies of renaming urban toponymy, and give account of the reasons why these particular strategies are preferred at a local level.

Analyses of the data show that renaming arises as a reconsideration and reconstruction of national identity, where history functions as an integral structural part. This toponymic ideology brings about the iconization of certain historical periods, such as Cossack times, 1917–1921 Ukrainian struggle for independence, and pre-Soviet and Soviet industrial growth—all of which are represented as commemorative, through association with specific personal and collective names. The multi-ethnic character of Ukrainian identity is iconized in the toponymic designation of the Roma minority, while this iconization is constrained by the major renaming ideology of belonging to the place.

The leading principle being "communist vs non-communist" opposition, the naming process redefines contemporary Ukrainian identity on the "non-communist" side, which evolves out of a general projection of the "our own vs foreign" dichotomy. Nonetheless, this logic also leads to the neglect in the renaming process of such historical periods as those of Kievan Rus and the Ukrainian Insurgent Army. These periods go unrecognized, and the communist period is erased altogether. Ukraine's political and military history is also largely unobserved, due to the perceived changeability of political values and the current time as a whole. Women's history is also unaccounted for, hardly represented at all at the city's local level. The Soviet-related toponymy, which characterizes local identity, is not associated with communist ideology—and therefore, is perceived in Kryvyi Rih to be "our own."

As shown by previous studies, Ukraine's decommunization renaming shares some common trends with other post-socialist European countries. The city of Kryvyi Rih is not an exception here. This study also suggests that appeals to the pre-Soviet era, as well as parts of the Soviet history of this particular city, arise as a result of an unclear nature of more recent historical events, and the general transience of any official state ideology. The decrease of political and military place names in favor of toponymy exhibiting local topographical features, as well as peculiarities of local industry and culture, can be seen as they are called forth by a desire to avoid any future renaming situations. The overall dominance of the local toponymy testifies to a growing ideology of individualization (as opposed to previous universalization) in the current process of identity formation we see across Ukraine.

Bibliography

Azaryahu, Maoz. (1997). German reunification and the politics of street names: the case of East Berlin. *Political Geography* 16(6): 479–493.

Azaryahu, Maoz. (2009). Naming the past: the significance of commemorative street names. In *Critical toponymies: the contested politics of place naming*, Berg, Lawrence D. & Vuolteenaho, Jani (eds). Farnham: Ashgate, 53–70.

Azaryahu, Maoz. (2011). The critical turn and beyond: the case of commemorative street naming. *ACME: An International E-journal for Critical Geographies* 10(1): 28–33.

Basso, Keith. (1996). *Wisdom sits in places: landscape and language among the western Apache*. Albuquerque: University of New Mexico Press.

Berezkina, Maimu. (2016). Linguistic landscapes and inhabitants' attitudes to place-names in multicultural Oslo. In *Names and naming: people, places, perceptions and power*, Puzey, Guy & Kostanski, Laura (eds.) Bristol: Multilingual Matters, 120–136.

Berg, Lawrence D. & Vuolteenaho, Jani (eds). (2009). *Critical toponymies: the contested politics of place naming*. Burlington, VT: Ashgate Publishing Company.

Bucher, Slavomir, Matlovič, René, Lukáčová, Alena, Harizal, Barbora, Matlovičová, Kvetoslava, Kolesárová, Jana, Čermáková, Lenka & Michalko, Miloslav. (2013). The perception of identity through urban toponyms in the regional cities of Slovakia. *Anthropological Notebooks* 19(3): 23–40.

David, Jaroslav. (2013). Street names — between ideology and cultural heritage. *Acta Onomastica* 54: 1–8.

Field, Margaret C. & Kroskrity, Paul V. (2009). Introduction: Revealing native American language ideologies. In *Native American language ideologies: beliefs, practices and struggles in Indian country*, Kroskrity, Paul V. & Field, Margaret C. (eds). Tucson: The University of Arizona Press, 3–28.

Gill, Graeme. (2005). Changing symbols: the renovation of Moscow place names. *The Russian Review* 64(3): 480–503.

Gnatiuk, Oleksiy. (2018). The renaming of streets in post-revolutionary Ukraine: regional strategies to construct a new national identity. *AUC Geographica* 53(2): 119–136.

Gomaniuk, Mykola. (2017). Dekomunizatsiini modeli pereimenuvannia naselenykh punktiv pivdnia Ukrainy (na prykladi Khersonskoi oblasti) [from Ukr.: Decommunization patterns of place renaming in the south of Ukraine (a case study of Kherson region)]. *Naukovyi visnyk Khersonskoho derzhavnoho universytetu* [from Ukr.: Kherson State University scientific bulletin] 6: 30–37.

The Law of Ukraine. (2015a). Zakon Ukrainy "Pro zasudzhennia komunistychnoho ta natsional-sotsialistychnoho (natsystskoho) totalitarnykh rezhymiv v Ukraini ta zaboronu propahandy ikh symvoliv" [from Ukr.: The Law of Ukraine "On the censure of the communist and national-socialist (Nazi) totalitarian regimes in Ukraine and the prohibition of propaganda of their symbols"]. *Zakonodavstvo Ukrainy*, https://zakon.rada.gov.ua/laws/show/317-19 (accessed 12 March 2020).

The Law of Ukraine. (2015b). Zakon Ukrainy "Pro pravovyi status ta vshanuvannia pam'iati bortsiv za nezalezhnist Ukrainy u XX st." [from Ukr.: The Law of Ukraine "On the legal status and commemoration of the strugglers for Ukraine's independence in the XX century"]. *Zakonodavstvo Ukrainy*, https://zakon.rada.gov.ua/laws/show/314-19 (accessed 12 March 2020).

Irvine, Judith T. (1989). When talk isn't cheap: language and political economy. *American Ethnologist* 16(2): 248–67.

Irvine, Judith T. & Gal, Susan. (2000). Language ideology and linguistic differentiation. In *Regimes of language: ideologies, polities, and identities*, Kroskrity, Paul V. (ed.). Santa Fe: School of American Research Press, 35–84.

Korotaiev, Oleksandr. (2017). Analiz protsesu dekomunizatsii u Kryvomu Rozi [from Ukr.: The analysis of the decommunization process in Kryvyi Rih]. In *Kryvorizhzhia: pohliad u mynule* [from Ukr.: Kryvorizhzhia: a glance in the past], Pechenina, Natalia, Tarasov, Andrii, Shliakhtych, Roman & Finicheva, Viktoriia (red.). Kryvyi Rih: Kryvyi Rih State Pedagogical University Press, 134–144.

Kostanski, Laura. (2009). 'What's in a name?': place and toponymic attachment, identity and dependence: a case study of the Grampians (Gariwerd) National Park name restoration process. *Semantic Scholar*, https://www.semanticscholar.org/paper/%27What%27s-in-a-name%27-%3A-place-and-toponymic-identity-%3A-Kostanski (accessed 5 December 2019).

Light, Duncan. (2004). Street names in Bucharest, 1990-1997: exploring the modern historical geographies of post-socialist change. *Journal of Historical Geography* 30(1): 154–172.

Light, Duncan, Nicolae, Ion & Suditu, Bogdan. (2002). Toponymy and the communist city: street names in Bucharest 1948-1965. *GeoJournal* 56(2): 135-144.

Melnyk, Oleksandr. (2015). *Naseleni mistsia Kryvorizhzhia (1750-1925): Kryvorizkyi i Shyrokivskyi raiony Dnipropetrovskoi oblasti* [from Ukr.: Settlements of Kryvorizhzhia (1750-1925): Kryvyi Rih and Shyroke neighbourhoods of Dnipropetrovsk region]. Kryvyi Rih: [without publ.].

Palonen, Emilia. (2008). The city-text in post-communist Budapest: street names, memorials, and the politics of commemoration. *GeoJournal* 73(3): 219-230.

Pavlenko, Aneta. (2011). Language rights versus speaker's rights: on the applicability of Western language rights approaches in Eastern European contexts. *Language Policy* 10(1): 37-58.

Pavlenko, Iryna. (2018). Urbanonimy yak zasib formuvannia istorychnoi pam'iati [from Ukr.: Urbanonyms as a means of shaping historical memory]. *Visnyk Zaporizkoho natsionalnoho universytetu* [from Ukr.: Zaporizhzhia National University bulletin] 2: 58-66.

Pipitone, Kaitlin E. (2019). *Mapping Ideologies: Place Names in Glacier National Park. Graduate student theses, dissertations, and professional papers*, https://scholarworks.umt.edu/etd/11393 (accessed 28 November 2019).

The Order. (2016). Rozporiadzhennia holovy Dnipropetrovskoi oblderzhadministratsii "Pro pereimenuvannia toponimiv u naselenykh punktakh oblasti" (dodatok 4) [from Ukr.: The order of the head of Dnipropetrovsk regional state council "On the renaming of toponyms in the settlements of the region" (attachment 4)], http://search.ligazakon.ua/l_doc2.nsf/link1/DN160098.html (accessed 12 December 2019).

Stipersky, Zoran, Lorber, Lučka, Heršak, Emil, Ptaček, Pavel, Gorka, Zygmunt, Koloś Arkadiusz, Lončar, Jelena, Faričić Josip, Miličević Mirjana, Vujakovič, Ana & Hruška, Anita. (2011). Identity through urban nomenclature: eight central European cities. *Geografisk Tidsskrift – Danish Journal of Geography* 111(?)· 181-194.

Viatrovych, Volodymyr, Shpak, Alina, Tylishchak, Volodymyr, Riabenko, Serhii, Hromenko, Serhii, Korolenko, Bohdan, Podobied, Pavlo, Budko, Serhii, Maiorov, Maksym, Karetnikov, Ihor & Horobets, Serhii (red.). (2015). *Dekomunizatsiia: shcho i chomu pereimenovuvaty j demontuvaty* [from Ukr.: Decommunization: what and why rename and dismantle]. Kyiv: Ukrainian Institute for National Memory.

Woolard, Kathryn A. & Schieffelin, Bambi B. (1994). Language ideology. *Annual Review of Anthropology* 23: 55-82.

2 The Friends So Far, the Foes So Near? Ambiguities of Georgia's Othering

Petra Colmorgen

In order to create a positive representation of its identity, Georgia emphasizes different aspects of belonging. Due to geography and geopolitics, history and heritage, there exists a big variety of potential identities to choose from and no less options to distance oneself from. Like the other South Caucasian small states Armenia and Azerbaijan, Georgia emerges with a unique scheme of who is considered to be friend and who is foe in immediate neighborhood and beyond. While Azerbaijan and Armenia found mighty supporters in the region with Turkey and Russia respectively, Georgia feels itself to belong to something spatially more distant. According to opinion polls, the thousands of kilometers distant United States are considered to be the main friend by a majority of Georgians (The Caucasus Research Resource Center 2019b). Neighboring Russia instead is considered to be the main enemy, followed by neighbor Turkey, though with significant distance (The Caucasus Research Resource Center 2019a). Due to different religious and ideological preferences, relations to Armenia and Azerbaijan are ambiguous as well. Accordingly, Georgia finds itself encircled by countries more or less strange to the construction of the Georgian Self. Or, as Stephen Jones put it:

> Many Georgians believe that they are European, but are trapped in a non-European environment. (Jones 2004: 99)

Stephen Jones has described the components of Georgianness through several "cultural paradigms"[1]. He argues that the country's Western orientation and its Orthodoxy are the most crucial identity elements. While there is consent in the literature about

---

1   Jones, Stephen. (2004). The Role of Cultural Paradigms in Georgian Foreign Policy. In *Ideology and National Identity in Post-Communist Foreign Policy*, Fawn, Rick (ed). London: Cass, 81–108.

those features being vital for Georgianness, the question has been neglected, how Georgianness is complemented by constructing a distance to its immediate neighbors, who represent a different faith or a different enthusiasm to westernize. This chapter aims to contribute to this discussion, and I will focus on the process of othering, which is necessary for the identity development through identification with and differentiation from the own Self. I will discuss the respective construction of Others vis-à-vis Westernness and Orthodoxy. As the analyses will show, a clear line between the Self and the Other might not always be drawn sharply. Instead of an Us versus Them dichotomy we rather look at a complicated net of entities and attributions. To begin with, Russia serves as the main Other to Georgia's crucial Western identity. Nonetheless, Russian Orthodoxy is in close proximity to the second essential part of the Georgian Self–its own religiosity and respective conservative values. Then, analogously the process of othering Islam based on Georgia's Orthodoxy as an identity marker produces also a complex picture regarding neighboring NATO member and EU candidate Turkey. Accordingly, one and the same object can be a source of identification or differentiation at the same time.

Thus, my objective for this chapter will be to discuss different aspects of who represents the Other for Georgia and to develop potential answers to the question, why the distinction between the Self and Other of Georgianness might be blurred. On one hand, I hope to shed light on the ambiguous processes of othering Georgia's two biggest neighbors Russia and Turkey. On the other hand, I aspire to discuss how Georgia's construction of Others affects different domestic groups within its state border as well. I will argue that the main reason for the complexity of Georgia's othering can be found in the Georgian Self: the country's main identity parameters Westernness and Orthodoxy are in conflict with each other. In their pure form, they appear to be mutually exclusive. Accordingly, in present day Georgia the construction of Georgianness between Orthodoxy and Westernness also constitutes a main cleavage in society. This ambiguity is transmitted into processes of othering, which remain accordingly rather flexible.

Othering as Identity Construction

With the collapse of the Soviet Union, constructions of national identities have been in high demand, aiming to support nation building in the now post-Soviet space (Jones 2004: 82). For relational constructivists, identity formation requires a negotiation process between the Self and Others, which results in demarcations between the two (Risse 2017: 83; Hagström & Gustafsson 2015: 5; Jensen 2011: 66; Göl 2005: 1; Neumann 1999; Wendt 1994: 386). For a domestic audience, discourses about who is friend and who is foe are perceived as important tools for mobilization and strengthening group cohesion (Szkola 2017: 7). Othering is not restricted to role identities, like ally or enemy, but the attribution of roles is unthinkable without the construction of Others (Rumelili 2004: 32) Applying discursive tools, the national Self emerges through precisely this differentiation from what an entity is not in relation to something other, thus constructing the "in" and "out", the "we" and "them" (Lindgren & Lindgren 2017: 381, 2017: 379; Staszak 2009: 43; Jørgensen & Phillips 2002: 50–51). According to Iver Neumann, to study the Self and Other nexus enables a better understanding about the constitution of various actors in foreign policy (Neumann 1999: 37). Kornely Kakachia argues that Georgia's foreign policy is particularly identity driven and not primarily based on realist assumptions like national interest or the balance of power (Kakachia 2012: 5).

In certain aspects, othering produces a moral order and reduces those who are othered to stereotypical negative characteristics. They also might be rendered as inferior or dangerous (Szkola 2017: 7; Hagström & Gustafsson 2015: 7; Brons 2015: 70; Jensen 2011: 65; Staszak 2009: 43). Particularly in postcolonial studies, scientific literature concentrates on analyzing relations between the imperial core and the formerly marginalized colonial Others (Mamadouh & Bialasiewicz 2016: 129). The formation of an European identity through othering Russia and Turkey has received a lot of academic attention in this respect (Lindstrom 2003: 319). Without question, othering as a process results in a certain judgement about the Other. But it does not necessarily have to produce a consideration of the

Other as inferior. Instead, there can be positive othering with an object of aspiration, of identification and negative othering with entities, who show undesired characteristics (Russo 2018: 132). Alexander Wendt emphasizes this aspect back in 1994:

> Identification is a continuum from negative to positive-from conceiving the other as anathema to the self to conceiving it as an extension of the self. (Wendt 1994: 386)

Lene Hansen observes that one Other might contain more than one attribution at the same time, when it quasi gets split into sub-Others. Using the US narrative about the war in Iraq, she demonstrates that the object of othering (Iraq) was split into the repressive Saddam Hussein regime on one hand and the oppressed Iraqi people on the other hand (Hansen 2006: 36).

The two last assumptions will play a crucial role in my analyses: First, the construction of an Other can but does not necessarily have to be negative. An Other can be perceived to be different from the Self, but might serve as a positive Other, an Other with whom similarities are shared. Second, one and the same Other can contain different attributions. A third important condition of othering is that it might have an internal, a domestic element as well. Although principally directed outwards, the construction of an Other might also have powerful repercussions inside the country. This aspect of indirect othering will also play a major role in this discussion.

The departure point for this chapter is Stephen Jones' study of Georgian identity markers. Jones developed four Georgian cultural paradigms: 1) Religious identity, 2) Western identity, 3) Anti-Russian Sentiment, and 4) Pan-Caucasian identity[2]. While the first two constitute the dominant elements of Georgianness, the Anti-Russian Sentiment will be discussed in this chapter in form of a constructed Other. Putting Turkey and Russia into the context of the Georgian Selves and Others demonstrates that we do not look

---

2   The relevance of the Pan-Caucasian/South-Caucasian identity aspect has been questioned by Jones himself. A full analysis of this parameter is outside the scope of this chapter. For further reading: Russo 2018: 128–139; Jones 2004: 90; Chikovani 2005: 52

simply at relations between the two, but rather at a complex net of different attributions and entities.

Western Self: "I am Georgian, Therefore I am European"[3]

According to Jones, Westernness is one of the two crucial features of Georgian identity (Jones 2004: 88–90). The affirmation of Georgian Westernness[4] is directed to an external international audience as well as to the internal domestic public. At home, Westernization is perceived as modernization and thus "the aspiration to establish Western-style democracy became a part of the Georgian subconscious" (Kakachia 2012: 6).

In order to convince international partners to advocate for Georgian accession to NATO and EU, a powerful pro-Western narrative was created and reinforced (Kakachia & Minesashvili 2015: 171–172). Westernness is portrayed as an intrinsic, century old feature of Georgianness. To be European is not a recent state of mind, but a historic continuation and even a "matter of historical justice" (Kakachia 2012: 5–6), a "return to the West" (Storm 2019: 137), the attempt to "retake its rightful place in Europe" (Beacháin & Coene 2014: 923). This claim to reconnect to Europe is stated in a strategy paper of the Ministry of Foreign Affairs as well:

> The highest priority of Georgian foreign policy is to achieve full integration into European political, economic, and security structures, thus fulfilling the historical aspiration of the Georgian nation to participate fully in the European community. (Georgian Ministry of Foreign Affairs 2000)

Implicit in this context is that Georgia is (still) not sufficiently European (Nakhutsrishvili & Lejava 2018: 12). The emphasize on the return to Europe includes the distance from it as well as the

---

3   Georgian Prime Minister Zurab Zhvania spoke these words in a speech on the occasion of Georgia's accession to the Council of Europe in Strasbourg in 1999.
4   In this context, Western identity and European identity are used interchangeably and might include identification with the United States as well. In line with Gamkrelidze, Europe is seen rather as a discourse and bearer of certain values than a coherent concept (Gamkrelidze 2019: 352).

aspiration to finally reach it (Gamkrelidze 2019: 351)[5]. At the same time, Europe is perceived to be on one hand superior and at the same time identical to the own identity (Hansen 2006: 35). Whether such popular historically and culturally grounded narratives about Georgia's ancient European identity are justified, is hard to tell. Donnacha Beacháin and Frederik Coene argue that such arguments are not "incontrovertible and waterproof". On the other hand, the authors state that there is no evidence of Georgia's non-European identity either and that to feel European might also be considered to be sufficient (Beacháin & Coene 2014: 928).

Although full accession to EU and NATO is out of sight for Georgia and despite changes in power, Western identity is stably featured since the mid 1990ies and has "become the point of national consensus that no party of any consequence challenged" (Nodia 2017: 18). Particularly the Saakashvili administration made Westernness the top narrative. Kornely Kakachia interprets this overload of identity rhetoric as an attempt to compensate for a lack of any tangible interest or military support of the West during the war in 2008 (Khelashvili 2012: 8). Then president Saakashvili presented the country as an integral part of the freedom and democracy seeking movements, as part of the "Arab Spring" regime change initiatives (Kakachia et al. 2018: 8). Fighting for democracy, Georgia was supposed to perform as a regional "norm entrepreneur"[6] in the post-Soviet space (Wivel 2016: 101). In this narrative, the Georgian democracy movement would spread into the entire region and cause a domino effect, sweeping authoritarian powers around peacefully out of office. It was hoped to receive respectively high credits for this pioneer role from Western states (Oskanian 2016: 5). Eventually, this democracy euphoria was hoped to also

---

5   A similar discourse took place in Slovenia and Croatia before their accession to the EU, focusing on Balkan, post-Yugoslav and European identity (Lindstrom 2003: 313–314).
6   Scandinavian small states have been originally described to act as such *"norm entrepreneurs"* on the international stage with respect to promoting sustainable development, peaceful conflict resolution and redistribution of wealth (Ingebritsen 2002: 20).

infect Georgia's secessionist entities Abkhazia and South Ossetia and thus reconnect them to Georgia proper.

It cannot be ignored that democratic aspirations and political realities have not always been congruent. The violent crackdown of opposition protests in 2007 under the Saakashvili administration was one such example. The sharp increase of Georgia's prison population, which quadrupled from 2003 to 2011 due to Saakashvili's zero tolerance policy was another alarming sign (Di Puppo 2019: 18). And also the Georgian Dream Coalition's handling of recent anti-government protest, aspects of the electoral reform, arrests of opposition members and the appointment of politically dependent judges do not look any more democratically mature (Jam News 2020). Society's reaction to such undemocratic steps is quite powerful and persistent (Roehrs-Weist 2018). Thus, the Georgian public might have internalized Western identity more successfully and sustainably than its political elite in the government.

Western Self Versus Russian Other: Favorite Foes Forever?

Out of all Georgian neighbors, in the recent discourse, Russia stands out as the most crucial, the most fundamental Other to Georgianness. While Jones discusses "Anti-Russiansism" (Jones 2004: 91-93) as a self-standing Georgian cultural paradigm, I contextualize Russia differently. I argue that Russia should be considered as the main Other to the Georgian Western Self. In this respect, Russia is framed to personify certain, specifically anti-Western characteristics. Since Russia has proven to be an assertive and hostile neighbor after the dissolution of the Soviet Union, sincere rapprochement cannot be on the agenda. Although Russia's ambitions as a Great Power might be comparable to those of the USSR, its ideational and material resources are scarcer (Timofeev 2017). In economic and innovative terms this lack of attractiveness becomes particularly obvious (Kakachia & Minesashvili 2015: 177).

Saakashvili had been particularly outspoken about this otherness of Russia. The war in 2008 had been contextualized in this respect as well. He claimed that Georgia had been attacked by Russia because of different values and its democratic and economic successes, which were not acceptable for Moscow (Atlantic Council 2010). Quoting Georgia's better ratings in the Corruption Perception Index (CPI) from Amnesty International, he emphasized Georgia's progressiveness and successes in combating corruption in contrast to the Russian Other with increased perceived corruption, which is expressed through a lower rank in the CPI:

> Coincidentally and curiously enough, Russia moved the same for the same period, 78 positions down, so exactly the opposite movements.[7] (Atlantic Council 2010)

Russia is portrayed to be the main obstacle to full Europeanization and accession to NATO and EU precisely because of the Russian otherness of its political system and values. Accordingly, all hostile actions of the northern neighbor are interpreted to target Georgia's Western Self (Szkola 2018: 245). In Saakashvili's view, Russia showed a certain degree of inferiority, since it could not reach the state of an open and democratic society yet (Atlantic Council 2010). This moral judgement is characteristic for othering processes and enables a positive self-image. After the transition of power in 2012, the ruling Georgian Dream Coalition sought a less confrontational course towards Russia and might be characterized to be more balanced in comparison to the uncompromising westernizing United National Movement under Saakashvili (Buzogány 2019: 98). Despite this re-orientation of the government, public anti-Russian sentiment remains high. According to 2019 opinion polls from the Caucasus Barometer, Russia is seen as the main enemy of the country by 49% of the population, the highest value since 2013 (The Caucasus Research Resource Center 2019a). One reason for the peak in 2019 might be the government's violent reaction to protests

---

[7] The rank in this index is of limited information value, though. This is due to the fact that the total amount of ranked countries varies each year and that it is relational to the other countries. A more objective criterion would be the absolute CPI score. Georgia was first analyzed in 1999 and scored 2,3 in comparison to 2,4 for Russia (10,0 is the best, corruption-free score). When the interview with the Atlantic Council was conducted in 2010, Georgia scored 3,8 and Russia 2,1. So while there is a significant decrease of corruption in Georgia, the increase of corruption in Russia is not equally strong.

in Tbilisi in June 2019. They were triggered by the speech of a Russian MP in the Georgian Parliament in Russian language (Machaidze 2019). Accordingly, they need to be understood as an expression of opposition to Russian policies as well as of the public impression of alienation from the Georgian Dream Coalition government.

Today, despite different agendas and instruments of the Tsarist Empire, the Soviet Union and present day Russian Federation, enmity is constructed as a continuum towards the "oppressing other" (Leonardis 2016: 48). However, the perceived Anti-Westernness of Russia is a crucial parameter, which defines the degree of attributed otherness. Russian annexation, which started in 1801 after Ottoman rule, was seen instead rather as an opportunity to reconnect to the Christian West and its ideas despite scarifying Georgian independence (Jones 2004: 89). Jones argues further that despite an anti-European image due to autocracy in the Tsarist Empire and anti-Western Soviet ideology, both systems did represent a link to European culture (Jones 2004: 92). Other authors emphasize the othering of the Soviet Union and describe Communism as an important Other again, isolating Georgia further from its Europeanness (Kakachia & Minesashvili 2015: 174). The attempt to other the Soviet Union is noticeable in many spheres. One example of this attitude is the renaming of central public spaces with Russian or Soviet names in the capital Tbilisi to "Western Ones" like Freedom Square or Europe Square (Leonardis 2016: 51). Another example is the Victory Day Celebration. This day can neither be ignored out of respect for the veterans, nor can it be celebrated in a Soviet traditional way, emphasizing the glory of the Red Army with a military parade. Tbilisi celebrates this day now in a "European way" on the 8th of May instead of the 9th. The main direction is to establish "mournful remembrance as the dominant emotional component rather than a celebration of glory crowned by a military parade, as it is in Russia" (Khutsishvili 2018: 74).[8]

---

[8] The question about how to deal with Stalin in his homeland Georgia and more specifically in his hometown Gori, which is home to a controversial Stalin

Western Self and Russian Other are mutually constitutive in a self-reinforcing process. Accordingly, othering is fostered by a high degree of perceived Russian Anti-Westernness. Russian assertive foreign policies for its part additionally deepen this otherness. On the other hand, the extensive use of various soft and hard power instruments against Georgia has so far rather strengthened Westernization efforts (Delcour & Wolczuk 2015: 462). This development materializes itself within the state borders as well. Promoting a Western identity and othering Russia resulted in unbridgeable conflicts between Georgia and its secessionist entities South Ossetia and Abkhazia.

Western Self Versus Secessionist Entities: Intrinsically Anti-Western?

Not all of Georgia's official state territory can share the enthusiasm about Westernization. In Georgia's secessionist entities, a feeling of ancient Europeanness is rather absent and reconnection to the West (and Georgia) is not attractive for South Ossetians and Abkhazians. That the West supports Georgia's maximum demand of territorial integrity is one of the reasons, why Abkhazia and South Ossetia cannot identify themselves with the West properly. This leads to intrinsic opposition to NATO and EU and might not come as a surprise (Cooley 2017: 3–4). Furthermore, Western players inhibit the recognition of the secessionists' main goal of independence. Not only do those factors prevent identification with the West in particular, in more general terms, cultural paradigms of the center cannot be shared by the secessionists anyway. This is due to the fact that, they need to establish their own identity narrative and precisely need to create their own boundaries of us and them (Szkola 2018: 245).

Since Georgia's aim is territorial integrity and the secessionist entities are therefore regarded as part of the Self, there is no direct othering of South Ossetia and Abkhazia. We rather look at a form

---

museum, remains ambiguous, too. For further reading: Leonardis 2016: 52; Kabachnik 2018.

of indirect othering, which contains three main aspects. First, the entities themselves are portrayed as anti-democratic with a low rule of law status. Thus, they are constructed as anti-Western per se. This view included accusations of a low level of human right protection as well as broad criminal activity in South Ossetia and Abkhazia (Civil.ge 2005b, 2005a). After 2005, the emphasis at least in the academic discourse about the state of democracy shifted towards the democratic achievements in secessionist entities (Kopeček et al. 2016: 89). The secessionists' democracy development does not necessarily have to be worse than in their parent states, since both might show similar scores in democracy ratings like the Freedom House Index (Blakkisrud & Kolstø 2012: 286). Another effect related to the Georgian Western identity narrative was that democratic ambitions were not always met by the Georgian reality itself. Repressive behavior like the violent crackdown of protests in 2007 harmed the logic of the democratization champion narrative and "did not make convincing the skeptical Abkhazians and Ossetians about the inevitable attractiveness of Georgian capitalist liberal-democracy easier" (Oskanian 2014: 12). An increasingly assertive reintegration course under Saakashvili and measures to enforce it, like the isolation of South Ossetia from 2004 onwards alienated them even further (Waal 2008). Finally, the war in 2008 did sustainably spoil Georgia's already complicated relation to its secessionist entities (Blakkisrud & Kolstø 2012: 290).

Second, othering is expressed indirectly, through aversion against Russia not against Abkhazians themselves (Khutsishvili 2018: 80). For Georgia, Russia's activity is solely interpreted as neo-imperialist (Atlantic Council 2010; Abushov 2009: 190). Blaming exclusively Russia to initiate and foster conflicts with Georgia's minorities was and is a popular nationalistic topos after independence from the Soviet Union (Sadigbeyli 2002: 54). This is strongly connected with the denial of any separate identity for the secessionist entities, but the perception that they are nothing else but "Russian puppets". Thus any potential Georgian responsibility can be externalized (Kakachia 2012: 5).

Third, there is a "spillover effect" of othering Russia. Because the negative sentiment against Moscow is not shared in the secessionist entities, South Ossetia and Abkhazia are indirectly othered as well. Their Russia friendly attitude is largely a consequence of the strong ethno-nationalistic Georgian course after independence (Oskanian 2016: 6). For South Ossetians and Abkhazians, who had certain autonomy rights during Soviet times, living under *georgifying* conditions in independent Georgia became increasingly "unthinkable" (Cornell 2003: 151). Massive Georgian isolation efforts have made Russian patronage inevitable (Ker-Lindsay & Berg 2018). Recent fieldwork has shown that Russia is not perceived as an Other there, but rather associated to the Self. Based on a survey from 2017, across all age groups (18 to over 60) more than 70% of the inhabitants of South Ossetia and even more than 80% of the Abkhaz population agree that they are part of the "Russki Mir"[9] (O'Loughlin et al. 2017: 18). In an earlier survey, the team around O'Loughlin asked whether the collapse of the Soviet Union was the right or the wrong step. A clear majority in Abkhazia[10] and to a bigger extent with over 70% in South Ossetia perceive the dissolution as the wrong step (Toal & O'Loughlin 2014). Finally, starting in the early 2000s, Russian passports were issued in both secessionist entities. Accordingly, the majority of inhabitants in South Ossetia and Abkhazia are Russian citizens (Gerrits & Bader 2016: 303).

---

9   The *"Russian World"* is a fluid idea, which moves between the promotion of Russian language and culture abroad and the protection and management of the relation with compatriots in the neighboring countries. It includes the understanding of a distinct Russian cultural space, which can be understood in contrast to imagined other concepts like "The West" (O'Loughlin et al., 2017, p. 7; Toal, 2017, p. 243).
10 The survey shows different results for different ethnic groups in Abkhazia. While the values for inhabitants from Abkhaz, Armenian and Russian origin do not differ significantly, Georgians/Mingrelians perceive the dissolution of the Soviet Union to a lesser extent as a wrong step and are less supportive of the Russian leadership.

Orthodox Self: I am Georgian, Therefore I am Orthodox?

Stephen Jones put "Religious Identity"[11] first when he described Georgianness (Jones 2004: 85–87). The Georgian Orthodox Church (GOC) is presented as the stable preserver and transmitter of Georgia's ancient heritage and therefore essential for the fight for independence during the most tumultuous times and occupations. In this respect, similar to constructing intrinsic Westernness, Georgia's antiquity and heroism as a defender of European Christianity is emphasized through its role in fighting non-Christian invasions (Kakabadze & Makarychev 2018: 493). Accordingly, the GOC is rather of national importance than of religious. "It represents politics, not metaphysics" (Jones 2004: 87). Its importance for the national liberation movement in the 1980ies and the role to protect Georgia's identity is described similarly to that of the Polish Catholic Church (Kakabadze & Makarychev 2018: 493; Jones 2004: 86). With 70% either trusting or very trusting the GOC (The Caucasus Research Resource Center 2019c), the Church is a highly respected institution. Another important criterion is its stability, which is particularly obvious in comparison to other institutions like a volatile party system (Reisner 2015: 99).

Starting with Shevardnadze, the GOC gained concrete political influence. The former member of the Politburo of the Communist Party Shevardnadze got baptized by Patriarch Ilia II in 1992 and a symbiosis between politics and the GOC began, where the latter would guarantee support, while the government would grant certain privileges to the GOC (Halbach 2016: 15). Saakashvili instead took office with a different approach. Promoting a Western democracy model, secularism was more in line with his vision of statehood. Emphasizing a civil instead of an ethno-religious understanding of Georgian nationalism, his government hoped to include minorities more successfully (Reisner 2015: 98). The year 2012

---

11 In this context, religious identity is used synonymously with Georgian Orthodoxy or more broadly Christianity and is institutionally represented by the Georgian Orthodox Church (GOC).

changed the power balance between the state and the GOC towards the Church again. Oliver Reisner argues that the GOC's support for the Georgian Dream Coalition already during the campaign caused the newly elected government to return those favors (Reisner 2015: 106–107). Consequently, the GOC takes an increasingly engaged stand as a political actor in domestic like in foreign policy (Siroky et al. 2017: 506; Halbach 2016: 20). Sophie Zviadadze concludes that the GOC is today "the most 'visible' actor in Georgia's public life" (Zviadadze 2015: 51).

In contrast to the recent omnipresence of the GOC in public discourses, during officially atheist Soviet times, religiosity was practiced rather in domestic spheres (Gurchiani 2017: 518). Ketevan Gurchiani argues further that despite the institutional invisibility, Orthodoxy was a vital element of Georgianness during Soviet times as well, differentiating the country's identity from others "in the vast pot of Soviet 'atheist' nations" (Gurchiani 2017: 517). Due to the deep religious permeation of politics, culture and society, Georgian identity is often equaled to being Georgian Orthodox (Minesashvili 2017b: 7; Ladaria 2002: 108). This construction "creates a normality in which the community expects its members to be Orthodox Christians" (Gurchiani 2017: 527). Such an assumption marginalizes other religious or ethnic minorities and became a source of serious dissent with these groups (Jones 2004: 86). Before we come to those domestic repercussions of the Orthodox Self, I want to discuss how this stark religious identity affects the construction of external Others. Except of Russia[12], all of Georgia's neighbor countries practice a religion different to Orthodoxy. Turkey, as the successor state of the Ottoman Empire and influential partner of recent Georgia stands out in this respect and is subject to a complex construction of othering.

---

12   In the bordering Russian region North Caucasus instead, Islam is the dominant religion.

Orthodox Self Versus Muslim Other: A Matter of Turkey's Heritage?

The construction of an ancient Orthodox Self differentiates the Georgian identity from surrounding neighbors of different faith, in particular Muslims (German 2015: 607). Jones does not dismiss the idea of othering Islam, but regarding Turkey he argues that its othering is based on "historical experience rather than religious differences" (Jones 2004: 97). Until the fall of the Iron Curtain and respective reconnection to the Turkish neighbor, Ottoman and Turkish heritage in Georgia has been mainly framed in terms of invasion and expansion (Kononczuk 2008: 32) or forced disconnection from Georgia's rightful cultural European and Christian habitat (Tsintskiladze 2019; Kakachia & Minesashvili 2015: 176). Experiencing vivid Turkish engagement[13] in various spheres after the dissolution of the Soviet Union, nevertheless, Islamophobic connotation prevails. Andrea Weiss and Yana Zabanova observe that Georgian-Turkish relations include "anti-Muslim and anti-Turkish sentiments in line with narratives prevalent in national historiography and with dominant currents in the Georgian Orthodox Church" (Weiss & Zabanova 2016: 5). In line with that, I would argue that it is impossible to separate the historic from the religious image of Turkey. Accordingly, the Orthodox Self is also constructed in differentiation to a Muslim Other, which is (externally) most significantly represented by Turkey.

The othering of Turkey is common practice in the public and political sphere. Monitoring 17 Georgian tabloid and mainstream media outlets, the Media Development Foundation issues annual Hate Speech reports with significant amounts of Turcophobic messages. In the respective report from 2018, Xenophobic messages were the third year in a row the most common objects of Hate Speech (Gogoladze 2019). Within this category, Turcophobic

---

13 Trilateral cooperation with Azerbaijan is flourishing around the Baku-Tbilisi-Ceyhan pipeline and had been extended by a military component. Furthermore, there is deep economic integration with a Turkish-Georgian Free Trade Agreement and a very liberal border regime, which allows border crossing only with ID cards.

statements were the second most voiced ones. The majority of those Turcophobic messages dealt with assumed Turkish cultural, economic and religious expansion. This perception can be partly explained by the activity of Turkish donors and their support for the construction of religious buildings and Islamic centers (Khalvashi 2012: 15). One persistent source of conflict is the reconstruction of the Aziziye Mosque in Batumi. Critics argue that the mosque will be a fully functioning religious center and a powerful symbol of Turkey's presence (Chedia 2012). Proponents argue, that mosques had been part of Georgia's heritage just as Orthodox churches and deserve preservation as well (Zviadadze 2015: 54).

The engagement of Turkish state and non-state-actors in the field of religious education is seen particularly critical. Finding no adequate institution at home, Georgian Muslims get educated directly in Turkey and are suspected to promote the interests of Turkish clerics back home (Ivanov 2011: 82; Sanikidze & Walker 2004: 15). Another ambivalent issue is that of the flourishing entertainment industry in Adjara. Adapting to the demands of Turkish tourists, businessmen or transit drivers had massive implications for the locals. Tamta Khalvashi discussed, how increased lorry traffic from Turkey replaced the traditional citrus fruit business in Gonio, a small village between Sarpi and Batumi. The truck drivers were not only in demand for parking spaces and restaurants, but their presence triggered the large scale appearance of illegal brothels in resident's buildings, crowding out traditional family life (Khalvashi 2015: 114).

The unease towards the Turkish visibility in Adjara led to political mobilization and took Turcophobic characteristics (Smolnik et al. 2018: 573). Turcophobia became a unifying tool for some politicians, particularly during the election campaign in 2012 (Weiss & Zabanova 2016: 6; Cecire 2013: 122; Goksel 2013: 2). The calculation of the Georgian Dream Coalition, which had the support of the GOC, can be roughly explained as follows: Since rapprochement with Russia is on its agenda, Turkey plays the role of the "only real alternative to the 'enemy' Russia" (Mindiashvili 2012). This framing is different to the rather inclusive character of the previous Saakashvili government, where Turkish investments and deepened bilateral ties have been fostered heavily. The hope was to overcome prejudices in society through prosperous economic relations and people-to-people contacts (Goksel 2013: 6). This aspiration seemed to have been over optimistic and Saakashvili's statement that "Turkey has won the hearts of every Georgian" (Kiniklioğlu 2004: 45) was surely too optimistic.

To reject Islam is considered to be naturally Georgian, but this othering does not only affect neighboring Turkey. Having traditionally and persistently complex relations to Ankara and being home to a significant Muslim minority, already mentioned Adjara is an internal object of this othering as well.

Orthodox Self Versus Muslim Minorities: Not Georgian Enough?

Like discussed, Orthodoxy is such a strong component of Georgian identity that those, who have a different religion might be subject to othering. Like in the indirect othering of South Ossetia and Abkhazia, all Adjarians are considered to be part of the national Self, of the Georgian nation. In reality instead, we look again at some indirect and internal othering. This is by no means a new development. Starting already from medieval times, Georgians could quasi be deprived of their Georgianness by practicing a faith different from Christian Orthodox:

> 'French' became the name used to describe Catholic Georgians, Muslim Georgians became 'Tatar', and those baptized in an Armenian church, 'Armenians'. (Gurchiani 2017: 517)

This othering of Muslims comes to the surface particularly in Adjara. Many inhabitants of the region bordering Turkey converted to Islam overtime after its incorporation into the Ottoman Empire starting from the 15th century. In the late 19th century, Russia controlled the province and later on it became an autonomous region within the Socialist Soviet Republic Georgia (Cornell 2003: 163). After Georgia's independence, urban inhabitants in Batumi converted in large numbers to Orthodoxy, but in the rural areas in upper Adjara, Islam dominates (Pelkmans 1999: 54). People from Adjara do not define themselves as a distinct ethnic group but identify as Georgian. Since the rebirth of Georgian nationalism in the 1980ies and the growing visibility of the GOC, this creates a particular identity dilemma for the local Muslim minority (Pelkmans 2003: 46). Dominant Orthodoxy creates stark assimilation pressure for those parts of the Georgian society, which are not Orthodox (Reisner 2015: 105). Uwe Halbach describes Adjara therefore to have become an arena of "Kulturkampf" between the Christian Orthodox majority and the Muslim minority, which intersects with resentments towards growing Turkish influence (Halbach 2016: 21).

Nonetheless, it shall be mentioned that besides of the othering and its political exploitation, there exists a valuable heritage of interreligious harmony in Georgia. Anthropologists have described traditional ceremonies, which mixed Muslim, Christian, pagan and secular elements like the Alaverdoba festival in Kakheti, whose religiously inclusive character came under threat recently due to restrictive interference from the local Orthodox Church authorities (Mühlfried 2015). In all day life, there seems to exist a rather high degree of religious flexibility in Georgia as well. People are able to switch codes between the Self and the Other easily, depending on whether they are in a Muslim, Christian or mixed context (Smolnik et al. 2018: 573).

Identity Flexibilities: Positive Others and Cleavage within the Selves

Like discussed, Russia is the most obvious Other to Georgia's Western identity construction. Emphasizing Russia's democratic inferiority, the othering of the Northern neighbor is clearly negative in this respect. Despite this differentiation from Russia's anti-Western position, Russia's ideas of religious conservatism fall on fertile ground in Georgia and are in line with those of the GOC. The Russian Orthodox Church (ROC) is a crucial actor in the traditional value discourse. The ideals of the ROC are very near to the Georgian Orthodox Self and rather an object of identification than of distinction.

Both Churches are connected through "Orthodox brotherhood" and the ROC is an important point of reference for the GOC (Kakabadze & Makarychev 2018: 493). Being the bigger brother in this relation, the ROC is an influential actor towards Georgian orthodox culture (Makarychev & Yatsyk 2017: 12). Both Churches agree about the superiority of Orthodoxy and the respective lack of morality in the West (Kakabadze & Makarychev 2018: 496). This orthodox consent is in stark contrast to the official pro-Western orientation of the government. Accordingly, religion might serve as a powerful soft power tool for Russia (Siroky et al. 2017: 513–514). Although this is obviously in line with Russia's interests, whether there is a strategy for that as such is disputed. Andrey Makarychev and Alexandra Yatsyk emphasize instead that the ROC lacks any specific policy towards Georgia. They argue further that instead of the ROC pushing its agenda it might be rather the GOC utilizing elements of the conservative discourse for their domestic purposes (Makarychev & Yatsyk 2017: 12). However, the GOC has its own communication channels to Russia, which became even more relevant after the war in 2008 (Russo 2018: 119). In 2013, Patriarch Illia II met with President Putin in Moscow and emphasized the need of pragmatic relations between both countries (Halbach 2016: 19). After meeting Putin, the Georgian Patriarch emphasized the eternal love between both countries (Kakachia 2014: 4–5). Stressing the unity between both Churches and states by the GOC, the othering of Russia in solely negative terms is accordingly not complete. Through Orthodoxy, othering Russia has a positive aspect as well.

To describe othering Turkey only as negative stays incomplete as well. Relations to the Western neighbor are rather multidimensional and go far beyond the construction of Turkey solely as a Muslim country. In one respect, the negative othering of Turkey is broken by vivid economic activities. Besides of trade relations, Turkish direct investments in Georgia are significant and Turkish companies got involved in several infrastructure projects, like the construction of a hydropower plant on the Chorokh river or the management of the airports Tbilisi and Batumi for the TAV airport holding (Goksel 2013: 1). Additionally, despite long lasting "historic enmity" following invasions and dominations, Turkey has never behaved subverting or destructive toward the Georgian state after independence. Although Ankara tolerates support for Abkhazia and thus de facto challenges the embargo, in Adjara, the province where it is perceived to play the role of a patron to some extent, Turkey did not attempt to ever question Georgia's territorial integrity (Waal 2010: 147). Even more important is Turkey's identity aspect Westernness. Jones goes as far as to say that the crucial role Russia once played for the modernization of Georgia in the 19th century is now performed by Turkey (Jones 2004: 97). For Georgia, "Turkey became a 'window overlooking Europe'" (Kononczuk 2008: 32). When both countries started to deepen their cooperation, Turkey was accordingly perceived to be vital for Georgia's Westernization. Holding the status of a member candidate for the European Union and being an active NATO member, Turkey was anticipated to actively promote Georgia's accession to these institutions. It was hoped that Georgia would be serving as a transit partner for oil and gas from Azerbaijan and the Caspian Sea to Turkey, good governance in return would flow to Georgia via Turkey from Europe. Thus, Turkey was seen to be a "proactive integration corridor"[14] (Goksel 2011: 6). Although those anticipations were often disappointed by a rather volatile foreign policy course of the ruling AKP in Turkey, at the end of the day, Turkey is Georgia's Western neighbor. It is still the only country within reach with direct and long-lasting ties to the West. Thus, Turkey is not only an object of negative othering in the Orthodoxy-Islam identity context but is object to positive othering as well. Accordingly, Georgia's Western identity construction leads also to a positive picture of and approach to the Turkish neighbor to a certain extent.

Having analyzed the othering of Russia and Turkey respectively, the question remains, why both are othered positively and negatively. I would argue that one of the main reasons is the inherent conflicting character between the two discussed Georgian

---

14 With new domestic and foreign policy priorities of the recent government, today, Turkey rather challenges and questions norms of the European Union (Fischer and Seufert 2018: 271). Despite anti-Western rhetoric, Turkey's anchoring in Western institutions, particularly in NATO is not seriously questioned.

identity parameters, Westernness and Orthodoxy. To find a suitable position between these two extremes is in constant negotiation in Georgia. The question is to which degree an Orthodox country can follow Western values or, vice versa, which degree of Orthodoxy is tolerable for a Western culture.

To find answers to those questions is a rather difficult and dynamic endeavor along the cleavage of conservatism versus progressiveness in Georgian society. The GOC has not only a pro-Russian position but shows a distinct anti-Western attitude. Western liberal values are doomed to conflict with Christian morality or Georgian traditions (Minesashvili 2017a: 21). At the same time, neither democracy itself (Minesashvili 2017b: 7), nor integration into EU and NATO was ever officially questioned by the GOC (Kakachia 2014: 5). There are even communication channels with both institutions and Georgian clergymen visited NATO and EU (Kakabadze & Makarychev 2018: 496). An obvious and often quoted battleground of this conflict is the question about minority rights and most evident the rights of sexual minorities. For the GOC, more equality is perceived to threaten the position of families and thus might potentially harm the nation (Minesashvili 2017b: 7). So far, the public space is rather dominated by the reactionary camp. This became obvious in 2013 when priests led a violent attack against pro-LGBT activists, who rallied against Homo- and Transphobia. An event, which also demonstrated "the impotence of the police, and the indifference of the political elite" (Beacháin & Coene 2014: 936). The controversy and impossibility to officially conduct a Pride March in Tbilisi in 2019 is another example (Civil.ge 2019).

The extent to which the GOC dominates the public and political discourse points to the second question of whether the GOC is granted too many privileges and that accordingly, religious freedom as a fundamental right and secularity as a state principle might not be given. The GOC enjoys for instance to be freed of tax payments (Minesashvili 2017b: 6). Furthermore it receives significant state funding as a compensation for damages and confiscations during the Tsarist Empire and afterwards by the Soviet Union (Grdzelidze 2010: 169). Religious minorities not only have fewer privileges, but also they are not sufficiently protected from discrimination or intimidations by the government. The reluctance of state authorities to secure the interests outside of the major religious group violates secular principles (Mikeladze 2013: 52). Nino Tsagareishvili sees the constitutional freedom of religion under jeopardy as well, since "law enforcement bodies have not adequately responded to the recent facts of religious intolerance in Georgia" (Tsagareishvili 2015: 4–5). The EU Association Implementation Report on Georgia from 2016 states as well, that "state institutions have on some occasions failed to act promptly and efficiently on human rights violations and discriminations against minorities, LGBTI community or religious minorities" (Association Implementation Report on Georgia 2016: 4).

Conclusion

Georgia's identity is constructed in differentiation from and identification with external Others. In the following diagram, this ambiguous process of constructing the Other against the Self shall be recapped. At the same time, certain symmetries in the process get visualized, since we look at three forms of othering: 1) negative as well as 2) positive othering which is both targeted externally. As a byproduct of the first, there also exists indirect othering directed inwards:

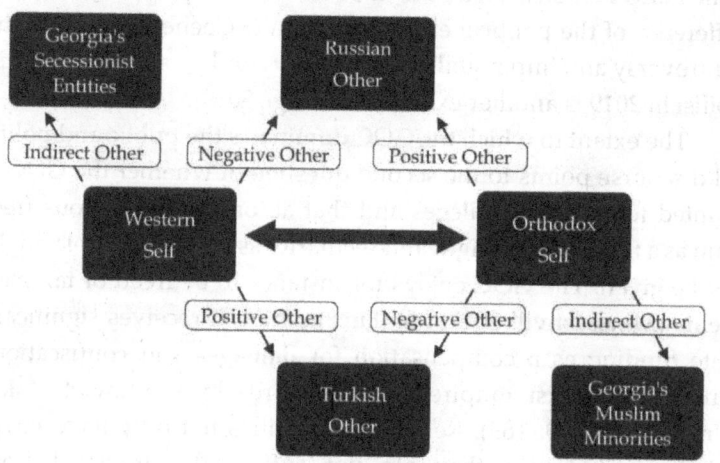

Looking at its immediate neighbors, Russia and Turkey respectively serve as important references for otherness to Georgian Westernness and otherness to Georgian Orthodoxy. This relatively straight forward relation gets blurred not only by a "spillover effect" of othering to either the secessionist entities South Ossetia and Abkhazia, but also by a transmission to its domestic Muslim minority in Adjara. In addition, the matter gets further complicated by certain characteristics of Russia and Turkey, which disrupt their solely negative othering. Since both countries represent elements of Orthodoxy (Russia) and Westernness (Turkey) as well, they function also as objects for identification and are thus positively othered. That leads to a rather complex relational net, where one and the same object can be perceived as a positive as well as a negative Other. This construction therefore stays incomplete and controversial. Since the same ambiguity is found in Georgia's main components of the Self as well, I have argued that the reason for this flexibility can be found precisely in the very construction of Georgian identity. Since Georgian Orthodoxy and Westernness are mutually exclusive in certain respects, despite all rhetoric and attempts, their equally strong existence in Georgian society cannot be a matter of fact, but rather a matter of permanent recalibration to either of the two extremes.

Bibliography

Abushov, Kavus. (2009). Policing the Near Abroad: Russian foreign policy in the South Caucasus. *Australian Journal of International Affairs* 63(2): 187–212.

Association Implementation Report on Georgia. (2016). Brussels: High Representative of the Union for Foreign Affairs and Security Policy.

Atlantic Council. (2010). *Saakashvili, Mikheil (Transcript)*, https://www.atlanticcouncil.org/commentary/transcript/saakashvili-mikheil-4-15-2010 (accessed 27 June 2020).

Beacháin, Donnacha Ó. & Coene, Frederik. (2014). Go West: Georgia's European identity and its role in domestic politics and foreign policy objectives. *Nationalities Papers* 42(6): 923–41.

Blakkisrud, Helge & Kolstø, Pål. (2012). Dynamics of de facto statehood: the South Caucasian de facto states between secession and sovereignty. *Southeast European and Black Sea Studies* 12(2): 281–98.

Brons, Lajos. (2015). Othering, an Analysis. *Transcience, a Journal of Global Studies* 6(1): 69-90.

Buzogány, Aron. (2019). Europe, Russia, or both? Popular perspectives on overlapping regionalism in the Southern Caucasus. *East European Politics* 35(1): 93-109.

Cecire, Michael H. (2013). The Merchant Hegemon: Georgia's role in Turkey's Caucasus system. In *Georgian foreign policy. The quest for sustainable security*, Kakachia, Kornely & Cecire, Michael H. (eds). Tbilisi: Konrad Adenauer Stiftung, 111-24.

Chedia, Beka. (2012). *Georgia: religious affairs pervaded with fear of Turkey's influence*, http://www.eastbook.eu/en/2012/03/18/georgia-religious-affairs-pervaded-with-fear-of-turkeys-influence/ (accessed 27 June 2020).

Chikovani, Nino. (2005). A United Caucasus: Reality Rooted in the Past or High-Flown Political Illusions? *Central Asia and the Caucasus* 35(5): 45-54.

Civil.ge. (2019). *First Ever Impromptu Pride Parade Held in Tbilisi*, https://civil.ge/archives/312596 (accessed 27 June 2020).

Civil.ge. (2005a). *Building the Case*, https://civil.ge/archives/107150 (accessed 27 June 2020).

Civil.ge. (2005b). *Saakashvili Focuses on Human Rights in Abkhazia in Talks with Annan*, https://civil.ge/archives/109235 (accessed 27 June 2020).

Cooley, Alexander. (2017). *Whose rules, whose sphere? Russian governance and influence in post-Soviet states*, https://carnegieendowment.org/2017/06/30/whose-rules-whose-sphere-russian-governance-and-influence-in-post-soviet-states-pub-71403 (accessed 27 June 2020).

Cornell, Svante E. (2003). *Small nations and great powers: A study of ethnopolitical conflict in the Caucasus*. Richmond: Curzon.

Delcour, Laure & Wolczuk, Kataryna. (2015). Spoiler or facilitator of democratization?: Russia's role in Georgia and Ukraine. *Democratization* 22(3): 459-78.

Di Puppo, Lili. (2019). *Policing as Spectacle in Georgia: The Creation of Boundaries in a Post-Revolutionary Country*. Moscow: National Research University Higher School of Economics.

Gamkrelidze, Tamar. (2019). The project of Europe: a robust attempt to redefine Georgian identity. *East European Politics* 35(3): 351-71.

Georgian Ministry of Foreign Affairs. (2000). *Georgia and the world: A vision and strategy for the future*, http://www.bits.de/NRANEU/docs/CFE/GeorgiaStrategy.pdf (accessed 27 June 2020).

German, Tracey. (2015). Heading west? Georgia's Euro-Atlantic path. *International Affairs* 91(3): 601-14.

Gerrits, Andre W. & Bader, Max. (2016). Russian patronage over Abkhazia and South Ossetia: implications for conflict resolution. *East European Politics* 32(3): 297-313.

Gogoladze, Tina. (2019). *Hate Speech 2018*. Tbilisi: Media Development Foundation.

Goksel, Nigar. (2013). Turkey and Georgia: Zero-problems? *On Wider Europe* (June): 1-8.

Goksel, Nigar. (2011). Turkish policy towards the Caucasus: A Balance Sheet of the Balancing Act. *Black Sea Discussion Paper Series* (1): 1-26.

Göl, Ayla. (2005). Imagining the Turkish nation through 'othering' Armenians. *Nations and Nationalism* 11(1): 121-39.

Grdzelidze, Tamara. (2010). The Orthodox Church of Georgia: challenges under democracy and freedom (1990-2009). *International journal for the Study of the Christian Church* 10(2-3): 160-75.

Gurchiani, Ketevan. (2017). How Soviet is the religious revival in Georgia: Tactics in everyday religiosity. *Europe-Asia Studies* 69(3): 508-31.

Hagström, Linus & Gustafsson, Karl. (2015). Japan and identity change: why it matters in International Relations. *The Pacific Review* 28(1): 1-22.

Halbach, Uwe. (2016). Religion und Nation, Kirche und Staat im Südkaukasus. *SWP-Studie* 18 (Oktober): pp. 1-35.

Hansen, Lene. (2006). *Security as practice: Discourse analysis and the Bosnian war*. New York, NY: Routledge.

Ingebritsen, Christine. (2002). Norm Entrepreneurs: Scandinavia's Role in World Politics. *Cooperation and Conflict* 37(1): 11-23.

Ivanov, Vladimir. (2011). Religious Dimension of Turkey's Policy in Ajaria and the Georgian Orthodox Church. *Central Asia and the Caucasus* 12(3): 79-90.

Jam News. (2020). *Could Georgia lose international support? Another critical letter from Washington*, https://jam-news.net/could-georgia-lose-internatio nal-support-another-critical-letter-from-washington/ (accessed 27 June 2020).

Jensen, Sune Q. (2011). Othering, identity formation and agency. *Qualitative Studies* 2(2): 63-78.

Jones, Stephen. (2004). The Role of Cultural Paradigms in Georgian Foreign Policy. In *Ideology and National Identity in Post-Communist Foreign Policy*, Fawn, Rick (ed). London: Cass, 81-108.

Jørgensen, Marianne. & Phillips, Louise. (2002). *Discourse Analysis As Theory and Method*. London: SAGE Publications.

Kabachnik, Peter. (2018). The power of place, or powerless places? Hybrid attitudes towards Soviet symbols in post-Soviet Georgia. *Central Asian Survey* 37(2): 265-85.

Kakabadze, Shota & Makarychev, Andrey. (2018). A Tale of Two Orthodoxies: Europe in Religious Discourses of Russia and Georgia. *Ethnopolitics* 17(5): 485-502.

Kakachia, Kornely, Minesashvili, Salome & Kakhishvili, Levan. (2018). Change and Continuity in the Foreign Policies of Small States: Elite Perceptions and Georgia's Foreign Policy Towards Russia: Elite perceptions and Georgia's foreign policy towards Russia. *Europe-Asia Studies* 70(5): 814-31.

Kakachia, Kornely & Minesashvili, Salome. (2015). Identity politics: Exploring Georgian foreign policy behavior. *Journal of Eurasian Studies* 6(2): 171-80.

Kakachia, Kornely. (2014). Is Georgia's Orthodox church an obstacle to European values? *Ponars Eurasia Policy Memo* 322(June): 1-6.

Kakachia, Kornely. (2012). Georgia's identity-driven foreign policy and the struggle for its European destiny. *Caucasus Analytical Digest* 37 (March): 4-7.

Ker-Lindsay, James & Berg, Eiki. (2018). Introduction: A Conceptual Framework for Engagement with de facto States. *Ethnopolitics* 17(4): 335-42.

Khalvashi, Tamta. (2015). *Peripheral affects: Shame, publics, and performance on the margins of the republic of Georgia*. Copenhagen: Faculty of Social Sciences, University of Copenhagen.

Khalvashi, Tamta. (2012). Can Muslim be a Georgian?: Historic Overview of Discourse on Georgian 'Essence'. In *Central Eurasian studies. Past, present and future*, Komatsu, Hisao (ed), T.C. Maltepe Üniversitesi yayınları. İstanbul: Maltepe Universität.

Khelashvili, George. (2012). Holding the Line amid Uncertainty. *Caucasus Analytical Digest* 37(March): 8-10.

Khutsishvili, Kristina. (2018). Myself and the Other: Competitive Narratives of Georgians and Abkhazians. *Region* 7(1): 69-82.

Kiniklioğlu, Suat. (2004). Turkish-Georgian Relations: An Interview with Georgian President Mikhail Sankashvili. *Insight Turkey* 6(2): 45-48.

Kononczuk, Wojciech. (2008). A Caucasian ally? Turkish-Georgian relations. In *Turkey after the start of negotiations with the European Union – foreign relations and the domestic situation*, Balcer, Adam (ed). Warsaw: CES Report, 31-40.

Kopeček, Vincenc, Hoch, Tomáš & Baar, Vladimír. (2016). De Facto States and Democracy: The Case of Abkhazia. *Bulletin of Geography. Socio-economic Series* 32(32): 85–104.

Ladaria, Konstantine. (2002). Georgian Orthodox Church and Political Project of Modernization. *Identity Studies* 4): 107–17.

Leonardis, Fabio d. (2016). Memory and Nation-Building in Georgia. In *Nation-building and identity in the post-Soviet space. New tools and approaches*, Isaacs, Rico & Polese, Abel (eds), *Post-Soviet Politics*. London, New York, NY: Routledge Imprint of Taylor & Francis Group, 24–45.

Lindgren, Wrenn Y. & Lindgren, Petter Y. (2017). Identity Politics and the East China Sea: China as Japan's 'Other'. *Asian Politics & Policy* 9(3): 378–401.

Lindstrom, Nicole. (2003). Between Europe and the Balkans: Mapping Slovenia and Croatia's "Return to Europe" in the 1990s. *Dialectical Anthropology* 27): 313–29.

Machaidze, Rusudan. (2019). *Tbilisi protests – what they mean and what to expect*, https://jam-news.net/tbilisi-protests-what-this-means-and-wh at-to-expect/ (accessed 27 June 2020).

Makarychev, Andrey & Yatsyk, Alexandra. (2017). Biopolitical conservatism and "pastoral power": a Russia–Georgia meeting point. In *Religion and Soft Power in the South Caucasus. Policy Perspective*, Georgian Institute of Politics (ed). Tbilisi.

Mamadouh, Virginie & Bialasiewicz, Luiza. (2016). Introduction to the Special Issue: Europe and its Others. *Tijdschrift voor economische en sociale geografie* 107(2): 129–33.

Mikeladze, Tamta. (2013). *Crisis of Secularism and Loyalty towards the Dominant Group: The Role of the Government in the 2012-2013 Religious Conflicts in Georgia*. Tbilisi: Human Rights Education and Monitoring Center (EMC).

Mindiashvili, Beka. (2012). *Pre-election Turkophobia*, http://www.tabula.ge /en/story/70462-pre-election-turkophobia (accessed 27 June 2020).

Minesashvili, Salome. (2017a). Foreign Policy of the Georgian Orthodox Church: Interplay between the West and Russia. In *Religion and Soft Power in the South Caucasus. Policy Perspective*, Georgian Institute of Politics (ed). Tbilisi, 17–24.

Minesashvili, Salome. (2017b). The Orthodox Church in the Democratization Process in Georgia: Hindrance or Support? *Caucasus Analytical Digest* 97(July): 6-9.

Mühlfried, Florian. (2015). Religion, Reinheit und Radikalisierung. Vom Ende des Alaverdoba-Fests in Georgien. *Osteuropa* 65(7-10): 587–98.

Nakhutsrishvili, Luka & Lejava, Nino. (2018). Einleitung. In *Georgien, neu buchstabiert. Politik und Kultur eines Landes auf dem Weg nach Europa*, Nakhutsrishvili, Luka & Heinrich-Böll-Stiftung (eds), *Edition Kulturwissenschaft*. Bielefeld: Transcript, 9–20.

Neumann, Iver B. (1999). *Uses of the Other: "The East" in European identity formation*. Minneapolis: University of Minnesota Press.

Nodia, Ghia. (2017). *Democracy and its deficits: The path towards becoming European-style democracies in Georgia, Moldova and Ukraine*: CEPS Working Documents 12.

O'Loughlin, John, Toal, Gerard & Kolossov, Vladimir. (2017). Who identifies with the "Russian World"? Geopolitical attitudes in southeastern Ukraine, Crimea, Abkhazia, South Ossetia, and Transnistria. *Eurasian Geography and Economics* 57(6): 1–34.

Oskanian, Kevork. (2016). The Balance Strikes Back: Power, perceptions, and ideology in Georgian foreign policy, 1992–2014. *Foreign Policy Analysis* 2(0): 1–25.

Oskanian, Kevork. (2014). Balancing a tightrope: Constraints, possibilities and ideology in Georgian foreign policy, 1991-2014.: Paper presented at the 2014 UACES Conference, Cork/Ireland.

Pelkmans, Mathijs. (2003). Shifting frontiers: Islam and Christianity in post-Soviet Ajaria. *ISIM Newsletter* 12(June): 46–47.

Pelkmans, Mathijs. (1999). The wounded body: Reflections on the demise of the 'Iron Curtain' between Georgia and Turkey. *Anthropology of East Europe Review* 17(1): 49–58.

Reisner, Oliver. (2015). Sakral-national Orthodoxer Glaube und Orthodoxe Kirche in Georgien. *Osteuropa* 65(7-10): 93–112.

Risse, Thomas. (2017). *Domestic politics and norm diffusion in international relations: Ideas do not float freely*. London, New York NY: Routledge.

Roehrs-Weist, Philip. (2018). Thomas de Waal: NATO membership is not necessarily essential for Georgia. *Caucasus Watch*, http://caucasuswatch.de/news/1154.html (accessed 27 June 2020).

Rumelili, Bahar. (2004). Constructing identity and relating to difference: understanding the EU's mode of differentiation. *Review of International Studies* 30(1): 27–47.

Russo, Alessandra. (2018). *Regions in Transition in the Former Soviet Area*. Cham: Springer International Publishing.

Sadigbeyli, Rovshan. (2002). Stability in the South Caucasus: The role of Russia and Turkey. Master thesis, Bilkent University Ankara.

Sanikidze, George & Walker, Edward W. (2004). Islam and Islamic Practices in Georgia. *eScholarchip*, https://escholarship.org/uc/item/7149d486 (accessed June 27, 2020).

Siroky, David S., Simmons, Alan J. & Gvalia, Giorgi. (2017). Vodka or Bourbon? Foreign policy preferences toward Russia and the United States in Georgia. *Foreign Policy Analysis* 13): 500–18.

Smolnik, Franziska, Weiss, Andrea & Zabanova, Yana. (2018). Political space and borderland practices in Abkhazia and Adjara: Exploring the role of Ottoman legacies and contemporary Turkish influences. *Eurasian Geography and Economics* 58(5): 557–81.

Staszak, Jean F. (2009). Other/Otherness. In *International encyclopedia of human geography*, Kitchin, Rob & Thrift, Nigel J. (eds). Amsterdam: Elsevier.

Storm, Karli. (2019). Flexible Memory Narratives in the Physical Landscape: A Case Study of Tbilisi, Georgia. *Demokratizatsiya: The Journal of Post-Soviet Democratization* 27(2): 131–62.

Szkola, Susanne. (2018). The Self/Other Space and Spinning the Net of Ontological Insecurities in Ukraine and Beyond: (Discursive) Reconstructions of Boundaries in the EU Eastern Partnership Countries Vis-à-Vis the EU and Russia. In *Crisis and Change in Post-Cold War Global Politics*, Resende, Erica, Budrytė, Dovilė & Buhari-Gulmez, Didem (eds). Cham: Springer International Publishing, 225–50.

Szkola, Susanne. (2017). 'Discursive reconstructions of boundaries in the South Caucasus countries vis-à-vis the EU and Russia and the crux of securitization. *UPTAKE Working Paper* 5.

The Caucasus Research Resource Center. (2019a). Main Enemy of the Country. *Caucasus Barometer*, https://caucasusbarometer.org/en/cb2019ge/MAINENEM/ (accessed June 27, 2020).

The Caucasus Research Resource Center. (2019b). Main Friend of the Country. *Caucasus Barometer*, https://caucasusbarometer.org/en/cb2019ge/MAINFRN/ (accessed June 27, 2020).

The Caucasus Research Resource Center. (2019c). Trust – Religious Institutions Respondent Belongs to. *Caucasus Barometer*, https://caucasusbarometer.org/en/cb2019ge/TRURELI/ (accessed June 27, 2020).

Timofeev, Ivan. (2017). Working Under the Radar: The Stealth Alternative in Russia's Foreign Policy. *Russian Council on Foreign Relations*, http://russiancouncil.ru/en/analytics-and-comments/analytics/working-under-the-radar-the-stealth-alternative-in-russia-s-foreign-policy-/ (accessed June 27, 2020).

Toal, Gerard & O'Loughlin, John. (2014). How people in South Ossetia, Abkhazia and Transnistria feel about annexation by Russia. Washington Post, March 20, http://www.washingtonpost.com/blogs/monkey-cage/wp/2014/03/20/how-people-in-south-ossetia-abkhazia-and-transnistria-feel-about-annexation-by-russia/ (accessed June 27, 2020).

Tsagareishvili, Nino. (2015). *Freedom of Religion in Georgia: Problems and Recommendations*. Tbilisi: Human Rights Center.

Tsintskiladze, Inga. (2019). European Integration and Identity Issues in Georgia. *Eastern Europe-Regional Studies*.

Waal, Thomas de. (2010). *The Caucasus: An introduction*. Oxford, New York: Oxford University Press.

Waal, Thomas de. (2008). South Ossetia: the avoidable tragedy. *Open Democracy*, August 12, https://www.opendemocracy.net/article/south-ossetia-the-avoidable-tragedy (accessed June 27, 2020).

Weiss, Andrea & Zabanova, Yana. (2016). Georgia and Abkhazia caught between Turkey and Russia.: Turkey's changing relations with Russia and the West in 2015-2016 and their impact on Georgia and Abkhazia. *SWP-Comments* 54(December): 1-8.

Wendt, Alexander. (1994). Collective Identity Formation and the International State. *American Political Science Review* 88(2): 384-96.

Wivel, Anders. (2016). Living on the edge: Georgian foreign policy between the West and the rest. *Third World Thematics* 1(1): 92-109.

Zviadadze, Sophie. (2015). Georgian Orthodox church and human rights: Challenges to Georgian society. In *Religion and Human Rights*, Ziebertz, Hans-Georg & Črpić, Gordan (eds). Cham: Springer International Publishing, 45-60.

3 The Splendid School Assembled
Studying and Practicing International Relations in Independent Ukraine

Nadiia Koval and Ivan Gomza[1]

International relations (hereafter: IR) sociology and, in particular, the development of IR studies around the globe has passed through consecutive phases and has covered different countries and regions for decades (Kristensen 2019). Ukraine, however, remains a vast blank spot on the map in the middle of Europe of such studies. The looming gap is evident even if one focuses solely on the post-Communist region. There are a plethora of studies on the organizational, theoretical, and ideological aspects of the development of IR studies in Russia (Lebedeva 2004; Lebedeva 2018; Tsygankov & Tsygankov 2010; Tsygankov & Tsygankov 2014; Morozov 2009; Sergounin 2009), Poland (Czaputowicz 2012; Czaputowicz & Wojciuk 2016; Czaputowicz & Ławniczak 2015), Czechia (Drulák & Drulákova 2000; Drulák & Drulákova 2006), Slovakia (Bátora & Hynek 2009), and Slovenia (Roter 2009). In addition, CEE-wide analyses (Drulák, Königová & Karlas 2004) and discussions[2] are

---

1 The authors are grateful to Prof. Michael Tierney, the Director of the Institute for the Theory and Practice of International Relations at the College of William and Mary (VA, USA) for his invitation to include Ukraine within the 2017 round of the TRIP research which made this study possible; to Denys Tereshchenko for his invaluable assistance with aggregating and structuring the raw data for this research.

2 See for example, the summary of the debate "The IR Scholarship in Central and Eastern European Countries: On Its Way to Cross the Regional Boundaries", which took place on September 21, 2012 during the 9th Convention of the Central and East European Studies Association in Cracow with contributions by Petr Drulák, Stefano Guzzini, Knud E. Jørgensen, Zlatko Šabič, Thomas J. Volgy, Anna Wojciuk, & Jacek Czaputowicz (*Przegląd Europejski*, 2003, 27(1): 9–36) or an earlier Introduction to the International Relations (IR) in Central and Eastern Europe Forum, with the contributions by Petr Drulák, Pinar Bilgin & Oktay Tanrisever, Petra Roter, Jozef Bátora & Nikola Hynek, Eiki Berg & Matthieu Chillaud, Viacheslav Morozov, & Vendulka Kubálková (*Journal of International Relations and Development* 12: 168–173).

relatively common. In stark contrast, of the former Soviet republics, only the most westernized Baltics can boast some attention in this regard (Berg & Chillaud 2009). A few selective mentions of Ukraine, Kazakhstan, and Belarus in a Russian reference book on IR development in Russia and CIS (Mezhdunarodnye issledovanija v Rossii i SNG 1999) did not initiate a meaningful discussion or research in the subsequent 20 years

More importantly, though, the Ukrainian IR scholars have hitherto not presented their own story and approaches to the international community. Even internally, the development of the discipline in its teaching, research, and practical policy dimensions has not been systematically investigated. Self-assessments that do exist are short, generalistic, and descriptive in nature. Predominantly, they address IR teaching and research developments at specific departments[3], provide some general non-academic information (Lysak 2014; Malsky & Moroz 2012), or celebrate another decade of IR studies in Ukraine (Instytut mizhnarodnykh vidnosyn 2004; Instytut mizhnarodnykh vidnosyn 2006; Instytut mizhnarodnykh vidnosyn 2014). While there was a heated discussion over the current state and (under)development of Ukrainian political science in general (Kudelia 2012; Matsiyevsky 2012; Starish 2012; Shevel 2015), the semi-autonomous IR community has never undertaken such a soul-searching exercise.

Still, in the absence of comprehensive analysis, the development of the Ukrainian IR community cannot be explained by the dynamics in the IR of the former metropolis, Russia (because of a different attitude to the Western experience and power-knowledge relationships), the scarcely studied dynamics in other post-Soviet republics or by the developments in the countries of Central and Eastern Europe which have experienced intense and consistent Westernization of their IR studies and research. This is not to say

---

3   See for example contributions of Valerii Kopiika on the "Kyiv School of IR" (Kopiika 2013), Oleksandr Krapivin & Ihor Todorov on the "Donetsk School of IR" (Krapivin & Todorov 2013), Ihor Byk on the development of IR studies in Lviv University (Byk 2013) and Anatolii Kruglashov on the development of European Studies in Chernivtsi University (Kruglashov 2013), published in *Visnyk of the Lviv University. Series International Relations* 33: 10–39.

that Ukraine beyond comparison, but that the mixture of different legacies, experiences, and policy choices make the case worth separate consideration.

Moreover, the country boasts robust number of research and teaching IR institutions: as of 2018, one could study "International relations, social communications and regional studies" at 91 higher education institutions of Ukraine. Besides, IR ranks among the most coveted specializations, attracting the students with the best grades (see: Kavtseniuk 2017); over 200 candidate and doctoral theses have been defended since 1991.

In addition, two non-academic developments make this study even more timely and relevant since 2014. The first one is the increased international visibility of Ukraine and different aspects of its foreign policy and regional dynamics due to Russian aggression. The second one is a set of Westernizing reforms in education and research that impose new accreditation regulations, encourage publishing in renowned international journals, and impose the requirements for the mastery of foreign languages (KAS 2017; Rumyantseva & Logvynenko 2018). Both developments impact the development of the IR discipline in Ukraine, pushing it towards more openness to the global research community. Therefore, it is high time to fill the gap and to study the Ukrainian IR community in detail.

This chapter is based on the results of the TRIP 2017 survey. It reflects the self-assessment of the Ukrainian IR faculty and offers insights on essential features of the scholarly IR community as well as its interaction with the social environment. Namely, we study the IR community's perceptions of (1) the place of IR among other social sciences in the Ukrainian context; (2) the level of integration into global IR scholarship; (3) the field's preferred paradigmatic framework(s) and research methods; (4) the particularities of Ukrainian IR caused by the global division of labor; (5) scholarly intentions to provide policy advice. We hope that this study will be followed by others so that the nascent field of IR sociology in Ukraine yields results that further the development of the discipline.

Data and Methods

To tackle the research questions outlined above, we decided to conduct an inductive study built upon the principles of the grounded theory commonly understood as "discovery of theory from data systematically obtained from social research" (Glaser & Strauss 2006: 2) with the utmost attention to "patterns of action and interaction between and among various types of social units" (Strauss & Corbin 1994: 278). In particular, we followed the fundamental procedures required for a grounded theory study (Charmaz 2006: 17–49): (1) we had no preconceived theories regarding our subject; (2) we used sensitizing concepts and disciplinary perspectives; (3) we followed leads defined in the data; (4) we applied primary coding to the obtained data; (5) discerning some regularities, we enlarged our data through other sources and applied textual analysis to extant texts; (6) after we reached the point of theoretical saturation we proceeded to interpretation and finally advanced a set of theoretical assumptions.

However, it is important to stress that, in some respects, we deviated from the grounded theory standard procedure. For example, we did not use open-ended questions and participant observation. Instead, we opted for a structured online questionnaire as our primary data-collection method.

The critical data for this research was obtained in the 2017 edition of the TRIP ("Teaching, Research and International Policy") Project, run by the Institute for the Theory and Practice of International Relations at the College of William & Mary, US. It was first launched in 2003 in order to study the role of expert opinion in the run-up to the Iraq War (Speed 2018). During the following decade, the project morphed into a multiple-round study on IR academic community. In early years TRIP encompassed predominantly English-speaking and North American countries, but the last round to date, the 2014 TRIP survey, included "IR scholars in 32 countries and 9 languages to examine teaching and research trends and foreign policy view in the IR discipline" (TRIP 2015). TRIP 2017 pushes the geographical boundaries of the research even further. Both authors of the chapter were the TRIP country partners in Ukraine responsible for translation, cultural fitting, and establishing contact with the relevant respondents.

According to the TRIP data-collection procedure, country partners are expected to pinpoint all the country's universities where IR is taught and where, consequently, a scholarly community is present. TRIP aims to "identify and survey all faculty member at colleges and universities... who do research in the IR subfield of political science and/or who teach international relation courses" (Maliniak et al. 2012: 2). These scholars/professors receive an invitation to fill in a standardized online questionnaire via personalized email with a link. Although the translation of the questionnaire is tailored to the country's cultural sensitivities and institutional logic, the questions are virtually universal for all participant countries. Moreover, the invitations are generated by the centralized software system hosted by the College of William & Mary and are distributed to all participants cross-nationally at the same time. As a result, a typical snowball data-collection method, when some respondents refer the scholar to other possible respondents, thus accumulating the dataset, was inaccessible. We had to identify all respondents in advance, contact them, explain the project's goals, receive their consent to participate, upload their emails (alongside affiliations) to the central software, and wait for the system to proceed in due course.

Initially, TRIP set the very ambitious goal of including all Ukrainian universities in the list of respondents. However, in 2017 IR was taught at 88 universities in Ukraine. Despite our best efforts, we did not manage to establish email contact with scholarly communities at all universities: respondents sometimes ignored our emails outright; sometimes they did not wish to participate in a project of which they had no previous knowledge; finally, in the worst cases, email contacts (or even university Web pages) were nowhere to be found. Eventually, we decided to focus on the most prominent universities with the most renowned IR programs. We deem them to be sufficiently representative of the first participation of Ukraine in the TRIP project.

Our contact list included 188 IR scholars from 25 top Ukrainian universities with IR programs or affiliations to prominent individual specialists. The geography of the study is relatively broad: we invited scholars from **Western Ukraine** universities (Lesya Ukrainka East European National University, Fedkovych Chernivtsi National University, Lviv Polytechnic National University, Ukrainian Catholic University, Uzhgorod National University, Lviv National University, Stefanyk Precarpathian National University, National University of Ostroh Academy), **Eastern and Southern Ukraine** universities (Honchar Dnipro National University, Zaporizhzhya National University, Sukhomlynsky Mykolaiv National University, Mechnikov Odesa National University, Karazin Kharkiv National University, Stus Donetsk National University, Mariupol State University), and **Kyiv region** educational and research institutions (Shevchenko National University of Kyiv, Pereiaslav-Khmelnytskyi State Pedagogical University, National University of Kyiv-Mohyla Academy, Kyiv National University of Trade and Economics, Grinchenko Kyiv University, NASU Institute of History of Ukraine, National Institute for Strategic Studies, Khmelnytsky National University of Cherkasy, Diplomatic Academy of Ukraine, National Aviation University).

97 scholars eventually filled in the 69-question long survey (with both open-ended and closed types of the question), the response rate thus being 51.5%. With the average response rate for TRIP-2012 of 49.5% (Maliniak et al. 2012: Table 1), the figure is well within the acceptable range. We are grateful to all respondents who contributed to the entrance of the Ukrainian IR community into the TRIP project. Our research, therefore, follows the grounded theory in its methodological rejection of qualitative/quantitative methods division: we used the quantitatively obtained data to formulate a qualitative interpretation of the subject.

Because of fidelity to the grounded theory principles, we do not offer a separate theoretical section at the beginning of the chapter; instead, we start each research section with a concise presentation of essential theoretical and contextual underpinnings. The chapter is, thus, structured as follows: First, we describe the particularities of the developmental trajectory of IR in Ukraine in historical and regional contexts; next, we present our findings regarding the five outlined research questions (each in a separate section) and discuss the results; finally, we offer general conclusions. Lastly, we acknowledge that according to the agreement with the TRIP project managers, we were granted access solely to surveys by Ukrainian participants; consequently, no cross-national comparison is possible at present. However, the aggregated data provide a unique view of Ukrainian scholars' self-positioning and their visions on IR.

History and Context

Soviet Legacies, Western Innovations, and East-European Struggles: The Context of Developing the IR Field in Ukraine

Ukrainian IR developed at the crossroads of two trends. The first and probably the defining one is the legacy of the Soviet period, which established initial structures and laid the foundation for the key and lasting perceptions of what IR is and how it should be practiced. The second tendency was the need to accommodate the US (Western)-centric IR approaches and theories, which arrived belatedly and inconsistently during the independence period. This initiated the struggle between "catching-up" Westernization and the Soviet-tainted tendency to nativism, common for post-Communist Central and Eastern Europe countries.

The Ukrainian Soviet Socialist Republic (hereafter: UkrSSR) occupied a peculiar position in the foreign policy of the Soviet Union, as it (together with Belarus SSR) joined the UN as a separate entity after World War II (for negotiation details, see Plokhy 2011). Undoubtedly, in a highly centralized Soviet system, nearly all foreign policy decision-making and foreign policy related research were conducted in Moscow. Nevertheless, due to the need for institutional support, a Republican People's Commissariat (later — Ministry) of foreign affairs was created in 1944 alongside a small Department of International Relations at the Kyiv State University to train future diplomats. The continuity in current Ukrainian IR could be traced back to the peculiarity of the Soviet approach to IR, modified according to the Ukrainian context.

Zimmerman (1969), Light (1989), Tyulin (1997), and Lebedeva (2004, 2018) outlined the key features of Soviet IR studies:

1. Initially, Soviet IR developed as a study of IR history and foreign languages. Any analytical and comparative research was introduced only later and to a limited degree. Throughout its development, the field had a practical and analytical dimension, providing policy analysis for the MFA of the USSR and the Communist Party of the Soviet Union.

2. Soviet IR mostly took the form of the area studies conducted by geographically defined research institutes in the Academy of Sciences of the USSR. In the words of Lebedeva, "region and country not only dominated in the fields of study and education but also actually subordinated everything to itself" (2018: 48).

3. Moscow State University of the International Relations (known after its Russian abbreviation *MGIMO*) was created as a critical educational and research institution within the structure of the MFA, securing direct links between policy training, research, and policymaking. The rotation between political and academic/research posts was not entirely unknown in Moscow but never reached the extent of that in the US.

4. There was only one valid and all-explaining theoretical framework, Marxism-Leninism; thus, Western IR and other social sciences were interpreted as bourgeois pseudo-science, confined to *spetshran* (limited access library collections), and inaccessible to most scholars. As Light observed:

> The official position under Stalin, and for some years after his death, had been that Marxism-Leninism was Political Science and provided a ready-made theory of International Relations. (Light 1989: 229)

5. While Marxism-Leninism could provide only the broadest framework, the primary theoretical approach was the "intuitive realism" (Lebedeva 2018). In practice, it meant non-theoretical empirical "common sense" driven narrative research, used chiefly for analytical work (but also for propaganda aims, according to Zimmerman (1969).

6. Political science did not exist in the USSR; thus, IR was the first field to establish itself as a separate branch of knowledge with different university departments and scholarly communities before political science per se entered the curricula.

These key features were also present in Soviet Ukraine, and some vestiges are revealed in the analysis of the TRIP responses (see below). Nevertheless, there were substantial differences, defined by the republic's peripheral status and its foreign affairs system. As Kaminskyi (2001) demonstrates, the local MFA was much more actively engaged in propaganda actions and ideology battles, especially with the Ukrainian diaspora in the West, than in genuine interstate relations. Thus, it had an oversized political department and severely downsized diplomatic structures. All in all, the Ukrainian ministry was over-dependent on the Center's decisions. The department at Kyiv University did not become the key institution in foreign policy research. Whenever the UkrSSR MFA sought academic support, it called on different institutions of the local branch of the Academy of Sciences or individual scholars at central and regional institutions. While in Moscow, the MGIMO was part of the MFA and directly linked to the policymaking, policy analysis, and sometimes even elite rotations, a small university facility had only sporadic non-institutional connections to the local ministry. All in all, the precarious and peripheral state of foreign policy research is demonstrated by the fact that the idea to create a republic-level Institute for International Studies failed because of the lack of trained staff (Kaminskyi 2001: 569).

Upon gaining independence, Ukraine's façade ministry turned into a full-fledged one, representations abroad were created from scratch as Moscow monopolized all Soviet offices, and diplomats were hastily recruited from all the possible backgrounds. Thus, the longest-serving minister of foreign affairs Pavlo Klimkin (2014–2019), is a physicist by training who entered diplomacy when disarmament and denuclearization became pressing international questions for Ukraine. The first Diplomatic Academy was opened in 1996, designed to train non-professional diplomats who entered the ministry *en masse*, as the Kyiv faculty was too small to train enough cadres for the diplomacy of the now independent state (in Moscow, an analogous institution functioned since 1934).

The department of international relations at Kyiv State University became a key state Institute of International Relations in the final years of the Soviet Union. New IR departments (Lviv National

University 1992, Lutsk 1998, Ostroh Academy 2008, Dnipro 2011) and chairs (Odesa 1994 (department since 2018), Chernivtsi 2001, Kyiv-Mohyla Academy 2017) were opened in the universities around Ukraine. They proliferated so extensively that, as of 2019, there are 91 IR-related programs in Ukrainian universities. This is partly due to high demand, as international relations were traditionally perceived as elite training. Considering this demand and given notoriously weak accountability within the educational system of Ukraine, many smaller universities ventured opening IR-related programs for rather commercial interests, namely, to entice students to expensive IR studies. One way or another, this contributed to a decline in the quality of IR teaching. Similar processes have been reported in Russia (RIAC 2013) and probably could be found in other post-Soviet countries.

While sharing a shared Soviet legacy and coping with similar organizational challenges, the roads of Ukrainian and Russian IR studies, in terms of content and approaches, diverged significantly after the USSR collapsed. Structurally, Russia entered the new era with the USSR-inherited institutional and research setup in a much better position. Politically and ideologically, it concentrated on identity-building, looking for a new place in the world system, defining its particular place in relation to the West, toying with the ideas of geopolitical thinking, great power politics, and multipolarity. In other words, while western approaches did enter Russia, the drive to develop some local, Russian theory of international relations became mainstream (Morozov 2009; Tsygankov & Tsygankov 2010; Tsygankov & Tsygankov 2014). The link between research/analysis and the needs of the current policy of Russia was further strengthened due to the state-centered approach and the lack of a robust civil society.

In Ukraine, the link between the state and IR studies was much weaker, and the question of separating the Ukrainian school of foreign policy studies never became a significant trend of public discussion. Following the Russian lead was out of the question due to mutually exclusive foreign policy priorities. Most importantly, Westernization was not perceived as a threat but rather a chance to strengthen the independence and catch up with the developed world. Thus, in the independence years, the IR development in Ukraine followed a path resembling that of other post-communist CEE states.

Indeed, the challenges of the former Warsaw block states in (re)building their diplomatic presence and non-Marxist IR studies seem very familiar to Ukraine's experience since independence, and some structural similarities can be traced even in the 2010s. Some were due to the unavoidable Marxist legacy: the TRIP 2014 survey, which embraced Poland as a first-ever country from the region, has demonstrated the prevalence of "common sense realism" (Czaputowicz 2012), lack of theoretical reflection in favor of the practical analysis, and a much stronger tendency towards area studies than all the other countries participating in the survey. As responses to the open questions have shown, "the respondents pointed out petrified hierarchical academic department structures, as well as their colleagues' psychological complexes, a general lack of academic originality, and parochialism within Polish universities and research institutes. The survey also mentioned the influence of Poland's communist past on some researchers and cited "post-communist thinking" (Czaputowicz & Wojciuk 2016: 97). Empirical and descriptive inclinations and preferences for the historical method of the post-communist CEE IR were also observed by Drulák (2009).

Another similarity of Ukrainian IR development with that of CEE countries was the rapid Westernization throughout the region. Like most other post-Communist countries, Ukraine missed the key discussions regarding the discipline's goals and scope. Since the 1990s, it has borrowed from Western academia many theoretical assumptions without grasping the complexity of discussions it has gone through. In particular, a peculiar formation of the IR discipline was practically ignored: Since the first registered spike in IR studies in the US in the early 1960s (see Fox & Baker Fox 1961), there was a state of "US dominance of International Relations" (Smith 1987: 190) to the extent that for a considerable period "international theory barely exist[ed] outside the anglophone countries" (Holsti 1985: 127). Even if one rejects this claim as somewhat extreme, the role of the US scholarship in building conceptual frameworks, analytical approaches, and methodological principles for the IR discipline is undeniable. Non-US scholars refined their arguments in discussions with US scholars, such as Barry Buzan, or worked within the US academia only to leave it in order to find a more receptive academic environment (e. g. Friedrich Kratochwil). Thus, the discipline bears an undeniable American influence.

Remarkably, the Marxist approach to the IR and the US approach sometimes ran parallel to one another. For instance, both traditions underline the policy relevance of the IR research. However, most of the "Great Debates" on theory in IR (occurred primarily in the US) and the ripples of the disturbance they provoked passed unnoticed for CEE countries and later Ukraine. On the contrary, after 1991, they borrowed almost unconditionally American IR paradigms, theories, and quality standards. New books and theoretical approaches were gradually introduced, some essential translations appeared, new contacts and international cooperation were established, and Westernizing educational reforms happened throughout the region, posing similar problems of the coexistence of the old and new. However, the implementation rate and the balance of continuity and change was uneven and created some rifts in the academic communities, observed by Drulák (2009: 169), which could be safely applied to Ukraine as well:

> All the national IR communities in the region are internally divided between two uneven groups of scholars. On the one hand, there is a small minority of those who consider themselves members of the Anglo-American IR and try to orient their academic activities accordingly, publishing with recognized international publishers or participating at international IR conventions. On the other hand, a vast majority of scholars are only active in their national contexts, focusing on teaching, textbook writing, policy advice and public intellectual activities. With a few important exceptions, the institutional power (department heads, deans, professors) usually rests with nationally oriented scholars who set the explicit and implicit criteria of further disciplinary reproduction.

Still, significant differences existed. First, most CEE states of the former Warsaw block were independent during the interwar period and experienced a kind of intellectual renaissance during Khrushchev's thaw, when foundations of foreign policies and IR studies were laid. Ukrainian IR scholars sometimes refer to the institutional experience of Lviv School of international law that functioned in the interwar period under Polish rule (Byk 2013) but to present this episode as a part of Ukrainian heritage would be misleading.

Second, unlike the other countries of the region, Ukraine's European perspectives have been clear cut, and its Westernization of education and research since independence has been inconsequential. These factors caused a significant divergence between Ukraine and its Western neighbors. The tempo of westernization is, thus, incomparable: the new standards for publications, increase in theoretical awareness, scholarly standards adoption (peer review, plagiarism) occurred more rapidly in the CEE, even if we take into account the recent educational reform in Ukraine after 2014. The result is that the IR scholars of the Western neighbors of Ukraine are already in the middle of the discussion whether or not IR in their respective countries has become too westernized and whether the model of relations with global IR should be modified from emulation to contribution of national (Czaputowicz & Wojciuk 2016) or regional (Drulák 2013) nature. In Ukraine, this discussion has yet to take place.

In this respect, it would be safe to say that Ukrainian IR suffers from double parochialization: its peripheral position under Soviet domination provided a weak starting position for developing IR studies and research. Second, due to irregular Westernization, it is still catching up with the Central and Eastern European IR, simultaneously fighting the temptation to protect the established hybrid structures. What bearing does it have over the essence of Ukrainian IR teaching and research?

Taking into account both the legacy of Soviet IR and incomplete westernization attempts, we analyze the Ukrainian IR community along five axes: (1) how it situates the IR discipline within the broader field of social sciences; (2) how deeply it is integrated into global IR scholarship; (3) what paradigmatic framework(s) and research methods it prefers; (4) what kind of regional studies it conducts; (5) whether it deems important, and tries to bridge the gap between, the scholarly community and policy-makers. When combined, these questions are interrelated; when combined, they offer a complex view of the status of IR scholarship in Ukraine and the ways IR scholars cooperate with the broader community both domestically and internationally.

Findings and Discussion

A Riddle Inside the Mystery: Looking for the Place of IR Within the Broader Field of Social Sciences in Ukraine

For laypeople, the IR discipline focusing on states, international conflicts, power politics, and the intersection of collective goals and personal ambitions in diplomacy often represents the essence of political science. Furthermore, universities no less frequently offer study programs in IR as a part of broader political science programs. For instance, *InternationalRelationsEDU.org*, a career counseling platform for those eager to start or advance a career in international relations, describes IR as a field of study in its own right but also as an "offshoot of political science" (2019). Finally, the TRIP project explicitly cites the "IR [as a] sub-field of political science" (Maliniak et al. 2012: 2). According to this point of view, IR belongs to the versatile domain of social sciences, thus sharing basic methodological assumptions and trends such as the "behaviorist revolution," the "cultural turn," and the advent of computational methods.

However, there is a significant counter-current that rejects IR's inclusion into social sciences tracing its genealogy instead of historical science. This makes some sense since many IR research interests (e. g., face-to-face diplomacy and transformations of international systems) are best studied through traditional historiographic approaches. Moreover, the notable IR sub-field of foreign policy analysis fully developed out of the *emphatically atheoretical* and *historically oriented* diplomatic analysis. Only later was it influenced by system-level theory (Potter 2010). Such lack of theoretical foundations is sometimes lionized by some IR scholars, for it constitutes the uniqueness of the discipline, thus setting it apart from other social sciences in general and political science in particular. Remarkably, Reynolds explicitly opposed the understanding of IR as a field within social science and suggested the discipline should focus on visions and choices by key players vested with the authority to take decisions at critical junctions of international politics (1973). History, being "a discipline of context" (Stone 1981: 34), is required to avoid overgeneralized theories and study particularities. The same preference for narrative-based explanations, where "the facts speak for themselves" instead of theory-based explanations, is a significant feature for some prominent IR scholars with historical training (see Gaddis 1986; Leffler 1995; Mayer 1969). One might trace the roots of IR in historical science back to Thucydides, who is considered one of the founding fathers of both history and IR.

The debate on whether IR should remain a separate branch of knowledge or be merged with the political or economic sciences is noteworthy in Ukraine for two reasons. First, the Soviet legacy, i. e. earlier establishment of IR, supports a separate standing, providing it with symbolic capital and political importance. This stands in contrast to political science, which mostly appeared only after the USSR had collapsed. This tradition grants some IR teaching and studying institutions (most notably the Kyiv Institute of International Relations) a privileged status. Secondly, the post-1991 process of new IR departments branching out from departments of history, geography, and political science and recruitment of specialists with various training to newly created IR departments contributed to the emergence of a particular setting, where IR and its subdisciplines are nested within other social sciences.

The conflict between the perceived privileged position of IR and the mixed reality revealed itself in 2015 when a higher education reform envisaged reviewing the list of higher education specializations in Ukraine. Among other innovations, it categorized "International Relations, Social Communications, and Regional Studies" and "International Economic Relations" as belonging to Social and Behavioral Sciences, on par with the economy, political science, sociology, and psychology. It also suppressed some lesser specializations like "International Information" and "International Business" and placed "International Law" as a subcategory of more general "Law studies" (CMU 2015). Although the reformers justified their decision by the need to align with the western standards, they did not go as far as to place IR under Political Science (see two interviews by the then deputy minister of education: Sovsun 2015a; Sovsun 2015b). The reform elicited a public outcry in student publications (Sherstiuk et al. 2015) and a lack of support from the MFA and the parliamentary committee on education, but no significant public discussion. Thus, the pressure went the informal way: after the change of the government, the status of International Relations as the standalone branch of studies, consisting of "International Relations, social communications and regional studies," "International Economy" and "International Law" in January 2017, has been reestablished (CMU 2017), which reflects the still significant lobbying power of Ukrainian IR faculty elites.

Our data suggest that the Ukrainian IR community holds a two-tiered status and would like this status to persist. When explicitly asked about their specialization, only 16.4% of the whole sample indicated political science related sub-fields (e.g., comparative politics or political theory), whereas 65.7% indicated international relations, area studies, or global politics. Another 17.8%, declared that they were not political scientists outright, claiming to be either historians or economists (see Figure 1).

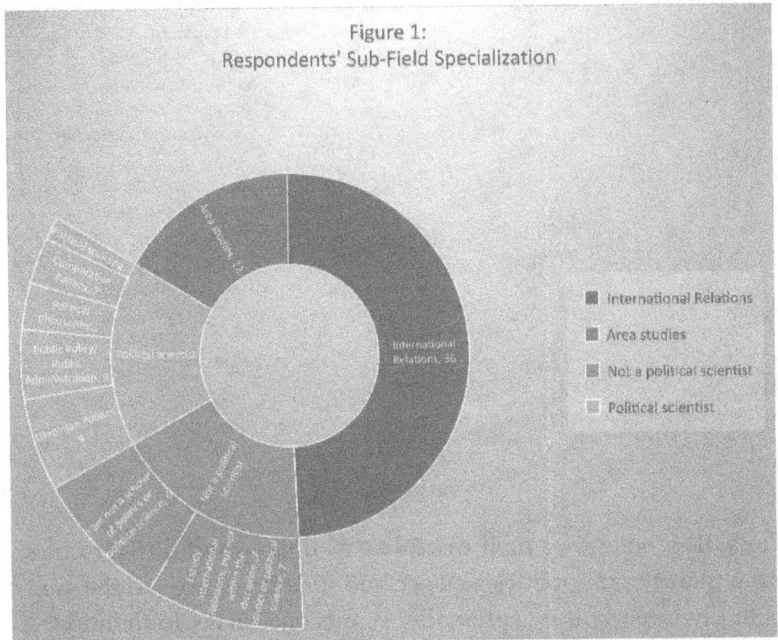

Figure 1:
Respondents' Sub-Field Specialization

Equally revealing Is that 48 TRIP survey respondents (48.5% of the total number or 61.5% of those who responded to the question) signaled that they would prefer standalone Ph.D. programs in IR (See Figure 2). Most Ukrainian IR scholars consider their field too distinct to be taught alongside either political science or history. It is also noteworthy that, unlike in other countries (e.g., the US or Germany), area studies specialists do not consider their craft as a separate branch of IR: none of those 9 people who advocate including IR Ph.D. programs into area studies do area studies. Conversely, all area studies specialists opt for standalone IR programs. The relations between IR and area studies will be elaborated upon below.

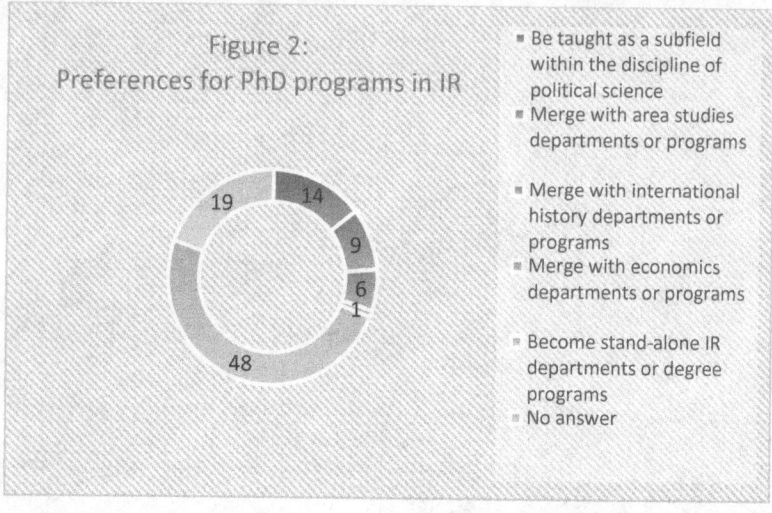

Figure 2: Preferences for PhD programs in IR

- Be taught as a subfield within the discipline of political science
- Merge with area studies departments or programs
- Merge with international history departments or programs
- Merge with economics departments or programs
- Become stand-alone IR departments or degree programs
- No answer

Thus, IR scholars see their discipline as unique and different both from mainstream political science and history. However, the symbolically important exceptionality stands on a shaky foundation. A doctorate and a professorship in IR are received when one defends one's thesis of a respected degree. Unlike for History or Political Science, there are no specialized "International Relations" boards. To be a Ph.D. or a Doctor of Science in IR, one should defend a thesis in Political Science sub-specialization No. 23.00.04 labeled "Political problems of international systems and global development." A Ph.D. (prior to 2014 "Candidate of Science") or a Doctor of Science holder is a Dr. or Prof. in Political Science with no mention of their sub-specialty. In other words, at a closer glance, the IR exceptionality seems to vanish. This, however, is a misleading conclusion because all the Scientific Councils that award honorary degrees are concentrated in the biggest IR departments controlled by the community. Albeit disciplinary related to political science, IR in Ukraine remains procedurally separate, supporting the power and self-reproduction of the faculty and administration.

All these findings suggest that despite the strong opposition from elites, post-Soviet inertia, and partial rollback of the reform, there is enough space and plenty of institutional capacity to strengthen the IR-Political Science connection typical for Western academia. It is the willingness of the Ukrainian IR community which lacks. Arguably, the double "political science—history" foundation provides the IR community with particular status among other sciences: it makes the discipline incommensurable, thus raising the status of IR scholars who are immunized from methodological critique by *both* social scientists and historians.

Please Call Later: The Connection of Ukrainian IR Scholars to the Global Scholarly Networks

Autarky is far from beneficial to the advancement of science. When excluded from communication with foreign scholars who bring new ideas, methodological innovations, alternative explanations, and research grants, national scholarly communities tend to lose vigor and focus. Numerous cases like information technology in the German Democratic Republic (Geipel 1999), physics in Franco's Spain (Herran & Roqué 2012), biomedicine in North Korea (Kim 1999), or even the whole scientific institutes like National Council for Research in Mussolini's Italy (Maiocchi 2015) prove that inertia and inefficiency reign supreme when scholars are enclosed in national autarkic systems. Inclusion into global scholarly networks does not automatically imply compliance with hegemonic discourses: one might voice his/her dissent disseminating alternative interpretations via specialized journals, find like-minded researchers abroad, or even achieve international acclaim as a non-conformist. Integration, in other words, brings exchange and cross-fertilization no less often than slavish copying of foreign patterns.

An autarkic attitude is not necessarily imposed on scientists by authoritarian regimes. Scholars may voluntarily seclude themselves in national contexts and topics culturally unimportant for the international audience. In this case, the proliferation of tiny "local schools" energetically demarcating and preserving their identities is expected. In addition, there will be a notable lack of foreign language proficiency among the scholarly community, for the inability to communicate with foreign partners effectively expels experts out of the "republic of letters."

The TRIP questionnaire is well-placed to monitor whether IR scholars cooperate with foreign partners or, instead, prefer to insulate themselves from international scholarly trends. Focused on questions of the most influential IR journal, the best publishing house, an individual scholar with the utmost impact over the field in the last 20 years, the most advantageous university to build a career in foreign policy, the most prestigious Ph.D. program in IR all, the survey provides quite an accurate assessment of whether scholars are well integrated into the global market of ideas and its underlying institutional machinery.

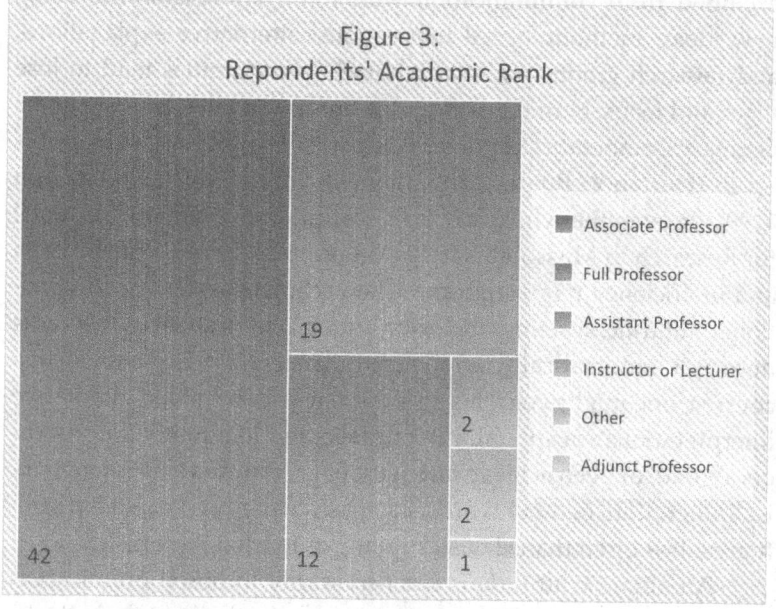

Figure 3: Repondents' Academic Rank

To interpret this part of TRIP data on Ukraine correctly, some information on the sociological background of the Ukrainian sample is necessary. With a **median of 48.5 years** (ranging from 28 to 83), 55% of the respondents are male and 43% female, the sample is a set of academicians in the prime period of their career. As shown in Figure 3, roughly half of the respondents are Associate Professors, and another quarter are Full Professors in their departments. None are Ph.D. students or a new Ph.D. holder in the early stage of his or her career. Therefore, one might expect our respondents to be active in editing articles and books as well as to be acquainted with a number of international scholars. It might also be predicted that being the most active age cohort in both research and teaching, the TRIP respondents should participate in theoretical and paradigmatic debates and policy discussions.

However, the picture presented by the TRIP survey is more complex in several respects. First, only 45% of respondents assessed their mastery of English explicitly as sufficient to read literature and policy documents, with another 20% claiming the same for German, 13% — for French, and 12% — for Spanish. If aggregated, these figures provide an optimistic picture suggesting that Ukrainian IR experts can communicate with international partners. In addition, 50% of the total sample (and virtually everyone who decided to respond to this particular question) stated proficiency in the Russian language. The data suggest that there is no solid language barrier separating the Ukrainian IR community from the world; however, there is still an essential space for improvement.

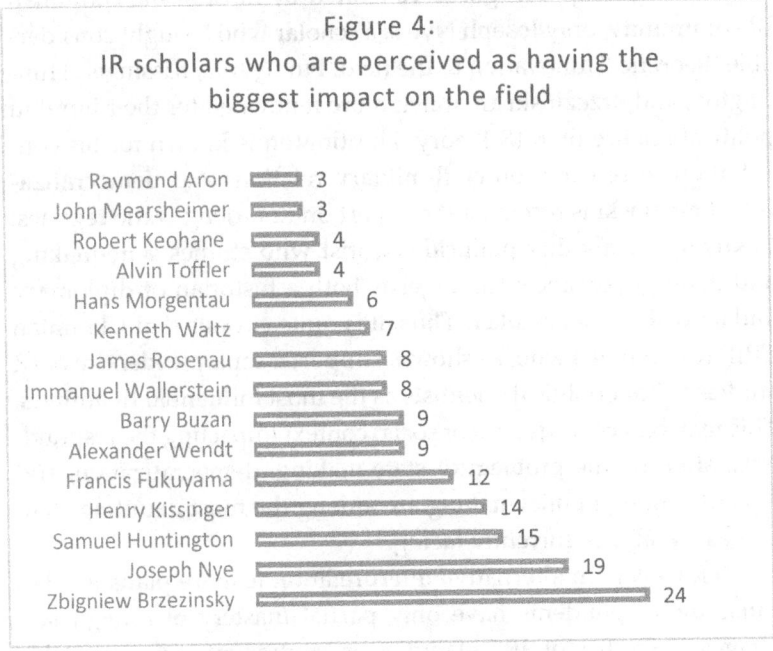

Figure 4:
IR scholars who are perceived as having the biggest impact on the field

Scholar	Count
Raymond Aron	3
John Mearsheimer	3
Robert Keohane	4
Alvin Toffler	4
Hans Morgentau	6
Kenneth Waltz	7
James Rosenau	8
Immanuel Wallerstein	8
Barry Buzan	9
Alexander Wendt	9
Francis Fukuyama	12
Henry Kissinger	14
Samuel Huntington	15
Joseph Nye	19
Zbigniew Brzezinsky	24

Second, due to the partial access to the market of ideas, different authors are perceived and incorporated into the local IR canon unevenly. When asked to list four scholars whose work has had the most significant influence on the field of IR in the past 20 years, Ukrainian respondents provided a host of answers climbing up to 99 personalities. The list is highly versatile, for it includes scholars of IR proper (e.g., Andrew Moravcsik and Robert Jervis), area studies specialists (e.g., Stephen Sestanovich and Gerard Toal), historians (e.g., Christopher Hill and Jean-Baptiste Duroselle), founders of the social sciences (e.g., Max Weber and Karl Marx), specialists in transitional studies (e.g., Guillermo O'Donnell and Philippe Schmitter), and even currently fashionable authors such as Nassim Taleb and Fareed Zakaria. Neither the list nor the categories we cite are exclusive. Most of the authors are mentioned only once or twice. Figure 4 shows all those who scored at least three votes.

Several noteworthy observations can be made from this data. To begin with, something which remotely resembles a commonly referenced pool of the most prominent experts is significantly selective. From the top-5 IR gurus venerated by most of the Ukrainian IR community, only Joseph Nye is a scholar who brought considerable theoretical innovation to the field. Fukuyama, Kissinger, Huntington, and Brzeziński are much more renowned for their input in political science than IR theory. Huntington is known for his contribution to research on civil-military relations and democratization; Brzeziński is foremost the expert on non-democratic regimes; Fukuyama is another political scientist who studies state-making and good governance; Kissinger is both a historian of diplomacy and a notable policymaker. Thus, it is quite curious that Ukrainian TRIP respondents who, as shown, support a separate identity of IR studies behold political scientists as the most influential IR authors. This may be a consequence of social context impacting the respondents: after all, the problem of state-making, democratization, and effective foreign policymaking are among the most daunting challenges Ukraine is currently facing.

However, an alternative interpretation is more plausible. Because the respondents have only partial mastery of foreign languages, their list of IR celebrities is contingent upon available translations. After the USSR collapsed, the uneven arrival of books and names provoked lopsided results in perceptions of the greatest IR scholar. Translated into Ukrainian in 2000, *The Grand Chessboard: American Primacy and Its Geostrategic Imperatives* by Brzeziński (2000) became a reference book due to the geopolitical importance it ascribes to Ukraine. In contrast, in the Global sample of TRIP-2014 Brzeziński does not make it to the top ten, and in the Polish ranking of TRIP 2014, he climbed only to the 10th position. The even more noteworthy translation of Fukuyama's *The End of History?* was first published as an article in 1990 (Fukuyama 1990) and became a reference text and, later, an object of critique. The same can be said about Fukuyama's former professor, Samuel Huntington, whose *Clash of Civilizations* became available in Russian in 1994 (Huntington 1994). The late 1980s and early 1990s were, presumably, the foundational years for most respondents from the Ukrainian TRIP sample; hence the importance they ascribe to the top-5.

Next, when considered as a whole, the data in Figure 4 reveals a curious post-Communist trend: Ukraine, Poland, and Russia share a specific corpus of preferred texts. This effect is also contingent upon available translations. As noted by Czaputowicz and Wojciuk (2016), Brzeziński, Kissinger, Fukuyama, and Huntington all appeared in Polish in the early 1990s and were widely discussed. Furthermore, in this particular genre, "books offering narratives describing current international phenomena, sometimes successfully combining IR scholarship with visions of global trends, were more popular than ambitious academic publications. In recent years, the Polish community of IR scholars has become more active and more open to international collaboration. Thus, the past several years have yielded certain overdue translations of classical writings, such as those of Morgenthau, Waltz, Wendt, and Nye" (Czaputowicz & Wojciuk 2016: 7). Likewise, in Russia, "the image of western international relations theory [is] almost exclusively based on the works of the political activists like Huntington, Fukuyama, and Brzezinski, who do not occupy any visible place in western university canon" (Astrov 2005). One of the most striking examples is the analysis of the "perception of western theories" in Russia is provided by Tsygankov, which is supposed to be comprehensive. However, in fact, his list of "western theorists" does not extend beyond Fukuyama and Huntington (Morozov 2009: 203).

Finally, as the Ukrainian TRIP survey reveals, the respondents hold their colleagues (or themselves) in great esteem, for they cite Ukrainian scholars as belonging to those with the greatest influence on the field of IR in the past 20 years. Our entire list of 99 personalities included 16 Ukrainians. However, none emerge as a local big-name whose prominence is recognized by the Ukrainian IR community as a whole. This might be due to a relatively short and tumultuous history of the IR in Ukraine: the local big-name is yet to arrive.

Another essential feature of global integration revealed by TRIP is participation in the scholarly publishing industry. The obtained results indicate the complex position of Ukrainian IR scholars. When asked to identify academic journals with the most influence on international relations, respondents are significantly unsure. To begin with, 50% of the total sample simply skipped this question. Moreover, the given answers are, once again, extremely versatile. 80 different titles were suggested altogether, 58 of them were mentioned only once. On top of that, the list includes a volatile mix of academic and non-academic, international and national journals, and even newspapers (See Figure 5). There is little consistency in this regard, suggesting that each scholar follows individual awareness and publication trajectory.

This reflects several noteworthy tendencies. First, written communications of findings in general and scholarly journals are not significantly important for the Ukrainian IR community. In this, the community follows the Ukrainian research tradition proper to all disciplines. It comes with little surprise that, given this tradition, none of the Ukrainian journals gathered more than 4 votes. Our respondents referred to *Zovnishni spravy* ("Foreign Affairs"), *Visnyk KNU* ("Kyiv National University Bulletin"), *Aktualni Problemy Miznarodnykh Vidnosyn* ("Current Issues in International Relations"), *Hileya* ("Hileya"), and *Almanakh "Hrani"* ("The Edges' Yearbook"), a very diverse set of national journals both style- and qualitywise. Therefore, we can argue that Ukrainian journals are not the key element of professional communication and that no single authoritative common-reference journal exists[4].

Second, the high placing of international non-academic *Foreign Affairs* and *Foreign Policy* suggests that the practical inclinations of Ukrainian IR scholarship make this type of publication more valuable than anything purely academic.

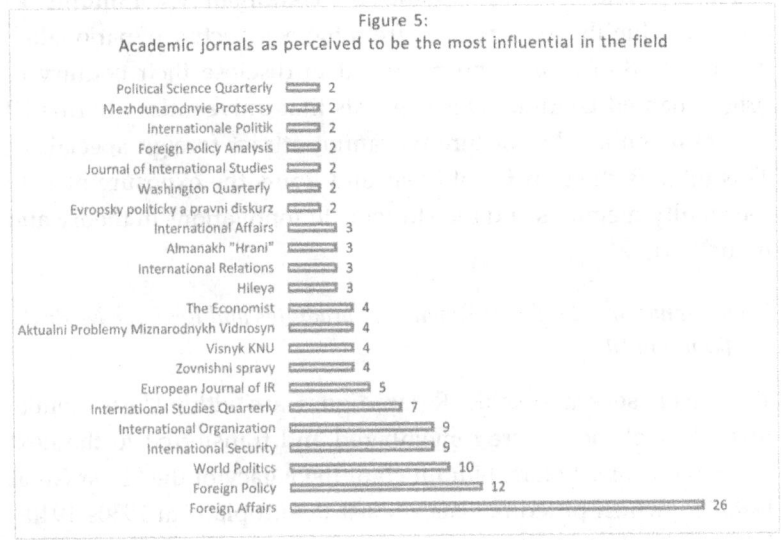

Figure 5:
Academic jornals as perceived to be the most influential in the field

- Political Science Quarterly — 2
- Mezhdunarodnyie Protsessy — 2
- Internationale Politik — 2
- Foreign Policy Analysis — 2
- Journal of International Studies — 2
- Washington Quarterly — 2
- Evropsky politicky a pravni diskurz — 2
- International Affairs — 3
- Almanakh "Hrani" — 3
- International Relations — 3
- Hileya — 3
- The Economist — 4
- Aktualni Problemy Miznarodnykh Vidnosyn — 4
- Visnyk KNU — 4
- Zovnishni spravy — 4
- European Journal of IR — 5
- International Studies Quarterly — 7
- International Organization — 9
- International Security — 9
- World Politics — 10
- Foreign Policy — 12
- Foreign Affairs — 26

Third, among the international journals mentioned, two types can be distinguished. The first one includes world-renown IR/Political Science journals, which suggests that Ukrainian scholars are aware of their existence, albeit they seldom publish there. The second type is newly established and less-rigorous international journals, often established in cooperation between Ukrainian faculty and their colleagues from CEE countries (e. g. *Journal of International Studies, Evropský politický a právní diskurz*), which provide a relatively

---

4   Although it is beyond the scope of our research, on the margins we would like to note that none of those journals is indexed within the international reference bases yet, and although they are slowly updating their submission requirements and peer-review processes, the threshold for being published remains remarkably low. A detailed study of the peculiarities of Ukrainian social sciences journals, like the one recently conducted in Russia (Istomin & Baikov 2013), is thus long overdue.

simpler possibility to obtain an international publication in response to the new standards imposed by the Ministry of Education and Science.

The last important piece of evidence on how deeply Ukrainian scholars and universities are integrated into the global IR community comes from a somewhat unexpected direction. According to the data provided by respondents, the Ukrainian IR community as a whole is highly homogenized from the perspective of nationality. 77 out of 78 of those who preferred to disclose their country of origin, named Ukraine. This suggests that universities offering IR programs either do not hire or cannot attract foreign specialists. This inhibits the transfer of ideas and limits the exposure of both the faculty members and the students to innovations in theory and in methods.

Same Framework, Different Practices: Paradigms and Research Methods in Ukrainian IR

There were several notable IR paradigm wars within US academia. Just a few of them were remembered and transferred to the next generations of scholars. Not much of the legacy of the "First Great Debate", which pitted realists against the utopians in 1930s-1940s, is considered of practical value for contemporary students of IR. The "Second Great Debate" between classicists, who preferred the historical narrative approach (Bull 1966), and behavioralists, heavily influenced by natural science and its methodology (Kaplan 1966), and the final victory of the latter gave the discipline a typical positivist outlook. Albeit the very incidence of the "Third Great" Inter-Paradigm Debate remains questioned (Waever 1996), it modified the field from now on more than ever focused on paradigms. Finally, the epistemologically driven "Fourth Great Debate," the rivalry between rational positivism and constructivism, produced the canonic repertoire of paradigms inculcated to any IR novice. There are the Big Three approaches (Realism, Liberalism, and Constructivism) supplemented with Marxism, English School, and Feminism.

Despite some efforts to reorganize the structure of IR textbooks so that the discussion gravitates toward pressing topics such as international terrorism, global inequality, and climate change instead of paradigms (see Frieden, Lake, & Schultz 2010), a typical US IR textbook and a typical class still focus on paradigms and the different answers they deliver (Maliniak et al. 2011: 441–444). Such a tendency might be responsible for the finding by Matthews & Callaway that although in the US "92% of the textbooks provide at least a foundational level of theoretical coverage in the theory chapters, the lack of theoretical application throughout the material robs students of the ability to see the real of strength of theories" (2015: 17). In other words, it is likely that nowadays, IR professors pay customary duty to presentations of theories but shy away from consistent and thorough usage of them as analytical frames, thus widening the gap between abstract theories and practical needs. Yet, it is premature to abandon paradigms in IR. Guzzini (2001) noticed that data never speak for itself, and any meaningful interpretation of events is theory-dependent. Therefore, it is not enough to accumulate information about past and ongoing events: all players within the IR domain need conceptual frameworks to have some impact and even be actors. Moreover, mastery of theories improves "the capacity of students to train in clear thinking" (Guzzini 2001: 103).

In the post-Soviet times, when IR studies proliferated in bigger and smaller universities, the previously peripheral department for international relations in Kyiv state university became the key national institution. Its study programs and curricula have been emulated by newly appeared regional universities (Malsky & Moroz 2012: 3). At the same time, Western IR theory became more accessible in Ukraine, although lack of the participation of Ukrainian (Soviet) scholars in the key theoretical debates of the previous decades, compounded by selective translations of books and limited access to the originals, played a role in the way IR paradigms were adopted. The fact that Ukrainian scholars are mindful of paradigmatic differences is corroborated by the handbook publishing. Since 2007, at least 5 university-level manuals on Theories of International Relations have been published in Ukraine (see Shepeliev

2004; Kamenetskyi 2007; Malskyi & Matsyakh 2007; Tsymbalistyi 2009; Trebin 2016). Each describes more or less extensively the key theoretical debates. In addition, there is a two-volume edition *Ukrainian Diplomatic Encyclopedia* (2004), which treats this question at some length.

In addition to numerous theoretical approaches, the IR discipline has witnessed a considerable proliferation of research methods. Nowadays, a typical research toolkit in IR includes simulation and modeling (Alker & Brunner 1969; Ruloff 1976; Snidal 2004), manual event analysis (McClelland 1970), computational event analysis (Bennett & Stam 2000; Schrodt 2000), cognitive mapping (Johnston 1995), case study (Bennett and George 2005), statistical analysis (King, Keohane, & Verba 1994; Braumoeller & Sartori 2004), and computer data mining (Unver 2019).

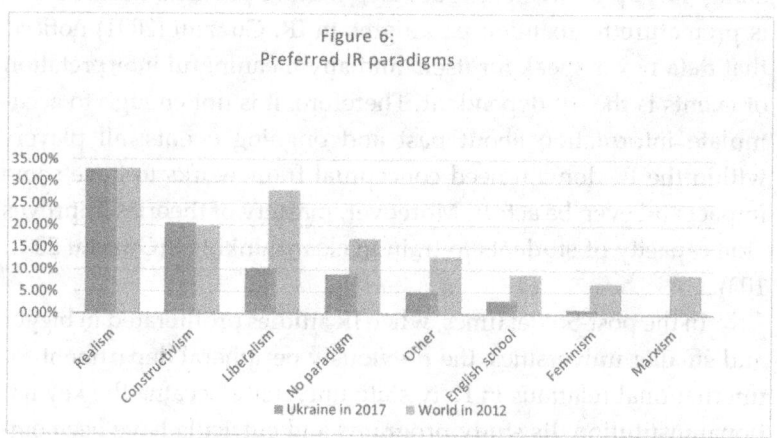

Figure 6: Preferred IR paradigms

This section analyzes the TRIP data to understand whether the Ukrainian IR community follows global trends in both theoretical approaches and preferred methods. There are several essential findings.

First, Ukrainian IR scholars are well aware of the existence of the discipline's main paradigms. None of them skipped the question on their paradigmatic approach to study of IR, and most of them (80 respondents) provided a definite answer (as opposed to 17 who checked "no answer"). And even though 9 respondents declare they do not use paradigmatic analysis, the theoretical preferences of the community are quite discernable: 32 are realists, 20 are constructivists, 10 are liberals, 3 lean to the English School, and 1 person espouses a Feminist approach to IR. Remarkably, no one adopts any variation of the Marxist approach (particular prompt invited respondents to choose either Marxist historical materialism or neo-Gramscianism or other critical theory). The distribution is consistent with the universal trends (as registered by TRIP 2012, see Maliniak et al. 2012). To illustrate this, we plotted both data on a chart (see Figure 6). Although the TRIP-2012 numbers add to more than 100%, which results from the methodological difference between two survey rounds (unlike in 2017, in 2012 respondents were asked a percentage for each paradigm), it is evident that Realism and Constructivism dominate globally. Ukraine evidently participates in the trend.

This is not surprising: despite their epistemological opposition, both Realism and Constructivism are mutually reinforcing, for Constructivism provides an additional ideational and identarian supplement to the state-centered realist approach. Thus, in the circumstances of post-Soviet IR traditionally focused on states, Constructivism was a fresh albeit not an incompatible innovation easily absorbed by the scholarly community. We find the apparent underestimation of Liberalism to be more noteworthy. The low esteem in which Liberalism is held makes Ukraine comparable to only two countries in the TRIP 2012 survey: Finland and Hong Kong. This is especially concerning given the high place that Ukrainian diplomacy accords to cooperation with partners and the peaceful resolution of conflicts, and its high esteem for international law and international organizations. It requires a further in-depth study into whether the lack of prestige for Liberalism corresponds to a particular political positioning of the countries outside military alliances.

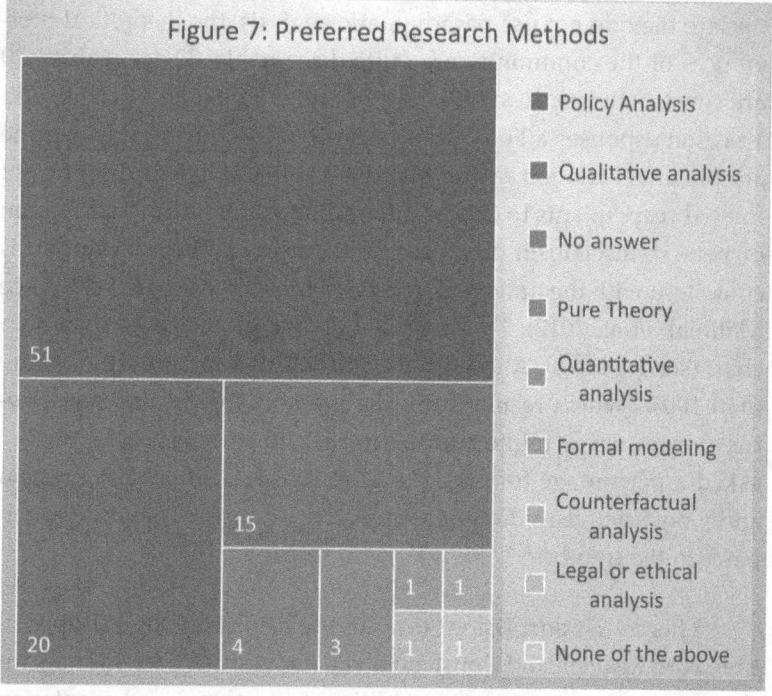

Figure 7: Preferred Research Methods

The most fundamental division between Ukrainian and global IR communities concerns methodology. In Western, and foremost in US IR studies, methodological preferences have been gradually shifting to empirical performance and measuring covariation in big data in particular to the extent that some scholars started voicing up warning signals that the field is moving towards "simplistic hypothesis testing... with most of the effort devoted to collecting data and testing empirical hypotheses" (Mearsheimer & Walt 2013: 438). This shift is a logical extension of the positivist research program, which, all epistemological debates notwithstanding, dominates in Western lecture halls and research centers. This would be impossible without the ever-increasing reliance upon quantitative methods that became almost compulsory for any research. The advent of quantitative-based science has had an enormous impact on both political science and IR, thus constituting an important bridge between two sub-disciplines.

In Ukraine, conversely, IR remains resistant to the quantitative drive, starting with basic statistical analysis. This might be a long-lasting legacy of the Soviet-style IR which relied heavily upon narrative policy analysis and thick description.

The TRIP survey corroborates this tendency among our respondents. (See Figure 7.) 51 scholars, which constitutes 52.5% of the whole sample or 62% of those who replied to the question, indicate policy analysis as their primary method. With other qualitative methods adding up to 28.6%, a meager fraction of 4% resorts to quantitative analysis or formal modeling ubiquitous in Western academia. When we pry open the "black box" of qualitative methodology, a clear tendency to narration and descriptive approach becomes obvious (See Figure 8): case studies, narrative analysis, process tracing, content, and discourse analysis prevail; even the dialectical research returns linking the Soviet past with the post-Soviet present.

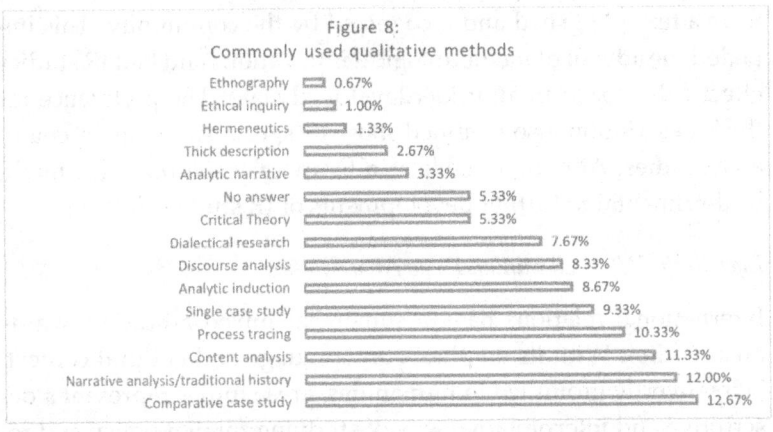

Figure 8:
Commonly used qualitative methods

Method	%
Ethnography	0.67%
Ethical inquiry	1.00%
Hermeneutics	1.33%
Thick description	2.67%
Analytic narrative	3.33%
No answer	5.33%
Critical Theory	5.33%
Dialectical research	7.67%
Discourse analysis	8.33%
Analytic induction	8.67%
Single case study	9.33%
Process tracing	10.33%
Content analysis	11.33%
Narrative analysis/traditional history	12.00%
Comparative case study	12.67%

Both dominant theoretical frameworks and preferred research methods suggest commonalities between Ukraine, other CEE countries, and Russia. Approaches inherited from the Communist times are responsible not only for Realism's lasting influence but also for the absorption of compatible aspects of Constructivism. Soviet Realism in IR was highly intuitive in its nature as its premise (the state is of utmost importance and its actions are not to be judged within the moral framework of individuals) came hand in hand with statism proper to the Soviet political agenda. Due to this reliance upon unproblematized assumptions, there were few theoretical elaborations. This gap was later filled with borrowings from Western academia and locally produced texts. In Soviet times, a methodological component of research remained underdeveloped: scholars typically relied upon highly descriptive policy analysis and narration, especially for case studies or area studies. Cross-national variations or large computational N-analysis, however, were scarce. In addition, unlike in the US, where the behavioralist revolution in IR brought the discipline closer to social sciences and was responsible for the quantitative revolution, in Ukraine, the double structure of IR simultaneously residing on historical and political science approaches has never been liberated from descriptive tendencies. To put it bluntly, scholars find that it suffices to provide a more or less detailed description of facts (e.g., recent political developments in a foreign country or preparation for a regional conflict) in order to have a text published and recognized by the community. This impeded the advent of methodological innovations and had IR studies effectively frozen in an underdeveloped state. The preference for thick description also confined most IR specialists to the arena of area studies. Although viable as a temporary solution, this might be detrimental to further developments of IR studies in Ukraine.

Eyes to the West: Ukrainian IR as Area Studies

International relations have a somewhat mixed attitude towards area studies. With its emphasis on language and cultural context, being overtly grounded in humanities, area studies represent a descriptive and interpretative way of studying foreign policy and relations between nations. It has much more in common with the atheoretical historical approach than the systematic approach to social sciences. Consequently, the fate and fame of area studies have been Inconsistent in recent decades. In the post-1945 bipolar world, with two superpowers competing for regional allies, it seemed essential to understand the mindset of populations in Asia, Africa, and Latin America as well as cultural sensitivities of local elites.

Cultural studies, regional history, and psychology coalesced to accomplish the mission (Capshew 1999). In addition, area studies experts collaborated extensively with the intelligence services (Cumings 1997), providing much-needed information through access to local media, field observations, and diplomatic back-channeling. Thus, the discipline evolved from a juncture of intelligence, statecraft, and soft power policy into strategic monitoring of regional integration policy.

As area studies proliferated, the expertise of its scholars contributed to many successful policies (notable examples include democratization of Japan, modernization of Turkey, viable state-building in Jordan) and was thus held in great esteem by experts and policymakers (see Kirk 1947; Hall 1948). During this honeymoon period, IR scholars did not shy away from the claim that "International Relations needs Area Studies" (Modelski 1961: 143). The situation was similar on the other side of the "iron curtain": whole institutes (e.g., the Institute of Asian and African Countries at Lomonosov Moscow State University, the Institute of Latin America, Institute for the Study of the USA and Canada, the Institute of the Far East, and the Institute of the Economy of the World Socialist System at the Academy of Sciences of the USSR) pursued area studies in the USSR, and some of the most prominent social scientists and politicians started their career as specialists in area studies (e.g., Georgi Derluguian was a specialist of Mozambique and Yevgeny Primakov specialized in Arab studies).

Much changed in US academia after 1991, when globalization seemed equivalent to homogenization, and the end of history was considered nigh. As a result, generous funding by government and private foundations went dry, universities cut expensive local language instruction (Katzenstein 2002: 131), and the area studies suffered methodological attacks as inadequate (Bates 1997). As one scholar sarcastically put it: "The problem with 'area experts' is [...] they are unable to define the theoretical structure of their field of study, to spell out the principles of their trade, to tell what the rules are of the game they are playing" (Kuijper 2008: 207). Nowadays, in the US, IR enjoys much more prestige than area studies.

In the post-Soviet world, however, area studies did not suffer such a drastic reversal of fortune. In Russia, up to 58 universities offer a BA in area studies (Zarubezhnoye regionovedeniye 2019). Furthermore, area studies degree proves to remain a good starting point for many politicians, diplomats, and statesmen. Unlike Soviet Russia, Soviet Ukraine used to be a backwater of diplomacy and great power politics, so no well-functioning conveyer belt would link area studies with statecraft. Nevertheless, integrated into many IR university curricula, area studies persevered and gained much of the veneer associated with diplomatic service. In short, no rupture between IR and area studies has occurred in post-Soviet academia; two sub-disciplines are considered more or less complimentary in their efforts to explain foreign policy.

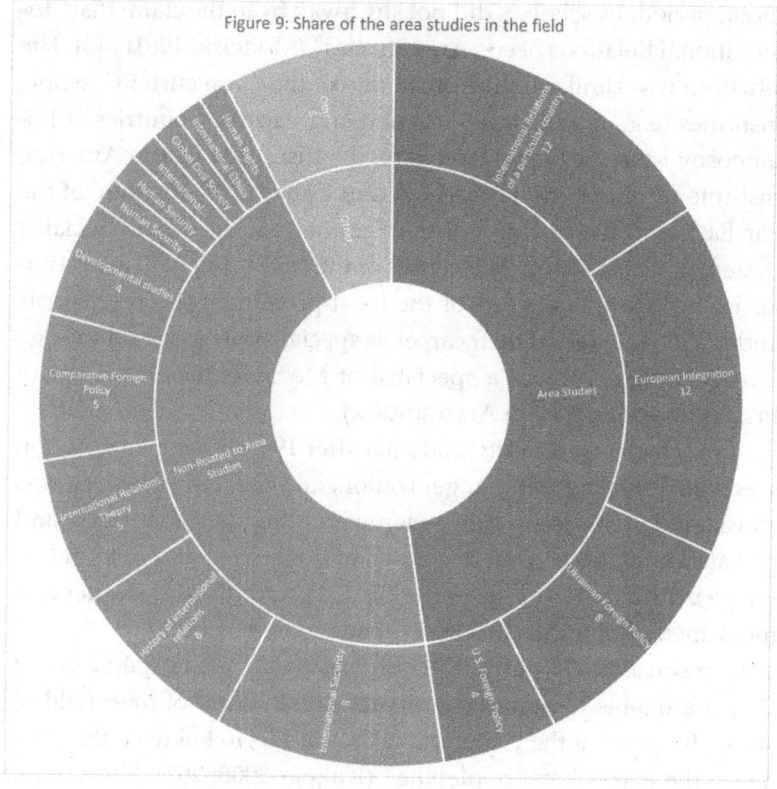

Figure 9: Share of the area studies in the field

The TRIP survey reveals the dominant position of area studies within the Ukrainian IR community. 40% of all respondents described focus on region or country to be their primary area of research as opposed to 38% of those who work in pure IR domains like "International Security" or "Human Rights" (see Figure 9). The figure for area studies should actually be even higher, for some respondents who opted for the "other" category specifically mentioned "International/Transnational Regionalism" or "Diplomacy and Ethnicity" as their main research agenda. None of the respondents considers himself/herself to be primarily specialists in international political economy, international law, international health, global environmental politics, Chinese foreign policy, gender in IR, and religion and IR. No doubt, there are specialists in international political economy and international law at Ukrainian universities, but they are concentrated in their respective chairs and departments and tend to affiliate with law or economics rather than with IR. Furthermore, when TRIP respondents were prompted to define their secondary areas of research, Ukrainian foreign policy (indicated by 10%), European Studies (9.34%), International Security (9%), and International Relations of a particular region or country (8.3%) emerged as the four most common answers. Yet another TRIP question corroborates the dominant status of area studies in Ukraine: 67% of participants conduct regionally focused studies, a towering figure compared with 16,5% of those who use global and cross-regional data instead.

Observing this data, we can safely conclude that **most IR experts in Ukraine are area studies specialists**. Given historical legacies, mastery of the Russian language, and the ongoing Russo-Ukrainian conflict, one might expect that Russia and the Former Soviet Union to constitute the primary research focus. This is not the case. The Russia/FSU region—as a primary region of studies—shares a relatively low-ranking 5th position with the North American region: only 5.15% of respondents study one of the regions. A significantly larger number of scholars focus on Central and Eastern Europe (30.93%) and Western Europe (13.40%). Moreover, when asked about the most critical region(s) for Ukraine now and in 20 years, respondents are notably consistent: the very same regions, Central and Eastern Europe and Western Europe, are considered of utmost importance for further research. (Remarkably, the Ukrainian IR community is confident that in the next 20 years, the North American region will lose its significance, whereas that of the North African region will increase (See Figure 10).

The predominance of area studies as *the* way to study international relations suggests that, in this respect, Ukraine has not shed its Soviet heritage. However, the developmental trajectory of area studies in Ukraine is somewhat particular and has more in common with CEE countries rather than with Russia.

There are, however, several significant inconsistencies in Ukrainian area studies. The most evident is the place of Russia. As noted, scholarly interest in studying Russia and FSU countries is unexpectedly low and appears in conceivably significant figures only as a secondary choice. This comes in a striking contradiction to the fact that most TRIP respondents described Russia's "aggressive foreign policy" as **one of the top three critical security threats** to Ukraine. So, they acknowledge the challenge but prefer to focus on other issues instead. This is a clear indication of a regrettable lack of academic Russian studies in Ukraine precisely at the critical juncture when expert opinion on the country is needed to guide Ukrainian foreign policy. Partially, the current state of affairs might be attributed to the fact that Ukrainian scholars do not categorize their region as the one belonging to Russia and FSU countries. This may be puzzling for Western experts, but the data suggest that the Ukrainian IR community identifies Ukraine chiefly with the CEE region.

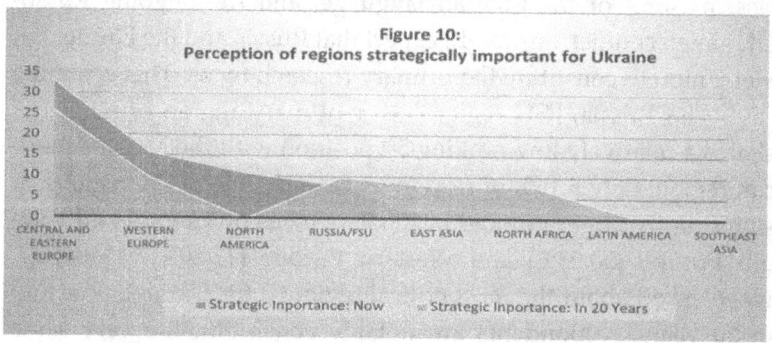

Next, there is an issue with primary source access. Notwithstanding the overt tendency to focus on Central and Eastern Europe, only 25.7% of the total TRIP sample indicated they master any region's language. Polish was the most popular answer, but some individuals speak Czech, Croatian, and Slovenian. None has declared proficiency in Hungarian, Bulgarian, Romanian, or any Baltic language. Thus, not only do specialists in the region have little access to original primary sources but also the sources they do deal with are lopsided towards the Polish case. Poland is undoubtedly one of the most important partners for Ukraine in the region, but it is far from being the only one, so there is a problematic imbalance to regional expertise. Moreover, when we looked at the specialization of respondents who speak Central European languages, we discovered that only 6 are area scholars, 7 study IR outside political science (e.g., economy or international law), and 17 are IR scholars. The data suggest that IR specialists or even jurists decide to focus on CEE at some period of their career rather than area studies expert offer their insights on the region built upon profound expertise in language and culture. In other words, area studies are practiced out of political expediency by people who were not trained to do it but decided to bridge the gap when the need arose.

Finally, the prevalence of area studies is a characteristic symptom of Ukrainian IR in general. There is a kind of international division of labor in the discipline with Western academia elaborating and refining general IR theories, while the rest of the world (global South) collects data and raw materials for this theory development. Still, the more non-Western scholars focus on data collection, the less time and resources they have necessary to develop original theoretical frameworks. They, therefore, grow increasingly dependent on theoretical approaches borrowed from the West. This division of labor amplifies the peripheral status of regional scholars whose data and localized insights are rarely published or cited compared to important theoretical generalizations. In the Ukrainian case, this amplifies the local traditions of isolated and practice-minded research.

Therefore, focusing exclusively on area studies induces peripheralization. This fate befell, among others, IR specialists in CEE:

they are inclined to produce texts that are not especially rich in theoretical insights but instead pay attention to their particular region of which they provide extensive descriptions of political developments. Since such minutiae are of interest primarily to other specialists in the area, the field grows increasingly isolated, the feedback loop perpetuates itself, and the peripheral status of the discipline with all the detrimental effects of scientific autarky we described above.

Middlemen Reaping the Benefits: Closing the Gap Between IR Research and Foreign Policy

One of the ever-open-ended questions for the IR discipline is: whether IR scholars should keep their research as practical as possible and avoid unwarranted theorization or, instead, they should uphold the high academic standards without compromising themselves to meet the needs of politicians. While too much theorization is likely to make scholars' messages inaccessible for policymakers, lack of theorization unravels the distinction between a scholarly point of view and a layperson's guess.

Some authors are apprehensive that the policymaking sphere and academia are converging more than they should. Hill and Beshoff invite scholars to avoid the "the siren song of policy relevance" cautioning: "where a dialogue with the world of policy is achieved, there are likely to be opportunity costs in terms of the time available for basic research." (1994: 220). Guzzini suggests that a simplification of the academic message, especially simplifications of theoretical models as a way to achieve higher policy-relevance might be counterproductive due to "the remoteness of applied studies from any direct practical value" (2001: 98).

Others, however, argue that IR drifted further away from the world of policymaking due to the effort to establish itself within the realm of pure theory. As stipulated by George, "most university professors write largely for one another and have little inclination or ability to communicate their knowledge in terms comprehensible to policymakers" (1993: 7). Wallace warns that "there is a danger that our discipline could follow the path that sociology took, becoming too self-preoccupied, too determined to leave its origins in applied research and policy-related work behind, to take refuge in increasing abstractions, theories, and meta-theories: to move from scholarship to scholasticism" (1996: 311). Lake concurs that "having created academic sects based on incommensurate assumptions and supported by selective evidence, we do not seek to assess which approach helps us understand world politics best" (2011: 471).

In the background of these mostly US-based discussions lies the fact that in the United States, a significant bridge links the ivory tower of academia to the keep of policymaking. Four presidents had been active in scholarly communities prior to entering politics; three prominent political scientists, W.W. Rostow, Henry Kissinger, and Zbigniew Brzezinski left their universities (MIT Center for International Studies, Harvard, and Columbia, respectively) to continue their careers as National Security Advisors. During his academic years, Kissinger beat Brzezinski for tenure at Harvard, who "retaliated," evicting Kissinger from office when President Carter came to power and teaching a future Secretary of State, Madeleine Albright. In fact, links between theory and practice influenced not only biographical twists of the key players but also the research itself: "the money and attention from the policy community came with strings attached—most notably, an expectation for immediately relevant research" (Potter 2010: 3).

Although in the USSR, the link between policymaking and research was not as strong, it contributed to the strong demand for practicality and application of scholarship for diplomacy. While formally framed within the only true Marxist-Leninist doctrine, the "IR community—policymaking circles" complex developed based on practical state-centered analysis, mainly concerning the questions of regional dynamics and some pressing issues on the international agenda with clear institutional links, and sometimes even elite rotations.

Soviet Ukrainian IR research followed the general trend on a lesser scale: it was undertheorized, practical, state- and region-centered, conducted via the framework of "intuitive realism." In the absence of a single Institute for International Studies, the expertise was used instead through the eventual individual involvement of scholars and remained markedly peripheral compared to Moscow. Even the CEE states were in a somewhat better position: they established connections with the local research institutions, as their sovereignty was not as drastically limited as in the case of the Soviet republics, and have further developed them since the independence. Nowadays, the CEE states boast relatively strong government-funded and -funded research and policy institutions.

While the differences between Russian and Ukrainian IR research and its political application in USSR seemed to be either those of scale or simplified center-periphery dynamics, they provoked profound distinctions between Russia and CEE states since the USSR's collapse. The Russian State has made a great effort to bring IR research closer to foreign policy needs. It consolidated key governmental and government-supported analytical centers and research divisions to develop and communicate its foreign policy abroad. The extent of the trend was so substantial that analyzing how Russia instrumentalizes its state and state-supported private think-tanks and academics for promoting its views has become a common subject of analysis (Vendil Pallin & Oxenstierna 2017; Smagliy 2018).

The TRIP 2017 data indicate that the Ukrainian IR community deems it necessary to pay attention to the needs of current politics. 45% of the total sample claim to have responded to significant world events by taking them into account in their research or making their research more relevant for policy practitioners as opposed to 15.5% who have not (regrettably, 37% ignored the question). Still, there are several inconsistencies between foreign policy priorities and foreign policy academic research. First, as mentioned in the subchapter on the specifics of the regional studies, Ukrainian IR scholars underestimate the need for Russian studies even in the middle of a half-decade of armed and political conflict. Second, although Ukrainian diplomacy relies heavily on diplomatic dialogue and the instruments of international law while dealing with Russia on the international scale, the Liberal paradigm remains among the least favored by Ukrainian academics.

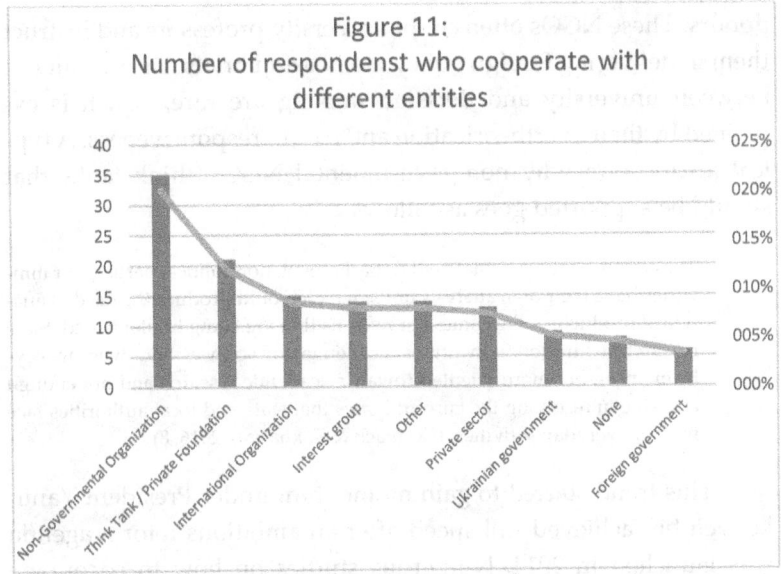

Figure 11: Number of respondenst who cooperate with different entities

Finally, as Figure 11 illustrates, despite all the emphasis on the practicality of their research, only a minority of Ukrainian IR faculty mentions working directly for the Ukrainian government (9 persons). A much greater fraction resorts to intermediaries, namely NGOs (35) and think tanks (21), to conduct practical research. While NGOs and think-tanks are more often than not mixed in Ukraine, fusing analysis and advocacy (Livny, 2013: 18), the combined data—56 persons contributing to NGOs/think-tanks explains a key difference between Ukraine on the one hand and her Eastern and Western neighbors on the other. Namely, in Ukraine, neither research institutions, nor universities, nor even state-funded think-tanks ever achieved significant influence on government policy analysis. A poll in 2016 (Bekeshkina et al. 2016: 44) has shown that while governmental institutions rely on old habits of requesting the expertise of individual scholars, they are less inclined to rely on the state think tanks than on non-state analytical institutions.

On the contrary, Ukraine experienced a push for government institutions to cooperate extensively with non-governmental organizations, supported organizationally and financially by external donors. These NGOs often coopt university professors and instruct them in delivering foreign policy memos and briefs. Direct contacts between university and decision making are rare, which is explained by their overtheorization and lack of responsiveness. A typical justification why non-governmental NGOs/think tanks that should be supported goes as follows:

> The circumstances are that neither parliament, nor political parties, nor ministries have their own analysis units, which would produce the needed analytical products in the context of reforms that are being implemented. State research institutions — institutes, academies of sciences and even agency-level ones — are more oriented towards academic research and not enough effective in resolving the current issues that state and local authorities face in their everyday activities. (Kermach & Sukharyna 2016: 8)

This trend started to gain momentum under President Yanukovych but achieved full speed after an ambitious reform agenda was launched in 2014. Numerous studies on how to encourage closer cooperation between government and think tanks appeared (Livny 2013; DIF 2015; Bekeshkina et al. 2016; Kermach & Sukharyna 2016; IRF 2017) often driven by normative reasoning. It did not concern foreign policy — it was only one among the other sectors that needed reform — but the foreign-policy think tanks benefited from the key program in the field — *International Renaissance foundation*'s program "Think-tank development initiative for Ukraine", scheduled to operate within the period between 2014 and 2020, and aimed at improving institutional, organizational capacities as well as the links with the government[5]. NGOs/think tanks have joined the initiative and started pushing the government for increased cooperation themselves through signing Memoranda of cooperation, inviting individual MFA representatives to public conferences and private opinion exchanges, as well as providing the research both on demand and proactively.

Thus foreign-policy NGOs/think tanks act partly as intermediaries for university faculties and partly as new and even more important players that offer analysis for governmental agencies.

---

5 See the webpage of the program for more information: http://www.irf.ua/en/programs/support-think/.

This does not necessarily mean that NGOs/think tanks have inherently better expertise, but the early studies indicated the key problems that must be overcome: the gap between policy demand and policy supply, poor methodological quality, descriptiveness, ineffective communication, and lack of engagement with policymakers (Livny 2013: 3). While in the PACT/KIIS survey of 2012, almost 70% (80 among the NGOs and academics themselves) claimed that "non-governmental think-tanks do not significantly affect public policy and management decisions," with meager impact in the spheres of national security and international relations (cited via Livny 2013: 10), the sustained effort and attention of the donors helped to reverse the situation, intensifying both the cooperation with the government and the participation of foreign policy experts.

It is safe to assume that NGO/think tanks attract many young specialists away from academia. It is equally significant that although in Ukraine the cadre rotation between academia and power is rather negligible, several former think-tankers penetrated practical politics in 2014, thus making a shift from analyzing and influencing the politics to make the politics. As Axyonova & Zubko (2017: 186) note, there were at the very least three experienced politicians with the background of think-tankers in the realms of foreign policy and security agenda in 2014-2019 government, namely Ivanna Klympush-Tsintsadze (vice-prime minister responsible for European and Euro-Atlantic integration), Oleksandr Lytvynenko (Deputy head of the Council of National Security and Defence), and Svitlana Zalishchuk (MP very active in the Committee for International Affairs). After the end of the 2019 electoral cycle, these personalities lost their respective positions. More importantly, none of the think-tankers have joined the MFA. Informing and influencing foreign policy remains the key agenda for the think tanks as mentioned above.

Given these developments, it is little wonder that, as revealed by the TRIP 2017, the Ukrainian IR community is unsure whether its work is applied or theoretically oriented. Two questions tested this particular aspect. The first one probed the perceived mission of courses taught to IR students: is it to introduce students to IR scholarship or rather prepare them to be informed about foreign policy issues. Answers are close to the even distribution (see Figure 12).

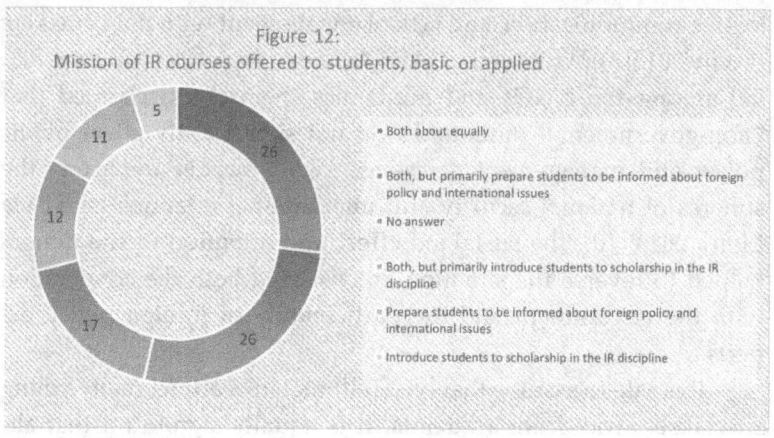

Figure 12: Mission of IR courses offered to students, basic or applied

The second question invited scholars to reflect on whether their research is basic or applied. Only a fraction took the "pure" options, primarily basic (8.2%) or primarily applied (10.3%). Most IR scholars claim they do "both equally" (21.6%), "both, but more applied than basic" (20.6%), and "both, but more basic than applied" (22.6%). Statistically, this is a normal distribution, but interpretatively the data suggest that Ukrainian IR scholarship is neither sufficiently theorized nor directly applicable to foreign policy.

Conclusions

In the post-Soviet period, the development of the IR discipline in Ukraine can be partially compared with that in Russia and the post-communist CEE states. While sharing some common past with Russian IR, it does not devote as much attention to creating a national school of foreign relations, and nor does it obsess over great power status or have as strong connections with the state as the Russian analog. The commonality with the CEE experience lies in the attempted Westernization, which, however, remains less consequential.

Arguably, IR in Ukraine is still going through a transitional phase. The conversion from the Soviet tradition of studying and practicing IR to the Western one is rather painful, incomplete, and prompts an isolationist attitude. The field thus faces two challenges: Integrating new standards in research methods and new theoretical approaches into the flimsy institutional framework of the post-Soviet high educational system, and the particular legacy of Soviet IR has also left some deep marks on the discipline itself.

To grasp the particularities of Ukrainian IR, we structured the analysis of the TRIP-2017 respondents' responses along five axes and reached the following conclusions:

First, the Soviet-inherited perception of IR as a knowledge area persists, separate not only from political science but even from all the other social sciences. Although in practice the extensive growth of IR studies since the 1990s prompted many IR departments to be situated within either history or political science departments, and current practices of awarding the doctorates squarely place IR into the political science framework, the power of IR scholarly elites is strong enough to thwart any formalization of this link via governmental reform. Thus, we observe the dual standing of Ukrainian IR, for it exists simultaneously in and out of the political science discipline framework.

Second, TRIP-2017 suggests that the Ukrainian IR community remains poorly integrated into the global IR network. Consequently, it nourishes vague and often inconsistent perceptions regarding influential IR thinkers, academic journals, publishing houses, and Master and Ph.D. IR programs worldwide.

Most conspicuously, Ukrainian scholars are virtually absent in international journals despite government efforts to incentivize publishing (see MESU 2016), which is corroborated by the data not related to TRIP. Even if compared to other countries of the region, Ukraine belongs to the second tier both according to the number of published articles (226 publications, 10th rank out of 23) and 2.22 citations per article (15th out of 23). The top three regional publishing countries are Russia with 3605 publications, Poland with 1036 publications), and Czechia with 729 (see SJR 2019), which transpires that the publication impact of Czechia, having four times less population and less extensive IR research institutions network, is almost three times more effective than that of Ukraine. Furthermore, the SJR data lumps together political science and IR publications so that the real presence of Ukrainian IR experts might be even smaller.

Third, the scholarly IR community in Ukraine is populated predominantly by experts who are relatively indifferent to developing theoretical aspects of IR. Although well aware of the major paradigms, the inherited preference for Realism limits the application of theoretical paradigms: skillful elaboration on conceptual assumptions of Constructivism, and especially Liberalism, is flagrantly lacking in Ukrainian IR scholarship. In addition to a lack of theorization, broader issues like human rights, global health, or climate change are also relatively unimportant for Ukrainian IR. On the contrary, the Ukrainian IR scholars primarily focus their research on regional studies, historical treatises, and immediate practical issues, accordingly opting for policy analysis and case studies as the preferred research methods.

Therefore, Ukraine fits within the cross-regional observation that working on theoretical issues remains the privilege of Western academia, whereas the rest of the world collects data and provides cases. This international division of labor decreases the global visibility of local scholars because theoretical generalizations are quoted more often than observations on regional developments. The CEE IR communities have well learned this lesson during the post-Communist transition. We do not invite Ukrainian IR scholars to create esoteric nativist paradigms. Still, finding a way to contribute to the global IR instead of either closing upon its community or (partially) following the Western trends is essential.

Fourth, while digging deeper into the peculiarities of the area studies *à la ukrainienne*, we discover that scholars conduct their research with two practical issues in mind: European integration and Ukrainian foreign policy. They believe two regions to be of utmost importance for the domains in question, namely Central and Eastern Europe and Western Europe. A highly problematic regional omission is Russia and FSU countries: despite the ongoing Russo-Ukrainian conflict, the Ukrainian IR community - although explicitly acknowledging Russia's role as a security threat - tends to eschew Russia studies. Other strategically significant regions also remain virtually uncharted. As the TRIP reveals both by direct answers and the self-assessed language proficiency, only a few scholars focus on East Asia, the Middle East, or Latin America. Thus, we could argue that partial Westernization has also impacted Ukrainian IR in choosing topics for their research, probably supported by more readily available funding and cooperation opportunities. This creates visible asymmetries in Ukrainian area studies.

Fifth, the responses to the TRIP 2017 show that, despite its manifestly practical, politically relevant, and state-minded approach, IR faculty in Ukraine cultivate limited and poorly institutionalized links to practical policy-making and providing informed advice. This role has been assumed by largely non-governmental think-tanks that have recently grown both in personnel and impact. The recommendations they provide are heeded more attentively so that today there is a better chance of influencing foreign policy via advocacy networks than via academia. Nowadays, different foreign policy NGOs/think tanks either directly compete with the academic community in the arena of foreign policy analysis or become an irreplaceable intermediary link, often luring young specialists away from the latter.

Bringing these five trends together, we argue that the perils of transition currently faced by the IR community in Ukraine are best conceptualized as "double peripheralization." The first aspect of double peripheralization is a visible gap with the global IR community, where Ukrainian scholars are poorly integrated. The second aspect of double peripheralization is the lack of prestige within the national community, where they have lost policy relevance to non-governmental think-tanks. Isolated and ignored, the IR community could decline rapidly, so it is imperative to overcome the double peripheralization in order to revive the discipline. We hope that better awareness of the peculiarities of Ukrainian IR, dealt with in this study, might suggest the ways for the IR community for further development.

In general, the TRIP-2017 survey provided an opportunity to take a snapshot of Ukrainian IR today, almost 30 years after the

USSR collapsed. Its 69 questions revealed noteworthy regularities in how it perceives and assesses its key challenges and characteristics, offering some vistas to be developed in further research. In particular, IR sociology offers particularly promising vistas. While conducting this study, we discovered that essential pieces of the puzzle remain to be found: for example, studying the evolution and content of IR publications and journals (both national and international) seems especially promising. Beyond that, the development of curricula, quality standards and their evolution, comparative development of IR teaching and research in different regional universities, the effectiveness of the higher education reforms on the discipline development could initiate a long-missing and evidence-based discussion on the current state and future developments of the IR studies in Ukraine.

Bibliography

Alker, Hayward & Brunner, Ronald. (1969). Simulating International Conflict: A Comparison of Three Approaches. *International Studies Quarterly* 13(1): 70–110.

Axyonova, Vera & Zubko, Diana. (2017). The European Union through the Eyes of Ukrainian Think Tankers: Studying EU Perceptions Post-Euromaidan. *Kyiv-Mohyla Law and Politics Journal* 3: 181–200

Bates, Robert. (1997). Area Studies and the Discipline: A Useful Controversy? *Political Science and Politics* 30(2): 166–169.

Bátora, Josef & Hynek, Nik. (2009). On the IR Barbaricum in Slovakia. *Journal of International Relations and Development* 12(2): 186–193.

Bekeshkina, Iryna & Kermach, Ruslan & Lutsevych, Orysia. (2016). Nezalezhni analitychni tsentry i orhany vlady: partner u prosuvanni reform chy dvi paralelni realnosti. *IRF Analytic report*, July 7, 2016, http://www.irf.ua/knowledgebase/publications/nezalezhni_anali tichni_tsentri_i_organi_vladi_partneri_u_prosuvanni_reform_chi_d vi_paralelni_realnosti/ (accessed November 13, 2019).

Bennett, Andrew & George, Alexander. (2005). *Case Studies and Theory Development in the Social Sciences.* Cambridge: MIT Press.

Bennett, David & Stam, Allan. (2000). EUGene: A conceptual manual. *International Interactions* 26 (2): 179–204.

Berg, Eiki & Chillaud, Matthieu. (2009). An IR community in Baltic states: is there a genuine one? *Journal of International Relations and Development* 12(2): 193–199.

Braumoeller, Bear & Sartori, Anne. (2004). The Promise and Perils of Statistics in International Relations. In *Models, Numbers, and Cases: Methods for Studying International Relations*, Detlef F. Sprinz & Yael Wolinsky (eds.). Ann Arbor: The University of Michigan Press, 129–151.

Bull, Hedley. (1966). International Theory: The Case for a Classical Approach. *World Politics* 18(3): 361–377.

Byk, Ihor. (2013). Mizhnarodni vidnosyny u Lvivskomu universyteti: istoriya i suchasnist. *Visnyk Lvivskoho universytetu* 32: 3–9.

Brzeziński, Zbigniew. (2000). *Velyka shakhivnytsia*. Ivano-Frankivsk: Lileya-NV.

Capshew, James. (1999). *Psychologists on the March: Science, Practice, and Professional Identity in America, 1929–1969*. Cambridge & New York: Cambridge University Press.

Charmaz, Kathy. (2006). *Constructing Grounded Theory: A Practical Guide Through Qualitative Analysis*. London: Sage Publications.

CMU, Cabinet of Ministers of Ukraine. (2015). Pro zatverdzhennia pereliku haluzei znan i spetsialnostei, za yakymy zdiisniuyetsia pidhotovka zdobuvachiv vyshchoyi osvity. *Decree No 266*, 29 April 2015, http://ooep.kpi.ua/news/266.pdf (accessed 15 December 2019).

CMU, Cabinet of Ministers of Ukraine. (2017). Pro vnesennia zmin do postanovy Kabinetu Ministriv Ukrayiny vid 29.04.2015 *No 266. Decree No 53*, 1 February 2017, https://zakon.rada.gov.ua/laws/show/53-20 17-п (accessed December 15, 2019).

Cumings, Bruce. (1997). Boundary Displacement: Area Studies and International Studies during and after the Cold War. *Bulletin of Concerned Asian Scholars*, n.d., https://www.mtholyoke.edu/acad/intrel/cumings2.htm (accessed December 10, 2019).

Czaputowicz, Jacek & Ławniczak, Kamil. (2015). Poland's International Relations Scholarly Community and Its Distinguishing Features According to the 2014 Trip Survey of International Relations Scholars. *Baltic Journal of Political Science* 4: 94–110.

Czaputowicz, Jacek & Wojciuk, Anna. (2016). IR scholarship in Poland: the state of the discipline 25 years after the transition to democracy. *Journal of International Relations and Development* 19: 448–474.

Czaputowicz, Jacek. (2012). Theory or practice? The state of international relations in Poland. *European Political Science* 11(2): 196–212.

DIF, Democratic Initiatives Foundation. (2015). Nezalezhni analitychni tsentry Ukrayiny v protsesi vyroblennia polityky: pereshkody, perspektyvy ta ochikuvannia u spivpratsi z orhanamy vlady. *Report*, n.d., https://dif.org.ua/uploads/pdf/1421935943_3402.pdf (accessed December 10, 2019).

Drulák, Petr & Königová, Lucie & Karlas, Jan. (2004). Continuity and change in the discipline of IR in Central and Eastern Europe Countries. *Paper presented at 2004 ISA Convention*.

Drulák, Petr & Druláková, Radka. (2000). International Relations in the Czech Republic: A Review of the Discipline. *Journal of International Relations and Development* 3: 256–282.

Drulák, Petr & Druláková, Radka. (2006). The Czech Republic. In *International Relations in Europe: Traditions, Perspectives and Destinations*, Knud Erik Joergenssen & Tonny Brems Knudsen (eds.). London and New York: Routledge. 172–196.

Drulák, Petr. (2009). Introduction to the International Relations (IR) in Central and Eastern Europe Forum. *Journal of International Relations and Development* 12: 168–173.

Drulák, Petr. (2013). Going native? The discipline of IR in Central and Eastern Europe. *Przegląd Europejski* 27(1): 10–13.

Fox, William & Baker Fox, Annette. (1961). The Teaching of International Relations in the United States. *World Politics* 13(3): 339–359.

Frieden, Jeffrey & Lake, David & Schultz, Kenneth. (2010). *World Politics: Interests, Interactions, and Institutions*. New York: W. W. Norton.

Fukuyama, Francis. (1990). Konets Istorii? *Voprosy filosofii* 3: 134–148.

Gaddis, John. (1986). The Long Peace: Elements of Stability in the Postwar International System. *International Security* 10(4): 99–142.

Geipel, Gary. (1999). Politics and Computers in the Honecker Era. In *Science under socialism: East Germany in comparative perspective*, Kristie Macrakis & Dieter Hoffmann (eds.). Cambridge: Harvard University Press, 231–258.

George, Alexander. (1993). *Bridging the Gap: Theory and Practice in Foreign Policy*. Washington, DC: US Institute of Peace.

Glaser, Barney & Strauss, Anselm. (2006). *The Discovery of Grounded Theory Strategies for Qualitative Research*. New Brunswick and London: Aldine Transaction.

Guzzini, Stefano. (2001). The Significance and Role of Teaching Theory in IR. *Journal of International Relations and Development* 4(2): 98–117.

Hall, Robert. (1948). *Area Studies: With Special Reference to Their Implications for Research in the Social Sciences*. New York: Committee on World Area Research Program, Social Science Research Council.

Herran, Néstor & Roqué, Xavier. (2012). An Autarkic Science: Physics, Culture, and Power in Franco's Spain. *Historical Studies in the Natural Sciences* 43(2): 202–235.

Higher Education in Ukraine: Agenda for Reforms. (2017). *KAS Policy Paper*, https://www.kas.de/c/document_library/get_file?uuid=1139 6582-8774-8a81-1492-9dee7e451d2d&groupId=252038 (accessed December 10, 2019).

Hill, Christopher & Beshoff, Pamela. (1994). *Two Worlds of International Relations: Academics, Practitioners and the Trade in Ideas.* London: Routledge.

Holsti, Kalevi Jaakko. (1985). *The Dividing Discipline: Hegemony and Diversity in International Theory.* Boston: Allen & Unwin.

Huntington, Samuel. (1994). Stolknoveniye tsivilizatsii? *Polis* 1: 33–48.

Instytut mizhnarodnykh vidnosyn Kyivskoho natsionalnoho universytetu im. Tarasa Shevchenka. (2004). Ed. V. Skopenko. Kyiv: Znannia Ukrayiny.

Instytut mizhnarodnykh vidnosyn Kyivskoho natsionalnoho universytetu im. Tarasa Shevchenka. (2006). Ed. V. Skopenko. Dnipropetrovsk: Balans-Klub.

Instytut mizhnarodnykh vidnosyn Kyivskoho natsionalnoho universytetu im. Tarasa Shevchenka. (2014). Ed. L. Huberskyy. Kyiv: Ukrblankovydav.

Istomin, Igor, Baykov, Andrei. (2013). Sravnitel'nye osobennosti otechestvennyh i zarubezhnyh zhurnalov. *Mezhdunarodnye processy* 13(2): 114–140.

Johnston, Alastair. (1995). *Cultural Realism: Strategic Culture and Grand Strategy in Chinese History.* Princeton: Princeton University Press.

Kamenetskyi, Maksym. (2007). *Teoriya mizhnarodnykh vidnosyn.* Kyiv: Natsionalnyi universytet Im. Tarasa Shevchenka.

Kaminskyi, Yevhen. (2001). Povoyenna dyplomatiya Ukrayinskoyi RSR. In *Narysy z istoriyi dyplomatiyi Ukrayiny,* Valerii Smolii (ed.). Kyiv: Alternatyvy.

Kaplan, Morton. (1966). The New Great Debate: Traditionalism vs. Science in International Relations. *World Politics* 19(1): 1–20.

Katzenstein, Peter (2002). Area Studies, Regional Studies, and International Relations. *Journal of East Asian Studies* 2(1): 127–137.

Kavtseniuk, Mariana. (2017). Vybir abituriyentiv 2016 roku: haluzevyi analiz. *CEDOS report*, 13 June 2017, https://cedos.org.ua/uk/articles/vybir-abituriientiv-2016-roku-haluzevyi-analiz (accessed December 10, 2019).

Kermach, Ruslan & Sukharyna, Andrii. (2016). Nezalezhni analitychni tsentry i orhany vlady: chy ye prosuvannia u dvostoronnii spivpratsi. *Analytic report*, 1 December 2016, http://www.irf.ua/knowledgebase/publications/nezalezhni_analitichni_tsentri_i_organi_vladi_chi_e_prosuvannya_u_dvostoronniy_spivpratsi/ (accessed December 10, 2019).

Kim, Geun Bae. (2017). Science and Ideology: The Rise and Fall of the Bonghan Theory in North Korea in the 1960s. *The Korean Journal for the History of Science* 39(2): 325–357.

King, George & Keohane, Robert & Verba, Sidney. (1994). *Designing Social Inquiry*. Princeton: Princeton University Press.

Kirk, Grayson. (1947). *The Study of International Relations in America Colleges and Universities*. New York: Council of Foreign Relations.

Kopiyka, Valerii. (2013). Kyivska shkola mizhnarodnykh vidnosyn. *Visnyk Lvivskoho universytetu* 32: 10–17.

Krapivin, Oleksandr & Todorov, Ihor. (2013). Donetska shkola mizhnarodnykh vidnosyn. *Visnyk Lvivskoho universytetu* 32: 18–25.

Kristensen, Peter Marcus. (2019). Southern Sensibilities: Advancing Third Wave Sociology of International Relations in the Case of Brazil. *Journal of International Relations and Development* 22(2): 468–494.

Kruhlashov, Anatolii. (2013). Rozvytok yevropeiskykh doslidzhen v rehionalnykh naukovykh tsentrakh: pryklad Chernivtsiv. *Visnyk Lvivskoho universytetu* 32: 32–39.

Kudelia, Serhii. (2012). Chy mozhlyva v Ukrayini politychna nauka? *Krytyka* 1–2: 24–25.

Kuijper, Hans. (2008). Area Studies Versus Disciplines: Towards an Interdisciplinary, Systemic Country Approach. *International Journal of Interdisciplinary Social Sciences* 3(1): 205–216.

Lake, David. (2011). Why "isms" Are Evil: Theory, Epistemology, and Academic Sects as Impediments to Understanding and Progress. *International Studies Quarterly* 55(2): 465–480.

Lebedeva, Marina. (2004). International Relations Studies in the USSR/Russia: Is there a Russian National School of IR Studies? *Global Society* 18(3): 263–278.

Lebedeva, Marina. (2018). *Russian Studies of International Relations. From the Soviet Past to the Post-Cold-War Present*. Stuttgart: Ibidem-Verlag.

Leffler, Melvyn. (1995). New Approaches, Old Interpretations, and Prospective Reconfigurations. *Diplomatic History* 19(2): 173–196.

Light, Margot. (1989). The Study of International Relations in the Soviet Union. In *The Study of International Relations. The State of the Art*, Hugh Dyer & Leon Mangasarian (eds.). New York: Palgrave-McMillian, 229–243.

Livny, Eric. (2013). "In Search of its Voice: Assessment of Policy Relevant Research in Ukraine." *UNITER Report*, 26 March 2013, https://issuu.com/uniter/docs/assessment_of_policy-relevant_research_eng (accessed December 10, 2019).

Lysak, Volodymyr. (2014). Dystsyplina "mizhnarodni vidnosyny" v systemi osvity ta nauky Ukrayiny. *Istorychni i politychni doslidzhennia* 3–4: 57–58.

Maiocchi, Roberto. (2015). The National Council for Research in the Context of Fascist Autarky. In: *Science Policies and Twentieth-century dictatorships: Spain, Italy and Argentina*, Amparo Gómez, Antonio Fco. Canales, Brian Balmer (eds.). Burlington: Ashgate, 141–158.

Maliniak, Daniel & Oaks, Amy & Peterson, Susan & Tierney, Michael. (2011). International Relations in the US Academy. *International Studies Quarterly* 55: 437–464.

Maliniak, Daniel & Peterson, Susan & Tierney, Michael. (2012). TRIP around the World: Teaching, Research, and Policy Views of International Relations Faculty in 20 Countries. *The Institute for Theory and Practice of International Relations*. Final Report.

Malskyi, Markiyan & Matsyakh, Mykhailo. (2007). *Teoriya mizhnarodnykh vidnosyn*. Kyiv: Znannia.

Malskyi, Markiyan & Moroz, Yurii. (2012). Pidhotovka fakhivtsiv-mizhnarodnykiv v umovakh transformatsiyi mizhnarodnoyi systemy. *Visnyk Lvivskoho universytetu* 30: 3–8.

Matsiyevsky, Yurii. (2012). Chomu v nas nemaye politychnoyi nauky. *Krytyka* 6: 10–12.

Matthews, Elizabeth & Callaway, Rhonda (2015). Where Have All the Theories Gone? Teaching Theory in Introductory Courses in International Relations. *International Studies Perspectives* 16(2): 190–209.

Mayer, Arno. (1969). Internal Causes and Purposes of War in Europe, 1871-1956. *Journal of Modern History* 41(3): 291–303.

McClelland, Charles. (1970) Some Effects on Theory from the International Event Analysis Movement. Working paper. *University of Southern California*.

Mearsheimer, John & Walt, Stephen. (2013). Leaving theory behind: Why simplistic hypothesis testing is bad for International Relations. *European Journal of International Relations* 19(3): 427–457.

MESU, Ministry of Education and Science of Ukraine. (2016). Pro zatverdzhennia Poriadku prysvoyennia vchenykh zvan naukovym I naukovo-pegahohichnym pratsivnykam. *Decree*, https://zakon.rada.gov.ua/laws/show/en/z0183-16/?lang=uk&fbclid=IwAR10wp6d6q6tqJcnq1jHdN6dP-BbT5RfRTktW_4SWXd6zraRIodmpT_mV1k (accessed December 12, 2019).

Mezhdunarodnyye issledovaniya v Rossii i SNG. (1999). Tsentr konvertiruyemosti obrazovaniya. Spravochnik. Moskva: Moskovskiy rabochiy.

IRF, Mizhnarodnyi Fond "Vidrodzhennia". (2017). Initsiatyva z rozvytku analitychnykh tsentriv Ukrayiny. *IRF Report for 2014-2017*, https://issuu.com/irf_ua/docs/ttf-ua-web_(accessed December 10, 2019).

Modelski, George. (1961). International Relations and Area Studies: The Case of South-East Asia. *International Relations* 2(3): 143-155.

Morozov, Viacheslav. (2009). Obsessed with Identity: The IR in post-Soviet Russia. *Journal of International Relations and Development* 12(2): 202-205.

Plokhy, Serhii. (2011). *Yalta: The Price of Peace*. London: Penguin Books.

Potter, Philip. (2010). Methods of Foreign Policy Analysis. *Oxford Research Encyclopedia of International Studies*. Ed. R. Marlin-Bennett, https://oxfordre.com/internationalstudies/view/10.1093/acrefore/9780190846626.001.0001/acrefore-9780190846626-e-34?print=pdf (accessed December 10, 2019).

Reynolds, Charles. (1973). *Theory and Explanation in International Politics*. London: Martin Robertson.

RIAC, Rossijskije issledovanija i obrazovanije v oblasti mezhdunarodnykh otnoshenij 20 let spustia. (2013). Rabochaja tetrad, *Rossijskij sovet po mezhdunarondym delam* 11.

Roter, Petra. (2009). At the centre and the periphery simultaneously: the incomplete internationalization of Slovenian International Relations. *Journal of International Relations and Development* 12: 180-186.

Ruloff, Dieter. (1976). Simulation and Gaming: The Analysis of Conflict and Cooperation in the Field of International Relations. In *Systems Theory in the Social Sciences*, Hartmut Bossel, Salomon Klaczko, & Norbert Müller (eds.). Basel: Birkhauser Verlag, 519-533

Rumyantseva, Nataliya & Logvynenko, Olena. (2018). Ukraine: Higher Education Reform and Dynamics of the Institutional Landscape. In *25 Years of Transformations of Higher Education Systems in Post-Soviet Countries: Reform and Continuity*, Jeroen Huisman, Anna Smolentseva, & Isak Froumin (eds.). London: Palgrave Macmillan, 407-433.

Schrodt, Philip. (2000). Pattern Recognition of International Crises using Hidden Markov Models. In *Political Complexities: Nonlinear Models of Politics*, Diana Eva-Ann Richards (ed.). Ann Arbor: University of Michigan Press, 296-238.

Sergounin, Alexander. (2009). Russia. IR at a crossroads. In *International Relations Scholarship Around the World*, Arlene Tickner & Ole Wæver (eds.). Abingdon, Routledge, 223-241.

Shepeliev, Maksymilian. (2004). *Teoriya mizhnarodnykh vidnosyn*. Kyiv: Vyshcha shkola.

Shevel, Oxana. (2015). Ukrainian Political Science and the Study of Ukraine within American Political Science: How Similar, How Different? *Journal of Ukrainian Politics and Society* 1(1): 23-32.

Sherstiuk, Andrii & Dluhach, Denys & Nahorna, Tayisiiya. (2015). Studenty Instytutu Mizhnarodnykh Vidnosyn KNU pro novyi perelik haluzei znan ta spetsialnostei. *Opinion,* http://osvita.ua/vnz/high_school/46985/?fbclid=IwAR3DUwUYoDUKFL8v3iAiVA-7YFUvPz XqDzgDIyb2JNUZxJyqUfpWLpgFxPI (accessed 15 December 2019).

SJR, Scimago Journal & Country Rank. (2019). *Official webpage.* Regional Ranking for Eastern Europe, https://www.scimagojr.com/countryrank.php?category=3320&area=3300&region=Eastern%20Europe (accessed 10 December 2019).

Smagliy, Kateryna. Hybrid Analytica: Pro-Kremlin Expert Propaganda in Moscow, Europe and the U.S. A Case Study of Think Tanks and Universities. Research Paper. *Institute of Modern Russia,* October 2018.

Smith, Steve. (1987). Paradigm Dominance in International Relations: The Development of International Relations as a Social Science. *Millennium – Journal of International Studies* 16: 189-206.

Snidal, Duncan. (2004). Formal Models of International Politics. In *Models, Numbers, and Cases: Methods for Studying International Relations.* Eds. Detlef Sprinz & Yael Wolinsky. Ann Arbor: The University of Michigan Press, 227-264.

Sovsun, Inna. (2015a). Bez novoho pereliku haluzei znan I spetsialnostei pidhotovky fakhivtsiv ne mozhemo rukhatysia dali, *Interview,* 3 March 2015, https://ukurier.gov.ua/uk/articles/inna-sovsun-bez-novogo-pereliku-galuzej-znan-i-spe/, (accessed December 15, 2019).

Sovsun, Inna. (2015b). V etom godu pervokursniki budut izuchat v dva raza menshe predmetov, chem ikh predshestvenniki, *Interview,* 17 April 2015, https://fakty.ua/198538-inna-sovsun-v-etom-godu-studenty-pervokursniki-budut-izuchat-v-dva-raza-menshe-predmetov-chem-ih-predshestvenniki, (accessed December 15, 2019).

Speed, Ashley. (2018). Carnegie Corporation of New York to fund TRIP research. *College of William & Mary Official Webpage,* https://www.wm.edu/news/stories/2018/carnegie-corporation-to-fund-wm-research-on-news-media-and-international-relations-issues.php (accessed December 10, 2019).

Starish, Oleksandr. (2012). Politychna nauka v Ukrayini: 20 rokiv nezalezhnosti. *Krytyka* 9-10: 27-29.

Stone, Lawrence. (1981). *The Past and the Present Revisited.* London: Routledge and Kegan Paul.

Strauss, Anselm & Corbin, Juliet. (1994). Grounded theory methodology: An overview. In *Handbook of qualitative research*. Norman K. Denzin, Yvonna S. Lincoln (eds.). Thousand Oaks: Sage Publications, Inc., 273–285.

Teoriya mizhnarodnykh vidnosyn. (2016). Mykhailo Trebin (ed.). Kharkiv: Pravo.

TRIP, Teaching, Research, and International Policy Project. (2015). *The TRIP Project Official Homepage*, https://trip.wm.edu/data/our-surveys/faculty-survey (accessed December 10, 2019).

Tsygankov, Andrei & Tsygankov, Pavel. (2010). Russian theory of international relations. *International studies Encyclopedia* 10: 6375–6387.

Tsygankov, Andrei & Tsygankov, Pavel. (2014) Russian IR theory: The Crisis of a Globally-Pluralist Discipline. *European Review of International Studies* 1(2): 92–106.

Tsymbalistyi, Vasyl. (2009). *Teoriya mizhnarodnykh vidnosyn*. Lviv: Novyi Svit.

Tyulin, Ivan. (1997). Issledovaniya mezhdunarodnykh otnosheniy v Rossii: vchera, segodnya, zavtra. *Kosmopolis. Almanakh*: 18–28.

Ukrayinska dyplomatychna entsyklopediya. (2004). [In 2 volumes.] Leonid Huberskyi (ed.). Kyiv: Znannia.

Unver, Hamid Akin. (2019). Computational International Relations: What Can Programming, Coding and Internet Research Do for the Discipline? *All Azimuth: A Journal of Foreign Policy and Peace*, https://dergipark.org.tr/allazimuth/issue/42171/476433 (accessed December 10, 2019).

Vendil Pallin, Carolina & Oxenstierna, Susanne. (2017). Russian Think Tanks and Soft Power. *Swedish Defence Research Agency (FOI) Report*, August 2017, https://www.foi.se/rapportsammanfattning?reportNo=FOI-R--4451--SE (accessed December 10, 2019).

Wæver, Ole. (1996). The Rise and Fall of the Inter-Paradigm Debate. In *International theory: positivism and beyond*, Steve Smith, Ken Booth, & Marysia Zalewski (eds.). New York: Cambridge University Press, 149–185.

Wallace, William. (1996). Truth and power, monks and technocrats: theory and practice in international relations. *Review of International Studies*. 22(4): 301–321.

What is International Relations? (2019). *InternationalRelationsEDU.org*. Official Webpage, https://www.internationalrelationsedu.org/what-is-international-relations/ (accessed December 10, 2019).

Zarubezhnoye regionovedeniye. (2019). *Vuzy, gde mozhno poluchit spetsialnost 5.41.03.01*. Webpage for students, https://postupi.online/spec ialnost/41.03.01/vuzi/ (accessed December 10, 2019).

Zimmerman, William. (1969). International Relations in the Soviet Union: The Emergence of a Discipline. *The Journal of Politics* 31(1): 52–70.

4 Toponymy and the Issues of Memory and Identity on the Post-soviet Tbilisi Cityscape

Augusto Dala Costa

Studies on aspects of memory, identity, and culture can embrace a great scale of subjects, since they are part of everyone's life, in their realities and environments. These aspects are always prone to be controlled by institutions, such as governments, to be modified and molded according to a particular discourse or ideology. Although more easily identified in larger instances, such attempts can happen in micro scales, such as street naming, and that aspect is what I will discuss in this particular research—specifically speaking of the toponymy of Tbilisi, the capital of the Republic of Georgia. As will be shown further, the post-Soviet country went through several renamings on the cityscape, all according to specific political events and shifts in power dynamics. Changing the name of a street does not only imply a simple modification of a marker in a city—it has a purpose, and an implication on a population's memory and identity. It can be used as a way of altering the cultural memory portrayed in an everyday place, reinforcing identity narratives that transform space into place by ascribing a certain meaning to a location (Assmann 1995; Connerton 1989, cited in Drozdzewski 2014: 67). A government can spread its political agenda by renaming streets, avenues, squares, or districts because this act works with the memory of the population. Giving places names of political figures, important political events, or historical peoples and places makes people remember and keep such concepts in mind individually and collectively, since toponyms like streets are used and referenced daily (Azaryahu 1996: 321; Drozdzewski 2014: 66). This is done to suppress possible threats to a regime's sovereignty and its political discourse (Sharp 2009, cited in Drozdzewski 2014: 66).

Around the fall of the Soviet Union, Tbilisi underwent a process of replacing the imposed toponymy by the Soviet regime by one that brought back its national figures, being significant on several aspects, such as religious, cultural, and historical ones. What is left for a research such as the present one is to analyze how the process of renaming was carried out, find patterns and see how the change of discourse took place, which figures got replaced, and which ones replaced them. To understand the commemorations placed on the cityscape, it is important to address the history of the city in question, making it possible to have an idea of which ethnonational and cultural aspects were chosen to be remembered and which ones were deliberately (or unintentionally) forgotten. Post-Soviet authorities had the power to choose which discourse they wanted to brand into Tbilisi's place names, for specific reasons and to evidence a certain national identity and ideology; in this work, I will assess which discourse was intended to be put forward and discuss the reasons for it in the light of the recent Georgian national idea of self. This is important to make sense of the recent political history of Georgia, how the most contemporary governments dealt with a reassertion of democratic power and how the Georgian national identity was built and commemorated.

It is important to mention the lack of data regarding the renaming of toponymy in Georgia on the academic literature in English; one of the few works on the subject in the language is an article by Elene Bodaveli, who drew her data from a book by Zurab Chelidze which is devoted to Tbilisi's street, avenue and square names – but is entirely in Georgian, with no translated version available. In the present work, the material gathered consists of decrees from the Tbilisi City Council and the aforementioned book about the capital's cityscape, and both sources had to go through translations into English to be used. These translations amount to a significant contribution to political science when it comes to the Caucasian studies, and one of the aims of this research is to bring them to light so that new knowledge can be reached by future works on the subject. As a way to start contributing, this work will take the data and make a first evaluation of what can be drawn from it, consisting of a general analysis of both sources followed by a division of the information present in them, so to make sense of the whole process of renaming and relate it to the building of the Georgian national discourse. The analyses are done to see how the Georgian identity came to be reflected in the cityscape of the country's capital on the eve of its return to be a Republic after decades of Soviet rule, and whether it has followed political trends and national discourses.

Theoretical Background

Memory and Commemoration on Toponymy

To start making sense of how the cityscape can be used to work with political discourses and participate in the process of commemoration, it is important to define some concepts, such as memory. In his seminal work about memory and history, Pierre Nora says that memory remains in permanent evolution, always susceptible to manipulation and appropriation, forgetfulness and remembrance (Nora 1989: 8). He maintains that history is always an incomplete and problematic reconstruction of the past, and while it is a representation of what has been and no more is, memory is "perpetually actual"; it is always present. Memory, however, chooses the most suitable facts to its interests (it is, to the ones manipulating it), so its recollections can be out of focus or telescopic, global, or detached. Memory "installs remembrance within the sacred; history, always prosaic, releases it again" (Nora 1989: 8-9).

> Memory is related to the objective notion of "history" but is often a selectively embellished or mythologized version of events, people, and places that serves social or political ends. (Foote & Azaryahu 2007: 126)

When the placement of memory occurs in an external place, a *lieu de mémoire*, a memory site, is created, and, in a way, is needed, because memories are not spontaneous, thus the creation of archives, commemorative anniversaries, celebrations and eulogies— as like if not commemorated, memories would be erased by history (Nora 1989: 12). Public memory is part of a symbolic foundation of collective identity, inscribing shared elements in the public space. Place names are not only symbolic but are also functional: while serving as spatial orientation elements, they reproduce official versions of history into daily life in a detached way from ideological contexts or communal obligations (Alderman 2000, 2003; Azaryahu 1986, 1996b; Ferguson 1988; Gill 2005; Palonen 1993; Stump 1988; Yeoh 1992, 1996; Foote & Azaryahu 2007: 128–129; Foxall 2013: 172). Public memory is the interface where the past is represented in the present, through shared cultural productions and reproductions (MacCannell 1976: 23–24, cited in Foote & Azaryahu 2007: 126). Memory is a vital component of identity formation, working as "a structural component of social memory of a group identity". Cultural approaches to memory maintain that shared memories are not produced accidentally, but are a consequence of cultural mediation, and its character is shaped by all kinds of mediation channels (Tamm 2013: 461).

Toponyms are important while being a representation of elements of culture and history of a place, describing the "geographical, political, social-economic and demographic conditions, historical moment and traditional, ethnographic, religious and lexical properties of certain people" (Sartania, Nikolaishvili & Ujmajuridze 2017: 49). Toponyms "represent the construct of social and power relations through which the identity of the city and society is being formed" (Berg & Voulteeenaho 2009). When political changes occur, politically motivated toponymy changes will be most certainly found (Azaryahu 1986, 1996; Bucher et al. 2013; Drozdzewski 2014; Foote & Azaryahu 2007; Kadmon 2004; Saparov 2003; Sartania et al. 2017). Toponyms express geopolitics of memory because they are palpable sites of contestation among competing ideologies; it is a process of determining "who gets representation, in what way and with what political outcomes" (Edkins 2003: 135; Yeoh 1996, cited in Drozdzewski 2014: 67). When people are subjected to multiple, overlapping geographies of history and politics, memories of past events may induce controversy instead of consensus; some renamings can generate "toponyms with contested pasts" (Wagner-Pacifi & Schwartz 1991: 376, cited in Foxall 2013: 176). Works on place and memory pertain to various fields of study and are especially useful in geographical studies. That is why I bring Drozdzewski's concepts and work on the geopolitics of memory, since her research done on Krakow's streetscape is very similar to the one in this work. The author points out that while totalitarian regimes had equivocal power of commemorative choice, even in autonomous governments a determined group's version of history is inevitably preferred over another; regardless of how democratic the choosing of the name is carried. This is related to the fact that memory is a social construction, and thus depends on the contexts of the groups it is recalled by — the ruling elite "use their power and resources to make and implement decisions about memorial landscapes" (Forest & Johnson 2002, cited in Drozdzewski 2014: 68). These decisions and the specific memories imprinted in the city of Tbilisi are, then, the main object of this research.

Building of the National Discourse

The Georgian capital, to this day, retains a series of characteristics that make it largely a Soviet city. Most people live in Soviet-built neighborhoods, and in general the spatial structure, even the transportation network, was built in that era (Salukvadze & Golubchikov 2016: 43). The capital went through noticeable changes in the cityscape since the 1920s, experiencing waves of renaming to incorporate Soviet ideology. New names were assigned to both existing and Soviet-built streets, squares, districts, and eventually metro stations (Bodaveli 2015: 156-158). Up to this point, the toponymy of Tbilisi was not particularly nationalistic. Instead, it reflected the capital's diversity on a certain scale, and the imperial domination in a larger setting; most referred to Russian emperors and their family members, noblemen, governors of Caucasia, and generals of the Russian Army (Bodaveli 2015: 163).

At first, the policy in Tbilisi was to mix local and Soviet identity. Russian imperial names were symbolically replaced by Soviet statesmen and important authors for the communist ideology, such as Engels, Marx, and Lunacharski; a few cases saw commemorations of Georgian figures who fought against russification, but for Georgian independence (Bodaveli 2015: 170, 176). This first part of the renaming process occurred from 1922 to 1923, with a second one from 1930 to 1934, as divided by Bodaveli. The second part removed the names of people who succeeded during the Russian Revolution or the first years of the Soviet Union, deemed "enemies of the people" (Bodaveli 2015: 158). The process underlying this second trend was part of the bigger intention of "forgetting" local heroes, traditional elements, and evidence of past regimes.

By the last years of the Soviet Union, radicalizations on the anti-Soviet opposition led to the Tbilisi Massacre of 9 April 1989, a violent repression of a demonstration in the capital. The revolutionary movement led the Supreme Soviet of Georgia to vote for condemning the 1921's Bolshevik occupation as an illegal act and call for new elections (de Waal 2010: 131–132; Salukvadze & Golubchikov 2016: 44). In the next year, Zviad Gamsakhurdia's Round Table bloc won the elections for the reconstituted Supreme Soviet, and on April 9, 1991, full independence from the Soviet Union was declared. Becoming autonomous involved taking control of institutions and having the challenge of building a new discourse. In the emergence of the post-Soviet nationalism, the making or re-making of national histories turned into one of the most important instruments for corroborating claims of political legitimacy and strengthening, if not even "inventing traditions" of peoplehood (Hirsch 2005; Hobsbawm 1983; Ushakin 2009; Yurchak 2003, cited in Batiashvili 2018: 13).

Stephen Jones discerns between three models of post-Soviet Georgian nationalism, which are: a model of cultural assimilation upheld by president Gamsakhurdia (1991–1992), who took cultural and ethnical distinctiveness as threats to national unity; Shevardnadze's (1995–2003) policies of reconciliation between distinct ethnic and cultural groups and inclusive citizenship; and finally Saakashvili (2004–2013) with a mix of his predecessors (Jones 2013: 216, cited in Polese et al. 2017: 55). Saakashvili, the most symbolic representation of a renovated, very anti-Soviet discourse, was elected as president in 2004. Determined to restore the authority of the state, he symbolically erected the Saint George's monument at Liberty Square in 2006, where the Lenin monument used to sit until 1991 (Jones 2013). The Soviet past is a very important part of Saakashvili's discourse; it has to be anthetisized, be shown as "the other", a symbol of backwardness. From 2004 to 2012, there was an iconoclast fury towards Soviet-era monuments and symbols, replacing them by "national" ones or "Western" ones (Isaacs & Polese

2016). Religion is also prominent in the Georgian national discourse — the Georgian Orthodox church came to institutionalize an ethno-nationalist doctrine into its orthodox practice, making religion political; Georgia's nationalism has been emphasizing the rule of the country as a stronghold of Christianity in a hostile Muslim environment since the 1980s (Shnirelman 1998: 58, cited in Batiashvili 2018: 14).

Tbilisi, once a myriad of nationalities and cultures, became very homogenously Georgian with the changes it went through in the Soviet times and its independent era. One, however, can still see hints of the cosmopolitan past in its remaining churches, mosques, and mansions. With this setting as a backdrop, we will analyze and see how the national Georgian elements were commemorated in the capital's cityscape in the light of the national discourse developed in contemporary years.

Research Methodology

As Drozdzewski (2014: 77) writes,

> [...] by investigating how, why, and when, names changed in the past, we construct better topographies for understanding the importance of geopolitics to everyday spaces, especially those which are silent witnesses to trauma.

One of the aims of this research is to analyze toponyms, paying special attention to those with contested pasts, to assess their importance, the political regime's process, and effectiveness in applying cultural and identity aspects to the toponyms and which instances of those were applied. Doing this is directly connected with the memory elements and concepts discussed before; the imprinting of historical elements in public places, as a form of commemoration — memory and its manipulation.

Bodaveli's 2015 work is an important one in this research, both because of the data and the inspiration it provides, so the exhaustive discussions and discourse analysis regarding place names are done similarly, as they are deemed essential for a thorough comprehension of the process. Since the bulk of the important renamings from Imperial Russian/First Republic of Georgia to the Soviet era are covered in her article, they will not be part of this research; however, whenever convenient, they may be part of the discussion—for example, when a street is returned to its pre-Soviet name or when a clear replacing of an undesired name from that time takes place instead of the replacing of a Soviet commemoration. Bodaveli decides to select a certain number of streets according to their location in Tbilisi, the time of their establishment or their significance because of the size of the material she works with; since the present chapter is dealing with all the renamings from 1988 to 2007, selecting this period is a sufficient measure to make the number of analyzed toponymy reasonable, and thus no place name was taken out of the research. It may be the case that more toponyms were indeed renamed in the selected time frame, and that such information was missing from the consulted sources. Since the portion of data analyzed here differs from that of Bodaveli's, different classifications were crafted so to group the streets; still, they are closely inspired by her work. Another important acknowledgment has to be made regarding Drozdzewski's 2014 work, from which the central theoretical ideas were drawn from and where the intention of analyzing the geopolitical implications of the renaming process came from (only transporting the setting from Poland to Georgia).

The data concerning the subject of this chapter, being it, Tbilisian street and place names (old and new), the year of such renamings, and the location of the places in the city is very scarce (if not nonexistent) in the English scientific literature. It was possible, however, to obtain such data in Georgian, in the book by Zurab Chelidze—The "Georgian Encyclopedia—Tbilisi: Streets, Avenues", published in 2008. Additionally, in the Tbilisi City Archives under the Georgian National Archives, it was possible to find an extensive list of renamed toponyms, with all their old names, and the correspondent districts; the list does not include the year of the renaming, though, whereas the book includes them. It was necessary to combine both sources to get a full, comprehensive list, which could be used for the present work. In the archives, it was also possible to find some of the decrees regarding the renamings, some of them explicating the reasons for that and the people responsible. The chapter on toponymy from Chelidze's book, due to its extensive nature, was translated by a translation office. The City Council Decrees were translated with the help of academics fluent in Georgian, nationals or not.

With such material in hand, it is possible to make a general, previously non-existent database. In that sense, a table was crafted out of crossing the available data from both sources. It includes streets with their current name and the previous names, according to the list provided by the National Archives of Georgia. Then, based on the translation of the renaming section of Chelidze's book, it was possible to assess the year of each renaming, when possible to find — unfortunately, some of the streets or the year of their renamings sometimes were not included in the book. With such a table in hand, it is possible to start separating toponyms by district, year of renaming, and other patterns that may be found during the research. From the patterns and the decrees, it will be possible to make conclusions regarding the political implication of the renamings — not only what is being commemorated on the toponymy, but also what has been forgotten, or rather chosen to be. The analyses, from the general to the individual scope, are all made having in mind the historical background of Georgia as a whole and Tbilisi, not only paying attention to the removal of old names but to the renaming itself, for example, if the new names imply on a direct antithesis to the old name or if the removal itself is what matters. This historical correlation is what leads the categorizing of renamings, as it places the figures of importance that are commemorated in the context of the imprinting of a national discourse in the cityscape. The goal of the analyses is, then, to make sense of how selective the process was, mainly concerning the national discourse built in the past decades, through discourse analysis. It is important so to understand how the cultural memory of Georgia is represented and make a clear map of the geopolitics of memory in the Caucasian post-Soviet environment.

To begin with, since the Renaming Policy Decrees provide the most concrete set of data for this research, a section will ensue to evaluate the information it can provide regarding the process, the reasons (when mentioned) and what can be drawn from those—an analysis of the whole operation and its outcomes. The first part of the section will be dedicated to a general analysis of documents, what they tell us as a whole and what inferences we can make regarding the renaming process based on them. According to the relevance of the information and to structure a more in-depth survey of the data, it was divided into subsections: Districts, with thorough explanations of their renamings and the meaning of it; and Streets, with a likewise dedicated unraveling.

Later on, another section will turn to the scrutiny of the table put together for this research. There, the toponyms will be divided by district and year of renaming. Then, another set of divisions will take place, dividing the names according to their role; since the majority refers to people, the division refers mostly to the activity that made them relevant. The categories, classified according to the names found rather than being pre-made to fit the data, are: Artists; Historical figures; Religious themes and people; Sportsmen; Scientists; Politicians; Foreigners; Geographical places; Concepts; and Unknown. The Artist category includes poets, writers, composers, singers, painters, sculptors, ballet dancers, actors, and directors. The Historical figures include people who were part of Georgian history like kings, princes, important military commanders, and also people who are commemorated because they took part in key events, like martyrs from civil wars and national symbols of resistance. The Religious themes and people include priests, bishops, patriarchs, saints, theologians, and more rarely, religious concepts (like "Transfiguration" or "Trinity") and names of churches or monasteries. Sportsmen include footballers, rugby players, chess players, cyclists, tennis players, and athletes in general. The Scientist category groups together linguists, philosophers, historians, psychologists, electrochemists, architects, political scientists, biochemists, physicians, and doctors. Politicians include people with contributions that made them famous in a specific area, like presidents, congressmen, and sometimes revolutionaries who became part of the government. Foreigners include the few instances when non-Georgian people were commemorated in the toponymy, and it overlaps with other categories, like politicians, artists, or even religious people. Geographical places include all references to cities, villages, countries, and other toponyms in general, like the names of mountains or gorges. Concepts is a self-explanatory one — it brings concepts deemed important enough for Georgians that they are commemorated, like "Freedom", "Friendship", and also important historical dates. The unknown category, as the name indicates, includes all the streets which names were not possible to be assessed, due to lack of information available.

Structurally speaking, the categories were presented in order of perceived importance, apart from the division based on the source materials, so more evident or even bigger toponymy like the names of entire districts and stations come first. When it comes to why certain patterns were chosen, they reflect the tendencies that were found to be intentionally considered for the renaming process, like the categories discussed above. When none were found, broader scopes were applied, like the analyses by year and district, so to make it easier to look at. Information about the commemorated people is drawn mostly from Chelidze's book, where there is a chapter dedicated to giving information about the names inscribed on Tbilisi's cityscape.

The final part of the research will be composed of a concluding section, bringing the findings of the present work and making sense of them as a whole, the impact they have on providing a better understanding of the subject — so to say, the impact of renaming practices on the geopolitical arena, specifically on the post-Soviet context, and the efficiency of this ideological battle.

Results and Discussion

Renaming Policy Decrees

General Analysis

The Renaming Policy Decrees provide a very unique and interesting source of data. First of all, they come with a heading and stamp which specifies the entity responsible for the issuance and official character of the decree. This is important because through it we can already start making inferences regarding the political implications of the renamings: while most of the decrees analyzed here refer to the "Executive Committee of Tbilisi City Council (Soviet) of People's Deputies", evidencing that they were produced during the agonizing stages of the Soviet Union in Georgia. There are two decrees from as early as August 1991 which claim to be issued by the "Cabinet of Ministers of the Republic of Georgia" — the government of the newly independent Republic of Georgia. Interestingly, those last two decrees are the ones treating directly with the end of the Soviet Rule in the country. It follows directly on the president's decision to call off the Soviet rule 3 days before, and demands that the responsible committees evaluate the worth of all property belonging to the Communist Party. Four days later, the second decree, this time issued by the City Hall of Tbilisi, calls for a similar action to take place, along with an *inventarization* of the belongings of the Communist Party and its bodies, but also giving the responsibility to the district prefectures and assemblies.

When Georgia and, consequently, Tbilisi as well were still part of the Soviet Union, the city administration was already changing the names of the local toponymy. The phenomena can already be assessed from as early as 1988, with the decree that changes a square and a street from their previous denominations to the name of the Georgian painter Lado Gudiashvili; it can be seen as a challenging act since Gudiashvili acted in opposition to the Soviet ideology in 1946 when painting religious motives in the Kashveti Church, which brought his dismission from the Academy of Arts two years later. Even though he was awarded the title of Hero of Labor of the Soviet Union in the 1970s, the fact that a "Georgian Hero" (as stated in this words by the decree) was being deliberately put on a square and street name meant that the administration didn't condone anymore with the creation of a "Soviet identity" (Bodaveli 2015: 157) and its expression in Tbilisi, and such a renaming can be seen as a way to protest. Feeling more confident to oppose Soviet rule, the administration of Tbilisi started to rename more toponyms in the city — the year of 1990 is particularly prolific in terms of issuing renaming decrees, comprehending nine of the documents present and investigated here. This evidences how the influence of the Soviet Union was waning throughout its republics. The renamings resonated with the events carried on the streets of Tbilisi and the councils; as commented on the historical background section, Zviad Gamsakhurdia was leading the revolutionary national movement, and it is certain to infer that this incentivized the reactions evidenced by the decrees, the rejection of the enforced Soviet elements branded in plain sight.

The decrees contain information that couldn't be directly found anywhere else in this research. They cite the renaming of entire districts, metro stations, and, on rare occasions, comment on the political situation of Tbilisi as the capital. One of them, from May 1990 states that:

> [...] as advised by workers, unions and students, and also by the institution's advisory council, decides to rename Shaumian Street to Ketevan Tsamebuli Street [...].

Another one, from August 30th, 1990, brings very interesting information: it mentions that people were unsatisfied because the process was being carried out too slowly, and seeing the first renamings, the own population wanted to bring back their cultural elements on the city namings, with all its aspects included — historical, religious and national figures. It is another solid evidence of how the liberation movement was resounding very loudly through the country and especially at the capital; the historical and religious character of the renamings was also, according to the narrative, being constructed for years, as aforesaid. Heeding the call of the populace, the City Council requests the district councils of Lenin and October (still to be renamed) to propose renamings which bring important historical names back, in collaboration with the residents — which is very interesting. It is possible to note that the "practice of returning historical names to Tbilisi districts and streets" does not refer directly to bringing back old street names, but rather historical figures on the toponymy, as none of the streets mentioned on the decree returned to their previous names. After all, before the Soviet renaming practices, the first independent Georgian Republic had a very limited time-frame to name its toponymy, and before that the imperial rule would not focus on commemorating distinct national

Georgian elements, so there was not much to bring back from previous times. Some other streets, however, got their previous names back, as well as the majority of districts.

The decrees also include the names of the City Council Chairman and the Secretary, giving crucial information about who issued the decrees. Although not including all the renamed toponymy in Tbilisi, they include a significant amount of those which underwent such process from 1988 to 1991, *ergo*, the period that is pertinent to this research. Other decrees from further and previous years could not be found in the research made in the Georgian National Archives.

Districts

On the Decree from the "Executive Committee of the Tbilisi City Council (Soviet) of People's Deputies" issued on April 26th, 1990, it can be read:

> The ECCCT has decided [...] that the following districts will be renamed:
> First of May District — Didube District
> Kalinin District — Mtatsminda District
> Kirov District — Krtsanisi District
> Orjonikidze District — Vake District
> Factory District — Samgori District
> 26 Commissars District — Isani District [...]

On another decree from November 7th, 1990, two other districts go through renaming: "[...] Lenin District — Nadzaladevi District [...] October District — Chughureti District [...]". It is not known, why there was a span of months between the renaming of those last two districts, and they were part of a decree that was most worried about renaming streets; it also included railways, medical and engineering institutes. One assumption we can make is that due to the sensitivity of times, some elements were deliberately kept due to their importance — after all, Lenin's name is still remembered and commemorated even nowadays in some post-Soviet places and is sometimes detached from the totalitarian nature of the later years. Nevertheless, it was to the Council's interest to remove that too. Since most of the districts had older designations, they were returned to those toponyms. It is possible to see traces of the rich history of Tbilisi on the names, given that many of them carry an etymology related to the language of the various peoples who were part of its formation.

Namely, the first decree was signed by the ECCT's Chairman I. Andriadze and Secretary V. Japaridze, and the second one, by N. Lekishvili.

Stations

A decree from November 7th, 1990 (issued the same date of the second decree changing the district names) asks the metropolitan leadership of Tbilisi to change the metro station names, as follows:

> Tbilisi City Council Presidium decides to change the names of Tbilisi Metropolitan Stations' names in collaboration with its advisory council workers of the capital, as well as the labor collective of the metropolitan workers.
> Stations: "October" to "Nadzaladevi"
> "Komsomol" to "Medical Institute"
> "26 Commissars" to "Avlabari"
> "Lenin Square" to "Freedom Square"
> "Polytechnical Institute" to "Polytechnical" [...]
> The City Council Chairman signature is from N. Lekishvili.

Streets

Since there is a large number of streets being referenced in the renaming decrees, the present analysis will be limited to choosing the ones which represent the whole process, instead of making a detailed and probably repetitive commentary on each one of them. A very symbolic renaming is from May 24th, 1990: "The Executive Committee of the City Council of Tbilisi, as advised by workers, unions and students, and also by the institution's advisory council, decides to rename Shaumian Street to Ketevan Tsamebuli Street (Ketevan the Martyr)". Shaumian was a Bolshevik revolutionary, leader of the Baku Commune that became the famous 26 Commissars, also commemorated on toponymy around the Soviet Union (and previously mentioned in this piece) (Chelidze 2008: 342). His name was replaced by Ketevan the Martyr—this is very significant because it is a religious expression, as evidenced by the name.

Another decree, from September 7th, 1990 concerns renamings done specifically in the district of Mtatsminda:

Changes for the following streets located in Mtsatminda area [...] The street names should be changed as:
1. A. Lunacharski st. – as Levan Laghidze st.
2. P. Makharadze st. – as Geronti Kikodze st.
3. M. Tskhakaia st. – as Vukol Beridze st.
4. A. Oboladze st. – as Vakhtang Kotetishvili st.
5. S. Kirova st. – as Giorgi Leonidze st.
6. G. Leonidze st. – as Brother Sargi (scientist) and Davit (artist) Kakabadzeebi st.
7. A. Japaridze st. – as Paolo Iashvili st.

As can be seen, it is posterior to the renaming of districts, since the district is not called "Kalinin" anymore. The fact that the renaming is not done at random, but focused on Mtatsminda, is most probably because the district is located in Old Tbilisi, rendering it an important location to include important historical figures from the Georgian pantheon. As for the streets, they replace names of Bolshevik revolutionaries for Georgian figures, in short; they either were opposed to the Soviet regime, or had no relation to it and represented important figures for the Georgian national consciousness, from painters and poets to scientists. The fact that they were all markedly ethnic Georgians is already a transgression to the "Soviet citizen", ethnic-free ideology.

On November 7th, 1990, yet another decree concerns the renaming of several streets located in different parts of the city. It is possible to see many very distinct names related to the Soviet ideology being replaced, like "Marx Street", "Kooperatsia Street" (Cooperation), "October Street", "Pioneris Street" (Pioneers), "Lokomotivi Stadium" (Locomotive) and "S. Ordzhonikidze Institute", for example. The names replacing them were once again of distinct Georgian people, also religious icons; Azizbekovi Street became Bellemi Street (Bethelem) and Cherniakhovski Street became David Gareja Street (after a monastery complex). A particularly important one is the renaming of Volodarski Street to Haidar Abashidze, a Muslim Georgian who was a key figure to keep Batumi under Georgia by the fall of the Russian Empire (Chelidze 2008: 249).

Toponymy Renaming Table

General analysis

Differently from the City Council Decrees, the table resulting from the combination of the data sources does not give us descriptions or direct information about the renaming process. On rare occasions, Chelidze's book gives a short commentary on it, usually when it is talking about streets named after people who lived in it or naming processes related to events, which happened on the toponym. Otherwise, there are no explanations. This requires that we make our conjectures based on what is possible to draw from the raw data, like the number of names commemorated on the same year or district, or nature of the names as a group. Let us have a look at sheer numbers first, then. There are 1,070 toponyms in the resulting table, out of which 244 were renamed between 1988 and 2007. It is relevant to mention that some of the renamings were applied to the same object, e.g. a street that was renamed in 1996 and, later, received a new name in 2000. This happened eight times, which amounts to a total of 251 renamings in 19 years. When talking about numbers, there are some assortments that we can make to have a clear view of the patterns. First, in Table 1 below, we see the nature of previous, replaced names.

Table 1. Number of renamed toponyms by category

Non-Soviet	Soviet	Previously unnamed or new street	Toponyms renamed twice	Toponyms renamed three times	Toponyms renamed four times	Toponyms renamed five times	Toponyms that returned to the old
107	99	36	74	47	21	6	32

Total number of commemorated names (1988–2007)	242

The table makes it evident already that most of the names that were taken out didn't contain ideologically Soviet elements. This grouping includes, among Georgians and foreigners, people who weren't connected to the Communist Party in any way, sometimes being detached completely from the period when the Soviet revolution took place. Since the vast majority of streets in Tbilisi were first named during Russian imperial times (as we can see in Chelidze's compilation) or at least included in city plans from the period, there were still instances when the most recent renamings were directed at them. Soviet instances, however, do not fall behind too much, with only 8 occurrences short of non-Soviet ones. However, as will be discussed further, even when the renamings were not directed at a Soviet toponym, the new names they carried were almost always Georgian (at least 90%), and thus serving as a way to reinforce the national narrative to the detriment of any previous ideology put forward in Tbilisi's cityscape. The remainder of substituted toponyms were previously unnamed streets or also unnamed stretches of old streets that were deemed to deserve a different name. When two names were given to different sections of the same street, but were still replacing an existing name, both occurrences were included separately in the first two categories of Table 1 — this causes the number of commemorated names to be different from the total number of renamings as presented on Table 3. The renamings counted in the columns to the right (the ones indicating how many times the toponymy was changed) include renamings that occurred before 1988, but on toponymy that got renamed again in the 1988-2007 period. It is useful so to understand how contested some toponyms are. The toponyms that returned to old names do not include some famous names like Rustaveli or Vakhushti Bagrationi, but are mostly geographical and with minor national references, not following a particular pattern regarding their location or function of the commemorated aspect; they just seem to be what the name states, a geographical return to a previous denomination. Regarding the themes present on the new names of the toponyms, a subsection follows to explore them.

Renamings by Theme

Jumping now to an analysis of the new imprinted names, we arrive at Table 2, where we can see a classification of the commemorated names according to the groupings mentioned in the methodology section.

Table 2. Commemorated people or concepts by theme and their percentage

Artists	Scientists	Historical Figures	Unknown	Religious	Geographical places	Sportsmen	Foreign people, concepts or places	Politicians	Concepts
69	47	42	19	17	16	13	13	7	7
27.6%	18.8%	16.8%	7.6%	6.8%	6.4%	5.2%	5.2%	2.8%	2.8%

Here some clarifications are needed. The concepts, first of all, do overlap sometimes, since it is possible for a foreign artist to be commemorated on a toponym, or a religiously relevant geographical place (for example, Jerusalem, which is also foreign). In this case, a decision was made to only include names in two categories when they are referring to foreign people, concepts, or places that already fall into other categories. This is done to make a better separation of the number of commemorated people on other categories, so for example, a medieval patriarch is included in the Religious category and not on the Historical figures one, according to which characteristic is more important or most salient. Another important note is that some names occur more than once in the namings, so they were only included once in the table. This makes it difficult to calculate a percentage of renamings that fall into a bigger group, like how many renamings commemorate certain people or concepts in absolute numbers; but we can have an idea of the proportion by just looking at the numbers and making general calculations.

The first inference we can make is the high number of local ethnic references, since the bulk of new names indicate Georgian people, places or related concepts, with an aforesaid number of at least 90%. Only 13 renamings refer to any kind of foreign people or place, and even then, some of them have some relation to Georgia or at least the Caucasus. As can be seen, the most populated category refers to artists, who are praised for their contribution to cultural production and their representations of national symbols, sometimes even revered internationally, and thus is an important expression of a national, independent regime. The second-biggest category, scientists, also play an important part in a country's development, materially and culturally speaking. Since the category includes historians, philologists, and professors, it also represents certain people who help the country to understand itself and pass that knowledge forward, being an integral part of a national identity's development. Historical figures, the third category, are all about a representation of the past, an integral part of one's perception of her group and its characteristics. A few of the later renamings in this category refer to more recent developments too, since they refer to people killed in the civil war in Abkhazia, in the early 90s. The fourth category includes all naming which meaning couldn't be assessed, it is, people whose information couldn't be found anywhere. It probably means that they commemorate local people from the neighborhood or street itself, with no big national importance; they are only known in the said neighborhood. The next category, Religious representations, is deeply tied to the revival of ethnic Georgian expressions, since the Orthodox Church is very important in the country and is in direct opposition to the atheist Soviet state. Geographical places also mostly refer to cities, villages, or mountains in Georgia itself, with only a couple of foreign references. The sportsmen category is made entirely from Georgian players or competitors, and most of the Politicians too. The concepts are tied to things deemed important for the Georgian culture, including "Freedom" (Square), "Artist" (Street), "Fighters for Georgia's Freedom" (Street), and "Rose Revolution" (Square). This category also groups important dates commemorated, like "26th of May" (Square), referring to Georgia's Independence Day.

Renamings by Year

As aforesaid in previous sections, renamings as a political act against the Soviet regime in Georgia already started before the end of the Soviet Union, most probably connected to the movements of national liberation. Here, a subsection is in order to analyze the renamings per year thoroughly, with investigation of the patterns found and the commemorations, along with reflections on the findings. The number of renamings per year can be consulted in Table 3 below:

Table 3.   Renamings according to year

Year	Number of renamings
1988	4
1989	5
1990	49
1991	17
1992	30
1993	12
1994	14
1995	21
1996	9
1997	6
1998	6
1999	17
2000	6
2001	8
2002	0
2003	18
2004	3
2005	6
2006	12
2007	8
Total number of renamings	252

It started with a shy number of four renamings in 1988, but they already carried a Georgian symbolism: Besides Lado Gudiashvili, as seen in the City Council Decrees section, other people commemorated on those renamings were Elene Akhvlediani and Davit Aghmashenebeli (David the Builder). Akhvlediani is revered as an important Georgian painter, and David the Builder (the medieval king) is one of the best-known Georgian figures of all time, both as a very successful ruler and as a religious character (Chelidze 2008: 277). 1989 had only one renaming more than the previous year, but they also carried symbolism: three of the renamings referred to important medieval Georgian kings (Tamar, Teimuraz, and

Pharnavaz) and another one to Merab Kostava, one of the most important Georgian revolutionaries who died in the same year (Chelidze 2008: 298), his commemoration on a street name makes it probably the most significant of all other renamings done before 1991. Along with these figures, the first foreign name appears: Alexandre Dumas, a French writer who visited the Caucasus, including Georgia, probably the reason for the commemoration (Chelidze 2008: 280). Dumas' name also replaced Zheliabov, who was a Russian revolutionary, one of the organizers for Tsar Alexander II's assassination (Chelidze 2008: 318).

Then we come to the most prolific year of renamings of all: 1990, with no less than 49 names changed. While some of them were carried so to name previously unnamed streets and new sections of existing ones, the majority of the renamings took out distinctly Soviet names, such as Lenin, Marx, Herzen, Ordzhonikidze, Perovskaya and Volodarsky. They were replaced by Georgian people, which compose all of the anthroponyms of this year. More direct religious names also start to come up on the year, such as Anton Catholicos (a Patriarch of the Georgian Orthodox Church), Transfiguration (of Christ), Bishop Gabriel, Ketevan the Martyr and Jerusalem (although being foreign, it is also important for the Orthodoxy). Geronti Kikodze, one of the members of the Constituent Assembly of the First Republic of Georgia, is commemorated in this year (Chelidze 2008: 336). It is also markedly the year when the main square of the city, Liberty Square, replaced Lenin Square, with an incredibly high symbolism. One medieval Georgian figure is present, too (Bagrat III). The next year, 1991, hosted way less renamings, 17. They were still following the trend to replace Soviet markers, though, and streets like "Communist Labor", "Tsiteltsqaro" (Red Spring), "Mogilevsky", and "Engels" were gone. Once again, predominantly Georgians names were brought back. "Dedoplistsqaro" (Queen's Spring) replaced Red Spring, since the name of the city commemorated also returned to that name (Chelidze 2008: 59), and Mogilevsky became Saint-Petersburg (before Mogilevsky, the street's name used to be Leningrad), a very political statement since it was also adhering to an old name of one of the most important cities in the late Soviet Union. Two medieval figures also appear (King Archil and Queen Tamar). A different kind of commemorated people (included in the Historical categorization) appear: the ones who died in the 9th of April protests or were directly related to it. Eka Bezhanishvili is one of these, who was only 16 when she died, in 1989 (Chelidze 2008: 263).

In 1992 the first year after Georgia's Independence, the renamings raised in number, almost doubled, with 30 occurrences — it can be seen as a renewal in the effort now that the country was free to express its cultural elements without any fear of reprisal. Other Soviet names were erased, with this trend now consolidated definitely. Streets such as "26 (Baku) Commissars", "Pravda", "Paris Commune", "Collective Agriculture", "(Rosa) Luxembourg" and "Matrosov" disappeared, to give way to a myriad of ethnic Georgian names, such as Erekle II, a historical king from the 18th century (Chelidze 2008: 281). Particularly important is the naming of a square as 26th of May, the aforementioned Independence Day of Georgia, and the anniversary of the massacre at Rustaveli Avenue. In 1993, the number of renamings dropped again, to less than half of the previous year: only 12. Soviet commemorations were starting to become rare now, with only a few of them removed, like "Traktor", "Grizodubov" and "Lunacharsky". All of the replacements were Georgian anthroponyms. 1994 kept it around the same number, with 14 renamings, but this time only two Soviet commemorations were erased — "Komsomol" (Leninist Young Communist League) and "Kakhovka", the city in Ukraine, which itself is not a great symbol of the Soviet Union, but the commemoration of another Soviet city can be seen as an ideological act. Georgian anthroponyms were the majority, with a few geographical places (one religiously relevant, Jerusalem Square) and a medieval king (Peter the Iberian, from the historical Georgian Kingdom of Iberia). Spiridon Kidia, a prominent figure during the First Republic, is commemorated as well (Chelidze 2008: 294). Another unique kind of commemoration, under the Historical theme, appears, with Koka Kldiashvili, a young man who died during the war in Abkhazia

(Chelidze 2008: 295). 1995 had a small spike in numbers, with 21 changes, taking out names like "Labor", "Deputies", "Pioneers", another "Lenin" and "Stakhanov". All the replacements, like 1993, were Georgian anthroponyms. One of them was Sergo Ksovreli, who died in the Abkhazian war in 1993 (Chelidze 2008: 337); other was Gia (Giorgi) Chanturia, who along with Zviad Gamsakhurdia and Merab Kostava, was a prominent figure of the national movement, leader of the National Democratic Party (Chelidze 2008: 352).

The year 1996 saw the beginning of a decline in the renaming process, as the Soviet commemorations were becoming more and more scarce. Only nine streets were renamed that year, and only one of the renamings carries the former regime's ideology: "Leninasheni". All the replacements are Georgian anthroponyms once again. Rostom Muskhelishvili is one of them—he was a colonel, Chief of Military Intelligence during the First Republic (Chelidze 2008: 308). 1997 dropped even more, with only six instances, with two of the replaced ones being heroes of the Soviet Union, "Shirshov" and "Voronin" (Chelidze 2008: 285). All the names that replaced the previous ones were of Georgian people in this year, too. In 1998, once again six toponyms were replaced; only one Soviet commemoration, however, "Budapest", which referred to a fellow Socialist country's capital, at the time. The only non-Georgian name to figure in the new commemorations was Hermann Gmeiner, a famous Austrian philanthropist (Chelidze 2008: 270). In 1999 a sudden spike on the renaming activity happened, with 17 instances. Nevertheless, it only got rid of three Soviet names, "Pisarev", one of the authors who influenced Lenin (Chelidze 2008: 316), "Gagarin", the famed first man to go to space under the Soviet Union and worldwide (Chelidze 2008: 268), and "Kurnatovsky", a revolutionary (Chelidze 2008: 298). One of the names of those years, which replaced a previously unnamed street, was "Fighters for Georgia's Unity", a very ethnically and politically Georgian name, very expressive of the national discourse. As expected, the other names are Georgian anthroponyms.

On the turning of the millennium, 2000, the practice decreased again, to six replacements. Two distinct Soviet names were put out, "Tchernichevski" (a revolutionary writer who influenced Lenin)

(Chelidze 2008: 343) and "Kaludin", a famous revolutionary worker, and a symbol of labor (Chelidze 2008: 293). The totality of new names amounts to all of them being Georgians again. 2001 saw only two more streets than the previous year, eight, but with only one Soviet toponymy replaced, once again a street name commemorating Gagarin. The only name which is not a Georgian anthroponym is Ochamchire, a city on the coast of Abkhazia (Chelidze 2008: 138). In 2002, for unknown reasons, there are no renamings registered. They were revived in 2003, with a good increase in numbers — 18 renamings, out of which only one Soviet commemoration was erased: "Kerch", the strait in the Black Sea, where many Soviet Georgians fought and died in combat during World War II (Chelidze 2008: 178). The majority of the names put in the toponyms were Georgian people, apart from "Artist" Street, rather a concept. Four of them were naming previously unnamed parts of existing streets, including "Artist" Street. Zurab Abuladze, one the commemorated people, was a young man killed during the war in Abkhazia (Chelidze 2008: 251); another street was named "Student Heroes" (Gmiri Kursantebi), a reference to the students of the police academy who died in Abkhazia (Chelidze 2008: 46). In 2004, only three renamings were carried, but one of them is quite relevant: it replaced Stalin Embankment by Zviad Gamsakhurdia Embankment, figuring the first president of Georgia for the first time and removing the most infamous Georgian of the Soviet Union from the toponymy. It was part of Saakashvili's anti-Russian, self-affirmation drive (de Waal 2010: 135, cited in Isaacs & Polese 2016: 32). Likely, removing Stalin's name from the embankment took so long because he was still revered by a good number of people and still is to this day, as evidenced very strongly by the street named after him in Gori, his hometown, and his museum there (Asatiani 2007, cited in Isaacs & Polese 2016: 31, 38). Another renaming put the name of Anatoly Sobchak on the commemorations; he was a prominent figure in the Soviet Union and demanded that the responsible people for the 9th of April massacre to be punished (Chelidze 2008: 324). Yet one more important name is Noe Zhordania, who had an important role in the socialist movement in the Russian Empire, becoming the prime minister of the First Republic. He is the only declared Georgian

Menshevik to be commemorated in the post-Soviet renamings (Chelidze 2008: 318). Only a bit more renamings were carried in 2005, six, and only one was replacing a Soviet element, "Atarbegov", a member of the Cheka at the time of the Soviet Occupation of Georgia. Notably, new streets were named George Bush (the American president at the time, named after he visited Georgia) (Chelidze 2008: 264), Rose Revolution Square, commemorating the recent developments in the country, and Europe Square, showing Saakashvili's Western orientation very clearly. Another one was renamed after Zurab Zhvania, the only Prime Minister of Georgia who died while in office, in 2005 (Chelidze 2008: 318).

In the penultimate year included in this research, 2006, there were 12 renamings. Three of them replaced streets bearing the same name, all of them after Gagarin, like in previous years; and all but three of the new names weren't Georgian, namely, Picasso (the Spanish painter), King Solomon (the biblical figure) and Peking (the Chinese capital, also known as Beijing). One of the new names was after Natia Bashaleishvili, another 16-year-old protester who got killed in the 9th of April events (Chelidze 2008: 263). Another was Kote Apkhazi, a General-major of Artillery during the First Republic (Chelidze 2008: 259). One more figure from the First Republic commemorated on the year is Giorgi Kvinitadze, the commander-in-chief of the army (Chelidze 2008: 295). An interesting name with a contested past commemorated in 2006 is Meliton Kantaria — he is the junior sergeant who (along with M. Egorov) raised the flag over the Reichstag in 1945, but his name was still chosen to be inscribed in the toponymy. It was part of Saakashvili's "nationalization" of Georgian war heroes, detaching the "Georgianness" from the "Sovietness". Later, in 2011, Saakashvili named a school after him as well, lamenting that "Kantaria is the most classical example of the tragic fortune of our country" (president.gov.ge 2011e, cited in Isaacs & Polese 2016: 31) because he was a Georgian living in Abkhazia and ended up his life as a refugee; in fact, Kantaria was expelled from Abkhazia and even found refuge in Russia, making Saakashvili's act a selective appropriation and manipulation of history, confirming his narrative of Georgian victimhood and stressing its resilience (Isaacs & Polese 2016: 31). In the last year, 2007, eight renamings figured, and again, two Soviet names stand out for how long it took for them to be removed from the toponymy; Stalin and Red Army Street. All but one name is not Georgian on the new names, Heidar Aliyev, Azerbaijan's former president, who was one of the most important post-Soviet figures in the country (Chelidze 2008: 254). It is probably a representation of the friendship between the two post-Soviet Republics, but also a commemoration of the liberation of the Soviet times since Aliyev was an important figure on the consolidation of the Republic of Azerbaijan.

From this set of information about the years and their commemorations, we can draw some conclusions. As made clear in other sections and reinforced here, the renaming process echoed the political events in Georgia. Starting slowly with an oppositional movement, it grew to become a big mobilization, as made apparent by the renamings carried in 1990. A decrease during the year of Independence is probably due to the political turmoil that took the country by assault. Even though it contributes to political freedom, which lets the process carry on without censorship, the abrupt change on the power structure is traumatic and the City Council must have had other priorities. As with other projects of nationalistic revival, it kept steadily going, and even if decreased in number, renamings were constant and most of the time substituting the previous regime's ideology. And when not doing so, still reinforcing cultural, ethnic, and nationalistic elements, as evidenced by the fact that the bulk of new names commemorated Georgian people. Odd years, like the renamingless 2002, are an exception, and it will only be possible to know whether the process of renaming stalled after 2007 if we get a grip of a new, updated set of data. Now, a more geographical kind of analysis will be carried in the next part.

Renamings by District

In this ensuing subsection, we'll take a look at the spatial distribution of the renaming process, dividing it by district and year. A compilation of this data can be seen in Table 4 below:

Table 4. Renamings by district and year

		District					
		Didube-Chughureti	Gldani-Nadzaladevi	Isani-Samgori	Mtatsminda-Krtsanisi	Old Tbilisi	Vake-Saburtalo
Renaming Year	1988	1	0	1	0	2	0
	1989	0	0	0	0	3	2
	1990	7	7	4	0	26	6
	1991	1	3	1	0	10	2
	1992	3	3	3	0	13	8
	1993	0	3	1	0	2	6
	1994	1	1	4	0	2	6
	1995	1	8	4	0	3	5
	1996	0	2	1	0	5	1
	1997	3	1	2	0	0	0
	1998	0	0	0	1	2	4
	1999	2	3	3	0	3	5
	2000	0	2	0	0	4	0
	2001	0	1	1	0	2	4
	2002	0	0	0	0	0	0
	2003	0	2	6	0	2	8
	2004	0	0	0	0	1	1
	2005	1	0	2	0	2	1
	2006	2	0	1	0	2	7
	2007	1	1	1	0	1	4
Total renamings by district		23	37	35	1	85	70

The district which bears the highest number of toponyms renamed is Old Tbilisi, with 85 names being replaced there. The high concentration on the district certainly has to do with its historical significance, as made obvious by its name. It is very symbolic that the oldest neighborhood in town sees the majority of the new names, almost all Georgian, put there. There also seems to be a deliberate effort to rename streets in the Vake-Saburtalo area. Both districts combine to form the famed part west of river Kura, where many universities are located, as well as a lot of bars and hotels and where the more economically active population lives; they were home to the "red intelligentsia" and the Communist Party nomenklatura (Jones 2013). One of the lines of the Tbilisi metro covers the most extension of Saburtalo and is named after the district. As for the other districts, they keep a constant number of renamings through the years and in total, so there does not seem to be a concerted effort to rename them. They are located in more peripheral areas of the city. The one exception is Mtatsminda-Krtsanisi, which recorded only one renaming, done in 1999. Though it is not known why the district received so little attention in the process, one possibility is that it felt victim to geographical disagreements. The National Archive's list only includes one street in the district, but if we consult the City Council Decrees, one of them places several renamed streets in Mtatsminda in a decree from 1990, which would put more commemorations on the neighborhood. This research is not a place to dwell into demarcation of districts in Tbilisi, and since the National Archive's list is the most comprehensive record of renamings done systematically, preference has been given to this source.

Conclusions

In the past 200 years, Georgia has only been an Independent Nation for 31 of them, having only a few decades in hand to assert its sovereignty in recent times. Marks of past regimes can still be seen in its cities, and particularly in the capital; most of them are from the Soviet period, the most recent former regime to assert its power in it. Along with the national liberation movement, the revamping of the cityscape of Tbilisi carried on with a process of commemorating elements associated with the rich Georgian history, running in an opposite direction from the Soviet ideological imprinting; Bodaveli (2015: 177) comments that more than 90% of their place namings were anthroponyms, with an almost total absence of Georgian historical people and events — while the post-Soviet Republic filled the capital with more than 90% of anthroponyms, almost all of them referring to Georgians, historical, religious, and cultural figures altogether, as evidenced by this research. It is paradoxical, however, that the Soviet nationality and development policies ended up incentivizing the "Georgianisation" of the capital (in detriment to other nationalities) and fueling the national discourse. While the Soviets only left Tbilisi with cultural aspects of identity, the Independent Republic revived national, religious, and ethnic aspects to the cityscape. Analyzing the data brought into this research shows clearly that the renamings intended to make the city a portrait of a homogenous Georgia, an assertion of a regained sovereignty over totalizing efforts. Branding memory in a place requires choosing elements from a real or even imagined past, and such choice was made — the capital, once famous for its diverse and cosmopolitan culture, now is more Georgian than ever. The Armenians and Azeris, once teeming in population and influence, were gone, and the toponymy is not the place where they are remembered. A lack of the own city's past is evident, when it comes to the representation of the city culture and the participation of others in the urban space.

This research intended to unveil the process of inscribing the geopolitical landscape of the post-Soviet Tbilisi and its intentions — and what has been found is that the function of the capital turned a lot more to the commemoration of national figures and aspects, mostly disregarding local figures and the urban identity, with only a few foreign mentions. The city shows only shy signs of its diverse past, mostly in derivative names of old neighborhoods and metro stations, a few survivors from the Russian imperial rule. A nationalistic discourse is the rule when it comes to toponymy now, not only downplaying the Menshevik nature of the First Republic, but also ignoring national minorities and a broader, shared Transcaucasian history — the city now displays broader national themes instead of a particular city history and culture. The cityscape reflects the politics of Gamsakhurdia and Saakashvili, most of all, in their effort to consolidate Georgia as a united, homogenous country and solidify this claim by etching it in shared, public elements. From 1988 to 2007, old names were returned or undesired names were renamed so to achieve such objectives (with a particular vigor on the first years of the free republic), and although no specific patterns were perceived, the commemorations were mostly after famous Georgian people and, after the wars in Abkhazia and South Ossetia, "martyrs" of the civil conflict. One thing that can be said for sure is that the naming process is consonant with the Georgian national narrative, adapting throughout the years to major political events and ideological changes, has been shown by the analysis of the data presented in this research. The public memory inscribed in the cityscape draws from history, but a specific and detached part of Georgian history, carefully sewn together so to reinforce the territorial and cultural claim.

The selective nature of the process, picking only the intended historical aspects in the memorial commemoration, is very clear. It is not only evident through the names, aspects, and events chosen but also the ones not chosen, and the ones which choice is deliberately oriented. There are important people from the First Republic present on the renamings, such as Noe Zhordania, and these commemorations, along with important dates from the time, are primarily concerned with bringing about the first democratic expression of power from the Georgian nation; it glosses over the Socialist, Menshevik nature of the First Republic, though, in a desire to forget everything related to the Soviet Union, even if sharing a few ideological traits. All other commemorated aspects from the First Republic were not party leaders or relevant participants, except for Zhordania, certainly only because he became president—a perfect example of the selectiveness of the process. These contested elements of the commemorative process express the troubles of Georgian people in dealing with the conflicting past they have—"toponymy with contested pasts", clearly seen in Zhordania's case and in other instances like the aforementioned commemoration of Meliton Kantaria, where the appropriation of the Georgian character of the historical figure is done while stripping him of his "Sovietness".

This is all part of what Assman calls cultural memory, the cultivation of which stabilizes and forms a society's self-image; and according to Bucher et al. (2013), it is an indivisible part of the formation of group identity, in what is called social memory. Whatever memorialization concept we choose to apply, what is been looking at in this work is the expression of a shared history and culture in the toponymy, filtered by institutions and for the sake of a particular national discourse.

As we can see, a predominantly Georgian presence in the population and the naming of Tbilisi is a very recent thing—only the past few decades have seen it. With its regained sovereignty, the Republic of Georgia is now tasting a full-blown commemoration of its culture, its heroes and martyrs, its religion, and its history. The etching of its national elements in the capital serves a reminder of these very elements so that the population gets reminded every day of who they are, which history they are intended to share and which fellow countrymen they can look up to in the journey to contribute themselves to the Georgian Nation's progress. In retrospect, nevertheless, this stressing eliminates the signs of a shared past with other Caucasian peoples, and even if not completely intentionally, erases their participation in an essential era of the city's development. There is no evidence that the reason for such disregard of the foreign influence on Tbilisi's history should be other than simply the reinforcement of the national, homogenous Georgian discourse. For instance, in discourses like Gamsakhurdia's, one can see nationalistic ideas that downplay the significance of national minorities, like Abkhazians and Svans, in favor of a uniquely Georgian nation; doing the same with other nationalities is just the next step. There are no xenophobic connotations to this lack of foreign representation, historical or not, but it would be interesting to analyze the impact this has on the population—whether they are aware of such shared past, what their opinion on the nations in question is, and other related questions. While we know that in their overall national discourse Armenians and Azeris also downplay the participation of others in their historical journey, it would be interesting to conduct similar research in their capitals to see how their discourse deal with commemorations of the past—they may be just like Tbilisi, or maybe not. Identifying such tendencies in blooming nationalistic revivals (or even births) like the post-Soviet ones might show us interesting things about political processes as a whole.

The influence of the renamings on the people, however, is the subject of other researches, probably through interviews. The present work's intention was not only to show how the independent Georgian regime has reinforced its narrative on the cityscape but also to bring data and knowledge to the international academic world and audience, so that more people can access and produce such kinds of work, letting us better understand how political and historical processes are carried and how they cope with it. I do not claim that this research has brought all the knowledge on the renaming process even on the period here discussed—many of the streets present in the City Council decrees lack information, especially on the year of renaming. Perhaps in the future more sources (especially archival ones) will be found, more accurate and complete, and the understanding of the process will be even bigger. Further studies could also try to correlate Soviet policies with the process of renaming and building of the national identity (like the indigenization policy), and apply the same analysis to other Caucasian republics. This serves as an invitation for more research and memory work to be done and new conclusions be made from the data presented here and eventually other data, sharing the rich Caucasian history which we have still much to know about.

Bibliography

Assche, Kristopher Van, Salukvadze, Joseph, & Shavishvili, Nick. (2009). *City culture and city planning in Tbilisi: where Europe and Asia meet.* Lewiston: Edwin Mellen Press.

Azaryahu, Maoz. (2012). Renaming the past in post-Nazi Germany: insights into the politics of street naming in Mannheim and Potsdam. *Cultural Geographies* 19(3): 385–400.

Azaryahu, Maoz. (1986). Street names and political identity: the case of East Berlin. *Journal of Contemporary History* 21(4): 581–604.

Azaryahu, Maoz. (1996). The power of commemorative street names. *Environment and planning. Society and Space* 14(3): 311–330.

Batiashvili, Nutsa. (2018). *The bivocal nation: memory and identity on the edge of the empire*. London: Palgrave Macmillan.

Bodaveli, Elene. (2015). The reflection of communist ideology in the street naming policy in Soviet Tbilisi (1922-1939). *Analytical Bulletin* 8: 156-178.

Buachidze, Ioseb Moses. ([1970]1979). Georgian Polytechnical Institute. In *The great Soviet encyclopedia* (3rd Edition). Farmington Hills: The Gale Group, Inc.

Bucher, Slavomír, Matlovič, René, Lukáčová, Alena, Harizal, Barbora, Matlovičová, Kvetoslava, Kolesárová, Jana, Čermáková, Lenka & Michalko, Miroslav. (2013). The perception of identity through urban toponyms in the regional cities of Slovakia. *Anthropological Notebooks* 19(3): 23-40.

Chelidze, Zurab. (2008). *Tbilisi: streets, avenues, squares*. Tbilisi: Irakli Abashidze Main Editorial.

de Waal, Thomas. (2010). *The Caucasus: an introduction*. New York: Oxford University Press.

Drozdzewski, Danielle. (2014). Using history in the streetscape to affirm geopolitics of memory. *Political Geography* 42: 66-78.

Foote, Kenneth E. & Azaryahu, Maoz. (2007). Toward a geography of memory: geographical dimensions of public memory and commemoration. *Journal of Political & Military Sociology* 35(1): 125-144.

Foxall, Andrew. (2013). A contested landscape: monuments, public memory, and post-Soviet identity in Stavropol', Russia. *Communist and Post-Communist Studies* 46(1): 167-178.

Isaacs, Rico & Polese, Abel. (2016). *Nation-building and identity in the post-Soviet space*. London: Routledge.

Jones, Stephen. (2013). *Georgia: a political history since independence*. London: I.B. Tauris.

Kadmon, Naftali. (2004). Toponymy and geopolitics: the political use—and misuse—of geographical names. *The Cartographic Journal* 41(2): 85-87.

Nora, Pierre. (1989). Between memory and history: les lieux de mémoire. *Representations* (26): 7-24.

Polese, Abel, Morris, Jeremy, Pawłusz, Emilia & Seliverstova, Oleksandra. (2017). *Identity and nation building in everyday post-socialist life*. London: Routledge.

Rose-Redwood, Reuben, Alderman, Derek H. & Azaryahu, Maoz. (2010). Geographies of toponymic inscription: new directions in critical place-name studies. *Progress in Human Geography* 34(4): 453-470.

Salukvadze, Joseph. & Golubchikov, Oleg. (2016). City as a geopolitics: Tbilisi, Georgia—a globalizing metropolis in a turbulent region. *Cities* 52: 39-54.

Saparov, Arseny. (2003). The alteration of place names and construction of national identity in Soviet Armenia. *Cahiers Du Monde Russe* 44(1): 179-198.

Sartania, Davit, Nikolaishvili, Dali & Ujmajuridze, Avtandil. (2017). Soviet toponymy: the history and the present. *Earth Sciences* 6(5-1): 49-55.

Suny, Ronald Grigor. ([1988]1994). *The making of the Georgian nation (2nd edition)*. Bloomington: Indiana University Press.

Tamm, Marek. (2013). Beyond history and memory: new perspectives in memory studies. *History Compass* 11(6): 458-473.

van Assche, Kristopher & Salukvadze, Joseph. (2012). Tbilisi reinvented: planning, development and the unfinished project of democracy in Georgia. *Planning Perspectives* 27(1): 1-24.

Vuolteenaho, Jani & Berg, Lawrence D. (2009). Towards critical toponymies. In *Critical toponymies: the contested politics of place naming*, Vuolteenaho, Jani & Berg, Lawrence D. (eds). Farnham: Ashgate, 1-18.

5 Mediatization of History
Introducing the Concept and Key Cases from Eastern Europe

Roman Horbyk, Yana Prymachenko and Yuliya Yurchuk

In "The History Manifesto" (Guldi & Armitage 2014) leading historians ruefully lamented "A spectre is haunting our time: the spectre of the short term" (p. 1). They saw the problem of short-termism as the main problem of humanities and vigorously called for the return of *longue durée*. Rather optimistically, they presented history as the sole academic discipline capable of speaking truth to powers and giving perspectives that exceed the lifetime of a generation. Likewise, several media publications have recently lamented the decline of interest in history as an academic discipline as faculties and departments all over the world fail to attract students who would choose history as their major (Alterman 2019 in *The New Yorker*; Brands & Gavin in *WarOnTheRocks.com* 2018).

These discussions among both historians and general public point out that the role of historians and role of history as an academic field is transforming. We look at this transformation as the change of habitus (Bourdieu 1990), a set of rules and norms governing a certain (professional) field and adopted by its participants as the necessary and successful way of behaviour. Habitus includes the entire range of practices, from types of discourse, vocabulary and rhetoric to the way an individual presents their body in a professional setting. The historical habitus, we argue, is changing in Eastern Europe, creating a new type of professional: a dynamic, media-savvy, blogger historian who is a public commentator and educator as much as a narrow expert. As a result of this work, a specific type of history—a "hashtag #history"—is produced.

This dynamic run hand in hand with a more obviously problematic development, especially relevant for Eastern Europe recently: the frequent use (and abuse) of history as a means to political ends (Assmann 20016, 2013; Erll 2008; Bell 2006; Blacker &

Etkind 2013; Jilge 2006; Nijakowski 2008; Portnov 2009, 2013). The practices of memory politics in the region are sadly all too often infested with nationalism and extreme instrumentalization, or even weaponization, of history. Even though a critique of it is frequently heard from academic circles, little is said about another aspect: the knowledge regime that connects mediated representations, historical narratives and short-term tactical political tasks in a powerful network of domination and control based on the power of media storytelling besides simply coercion. We call the process of the constant adoption of media logic by history writing the mediatization of history.

We therefore introduce mediatization of history as a concept that we propose for capturing a broad and growing range of interconnecting points, mutual saturations and influences between history and media. Clearly, the merger of history and media product (often light-brow or outright entertainment) is central to this knowledge regime. Yet can mediatization of history be not only the tool that drives this regime, but also the tool used to subvert it, or at least try and contain the most significant threats?

Taking our point of departure in memory studies and studies of uses of the past (Ankersmit 2001; Aronsson 2005; Assmann 2008; Karlsson & Zander 2014; Redin & Ruin 2016; Russen 1994, 2004), we lift the discussions on the uses of history and the role of media in memory to a new level of empirical and theoretical development aiming to explain how media logics influence history writing in Ukraine, specifically in a particular historians' project "Likbez". To show that mediatization of history is not unique only for Ukraine we put our discussion into a broader context of the countries of Eastern Europe, such as Belarus, Lithuania, or Poland. Due to the limits of this study, though, we cannot discuss the similar trends in history-writing in all the countries in detail.

History Meets Media: Theoretical Framework

We propose the theoretical framework for analyzing these cases based on mediatization theory that posits the increasing adoption of media logic outside media, particularly in academia (in our case, in historical scholarship). This changes the acceptable habitus in the field of academic history, creating a space for publicly visible, media-friendly historians that dramatically differ from both the rigid Soviet academic establishment and the flexible post-Soviet intellectuals. Their activity creates a body of "prosthetic memory" allowing to experience history through a range of media products. The example of the Eastern European countries that share significant parts of their histories allows to trace this process on a rich material of shared history (for example, in the differences between the mediatisatin-driven "prosthetic memories" of the Polish-Lithuanian Commonwealth in present day's Poland, Lithuania, Belarus and Ukraine). These conceptual approaches interlink in a way that allows for a complex and multi-perspective view of the process we describe as mediatization of history. Below, we are considering these elements of our theoretical approach in a more detailed way.

Mediatization has of late become one of the key concepts to interpret social transformations in the current media-saturated environment. In one of the most popular definitions (Hjarvard 2008), mediatization is explained as an increasing adoption of media logic by other spheres of life (such as politics, economy, education, arts, science etc). While in the classical Bourdieusian analysis the media are seen as dependent on other social fields (typically politics and business), the growing presence of media technologies and forms has led to intervention of the media field into other fields that have to adapt to its dominance and adopt patterns and types of behaviour ensuring public visibility and success. "In late modern societies, media have become co-constitutive for the articulation of various social fields in their present form: politics, economics, education, and so on" (Hepp, Hjarvard & Lundby 2015: 321).

Hjarvard (2008) regards mediatization as a merger between media and other social institutes whereby the media "have become an integral part of other institutions' operations" (106). Historically, the theory of mediatization is regarded as "consonant" with the so-called medium theory initiated by Harold Innis, Marshall McLuhan, and Joshua Meyrowitz (Ibid. 109) in its focus on an overall impact of the media but more empirical in its study of "specific mediatization processes among different groups" (ibid.: 110, following Krotz 2007).

Several approaches to mediatization have been outlined (Bolin 2014) but it is the institutional one we rely on most since it facilitates the analysis of interaction between different institutions and fields. From this perspective, mediatization is understood as "the process whereby society to an increasing degree is submitted to, or becomes dependent on, the media and their logic. This process is characterized by a duality in that the media have become integrated into the operations of other social institutions, while they also have acquired the status of social institutions in their own right. As a consequence, social interaction—within the respective institutions, between institutions, and in society at large—takes place via the media. The term 'media logic' refers to the institutional and technological modus operandi of the media, including the ways in which media distribute material and symbolic resources and operate with the help of formal and informal rules" (Hjarvard 2008: 113).

Following Hepp, Hjarvard & Lundby (2015) we emphasize the importance of being media-centred rather than media-centric, which "involves a holistic understanding of the various intersecting social forces at work at the same time as we allow ourselves to have a particular perspective and emphasis on the role of the media in these processes" (316). Couldry & Hepp (2013) speak about social-constructivist tradition: "The term 'mediatization' here is designed to capture both how the communicative construction of reality is manifested within certain media processes and how, in turn, specific features of certain media have a characterized 'consequence' for the overall process whereby sociocultural reality is constructed in and through communication" (196).

Even though not in the main scope of this article, we approach the national histories of Eastern Europe from the perspective of "shared" or "entangled history", which is also sometimes called "*transferts culturels*" and "*histoire croisée*". This approach characterises the interconnectedness of societies. The main argument is that no singular units of studies (neither nations, nor empires) can be the exclusive and exhaustive units and categories of historiography (Kasianov & Ther 2009). This approach allows to overcome methodological nationalism, on the one hand, and put the whole region into a broader global perspective. The fact that once shared history of people who belonged to different transnational configurations is now written and interpreted in shattered spaces constrained by the boundaries of national states makes media's role even more visible. Often, these are media that channel different historical narratives across the boundaries so that historians in different countries engage in dialogue or, indeed, polylogue (as it happened with the film *Wołyń* which will be discussed below). Approaching history of the region as entangled history helps us put a stronger focus on interferences, interdependencies, and entanglements, and highlight the multidirectional character of the transfers (Barkan, Cole & Struve 2007). We suggest, particularly for future studies of the problem of mediatization of historical scholarship in Eastern Europe, focusing on exactly such episodes of "shared history", such as the WWII controversies or the shared legacy of the Polish-Lithuanian Commonwealth. In our article, we are touching upon this approach, which must be extended and deepened further in future research.

Media representations of history are approached here through the concept of prosthetic memory. Introduced by Alison Landsberg, the concept "prosthetic memory" describes a new form of public cultural memory formed under the influence of media. Landsberg showed how films can produce historical knowledge. She argued that this knowledge has a potential to awaken social responsibility and political alliances that transcend the essentialism and ethnic particularism of contemporary identity politics (2004; 2015). Landsberg and other scholars interested in media representations of the past concentrated on the media side of the process of "telling history" in which the role of historians was overseen or just pre-supposed to be the same as that of media producers. In the same way, the scholars who are interested in "reception" end of the media representations of history are focused on the reception by the audiences while the historians are left out of the picture. We would like to put historians and their professional work into the light.

Habitus (Bourdieu 1990) is another important concept we are going to employ in relation to how the profession of historian is changing under the effects of media logic. Habitus includes a set of rules governing behaviour, work and competition in a specific social field, from abstract professional norms to body language. We are particularly alert to how the historical habitus is changing in Eastern Europe as a new type of professional historian, who is also a media persona, is increasingly normalized and popularized.

In Search of the Mediated Past: Survey of the Field

The mediatization of politics or cultural production is increasingly documented but there has been little to no research into how science and knowledge, particularly history as a discipline, transform and become mediatized. One can but mention Schäfer's (2014) account of the mediatization of science (dealing mostly with internal communication within the field) and Rawolle and Lingard (2014) pinpointing the mediatization of education. Hoskins (2014) traced how the mediatization of memory made the archive of memory more networked and hybridized, and Senie-Demeurisse's (2010) doctoral dissertation discusses the mediatization of history in France and shows that it results in vulgarized, oversimplified multimodal narratives. Other than these distant approaches, our article is a pioneering attempt to discuss the study of the mediatization of history, especially in Eastern Europe.

Different scholars have been emphasizing the role of communication in formation of memory since the very beginnings of memory studies as the field of research. The "father" of memory studies, the French sociologist Maurice Halbwachs, emphasized that communication forms collective memory. Without interpersonal communication, there cannot be any memory shared by the community (Halbwachs 1992). Jan Assmann in his studies of memory underlined the role of communication on personal and institutional levels as he introduced his theory of communicative and cultural memory (2008). The role of media in this communication was constantly accentuated. The most important works in this regard are Alison Landsberg's "Prosthetic memory" (2004) and Marianne Hirsch's "Family Frames: Photography, Narrative, and Postmemory" (1997) where the authors show how media can allow a mediated access to the past for those who never experienced it. Media narratives can even substitute history understood as the experienced past, as in case of prosthetic memory formed under the influence of films we watch and books we read. Digital technologies have intensified the relationship between memory and media even more. As Andrew Hoskins pointed out, "In 'post-scarcity culture' (Hoskins 2011, 2014, forthcoming) the flux of the digital ushers in a frenzy of seeing and imagining past and present; what was once scarce and relatively inaccessible from the past in the past is suddenly and inexorably visible, searchable, and mineable" (2014: 670).

The ever-intensifying "growth" of the past due to the media technologies influences the ways history is perceived in, and, as we argue, influences the way history is written nowadays. Aleida Assmann (2008: 98) suggested that "[t]he institutions of active memory preserve the *past as present* while the institutions of passive memory preserve the *past as past*" (original italics). For her, the institutions of active memory are those that enable the daily communication, and the institutions of passive memory are historians and archives which form the historical narratives. We follow Hoskins who suggested blurring of these boundaries between "passive" and "active" institutions (2014: 674) as media technologies enable these institutions to be both passive and active at the same time. As Hoskins noted, "the productions of memory and the data used to forge history are made in an ongoing present" (2014: 673). It is exactly this "ongoing present" we aim to approach so as to analyze which history is forged in the context of accessibility of "inexorably visible, searchable, and mineable" data and overwhelming presence of media.

A lot of research has been done on memory in this region. Scholars analyzed memory discussing it in the context of political discourses, international politics, literature, and monuments (Karlsson, Petersson, and Törnquist-Plewa 1998; Törnquist-Plewa 1992, 2001; Shevel 2016; Mälksöö 2010; Lewis 2018; Etkind and Blacker 2013; Zhurzhenko 2013; Portnov 2009, 2013; Yurchuk 2014). Scholars also have written on media and their role in cultural memory construction (Erll and Rigny 2008; Erll and Nunning 2008).

What is, though, largely overlooked by scholars working within memory studies is the relation between history-writing and media where the work of historians comes into the center. Barbie Zelizer (2008) noted how historians have extensively used journalist's works in history writings while journalism's work of memory is not sufficiently recognized, this in spite of journalists producing the stories which form perceptions of the past in a similar way as historians do. We propose that, in order to fill this gap, the relation between history and media should in principle be approached from two directions: from the vantage point of historians who are using media in writing history and from the vantage point of media professionals who extensively use the past in producing their media content.

Mediatization of History at Work: Evidence from Eastern Europe

The region of Eastern Europe has lately shown an especially strong re-actualization of the past in the present, most often driving and driven by political conflicts. Narratives of the past are constantly framed as matters of security (Mälksöö 2010; Horbyk 2013; Horbyk 2015; Budryte 2018; Yurchuk 2017a; Yurchuk 2017b; Törnquist-Plewa & Yurchuk 2017). In this regard, researchers even started to speak about "mnemonic security" (Mälsköö 2015). Historians and historical texts become key actors in the political conflicts. This can be observed, for instance, in the case of the feature film *Wołyń* (2016, dir. Wojciech Smarzowski, translated into English as "Hatred", the same title as original Smarzowski's screenplay) that encapsulated the argument between Poland and Ukraine about the 1943 massacres of civilians as the defining problem in relations between the countries (Motyka 2009; 2011). The film was banned in Ukraine while met with universal acclaim in Poland, and perceived on both sides as a historical account rather than a work of fiction (Yevropeiska Pravda 2016; Kozubal 2016). Leading historians took the position of cinema critics in this "film controversy" and participated in the discussions on the film on TV and in newspapers (Yekelchyk 2016; Khomenko 2016; Zychowicz 2016). This short example shows that historians at present take new roles in the society using media extensively for reaching the public. This influences the ways historians form their argumentation and even the way they write history. A media product, primarily designated to entertain or satisfy the audience's cultural needs, practically set the agenda for the public debate on a historical problem, and to a large degree constituted (or substituted) the historical narrative. This case has also demonstrated the blurring of boundaries between institutions of active and passive memory (Hoskins 2014: 674) as historians actively sought to enter the field of representation where the past is as projected as part of the present rather than reflecting on the past as simply past. This is a rather powerful example of how history is currently being mediatized by way of creating a "prosthetic history" of a shared—entangled, indeed—historical moment (as the histories of Ukraine and Poland are shared and entangled around the shattered space of Volhynia in 1943).

We argue that media play one of the leading roles in the process of reformation of the historians' profession. In Poland itself, history became a burgeoning ground for media businesses, evident in the thriving environment for glossy historical magazines and supplements (*Nasza Historia, Pamięć.pl, Historia Extra, Historia Polski, Fokus Historia, Newsweek Historia, Wyborcza's Ale Historia, Uważam Rze Historia* and others). The Ukrainian situation, at the same time, is characterised by the lack of a developed market for historical magazines (*Lokalna Istoriia* magazine founded in 2018 is perhaps the only exception), while at the same time popular historical books are increasingly in demand and historians engage *en masse* in educational activity on Facebook and in other social media and digital initiatives. With the beginning of the conflict with Russia, some Ukrainian historians gathered into the "Likbez. Historical Front" project and saw themselves as the actors in the war (a more detailed analysis of this case follows in the next section). In Ukraine, film market is dominated by the state commissions of historical films that often create controversies in the historical community, such as *Kruty 1918* causing a public scandal between leading historian Kyrylo Halushko and the filmmakers in February 2019 (Shurkhalo 2019; Slipchenko 2019; Sakovska 2019).

In Belarus, oppositional historians are often trying to engage in a similar educational activity on a much smaller scale, but the format they use is more akin to the Polish case, an illustrated magazine (*Naša Historyja*); the popular historical books are much more few and far between than in Ukraine. At the same time, historians often voice their perspectives in the more independent media in interviews or opinion pieces, and several public initiatives produce easily accessible YouTube videos popularizing Belarus-centric historical narratives. A small but active market of historical role-playing tours is burgeoning, typically inviting urban dwellers on trips to medieval or early modern castles and palaces with some performance and game activity. This history-related mediated activity (often by historians themselves) can be seen as one of the key factors preparing the ground for and leading to the rapid outburst of collective indignation and national consciousness during the 2020 Belarus civil unrest.

In Lithuania, professional historians are becoming ever more visible figures in the mass media and are ever more active in the social media, for instance, Facebook. As an example: a historian Aurimas Švedas has his own radio show dedicated to history. A number of shows dedicated to historical issues gain popularity in Television and Radio (for instance, the TV show called *Istorijos detektyvai*, The Historical Detectives, Lithuanian Television channel) and are attracting bigger and bigger audiences. Many controversies, however, exist in the field of historical cinema, which is currently focusing on many controversial topics (such as the collaboration of Lithuanians with the Nazi Regime and their role in the Holocaust, as in the film called *Purpurinis rūkas*, Purple Mist, by Raimundas Banionis).

Considering mediatization of history in Eastern Europe through the focal lens of shared history, we observe that one particular case that requires more attention (apart from the WWII entanglements) is the Polish-Lithuanian Commonwealth period, in which all four national histories were especially closely knit together in a single state formation. As prosthetic memory increasingly takes over the institutions of passive memory in claiming authority over representation of the past, Polish media product focuses on glorifying the era as the time of the unquestionable Polish domination and prosperity, from glossy representations in popular historical magazines to the films and other audio-visual product. Lithuanian prosthetic memory (evident in the recent cases of blurred active/passive institutions of memory, such newly reconstructed Palace of the Grand Dukes in Vilnius) seeks to delineate the Lithuanian state and its position in the Commonwealth while also glossing over the period as an unmistakable golden age of Lithuanian nation. Belarusian discourses, in both more oppositional narratives (such as presented in the *Naša Historyja* magazine) and to some extent the more official knowledge production of the state-controlled institutions of "passive memory", try to claim the era for Belarus and frame the Grand Duchy of Lithuania as the precursor of the modern Belarusian state formation, thus especially clashing with Lithuanian mediated representations of prosthetic memory. At the same time, Ukrainian active memory builds mainly on the Cossack myth as well as the Kyiv Rus' origins for modern Ukraine (cf. recent movies such as *Pekel'na khoruhva, Storozhova zastava, Zakhar Berkut* etc) and rather looks away from the shared history of the Polish-Lithuanian Commonwealth, thus presenting a deviation in the otherwise relatively high interest in the early modern period in the other countries; it is more evident in popular books as well as the work of the more traditionally academic passive memory institutions.

Through looking at key history writing and history representation projects we could see that quite often and to a large degree, historians in these countries act akin to journalists interested in explaining the present moment rather than the past. Here, Barbie Zelizer's argument about journalism doing history's work sounds especially relevant. The most resonant historical discussions happen in media (not in journals, academic books, etc.). To paraphrase, *Historikerstreit* in Eastern Europe ever more often takes the form of a Twitter storm, a comments war on Facebook, very often degrading into trolling and infamy of a "shitstorm". Rather than a rigid and scrupulously guarded academic field, history in these countries is a communicative free-for-all where professional historians, state actors, journalists, public figures and celebrities, activists,

NGOs, and ordinary people engage in often vitriolic debates on how exactly the present is determined by the past. Borrowing from Simon Cottle's (2006, 415) conceptualization of mediatized rituals, they engage in creating "those exceptional and performative media phenomena that serve to sustain and/or mobilize collective sentiments and solidarities on the basis of symbolization and a subjunctive orientation to what should or ought to be". What we observe can be interpreted, therefore, as a merger of media and academic history.

Likbez: Between historical fact-checking and a memory war

Formally, the LikBez[1] project was presented on 8 September 2014. But the prehistory of the project is quite long. In 2010 the Tempora publishing house released a book "Ukrainian nationalism: *Likbez* for the Russians, or Who and why invented Ukraine" written by the Ukrainian historian Kyrylo Halushko (Halushko 2014). The book was written in Russian, because its target group was the Russophone audience in Ukraine and abroad. In the preface the author emphasized:

> This book is *likbez* for the uninitiated, i.e. the review of the facts, mostly vivid ones, well-known for the experts but unfamiliar for the majority of Russian-speaking (and not only) citizens of Ukraine (and former Soviet Union), because these facts are 'forgotten', 'unpopular', 'unpleasant', 'politically incorrect' or 'unfavourable'. (Halushko 2014: 16)

First of all, the book aimed to fill the gap that existed in Ukraine between academic research and public history, where, since the collapse of the Soviet Union, the folk-history[2] genre had

---

1   Likbez is the Soviet neologism that emerged in 1919 as a syllabic abbreviation of two words, "elimination" and "illiteracy" (in Russian, "ликбез" for "ликвидация безграмотности"). The term Likbez refers to the state campaign of elimination of adult illiteracy initiated by the Bolsheviks and aimed at teaching all illiterate adults to read and write in a short period of time.
2   Folk-history is a term used in post-Soviet area to mark quasi-historical literature and concepts that became popular in 1990s and have remained popular with the mass public ever since.

been predominant (Volodikhin 1999; Makhun 2007). In that sense, the purpose of the project was not unlike a form of "historical fact-checking" tasked with creating an easily accessible alternative to conspiracy theories and "fake news" dealing with history. At the same time, it was likewise a reaction to the aggressive Russian public discourses that had become especially active since 2007 and presented Ukraine as failed and artificial state that had no profound historical background. Thus, history became a real battlefield.

During the Revolution of Dignity (November 2013 – February 2014), Russian media actively used historical themes to discredit pro-European activists of Euromaidan as well as the whole idea of Ukrainian statehood (Okara 2014; Gaufman 2017). It was the continuation of the "memory wars" between the Russian Federation and Ukraine launched after the Orange Revolution. Mediated narratives, including popular entertainment genres such as period blockbuster movies and TV series, and not the least computer games, signified the advent of mediatization of history in Russia. Since 2014, however, it was used to cover up and justify the Russian military intervention in Ukraine. One of the key moments in the Russian public discourse was the film *Project Ukraine*, released in 2015, where a group of Russian and Polish historians denounced the existence of Ukrainians as a separate nation as well as depicted the whole idea of Ukrainian statehood as sabotage inspired by the Austrian General Staff in order to weaken Russian Empire in World War I.

This was the background against which in 2014, after the annexation of the Crimea, a group of Ukrainian historians from different institutions joined forces in a volunteer project "Likbez: The Historical Front". The idea as well as the name of the project were suggested by Kyrylo Halushko who became the coordinator of the project. Firstly, all texts were published in Russian because the target group was constituted by Ukrainian Russophone citizens, primarily in Eastern and Southern Ukraine. The Likbez official site lists the aim of the project as "to inform everyone interested in the key debate 'what's Ukraine', 'what's the history of Ukraine' and 'what's territory of Ukraine'. We take major myths and stereotypes and give answers based on facts and documents. Our readers can make their own conclusions and use this information as they please. Our aim is not to impose some perspective but to offer information". Obviously, the logic of Likbez team was in synch with the logic of its coordinator as stated in his eponymous book. In such way, the experts tried to make knowledge available to a large audience as well as for journalists who deal with historical topics. Halushko ironically calls his team "the fighters against obscurantism" who debunk both Russian and Ukrainian patriotic myths. Since the project united historians with different ideological and political background, the credo of the Likbez team can be expressed as "we are not marching together". This ideological diversity becomes apparent in personal books and interviews of the members of Likbez.

During the seven years of the project's existence, Likbez managed to publish a 10-volume series "History Without Censorship" covering Ukrainian history from the ancient period till the end of the Second World War. This series has become a phenomenon on the Ukrainian non-fiction market as the amount of sold copies totals over 120,000 (something of a "bestseller" status for Ukraine, where the book market remains notoriously underdeveloped and where leading writers' novels often sell but several thousand copies). The other significant project was "The History of Ukrainian Army" that became a textbook for Ukrainian military institutions.

In 2018 the reach of the Likbez website reach was 21,000 per month. The average reader of Likbez is a Russophone aged 18 to 35. Top five countries whose citizens visited Likbez site in 2018 were Ukraine, Russia, the United States, Germany and Poland. The public interest towards the project culminated in 2015. Yet until now Likbez, together with the Istorychna Pravda web portal, has remained the most popular historical NGO and the only historical "mythbuster" in Ukraine.

Among other activities Likbez is carrying out are public lectures, historical reconstruction festivals, media publications, and even films—a vast range of media products catered to very different audiences. For example, a recent production saw Likbez cooperate with film professionals to release a documentary, including fictionalized scenes, on the Ukrainian State in 1918. Inspired by Kyrylo Halushko, who was deeply dissatisfied with the portrayal of history in *Kruty 1918*, the film has become one of the most large-scale media ventures of Likbez and marked the intervention of professional historians in media entertainment field. This case is a strong evidence for the fusion of "active" and "passive" institutions that create history (i.e., historians who do research and create the narrative, and the media that convey it to the broader audience), as postulated by Hoskins (2014). Undoubtedly this is also a key manifestation of history being mediatized.

When it comes to confronting the shared history of the Polish-Lithuanian Commonwealth, one interesting feature in comparison with the other three countries is the relatively lower interest to this theme. Ukrainian narratives of the era are presented in several book projects and website articles debunking certain historical myths (especially romanticized Ukrainian nationalist imagery); however, there seem to be other more pressing concerns of the twentieth century history to deal with.

In some projects, Likbez acts as a co-organizer. The last one was the common project with Internews Ukraine and Ukraine/World, where six Likbez team members contributed to the book "Re-vision of History: Russian Historical Propaganda and Ukraine". The book gives a brief historical refutation of the most popular historical myths created by Soviet/Russian propaganda.

Therefore, Likbez is one of the NGO actors influencing the formation of public historical narrative in Ukraine. This activity has a lot of support as well as many critics. The major debate is about propaganda. How should one estimate the role of academic community in the promotion of public history? Where is the boundary between professional standards and propaganda? What is the role of intellectuals and experts in the formation of political agenda in the period when history became the object of mediatization and instrumentalization?

In Ukraine there are two opposite visions. The first one belongs to the former director of Ukrainian Institute of National Memory and promoter of de-Communization policy Volodymyr Vyatrovych who believes that media messages start to form historical concepts, so professional community should be active and suggest its expert knowledge to the society (Vyatrovych 2016 in *Ukraine*

Crisis Media Center). On the other hand, the leading historian Georgiy Kasyanov is rather skeptical about the active position of historians in the public sphere as well as the necessity for the institutions and laws that regulate historical policy (Kasyanov 2019). Though he defends the ideal of "pure" academic history, one can still find a lot of his interviews and columns in the media. The media, especially social ones, became platform not only for public but also for academic debate. This is the epitome of the mediatization of history.

It should be noted in general that Likbez has generated significant reception not only among the broad public (which is understandable, given the deficiencies and weaknesses of the national book market and media debates in general) but also in the professional community. For example, Georgiy Kasyanov in a different text (2017: 257-258) revived the Soviet concept "the fighters of the ideological front" to describe his interpretation of the activity of Likbez. While analytical or theoretical sophistication of such labelling can be questioned, it does reflect the historian's conceptual toolkit and his emotional reaction to the project. In a different style and tone, Andriy Portnov (2014) reacted to the language Likbez was using finding it positivist and positional. At the same time, Iryna Vushko (2018) in her review explained it by the objective condition of Ukrainian historical scholarship marked by a turn towards the national narrative—de facto banned in the Soviet Union—since Ukraine became independent in 1991, when Western historians had already moved away from national narratives.

> The project brought together more than two dozen historians to write ten books in less than two years and sold thousands of copies of each volume. No other country, to my knowledge, has carried out such a major review of its history on a similar scale over such a short span of time. Designed to debunk historical myths and propaganda, it should mark a new phase in historical discussion in Ukraine as well as create new professional standards in Ukrainian historiography. By covering over one thousand years, it also demonstrates the contingency of history, drawing our attention to events and processes from the Middle Ages and even earlier eras that affect memory, historiography and politics today. (Vushko 2018: 123-124)

Given this, we should acknowledge that mediatization of history is an accomplished fact. In modern world the state has completely lost its monopoly on historical policy. Different actors have provided their own visions of the past. The main challenge for the community of historians is how to act in the media sphere and stay within the professional standard, especially when the history becomes politically instrumentalized as we can see in Eastern and Central Europe. The Likbez case is an interesting phenomenon that emerges on the brink of national mobilization and acting in the era of extreme mediatization of all spheres of everyday life. It is a telling case of blurring the boundaries between passive and active memory institutions as professional historians whose only task was ever supposed to consist of creating academic knowledge in an internal professional discussion begin to seek media presence and adopt media logic alongside their academic field's logic in order to influence the formation of prosthetic memory, of course, in the shape of mediated representation. And this reaches farther than the change of logic; the habitus is modified and the rules and norms of behavior accepted in the media field become domesticated by this emerging type of historians. The mediatized historian's habitus includes, apart from the traditional professional norms, more informal, personal and direct style of speech and writing, broad use of storytelling techniques, soundbite-style rhetorical devices, social media management, cherishing of a certain persona and style (often more informal and/or more aimed at attracting the audience) when it comes to mere looks. Even though young women remain on lower positions in the hierarchy of Ukrainian academy, and often a minority in working teams and other formal and informal groups, they are uniquely positioned to benefit from this situation. Epistemologically, this new habitus may allow sacrificing superficial semblance of balance for the sake of presenting more emphatically what is accepted as historical knowledge when the media logic of storytelling demands it. What it also requires, rather self-evidently, is a recourse to technical resources pertaining to filming, editing, layout, design and other media production skills.

When this is contrasted with evidence from other fields, the case of Likbez also seems to fall within the range of similar grassroot, do-it-yourself "knowledge institutions" that popped up in Ukraine since 2014 to compensate for the deficiencies of the Ukrainian state at a critical moment, oftentimes taking advantage of modern technology and the changing media and communication trends. Just as the fact-checking resource StopFake organized by journalists and teachers of journalism has become a leading fact-checker in Eastern Europe and proved effective at debunking propaganda in a hybrid war (Horbyk 2015), or Ukrainian Crisis Media Centre—a communication professional's initiative—took a central position in media relations and nation branding (Bolin & Ståhlberg 2016), Likbez serves a similar function: it helps activist professionals and intellectuals cover the gaps in Ukraine's ineffective state policies and more official passive knowledge institutions. The media apparatus is becoming a vital element to this activity and harnesses the potential of mediatization of history to mitigate the flaws and weaknesses of the power/knowledge apparatus in the Ukrainian context.

Conclusion: Writing History for the Mediatized Age

"The glut of media is also a glut of memory: past is everywhere" wrote Andrew Hoskins (2014: 662) to emphasize the close link between media and perception of the past. This is especially perceptible in Eastern Europe, where so much public debate, from media polemic to trolling on Facebook, is rooted in historical problematic. As we have demonstrated, the countries in the region, including Belarus, Lithuania, Poland, Russia, and Ukraine, have all witnessed an increasing transfusion between fields of academic history and media/entertainment. Not only the media are intervening in history, setting the agenda and creating prosthetic memory artefacts, but also historians are actively pursuing the path of being visible, vocal and viral in both traditional and social media. *Historikerstreit* is happening on Facebook and in professional web forums as much as in peer-reviewed journals, sometimes even more intensively in the new and social media. Ever more often historians also create media product, ranging from popular articles for glossy magazines to popular books to YouTube videos to full-length films. The very habitus of historian is changed; no longer confined to a narrow problem or a cabinet hermit, the present-day historian in Eastern Europe—now more often than previously female—is in ever more cases a social media persona, skillful at using new media, and maintains a permanent media visibility.

Such situation creates opportunities for both hegemonic manipulation of history and counter-efforts to it. As demonstrated in the article, mediatized history opens up for memory wars around contested issues of shared, entangled histories, and suits well to propagating nationalist versions of those histories. Yet mediatization of history also creates space for counterefforts striving to set the historical record right and debunk myths and conspiracy theories wherever it is possible. It is only logical that the media, where much manipulation takes place, becomes also a space contested by historians willing to mitigate the consequences of the "use and abuse of history for life", to use the title of the famous essay by Nietzsche. Perhaps, mediatization of history is as much of a blessing as it is a curse—not unlike Platonian "pharmakon" in Derrida's reading; both poison and medicine for the region shattered by mutual attacks on the shared history. Whether this proposition is true remains to be seen, and most certainly invites further research.

Bibliography

Alterman, Eric. (2019). The Decline in Historical Thinking. *The New Yorker*, February 4, https://www.newyorker.com/news/news-desk/the-decline-of-historical-thinking (accessed February 4, 2019).

Ankersmit, Frank. (2001). The Postmodernist 'Privatization' of the Past. In Ankersmit F.R. *Historical Representation*. Stanford: Stanford University Press, 149–175.

Aronsson, Peter. (2005). *Historiebruk : att använda det förflutna*. Lund, Studentlitteratur.

Assmann, Aleida. (2006). *Der lange Schatten der Vergangenheit, Erinnerungskultur und Geschichtspolitik*. Munich: C.H. Beck.

Assmann, Aleida. (2013). "Europe's Divided Memory." In *Memory and Theory in Eastern Europe*, Uilleam Blacker, Alexander Etkind and Julie Fedor (eds.). Palgrave Studies in Cultural and Intellectual History. New York: Palgrave Macmillan, 25–42.

Assmann, Jan. (2008). Communicative and Cultural Memory. In *Media and Cultural Memory: an International and Interdisciplinary Handbook*, Astrid Erll and Ansgar Nunning (eds.), Berlin: Walter de Gruyter, 109–118.

Astrov, Alexander. (2012). The 'Politics of History' as a Case of Foreign-Policy Making. In *The Convolutions of Historical Politics*, Alexei Miller and Maria Lipman (eds.). Budapest, New York: CEU Press, 117–140.

Barkan, Elazar, Elizabeth A. Cole and Kai Struve (eds.) (2007). *Shared History, Divided Memory: Jews and Others in Soviet-Occupied Poland, 1939–1941*. Leipzig: Leipziger Universitätsverlag.

Bell, Duncan (ed.) (2006). *Memory, Trauma and World Politics: Reflections on the Relationship between Past and Present*. New York: Palgrave Macmillan.

Blacker, Uilleam and Alexander Etkind (2013). Introduction. In *Memory and Theory in Eastern Europe*, Uilleam Blacker, Alexander Etkind and Julie Fedor (eds.). Palgrave Studies in Cultural and Intellectual History. New York: Palgrave Macmillan, 1–24.

Brands, Hal and Gavin, Francis J. (2018). The Historical Profession is Committing Slow-motion Suicide. *War on the Rocks*, December 10, https://warontherocks.com/2018/12/the-historical-profession-is-committing-slow-motion-suicide/?fbclid=IwAR1oHpkwNNcYevZF8HKVmYxMNfpSgf2u1K9FLPYyE283tcyV02rEsvKJWIA (accessed October 10, 2019).

Bolin, Göran (2014). Institution, technology, world: relationships between the media, culture, and society. In *Mediatization of Communication*, Knut Lundby (ed). Berlin: De Gruyter Mouton, 175–198.

Bolin, Göran, & Ståhlberg, Per. (2015). Mediating the nation-state: Agency and the media in nation-branding campaigns. *International Journal of Communication*, 9(19).

Bourdieu, Pierre. (1990). *The Logic of Practice*. New York: Polity Press.

Budryte, Dovile. (2018). Memory, War, and Mnemonical. In *Security: A Comparison of Lithuania and Ukraine, in Crisis and Post-Cold War Global Politics: Ukraine in a Comparative Perspective*, Resende E. et al. (eds). Palgrave, 155–177.

Couldry, Nick & Andreas Hepp. (2013). Conceptualizing mediatization: Contexts, traditions, arguments. *Communication Theory* (23): 191–202.

Cottle, Simon. (2006). Mediatized rituals: beyond manufacturing consent. *Media, Culture and Society* 28 (3):411–432.

Erll, Astrid and Ann Rigney (eds.) (2009). *Mediation, Remediation, and the Dynamics of Cultural Memory*. Berlin, Boston: De Gruyter.

Erll, Astrid and Ansgar Nunning (eds.) (2008). *Media and Cultural Memory: an International and Interdisciplinary Handbook*. Berlin, DEU: Walter de Gruyter.

Gaufman, Elizaveta. (2015). Memory, media, and securitization: Russian media framing of the Ukrainian crisis. *Journal of Soviet and Post-Soviet Politics and Society. Special Issue: Russian Media and the War in Ukraine* 1(1):141–173.

Halbwachs, Maurice. (1992). *On Collective Memory*, Chicago, The University of Chicago Press, 1992.

Halushko, Kirill. (2010). *Ukrainskii natsionalism: likbez dlya russkikh, ili kto I zachem pridumal Ukrainu?* [From Rus.: Ukrainian natiolalism: likbez for the Russians or who and why invented Ukraine] Kyiv: Tempora.

Hepp, Andreas, Stig Hjarvard & Knut Lundby. (2015). Mediatization: theorizing the interplay between media, culture and society. *Media, Culture and Society* 37(2): 314–324.

Hirsch, Marianne. (1997). *Family Frames: Photography, Narrative, and Postmemory*. Harvard University Press.

Hirsch, Marianne. (2010). *Ghosts of Home: The Afterlife of Czernowitz in Jewish Memory*, co-written with Leo Spitzer. University of California Press, 2010.

Hirsch, Marianne. (2012). *The Generation of Postmemory: Writing and Visual Culture After the Holocaust*. Columbia University Press.

Hjarvard, Stig. (2008). The mediatization of society: A theory of the media as agents of social and cultural change. *Nordicom Review* 29(2): 105–134.

Horbyk, Roman. (2013). Paper empires. Orientalism in the mediated portrayals of India and Ukraine: A case study of British and Russian Press. *East/West: The Scholarly Journal for History and Culture* 16: 203–222.

Horbyk, Roman. (2015). Little Patriotic War: Nationalist Narratives in the Russian Media Coverage of the Ukraine-Russia Crisis. *Asian Politics & Policy* 7(3): 505–511.

Hoskins, Andrew. (2014). The mediatization of memory. Knut Lundby (ed). *Mediatization of Communication*. Berlin: De Gruyter Mouton, 661–680.

Jilge, Wilfried. (2006). The Politics of History and the Second World War in Post-Communist Ukraine. In *Gespaltene Geschichtskulturen? Zweiter Weltkrieg und kollektive Erinnerungskulturen in der Ukraine*, Wilfried Jilge und Stefan Troebst (eds.), Jahrbücher für Geschichte Osteuropas 54, H. 1, Stuttgart, 50–81.

Karlsson, K.-G., Petersson, B. & Törnquist-Plewa, B. (1998). *Collective Identities in an Era of Transformations. Analysing Developments in East and Central Europe and the Former Soviet Union*. Lund University Press.

Karlsson, Klas-Göran and Zander, Ulf. (2014). *Historien är närvarande : historiedidaktik som teori och tillämpning*, Studentlitteratur AB.

Kasianov, Georgiy and Philipp Ther (eds.) (2009). *A Laboratory of Transnational History: Ukraine and Recent Ukrainian Historiography*. Budapest: Central European University Press, 2009.

Kasyanov, Georgiy (2017). Istoryky ta istorychna polityka [From Ukr.: Historians and historical policy]. In *Istoiohrafichni ta dzhereloznavchi problemy istoriyi Ukrayiny: Istoryk na zlamakh istorii: dosvid perezhyvannya*, 243–261.

Kasianov, Georgiy. (2019). Ukraine prepares to grasp the nettle of its history politics — again. *Carnegie Moscow Center*, October 7, https://carnegie.ru/commentary/80001 (accessed October 7, 2019)

Khomenko, Sviatoslav. (2016). 'Volyn' polskyi film pro "henocyd" ['Volyn' polish movie about "genocide"]. *BBC Ukraine*, October 8, https://www.bbc.com/ukrainian/society/2016/10/161008_wolyn_volynia_film_sx_it (accessed November 18, 2019)

Kozubal, Marek. (2016). Recenzja filmu "Wołyń" Wojciecha Smarzowskiego [From Pol.: Review on Smarzhevskyi movie "Volyn"]. *Rzeczpospolita*, September 23, https://www.rp.pl/Gdynia-2016-/160929675-Recenzja-filmu-Wolyn-Wojciecha-Smarzowskiego.html (accessed November 18, 2019).

Krotz, Friedrich. (2007). *Mediatisierung: Fallstudien zum Wandel von Kommunikation*. Wiesbaden: VS Verlag für Sozialwissenschaften.

Landsberg, Alison. (2004). *Prosthetic Memory: The Transformation of American Remembrance in the Age of Mass Culture*, Columbia University Press.

Landsberg, Alison. (2015a). *Engaging the Past: Mass Culture and the Production of Historical Knowledge*, Columbia University Press.

Landsberg, Alison. (2015b). 'This isn't usual, Mr. Pendleton, this is history' Spielberg's Lincoln and the production of historical knowledge. *Rethinking History* 19(3): 482–492.

Lewis, Simon M. (2018). *Belarus - Alternative Visions: Nation, Memory and Cosmopolitanism*, London: Routledge.

Makhun, Serhii. (2007). Ukrainogenezis v silkakh mifotvorchestva [From Rus.: Ukrainian genesis in the net of mythmaking]. *Zerkalo nedeli*, March 3–7, https://web.archive.org/web/20071209182327/http://www.zn.ua/3000/3150/55989/ (September 5, 2019).

Motyka, Grzegorz and Dariusz Libionka. (2002). *Antypolska Akcja OUN-UPA 1943-1944. Fakty i interpretacj* [From Pol.: Anti-Polish Action of OUN-UPA 1943-1944. Facts and interpretation]. Warszawa: Wyd. IPN.

Motyka, Grzegorz. (2011). *Od rzezi wołyńskiej do akcji Wisła* [From Pol.: From Volyn massacre to action Vistula] Kraków: Wyd. Literackie.

Nijakowski, Lech M. (2008). *Polska polityka pamięci. Esej socjologiczny* [From Pol.: Polish memory politics. Sociological essey]. Warszawa: Wydawnictwa Akademickie i Profesjonalne.

Mälksöö, Maria. (2010). *The politics of becoming European: A study of Polish and Baltic post-cold war security imaginaries*, Routledge.

Mälksöö, Maria. (2015). 'Memory Must Be Defended': Beyond the Politics of Mnemonical Security. *Security Dialogue*, 221-237.

Okara, Andrey. (2014). Novorosiya... chto za zemlya? [Fron Rus.: Novorosiya... what is the region?]. *Radio Svoboda*, 26 April, http://www.svoboda.org/content/article/25363270.html (accessed 15 September, 2019).

Portnov, Andriy. (2009). Velyka Vitchyzniana viina v politykach pamiati Bilorusi, Moldovy ta Ukraiiny: kil'ka porivnial'nych sposterezhen [From Ukr.: Great Patriotic war in memory politics of Belarus, Moldova, Ukraine: some comparative observations]. *Ukraiina Moderna*, 15(4): 206-218.

Portnov, Andriy. (2013). Memory Wars in Post-Soviet Ukraine (1991-2010). In *Memory and Theory in Eastern Europe*. Uilleam Blacker, Alexander Etkind and Julie Fedor (eds). Palgrave Studies in Cultural and Intellectual History. Houndmills: Palgrave Macmillan, 233-254.

Portnov, Andriy. (2014). Pro proekt LikBez u videoblozi Andriya Portnova [About the project LikBez in video-blog of Andrey Portnov]. *Likbez*, October 28, http://likbez.org.ua/ua/o-proekte-likbez-v-videoblog e-andreya-portnova.html (accessed September 15, 2019).

Rawolle, Shaun and Bob Lingard. (2014). Mediatization and education: a sociological account. In *Mediatization of Communication*, Knut Lundby (ed). Berlin: De Gruyter Mouton, 595-616.

Redin, Johan and Ruin, Hans. (2016). *Mellan minne och glömska: studier i det kulturella minnets*, Bokförlaget Daidalos.

Schäfer, Mike S. (2014). The media in the labs, and the labs in the media: what we know about the mediatization of science. In: *Mediatization of Communication*, Knut Lundby (ed). Berlin: De Gruyter Mouton, 571-594.

Semesyuk, Ivan. (2019). «Dolenosnyi 1918»: v Kyevi vidbudetsya prem'trnyi pokaz serialu, znyatoho istorykamy ["Crucial 1918": there will be first night of serial shot by historians]. *Hromadske radio*, https://hromadske.radio/podcasts/hromadska-hvylya/dolenosny y-1918-v-kyyevi-vidbudetsya-prem-yernyy-pokaz-serialu-znyatogo -istorykamy (accessed 18 December 2019).

Senie-Demeurisse, Josiane (2010). *Médiatisation de l'histoire: contribution à la définition du concept de document*. Toulouse: Université Toulouse 2.

Sakovska, Anastasiia. (2019). Kino, iake ne zmohlo: desyat' vidhukiv pro film "Kruty" [From Ukr.: The movie that have failed: ten opinion about "Kruty" movie]. *Radio Svoboda*, February 17, https://www.rad iosvoboda.org/a/vidguky-pro-film-kruty-1918/29775104.html (accessed September 18, 2019)

Shevel, Oksana (2016). The Battle for Historical Memory in Postrevolutionary Ukraine. *Current History* 115(783): 258–263.

Shurkhalo, Dmytro (2019). Film "Kruty 1918": shcho lyshylosia vid realnyck podii? [From Ukr.: 'Kruty 1918' movie: what remains from real events?]. *Radio Svoboda*, February 17, https://www.radiosvoboda. org/a/29773978.html (accessed October 15, 2019).

Slipchenko, Kateryna (2019). Film "Kruty 1918" zibrav u prokat 3,5 mln hryven: Shcho pereshkodylo iomu staty liderom? [From Ukr.: 'Kruty 1918' movie gathered 3.5 million hryvnas in distribution: what prevented it from become a leader?]. *Zaxid.Net*, February 13, https://zax id.net/film_kruti_2018_zibrav_u_prokati_35_mln_griven_n1475610 (accessed October 20, 2019).

Törnquist-Plewa, Barbara. (1992). *The Wheel of Polish Fortune: Myths in Polish Collective Consciousness during the First Years of Solidarity*, Lund Slavonic Monographs.

Törnquist-Plewa, Barbara. (2001). *Vitryssland: Språk och nationalism i ett kulturellt gränsland*. Studentlitteratur AB.

Törnquist-Plewa, Barbara and Yurchuk, Yuliya. (2017). Memory Politics in Contemporary Ukraine. Reflections from the post-colonial perspective. *Memory Studies Journal*, 12(6): 1–22.

Volodikhin, Dmitrii. (1999). 'Fenomem folk-khistori' [From Rus.: Phenomenon folk-history]. *Nauchno-prosvetitelskyi zhurnal Skepsis*, n.d., http:// scepsis.net/library/id_148.html (accessed September 18, 2019).

Vushko, Iryna. (2018). Historians at War: History, Politics and Memory in Ukraine. *Contemporary European History* 27(1): 112–124.

V'yatrovych, Volodymyr. (2016). Lektsiya Vladimira Vyatrovicha "Tabloidizatsiya istorii: rol' SMI v osveshchenii polsko-ukrainskoy voyny 1942–1947 hodov" [From Rus.: Vladimir V'yatrovich lection "Tabloid history: how media highlights Polish-Ukrainina war on Volyn in 1972–1947"]. *Ukraine crisis media center*, July 12, http://uacrisis.org/ru/45310-lektsiya-volodymyra-v-yatrovycha (accessed August 15, 2019).

Yekelchyk, Serhy (2016). Ukrainskyi istoryk pro film Volyn' [From Ukr.: Ukrainian historian about "Volyn" movue]. *Hromadske TV*, October 6, https://www.youtube.com/watch?v=c3hqan-N4jw (accessed November 12, 2019).

Yermoleko, Volodymyr, Hrytsak, Yaroslav (eds.) (2019). *Re-Vision of history. Russian historical propaganda and Ukraine*, Kyiv: K.I.S.

Yevropeiska Pravda. (2016). Skandalnyi film "Volyn'" pokazhut v Ukraini, ale v inshi terminy [Scandal movie 'Volyn' will show in Ukraine but in another time]. *Yevropeiska Pravda*, October 18, https://www.eurointegration.com.ua/news/2016/10/18/7056035/ (accessed November 19, 2019)

YouTube. (2015). *Proekt Ukraina*. Film Andreya Medvedeva, April 9, https://www.youtube.com/watch?v=bvpAeGeqd4Q&t=746s (accessed October 15, 2019).

Yurchuk, Yuliya. (2017a). Global Symbols Local Meanings: The "Day of Victory" after Euromaidan. In *Transnational Ukraine? Networks and Ties that Influence contemporary Ukraine*, Timm Beichelt and Susann Worschech (eds). Stuttgart: ibidem, 66–89.

Yurchuk, Yuliya. (2017b). Reclaiming the Past, Confronting the Past: OUN-UPA Memory Politics and Nation-Building in Ukraine (1991-2016). *War and Memory in Russia, Ukraine, and Belarus*, Julie Fedor, Markku Kangaspuro, Jussi Lassila, and Tatiana Zhurzhenko (eds.), Palgrave Macmillan Memory Studies.

Yurchuk Yuliya. (2017c). "Writing history in the times of trouble. Popular history projects in Ukraine since 2014: a response to propaganda or a tool in information wars? The case of Likbez historians' project", presented at ASN, New York, May 4–6.

Zhurzhenko, Tatiana. (2013). Memory Wars and Reconciliation in the Ukrainian-Polish Borderlands: Geopolitics of Memory from a Local Perspective. In *Memory and Politics in Central and Eastern Europe: Memory Games*, Georges Mink and Laure Neumayer (eds.). New York: Palgrave Macmillan, 173–192.

Zychowych, Piotr. (2016). Wołyń - film prawdziwy [Volyn is a real movie]. *Do Rzeczy*, September 29, https://dorzeczy.pl/11242/Wolyn-film-prawdziwy.html (accessed November 19, 2019).

II
Post-Soviet Sovereigntism in Comparative Perspective

II

6 The Rise of Precarious States
A Shadow Side of Sovereignity Loss

Oleksandr Fisun and Nataliya Vinnykova

The early 21st century had been marked by many upheavals, e.g. the terrorist attacks of September 11, 2001, the global economic crisis of 2008, Arab Spring 2011, the COVID-19 coronavirus pandemic, that have revealed the institutional weakness and vulnerability of the national and international regulatory mechanisms in the setting of ongoing globalization. In recent years, many states have faced a legitimacy crisis, which is expressed in frequent changes of government, the deconstruction of representative systems, the volatility of electoral preferences and large-scale protest movements. The apparent trend in the exercise of state sovereignty is toward a changing role for the national government. This is occurring because of the multiplicity of actors participating in policymaking, the forms of interaction between them, and the move from hierarchically organized governance to its deverticalization in the interstices of the network.

State power is fragmented among many actors involved in policymaking and influencing decision-making at every level of governance: international structures and supranational entities with varying degrees of integration and institutionalization, global clubs, multinational companies and foundations, non-governmental organizations (NGOs). The heterogeneity of governance is exacerbated by the increase in the number of public actors seeking recourse to international organizations and institutions to address domestic political issues. Although political governance, by definition, is run by public authorities and aims to ensure the "public good," its implementation more often takes place through hybrid channels of private and public structures. Not all of them are publicly accountable. This area of policy-making is often too vague for recognizing the true power-holders, influencers and beneficiaries. Overwhelming impact on governance on the part of informal entities, e.g. clans, oligarchic networks, drug cartels, seem an explicative feature of the undemocratic regimes. Yet, the influence of transnational non-public bodies and informal networks on state governance increases with the enhancing globalization. Developed democracies cannot avoid the growing pressure of informal entities (both national and transnational ones) on statehood either.

The conceptual revision of the classical definition of sovereignty as "complete power to govern a country" (Oxford Learner's Dictionaries, 2021) is built on the fundamental question: Does "the complete power" can be achieved over any political entity in the age of globalization?

The scholar literature stresses the functional role of the state as a provider of services to ensure the welfare of citizens (Fisun & Vinnykova 2021, Miller 2020, Crouch 2017, Pabst 2010). For instance, Caleb Miller's (2020) argues that it is Hobbes's interpretation of sovereignty as a form of domination through the dichotomy of "subject" and "servant" models that reflects modern trends in governance. While the Hobbesian subject has a conscious attitude toward sovereignty as shared and mediated by the community and guaranteed by the agreement, the servant perceives sovereignty as an accidental phenomenon, unmediated and guaranteed by violence.

Miller (2020) underlines that in contrast to the ideal of citizens in a democracy, namely, that political practices meet or at least approach democratic criteria, citizens today recognize the impossibility of popular sovereignty and political equality. It is self-perception through the service format (the servant model) of building relations with institutions of power that makes the political involvement of citizens more productive and reduces the stressful consequences for providing state sovereignty.

Adrian Pabst points out that "late-modern democracy is no longer predominantly defined on the basis of territoriality, nationhood, or the self-determination of people composed of persons and citizens" (Pabst 2010: 59). Thus the main purpose of modern democracy is to regulate risks and maximize individual choice and the economic opportunities of consumers as regards material goods (ibid.).

In this chapter we lay bare the factors that determine the de-etatization of the sovereignty of modern states, focusing on informal ones. We interpret the concept of sovereignty in terms of legitimacy. Legitimacy as one of the main factors guaranteeing the full realization of sovereignty is at the heart of the matter. In the context of deterritorialization of the concept of state sovereignty and the transformation of political governance, the legitimacy of sources of power becomes crucial for understanding the growing social frustrations in different countries as a global trend in the last twenty years. Since the sovereignty of the state is based on the exercise of power and decision-making, with results that are binding on all members of society, according to rules (normative aspect) that determine who can make political decisions, when, and in what order, and also depends on the commitment of those affected (perceptual aspect), the top-down rules and bottom-up social commitment together are important for legitimating sovereignty, as they serve to guarantee the stability of the political system.

Taking into account the above, our study is based on the following assumptions. First, we assume that the trend of widespread protest activity in the world in the last decade can be attributed to the delegitimization of institutions of state power in the eyes of citizens and the simultaneous lack of alternative institutionalized channels for representing their interests. The second assumption is that the key factor in the de-etatization of the sovereignty of modern states is the actual policy-making in multi-actors' networks, which mostly do not have channels of public control. Under shortage of developed democracy pillars and statehood experience this may have a destructive effect on the stability of political system, and even on the integrity of the territory, thus undermining the primer function of sovereignty. This is particularly apparent in some post-Soviet states that have undergone through striking political crisis and riddance of control of the part of the territory. The case of Ukraine can serve as an illustration of sovereignty de-etatization due to overwhelming interference of non-state actors (both domestics and transnational ones) in government processes and policy-making. The Chapter consists of three parts. The first part introduces recent conceptual reflections on contemporary trends in state functioning and rising protest activism worldwide and provides some empirical justification of the issues. The second part discusses the challenges to the legitimacy of state sovereignty, caused by interfere of non-state actors in the governance as well as informal interlinks between public officials and private entities. In the last section we present the case of Ukraine as an exemplification of the loss of sovereignty in functional and territorial domains due to mentioned factors.

Political Disengagement as the Background for Sovereignty De-Etatization

One of the more obvious world trends in sociopolitical development is the surge of protest activity, political dissent, and other public expressions of dissatisfaction with the actions of governments and representative systems in established democracies and countries undergoing regime transformation (Brannen, Haig, & Schmidt 2020). Indeed, mass antigovernment protests rose annually by an average of 11.5% from 2009 to 2019 in all regions of the world, with the highest concentration of activity in the Middle East (16.5%) and the fastest growth rate in sub-Saharan Africa (Brannen, Haig, & Schmidt 2020:4). Even under severe quarantine restrictions in 2020 one can witnessed a lot of antigovernment protests in various countries.

Despite the variety of procedural mechanisms for public participation in policymaking, people in different countries with distinguished political modes more and more often take to the streets to declare their needs and interests. Does that mean that modern states can no longer provide the appropriate representation of public interest? The question is of interest insofar as representation is crucial for modern states. As Frank Ankersmit (2002: 115) has written,

> Without representation there is no represented — and without political representation there is no nation as a truly political entity.

Political representation has always been a complex mechanism, as relations between citizens and their representatives are mediated by political parties, interest groups, and corporate organizations. In addition, the common interest is based on the social identity of the representatives and those they represent. However, modern societies are becoming increasingly diverse in economic, cultural, religious, and gender aspects. That makes it a very complex task to provide means of representation that would satisfy the variety of public interests. Simultaneously, the political representation, embodied in the activities of parties, political movements, and parliamentary, is gradually losing its legitimacy as a mediator between government and society, as evidenced by the widespread decline in membership in political parties and confidence in political institutions.

Citizens' attitudes toward traditional party policy are reflected in the quantitative indicators of party membership and confidence to them.

According to the World Values Survey Wave 7 (first part) covering 48 countries only 14% of respondents are members of political parties, and of these, only 5% are active members, while 84.8% declare no party affiliation at all (Haerpfer et al. 2020: 215) and just 28.7% have confidence in political parties (Ibid: 178).

Additional evidence of delegitimization tendencies in established systems of representation comes from the decline in confidence in national parliaments. Overall, only 36.4% of citizens in the world trust national parliaments (Haerpfer et al. 2020: 179), and the proportion of those who do not trust parliaments increased from 49.2% in 2000 to 60% in 2020 (Inglehart et al. 2018: 167; Haerpfer et al. 2020: 179). Along with falling confidence in governments — more than half of citizens, 51.3%, do not trust national governments (Ibid: 177) — such figures highlight the inability of state policies and guidelines to satisfy social needs and public demands.

The de-affiliation from political parties is associated not only with a decline in trust in them and in parliaments but also with a change in the substantive component of representation, namely, the transformation of the social structure and a shift in the "traditional" electorate from left and center parties to the extremes of the ideological spectrum.

Structural transformations in modern societies occur mostly under labor market changes and migration flows. The IT sector and robotics, online systems, and multinational production have significantly changed the nature of professional employment over the last quarter of a century. The increasing use of robots in manufacturing and the introduction of electronic services have displaced blue-collar workers from the labor market. According to a report by the analytical group Oxford Economics, technological changes in production and services will lead to the loss of more than 20 million jobs by 2030 (Cone & Lambert 2019).

This trend casts into sharp relief the problem of marginalization of large professional groups related to the manufacturing sector and certain industries. At the same time, the ranks of such marginalized groups are replenished by graduates of higher education institutions who cannot find employment but have to make payments on loans for their education and by young people who cannot afford higher education at all. These groups—workers who are unskilled for the labor market, young educated people who cannot find jobs, migrants and refugees from conflict zones—form a new large social stratum that is neither tied to certain labor groups nor has a clear political identification. This stratum is Guy Standing (2011) conceptualized as a precariat.

The attitude of the precariat to production is defined as partial participation in the labor process in combination with the so-called "work for job," a term that refers to the constantly rising amount of unpaid activities workers must carry out in order not to lose a job. The precariat is often deprived of certain civil rights that other members of society have. However, the precariat is not yet a class *for itself*; so far it is a class *in itself*, but it is dangerous in terms of conflict because of the features that Standing identified and summed up as the "4As." Precariousness is characterized by constant *anxiety* due to uncertainty; by *alienation*, in the sense that workers do not do what they want and do a lot of things they do not want to do; by *anomie*, a despair caused by a lack of way out of a situation; and by *anger* as a result of the previous three points (Standing 2011: 9–24).

Unlike the proletariat, the industrial working class, whose existence formed the basis of the social democratic policy of the 20th century, the precariat does not have a definite political platform owing to its eclectic composition. Without seeing the "old" political parties and programs as reflecting its interests, the precariat becomes an object of manipulation by radical political forces. Radical populist parties have the greatest electoral influence in matters of domestic policy, upholding the principle of "national preferences" for employment and social security. By mobilizing the electorate against labor immigration, they are in favor of restricting the supply of labor in the labor market. Another reason for alienation is the weakening of traditional loyalty to political forces that previously acted as representatives of the interests of the working class. Increased support for radical parties can be seen as an expression of protest and frustration in centrist parties. Citizens show their dissatisfaction with the political elite by choosing parties that were outsiders to the political arena for decades.

Modern systems of political representation also face the pressure of participatory practices that utilize online technologies, through which citizens can independently represent their interests in policymaking. Citizens are less interested in unilateral participation in traditional political activities, such as maintaining formal party membership. As political organizations are unable effectively to represent the existing diversity of interests and values, online activities take over and complement the activities of public organizations and social movements. But are such technology-based activities able to fill the functional gaps in representation left by party activities?

Nowadays, the phenomenon that highlights the above-mentioned tendencies in public representation and the decline of trust in governmental bodies is the lightning rise of social movements worldwide, from small, local protests to protests of national or even global scale. The most vivid examples of such movements in recent decades include Occupy Wall Street, the "Arab Spring" uprisings, Ukrainian Maidans, the Indignados, Fridays for Future (a youth climate movement), the Umbrella Movement, the Yellow Vests, and Black Lives Matter. These social uprisings can be considered separate from the institutional pillars of state functioning, particularly in the state's mission of moderating plurality of public interests.

The diversity and multiplicity of non-governmental-sector organizations are growing exponentially, in particular in the scale of activity and influence on policymaking processes at all levels of government, from local to global. Surveys show that social movements and NGOs generally enjoy more trust among citizens than parties do. According to the Edelman Barometer, the level of trust in NGOs in 28 countries in the decade from 2010 to 2020 remained constant and even increased slightly, from 57% to 58% of respondents, respectively (Edelman Trust Barometer 2011:6; Edelman Trust Barometer 2020: 39).

The effectiveness of the representation of interests by social movements and public organizations depends on the influence they can exert on the institutions responsible for the implementation of laws. However, against the background of the transformation in the systems of political representation and the delegitimization of mass traditional parties, social movements and NGOs still have not supplanted them as representatives of social interests in the political arena. Social movements and NGOs draw attention to unanswered demands from government agencies and relay them through nonelectoral public channels. At the same time, such organizations are less interested in mediating between competing requirements for consistent policy development. Their campaigns are sporadic and fragmentary. Social movements do not fully compensate for the consequences of party withdrawal, as they perform only partially the functions that help ensure stable representation.

Among other challenges of political representation, it is necessary to point out the substantive aspect, the attributive characteristics of representatives, because the socioeconomic and value gap between those who delegate their right to represent interests and those who have to convert them into decisions is obvious. The problem of the lack of mechanisms for aggregating the existing multiplicity of interests with a simultaneous demand for their articulation in the political plane has become increasingly acute. After all, the spectrum of political representation, in our opinion, can no longer be reduced exclusively to a right-left dichotomy. A concomitant factor contributing to social anomie and declining public confidence in public institutions is the structural and organizational transformation of policymaking processes, namely, the fragmentation of state power between private and public actors at the subnational, national, and transnational levels. Through a domino effect, these several manifestations of the dysfunction of political representation systems form a global trend of de-etatization. The assertion of the universalist role of nation-states in representing the common interest rather than the collective interests of the inhabitants of a given territory, in relation to actions that take place within national borders, is in dispute (see: Crouch 2017: 63). This is especially relevant to countries which are missing functional efficiency in providing statehood and/or loss control over part of the territory.

Eroding State Sovereignty through the Economization of Its Legitimacy

Widely recognized factors in sovereignty transformation of state are globalization and the influence of supranational entities. Nonetheless, we argue that the political, institutional, and social changes taking place within the states are no less significant in their impact on the de-etatization of sovereignty and the shift to new organizational forms of governance. The legitimacy of decisions and the status of political institutions that must ensure the execution of state sovereignty are more often being disputed, as indicated by the frequency of changes in parliamentary coalitions and governments and the intensification of protest activity across the globe. The rules of the political game are becoming less clear owing to the fragmentation, deterritorialization, and diffusion of political power.

Despite numerous studies of political legitimacy, its conceptual rationale is still not clear enough. Various evaluation indicators can be adduced in support of legitimacy, such as the level of political activity of citizens or compliance with norms and rules. In a general sense, legitimacy can be represented as the perception of the population of political power that is acquired and exercised in accordance with certain social norms and criteria. Legitimacy is formed in accordance with the legal framework and through trust-building between stakeholders. These two forms of legitimacy, normative and perceptual, are complementary.

Thus, the state sovereignty one can interpret in two-fold manner: in normative one, fixed in law arrangements, and in political one, embedded in actual (perceptive) legitimacy of power-holders. Legitimacy presupposes the voluntary acceptance by society of power and the decisions the power-holder makes as meeting the requirements and challenges of today. Since trust is the basis of the legitimacy of policy-making, and legitimate requests from society are manifested primarily in the expectations of public authorities, to clarify the state of their perceptive legitimacy, one should examine what is important for citizens in terms of priority issues of state functioning. Cross-national monitoring studies show that the concerns of citizens are primarily related to the socioeconomic aspects of life. Ensuring stable economic growth is a priority for the state, according to 48.1% of respondents (Haerpfer et al. 2020: 204), while only 18.6% of respondents saw increasing the involvement of citizens in the discussion of government as a priority (ibid). An important finding was that at the individual level, among the priority goals, the majority of respondents (40.9%) indicated the maintenance of the order in the country. The fight against rising prices was identified by 23.6% of respondents, but giving more power to citizens in making important government decisions as a priority was selected by 22.4% of respondents only (ibid., 206).

Thus there is a public demand for solutions to economic problems amid low levels of trust in government. For their part, governments, caught between the need to keep their promises to citizens and their obligations to international institutions, must seek solutions that can satisfy both parties. The only factor that seems capable of yielding a compromise in such a contradictory situation by maintaining stability in society and the status quo for the pro-government forces is the successful functioning of the economy. If socioeconomic indicators are determinants of the legitimacy of political governance, then fluctuations in economic growth can have a significant impact on the maintenance of the political system because increasing the welfare of citizens increases the legitimacy of political decisions, while economic deprivation reduces the legitimacy of governance strategies and can cause frustrations in society. Problems of concern to citizens prove that the basis for recognizing or not recognizing modern policymaking processes is performative legitimacy, which is achieved by demonstrating the effectiveness of governance, mostly through the receipt of benefits.

In the context of modern sociopolitical trends, the two-dimensional format of the government–citizens seems insufficient to fully understand the features of legitimization of policymaking. After all, the effectiveness of governance depends not only on the ability of public institutions to provide public goods in general but also on the ability to effectively implement the program objectives of international entities. The study of international organizations such as the UN, the IMF, the World Trade Organization, and supranational entities such as the EU also highlights the importance of citizens' perceptions of problem-solving as a major factor in their legitimacy. States and their citizens support power through the collective benefits they receive (see: Tallberg & Zürn 2019: 595–596).

The transformation of state sovereignty under the influence of globalization has led to a change in the formats and principles of interaction between political actors, as many of the issues related to the domestic policy of the state are mediated by decisions made outside the state. As a result of the institutionalization of powers to set the agenda and make, implement, and enforce decisions, powers transferred from states to international organizations, the latter have expanded the scope of regulation beyond the original functional powers and have gained more imperative influence. The most powerful stakeholders choose legitimization strategies that allow them to maintain control over the process. They implement dependency mechanisms that are difficult to change. This is especially evident in governance formats with the participation of international institutions. For instance, the IMF, the World Bank, and the World Trade Organization are powerful sources of direct influence on both the economies and policies of member states. Adherence to the rules and recommendations of the IMF and the World Bank not only affects the possibility of obtaining a loan or grant, but also is a key aspect of a recipient country's international reputation, which is of interest to other international institutions and governments. Delegated authority can be restored only by terminating membership in a particular international organization. However, the consequences of such independence can be seen not only in reputational but also in real economic losses for the private and civil sectors of the state.

The fragmentation of state powers between a multitude of public and private stakeholders at the subnational and supranational levels of governance changes the structural modularity of legitimizing policymaking. First, in multistakeholder governance, the sources of legitimacy are fragmented, as each participant in a network partnership—a public institution, private or public organization, or international entity—may be seen as differently legitimate from the perspective of other actors and society as a whole. Legitimacy requirements vary depending on the audience. They are formed by the interaction of the legitimizing efforts of stakeholders and the reactions of target or other groups to such efforts. Even if there is trust and agreement among the members of a certain political and managerial network, they may have a low level of trust on the part of the general public. Citizens are not asked to consent to the participation of specific non-state actors in decision-making, and public trust is mostly assessed through attitudes toward government and government agencies.

Second, participants in multistakeholder formats of political decision-making may have their own unique strategies to legitimize political decisions, especially in the normative aspect.

Third, multistakeholder political and managerial processes lack mechanisms for legitimizing decisions that could simultaneously meet the legitimizing demands of all stakeholders and their legitimizing audiences.

Traditional formal accountability mechanisms are not suitable for assessing the legitimacy of decisions made in multistakeholder governance formats. To whom and on what grounds should each participant in the multistakeholder decision-making network be accountable?

International organizations (actually, their governing bodies) are accountable to member states; NGOs are accountable to donors and sponsors. The accountability of commercial organizations involved in decision-making and ultimately the provision of services applies only to shareholders and is not relevant to the accountability of public institutions to citizens. Even if multistakeholder governance is associated with multilateral decision-making goals to be implemented on behalf of governments, this format is not required to report on its activities or to follow the instructions of the intergovernmental community. Multistakeholder governance with an emphasis on organizational efficiency and managerial autonomy is not relevant to traditional models of political control and accountability.

The provision of services is influenced by the authorities and can be adapted to their particular interests. Principles of democratic governance, such as procedural transparency, distributive justice, and the civil status of individuals, can be undermined. These problems are particularly acute in countries with a low efficacy of democratic institutions and an underdeveloped civil society. The informal nature of multistakeholder governance here is the result of the close merging of the interests of public officials and large financial and industrial groups. The latter, together with the privatization of entire sectors of the public service, gain significant advantage over policymaking processes in the state while remaining out of the control of citizens, further strengthening their positions.

Studying strategic decisions made behind the scene by the American neoconservatives, who helped carry out large-scale privatization in the post-Soviet countries, and the numerous private players, who daily make public decisions without the public's engagement in the process, Janine Wedel (2009) defined them "flexions". She points out that "when such operators work together in longstanding groups, thus multiplying their influence, they are flex nets. Flexions and flex nets operate at one extreme of a continuum in crafting their coincidences of interests" (Wedel 2009: 7). Wherever they maneuver, the elitist circles of any level (from local to global) will blatantly defy the boundaries between the state and private sectors that used to be sacred.

In the countries lacking strong democratic traditions, which surfer from unstable economy, the multistakeholder governance of public-private networks seeks to what in scholars defines as "political rigging":

> [T]he process in which actors, blurring (or even fusing) official and private power, transform a system, in part or in whole, so that it favors an elite few at the expense of the less privileged many. In so doing, the actors blur the boundaries not only among official and private spheres, but often also among political, economic, media, cultural, and social arenas. (Wedel, Hussain & Dolan 2017: 6)

Another definition to this phenomenon is "policy capture – the process of consistently or repeatedly directing public policy decisions away from the public interest towards the interests of specific interest group or person" (OECD, 2017: 9). It takes place through a variety of illegal instruments, such as bribery, and at the same time through legal channels, including lobbying and financial support for political parties and election campaigns. Illegal influence can also be exercised without direct intervention or interaction with decision-makers, by manipulating the information provided to them or by establishing close social ties with them (Ibid: 9–10).

The normative aspect of the legitimacy of such multistakeholder governance is questionable because of procedural opacity and the lack of advisory mechanisms and compensation systems: those, affected by the decisions made in such a format, are excluded from the decision-making process and do not have adequate political and legal mechanisms to bring the decision-makers to justice. The lack of developed control mechanisms leads to problems of public legitimacy of decisions and causes social anomie and a sense of alienation from citizens owing to their inability to influence policy-making processes. Thus, state power bodies, in particular governments, as socially accountable stakeholders (at least in developed democracies), find themselves at the epicenter of public discontent. The relationship between efficacy and legitimacy takes the form of a vicious circle where increasing the efficacy of the state increases its legitimacy and where increased legitimacy increases the efficacy of the state. The issue of ensuring democracy in this context recedes into the background.

The predominance of market forces in the current wave of economic globalization has not only undermined the autonomous decision-making potential of governments in states, but also turned the state mechanisms into promoters of capitalistic interests. While current problems, such as poverty or climate change, impel the states to overcome their prejudices and to cooperate for working out collaborative decisions, the managerial mechanisms being implemented are intended to help in these attempts, and reflect the projects of transnational elite networks, substantially undermining the progress in solving these problems. Global cooperation largely mirrors political bargaining among the transnational capitalist elites, who regulate access to formal and informal institutes and networks, and thus shape the global political agenda and, as a rule, decide in favor of profit maximization rather than addressing socially oriented concerns. The authorities of developing countries, most of which bear the burden of trade liberalization, including inequality, violation of labor rights, and environment deterioration, are related to the global governance system not necessarily to challenge the foundations of underdevelopment, but more often for the sake of concessions meant to satisfy the interests of the internal business groups.

It is evident that the modern forms of political governance, particularly those of democratic nature, have failed to eliminate the rule of oligarchy. Accordingly associated not only with the presence of the so-called "democratic elites", but also with the accompanying anchoring of groups acting as subjects of democratic life, the democratic regimes are obviously involved in "representing" of what, in its essence, can be just group interests. Civil forces do not get a chance to affect significantly decision-making, which can have a legitimacy gap threatening to trigger the spread of alienation from the political process. These tendencies more or less evidently occur in post-Soviet countries, where government processes under the impact of business groups and oligarchic clans mutated into the neopatrimonial rule (see Fisun 2019).

The Ukraine is an eventual example of the loss of sovereignty simultaneously in functional and territorial aspects due to actual multistakeholder governance with domination of informal non-state actors' interests.

Ukraine as a "Precarious State"

Experiencing thirty years of its independence, Ukraine pricesly fits into the trends relevant to sovereignty's de-etatisation. Weakness of the economy and low level of trust in political institutions are permanent characteristics of the development of Ukrainian state. According to opinion polls, the most pressing threats to Ukraine, even against the background of military conflict (47%) and epidemic of coronavirus Covid-19 (35%), are socio-economic factors: the unemployment (37%), the low payments of wages and pensions (27%) (Rating 2021:4). Corruption in government (21%) as well as ineptitude of governmental officials (19%) is the main concerns of Ukrainians (Ibid).

The social and political anomy becomes the inherent part of Ukrainians' life-being. According to surveys only 17.1% Ukrainians trust the parliament, Verhovna Rada, and 18,3% have confidence in government (Razumkov center 2021). Political parties do not gain much public support either: just 17.9% respondents express trust to them (Ibid 2021). Despite the mosaics of political parties, only 8.1% of Ukrainians declare their party membership (Haerpfer et al. 2020: 215). Labor unions have a little higher degree of social reliance in Ukraine, i.e. 26.7% of approval (Razumkov center 2021).

Unstable economic situation, unemployment, loss of perspectives in tackling corruption compel Ukrainian citizens seek for jobs and better life abroad. According to various estimates, over 3 million Ukrainians work in other countries (Radiosvoboda 2019).

Yet, the delay of reforms and destructive consequences of Russia's invasion into Crimea and Eastern regions of Ukraine are predominantly caused by overwhelming influence of domestic as well as foreign non-state actors on the governmental system of the state.

After gaining sovereignty in 1991 Ukrainian political system rapidly transformed into something as "Republic of clans" (see Minakov 2019c), inducing oligarchic rule. The particularistic clan interests were embodied in policymaking that hampered the crucial political, economic, legal reforms:

> Subsidizing policy-making to the interests of financial and industrial groups and rent-seeking governmental officials led to total corruption that reached all levels of governing and all spheres of social life. Political particularism in decision-making became the only possible *modus vivendi* of governmental process in Ukraine. Particularism was enhanced by localism. Social and cultural specificities of Western and Eastern Ukraine provided a strong basis for dividing electoral fields and lobbying interests of local political elites and business groups included into clan governing networks. (Vinnykova, 2017: 74)

Along with pressure from the international agencies, due to borrowed loans in IMF and financial support of the World Banks, as well as the USA, the European Union and Russia, the effect of entire fragmentation of central power among regional oligarchic groups led to de-etatization of Ukraine's sovereignty. The last factor seems even more significant in entailing such phenomenon:

> Sub-national political regimes are based on the dominance of relatively autonomous local patron-client systems and political machines that enter into various arrangements with national political players and the party of power. Oftentimes, however, these networks maintain forms of autonomy. This trend produces multiple configurations of political settlements at the local level and promotes the emergence of regional party projects and electoral blocks. (Fisun 2017: 3)

Moreover, the particularistic approach to the foreign policy led to the events that happened in Ukraine in 2013-2014.

Ukrainian political officials from the very beginning induced foreign policy on tactic of "the rule of anticipated reactions" towards former Soviet metropoly, particular in the issue of border demarcation with Russia.

> Along with many other reasons, it happened due to Ukraine's dependence on Russian energy supplies and the interconnections of markets in both countries. Russia repeatedly used the energy factor and trade embargo as tools for pressuring the Ukrainian government. Additionally, after the rejection of nuclear weapons and its destruction during the 1993-1996 Ukraine had become vulnerable to any external assault. ...
> The status of the Black Sea fleet, which was commonly inherited by Ukraine and Russia from the USSR, also was not long imposed on the agenda in Ukraine. In 1997, an Agreement was signed on the conditions of the Russian

Black Sea fleet in the Crimea peninsula (Verhovna Rada of Ukarine, 1999). However, that document did not include a clearly fixed status of the Black Sea Fleet in Ukraine. Note that the Russian Black Sea Fleet in Ukraine was among numerous significant legal barriers to applying for membership in the North Atlantic Alliance. This situation was favorable for Russia that did not want to release Ukraine from its geopolitical pool. (Vinnykova 2020: 37)

The priorities of domestic policies and foreign strategies were changed according to interests of regional clans after the last gained the central power. For instance, at the time of Leonid Kuchma's presidency the idea of diverse vectors of foreign policy was dominative, meanwhile at the time of Viktor Yushchenko's presidency the priorities in foreign policy turned exclusively to the enhancement of interrelation with the USA and EU. The period of Viktor Yanukovych's presidency can be characterized by clear double standards in foreign policy: an official declaration of integration into the European Union co-existed with actual lobbying of economic interests of ruling clans, primarily from Donetsk region, oriented towards Russia. During the Petro Poroshenko's rule the whole foreign strategy have been turned to the West emphasizing the need of help in struggling with Russia's aggression and occupation of part of Ukraine's territory. The President Volodymyr Zelensky declaring strong affiliation to the European and Trans-Atlantic structure makes effort to set up contacts with Kremlin for getting a chance to reestablish state sovereignty on the occupied Eastern regions and Crimea. Such swing foreign policy did not meet full legitimacy both from external actors (states, international organizations and agencies) and citizens of Ukraine.

A pattern of oligarchic weightiness on the policy-making can be recognized in the official refusal from signing the Association Agreement. The rejection of the fact that the strategic choice for the whole state is determined solely by the interests of Yanukovych family's network eventually led to social unrest and protests, which quickly escalated into armed confrontation between pro-government forces and citizens. The consequences of social and political crisis in Ukraine included annexation of Crimea by Russia; separatism in Luhansk and Donetsk regions ended with a self-declaration of quasi-state entities; and a medium scale military conflict with thousands killed or wounded plus over a million of refugees or "internally displaced" citizens. Using antagonistic attitudes on external priorities of residents of Eastern and Western region, politicians, structured their electoral fields and provided regional clans with political capital. Incidentally, the public discourse on European integration was limited to mutually exclusive possibilities of relations with Russia, as Western vector acts versus Russian direction:

> Appealing to common culture and historical past, proponents of Russia were passing concepts of brotherly Slavic peoples, i.e. Ukrainians and Russians. The residents of the eastern regions bordering Russia were particularly vulnerable to such manipulative allegations. Residents of the Western regions of Ukraine, who are more likely to have been in the EU mainly for low earnings, perceived pro-integration slogans as an opportunity to transfer to Ukraine the experience of Central and Eastern Europe where the standards of living of ordinary people are much higher. (Vinnykova, 2020: 39)

The dominance of oligarchic network influence in the political system of Ukraine has led to the distortion of the main objective functions of state: articulation, integration coordination of the interests of different social groups. Therefore the social cohesion had been disrupted. Along with mentioned factors the precarious position of the state as an actor in international arena had put the sovereignty of Ukraine under threat. The perspectives of restoring sovereignty on the whole territory seem opaque, yet probable:

> The "Donets'k and Luhans'k republics" are new statelets that have only begun their state-building processes. They both depend on the political, military, and economic support of Russia. So far, their state identities and political systems are very fragile, which provides Ukraine with an opportunity for the reintegration of these breakaway communities/territories. (Minakov, 2019b: 190–191)

Meeting its 30-years anniversary, Ukraine seems to have less of its statehood than it had at the point of gaining independence. Its fourth part of territory is out of control. It has lost more than 10 million of its population, accordingly from 51 944 in 1991 to 41 442 million in 2021 (Ministry of Finance of Ukraine 2021).

Ukraine is one of the largest IMF's borrowers (IMF 2021a), with the 7496.24 million of outstanding purchases and loans (IMF 2021b).

Despite permanent demands of international bodies and Ukrainian authorities' declarations of inducing anti-corruption measures, the data shows the state's reluctance in tackling the shadow side of its functioning. According to monitoring of Transparency International, Ukraine stays in the low set of countries in Corruption Perception Index: starting from 144 (among 176 countries ranged) in 2012 (Transparency International Ukraine 2012) to 117 (among 180 countries ranged) in 2020 (Ibid, 2020).

The Ukraine is just one among numerous cases that reveals the backstage of de-etatization of state sovereignty. Global trend of fragmentation state's power among non-state actors both domestic and transnational one in post-Soviet subregion featured by neo-patrimonial modes of rule and Russia's claims on geopolitical dominance. Here, on "extreme periphery" (Minakov 2019a) the losing sovereignty by ones does not mean gaining it by others. Donetsk People Republic and Luhansk People Republic remain mostly unrecognized entities with tough dependence on Russia's support. Still de-etatization of sovereignty occurs in the countries that have full control over territory and enjoy full set of democratic governance. The ultimate power over political entity (country) does not belong any more to the state. Globalization empowers forces which are beyond the control of the state and international agencies. Client-patronage relations embedded both in domestic and global modes of governance reduce the power of people as the initial source of sovereignty in modern states.

Conclusion

The last two-decade global trend of mass-protests and upheavals experienced by countries with different type of political regimes and economic development is rooted in apparent global political anomy. The loss of public confidence in political institutions and representation systems caused by state losing its conventional functions due to fragmentation of state power between public and private sector actors. The shift of decision-making authority to non-state actors, leads to the alienation of citizens from policymaking.

The legitimacy of state sovereignty as a form of domination is ensured primarily through the ability of state institutions to provide socioeconomic benefits, though the transfer of public functions to wholly or partially controlled public service companies and joint forms of governance, such as networked public-private partnerships, displaces political control and weakens the link between public preferences and policymaking. In multistakeholder formats of policymaking, the sources of legitimacy are fragmented, as each participant in a network partnership may differ in the legitimization demands of external audiences and in its own legitimization strategies. The most powerful stakeholders, such as international organizations or financial industry groups, use strategies to legitimize decisions that make governments dependent on regulatory requirements or government claims. The lack of developed institutional mechanisms of accountability and control in citizens to feel alienated from the processes of policymaking. Institutions of state power, in particular governments, as socially accountable stakeholders are the focus of public discontent. The de-etatization of state sovereignty leads to the delegitimization of state institutions and downgrading of the status of states in general.

The states that experience the multi-stakeholder governance through interference of oligarchic clans, cartels, and other informal networks actors, are much more vulnerable to sovereignty de-etatization. The public-private partnership turns here into privatization of state's functions. Ukraine is an example of failed statehood building and sovereignty lose both in functional and actual, i.e. territorial, dimension due to diffusion of governance among non-state actors. Being in the grip between regulatory demands of international bodies and business inquiries of domestic oligarchic clans, Ukrainian government institutions lose the preliminary function of providing state sovereignty. Accounting Russia's harmful affect on Ukraine's territorial control lose in Crimea and partially in Eastern regions, still there are apparent evidences of entire forces that lead to state sovereignty destruction. Throughout history of new Ukraine' state-building one can observe the substitution of the major state's mission, i.e. serving and representing nation's interests, into granting particularistic inquires of oligarchic clans.

The 30-years old state now seems much more unguarded then in the early 90-s just after gaining its independence. Paradoxically, but preserving Ukraine's sovereignty toughly depends on international bodies affect. The deepening interference into national governance and strict control on taken commitments by governmental officials are the means that can mitigate the destructive effect of oligarchic rule and keep the Ukraine from seizing by Russia.

Bibliography

Ankersmit, Frank. (2002). *Political representation*. Stanford: Stanford University Press.

Brannen, Samuel, Haig, Christian Stirling & Schmidt, Katherine. (2020, March 2) *The Age of Mass Protests: Understanding an Escalating Global Trend. A Report of the CSIS and Foresight group*. Washington D.C.: Center for strategic and international studies. https://www.csis.org/analysis/age-mass-protests-understanding-escalating-global-trend (accessed June 19, 2021).

Cone, Edward & Lambert, James. (2019). How Robots Change the World. What Automation Really Means for Jobs and Productivity. *Oxford Economics*, n.d., https://www.oxfordeconomics.com/recent-releases/how-robots-change-the-world (accessed June 19, 2021).

Crouch, Crouch. (2017). *Can Neoliberalism be Saved from Itself?* UK, London: Social Europe Edition.

Edelman Trust Barometer. (2011). Annual Global Opinion Leaders Study. *Edelman Trust Barometer website*, n.d., https://www.slideshare.net/EdelmanInsights/2011-edelman-trust-barometer (accessed June 19, 2021).

Edelman Trust Barometer. (2021). Spring Update: a World in Trauma. Global Report. *Edelman Trust Barometer website*, n.d., https://www.edelman.com/sites/g/files/aatuss191/files/202105/2021%20Edelman%20Trust%20Barometer%20Spring%20Update_0.pdf (accessed June 19, 2021).

Fisun, Oleksandr. (2019). Neopatrimonialism in Post-Soviet Eurasia. *Stubborn Structures: Reconceptualizing Post-Communist Regimes*. Edited by Balint Magyar. Budapest: Central European University Press, 75-96.

Fisun, Oleksandr (2017, August) Ukraine's Semi-Managed Democracy on the March. *PONARS Eurasia Policy Memo*. Washington DC: Elliott School of International Affairs, 482, https://www.ponarseurasia.org/wp-content/uploads/attachments/Pepm482_Fisun_August2017.pdf (accessed June 19, 2021).

Fisun, Oleksandr & Vinnykova, Nataliya. (2021). De-etatization of State Sovereignty and the Formation of Global Maidan. *The Ideology and Politics Journal*. 1(17): 72–86.

Gleckman, Harris. (2018). *Multistakeholder Governance and Democracy Global challenge*. London: Imprint Routledge.

Haerpfer, Christian, Inglehart Ronald, Moreno Alejandro, Welzel Christian, Kizilova Kseniya, Diez-Medrano Jaime, Lagos, Marta, Norris, Pippa, Ponarin, Eduar, Puranen, Bi et al. (eds.). (2020). *World Values Survey: Round Seven – Country-Pooled Datafile*. Madrid, Spain & Vienna, Austria: JD Systems Institute & WVSA Secretariat. doi.org/10.14281/18241.1.

Inglehart, Ronald, Haerpfer Christian, Moreno Alejandro, Welzel Christian, Kizilova Kseniya, Diez-Medrano Jaime, Lagos, Marta, Norris, Pippa, Ponarin, Eduard & Puranen, Bi et al. (eds.). (2018). *World Values Survey: Round Four – Country-Pooled Data file* Version: Madrid: JD Systems Institute, doi.org/10.14281/18241.6.

International Monetary Fund (IMF) (2021a). Fast Facts about the IMF. *The IMF at a Glance*, March 3, https://www.imf.org/en/About/Factsheets/IMF-at-a-Glance (accessed June 26, 2021).

International Monetary Fund (IMF) (2021b). Ukraine. At a Glance. *The IMF at a Glance*, February 28, https://www.imf.org/en/Countries/UKR (accessed June 26, 2021).

Miller, Caleb R. (2020). *Living under Post-Democracy Citizenship in Fleetingly Democratic Times*. New York: Routledge.

Minakov, Mikhail (2019a). On the Extreme Periphery. The Status of Post-Soviet Non-Recognised States in the World-System. *The Ideology and Politics Journal* 1(12): 39–72.

Minakov, Mikhail (2019b). Post-Soviet Eastern Europe. Achievements in Post-Soviet Development in Six Eastern European Nations, 1999-2020. *The Ideology and Politics Journal*. 3(14): 171-193.

Minakov, Mikhail (2019c). Republic of Clans: Evolution of Ukrainian Political System, in Stubborn Structures: Reconceptualizing Post-Communist regimes (ed. Magyar, Balint). Budapest: CEU Press, 88–99.

Ministry of Finance of Ukraine (2021, May). Population of Ukraine in 2021 without occupied territories of Crimea, Sevastopol and part of Donbass). https://index.minfin.com.ua/reference/people/ (accessed June 19, 2021).

Organisation for Economic Co-operation and Development (OECD) (2017). Preventing policy capture: Integrity in public decision making. *OECD Public Governance Reviews*, OECD Publishing, Paris, doi: 10.1787/9789264065239-en.

Oxford Learner's Dictionaries. (2021). Sovereignty. Oxford Learner's Dictionaries, https://www.oxfordlearnersdictionaries.com/definition/english/sovereignty (accessed June 19, 2021).

Pabst, Adrian (2010). The Crisis of Capitalist Democracy. *Telos* 152: 44–67.

Radiosvoboda (2019, Augus 1). Ministry of Social Policy: more than 3 million Ukrainians work abroad on a permanent basis. *Radio Svoboda*, https://www.radiosvoboda.org/a/news-trudovi-mihranty-z-ukrainy/30087119.html (accessed June 19, 2021).

Razumkov Center (2021). Assessment of the situation in the country, trust in the institutions of society and politicians, electoral orientations of citizens (March 2021). *Razumkov Center*, March, https://razumkov.org.ua/napriamky/sotsiologichni-doslidzhennia/otsinka-sytuatsii-v-kraini-dovira-do-instytutiv-suspilstva-ta-politykiv-elektoralni-orii entatsii-gromadian-berezen-2021r (accessed June 19, 2021).

Sociological Group «Rating» (2021, March 24-28). Assessment of Medical Reform. *Sociological Group «Rating»*, April, http://ratinggroup.ua/files/ratinggroup/reg_files/rg_ua_medicine_042021_press.pdf (accessed June 19, 2021).

Standing, Guy. (2011). *The Precariat: The New Dangerous Class.* London: Bloomsbury Academic.

Statista. (2020). Number of Chinese Communist Party (CCP) members 2009-2019. *Statista*, n.d., https://www.statista.com/statistics/281378/number-of-chinese-communist-party-ccp-members-in-china/ (accessed June 19, 2021).

Tallberg, Jonas, & Zürn, Michael. (2019). The Legitimacy and Legitimation of International Organizations: Introduction and Framework. *The Review of International Organizations* 14: 581–606.

Transparency International (2012). Ukraine. CPI-2012. Press Release. *Transparency International*, December 5, https://ti-ukraine.org/en/research/cpi-2012/ (accessed June 26, 2021).

Transparency International (2020). Ukraine in the Corruption Perception Index 2020. *Transparency International*, June 19, https://ti-ukraine.org/en/research/ukraine-in-the-corruption-perceptions-index-2020/ (accessed June 26, 2021).

Wike, Richard, and Castilio, Alexandra. (2018). Many around the World Are Disengaged from Politics. *Pew Research Center. Global attitudes and Trends*, October 17, https://www.pewresearch.org/global/2018/10/17/international-political-engagement/ (accessed June 19, 2021).

Verhovna Rada of Ukraine (1999). *Agreement between Ukraine and the Russian Federation on the Status and Conditions of Black Sea Fleet Russian Federation in Ukraine*. Signed May 28, 1997. Ratified by Law No. 547-XIV (547-14) March 24, 1999, (in Ukr/Rus), http://zakon3.rada.gov.ua/laws/show/643_076 (accessed June 19, 2021).

Vinnykova, Nataliya. (2020). Risks of political non-decision-making (applications to Ukraine). *Politicus*, 5: 35-43.

Vinnykova, Nataliya. (2017). Particularism in decision-making: Constractive or descructive? *Studies of Changing Societies: Comparative and Interdisciplinary in Focus*, Vol.1, 61 – 83.

Wedel, Janine (2009). Shadow Elite: How the World's New Power Brokers Undermine Democracy, Government, and the Free Market, Publisher: Basic Books; First Edition first Printing edition.

Wedel, Janine, Hussain, Nazia & Archer Dolan, Dana. (2017). Political Rigging. A Primer on Political Capture and Influence in the 21st century. *OXFAM America Research Backgrounder, n.d.*, https://www.oxfamamerica.org/explore/research-publications/political-rigging/ (accessed June 19, 2021).

7 Sovereigntism as a Vocation and Profession Imperial Roots, Current State, Possible Prospects

Ruslan Zaporozhchenko

> *"Universal law is for lackeys; context is for kings."*
> Captain Gabriel Lorca, *Star Trek: Discovery*

Social movements,[1] whose positive dynamics increased in 2020, have reactualized sovereignty as one of the key concepts of sociopolitical scientific discourse. Sovereignty is related to issues of state organization, the principle of territorialism, the method of organizing power relations within a specific sociopolitical order, the codification of social space, and political decision-making. On the one hand, sovereignty is interpreted as a configuration of power and domination, that is opposed to sociopolitical plurality (systemic, institutional, or structural). On the other hand, sovereignty denotes the rule and completeness of political power in various forms of (self)organization of the population (a state, an empire, etc.). The expression of political power occurs through (1) political decision-making; (2) the codification and formalization of social relations and the social space; and (3) the reproduction of decisions, actions,

---

[1] According to the Carnegie Endowment for International Peace (CEIP 2021), from January 2020 to June 2021, more than 120 discrete kinds of protest took place in the world: electoral, political, related to the COVID-19 pandemic, economic, social, and others. Among the most recent important events of this kind are (1) the military coup in Myanmar and the beginning of mass protests (from February 4) against the interim government, the State Administrative Council, led by Min Aung Hlaing; (2) protests in the Russian Federation against the arrest of Alexey Navalny, which began on January 23, 2021; (3) an attempt to seize the US Capitol by supporters of Donald Trump on January 6, 2021; (4) protests against restrictions related to the COVID-19 pandemic that took place in the Czech Republic, Brazil, the Netherlands, and Mongolia in January 2021; and (5) a series of "December" protests in Albania, Haiti, Montenegro, Nepal, and Peru.

communications, symbols, and structures that are accepted by the society's system as "our own," separate from "alien."

The heterogeneity and plurality of the substantive part of the concept of sovereignty, as well as the lack of a comprehensive conceptualization and categorization of the concept under study, led to the (co)existence in the discourse of political science of three dominant forms of sovereignty. The first one is *state sovereignty* (as a legal norm for codifying power relations within a particular state). The second one is *national sovereignty* (as an appeal to national self-determination, which presupposes the existence of a political or cultural nation within a multicomponent society). The third one is *people's sovereignty* (as a way of legitimizing "people" in the system of power relations, the constitutionalization and legitimization of the rights of "people" to participate in the public policy of the state, i.e., political decision-making).

Over the past few years in the social sciences, sovereignty researchers have emphasized the following areas:

> sovereignty as a derivative of territorialism, that is, the influence of geographic determinism on the changing dynamics of sovereignty (Stilz 2019; Billé 2020);
> the impact of global processes, primarily globalization and building a network society, on the unsustainability of sovereignty (Agnew 2017; Mitchell & Fazi 2017; Craig 2019);
> historical analysis of sovereignty and its rethinking, taking into account the development of society as a social system and the state as a political institution (Bourke & Skinner 2017; Waltermann 2019; Herzog 2020);
> the study of sovereignty through the prism of nationalism, cosmopolitanism, and the modernization of political systems of economically developing "third world" countries (Margariti 2017; Walshe 2019; Bennett 2020).

Two areas of research are sovereignty, primarily in the political system of the EU (Baldassari, Castelli, Truffelli, & Vezzani 2020; Damiani 2020), and the role of sovereignty in the political system of national and modern states (state-nation, nation-state) and in the system of the liberal democratic order (Kallis 2018; Scholte 2020).

The positive dynamics of social movements around the world, mentioned earlier, also demonstrate the key tendencies of modern society:

1. attempts to increase the practice of the population's participation in (re)producing political decisions, as well as attempts to increase direct control over the implementation of these decisions;
2. the desire to narrow the established distance between the center of decision-making (the subject of political power) and the periphery of the execution of these decisions (the object of political power);
3. de-etatization of the sociopolitical space and the fragmentation of the structures of sovereignty; and
4. the growth of antiglobalization and nationalist, and populist tendencies.

Such tendencies become the basis for the development of sovereignty as one of the key concepts in sociopolitical discourse over the past ten years.

However, examining the category of "sovereignty," researchers have typically engaged with the issues of populism, nationalist movements, and the crisis in the system of governance that has developed in liberal democratic systems, missing the conceptual and structural features of sovereignty. Sovereignty is thereby transformed into a social and political movement, ideologizing (constructing social reality) claims to the sovereignty of the state, a power within a political organization.

Taking into account all the above-mentioned factors, my aim in this chapter is to conceptualize sovereignty as a mechanism for deconstructing[2] sovereign power. In this respect, sovereigntism as such a mechanism:

1. acts as a political movement that does not have a clearly expressed ideology;
2. manifests in crisis situations related to issues of legitimation and the legitimacy of political decisions within the state; and

---

2 I borrow the term deconstruction from the work of Jacques Derrida. Deconstruction is the understanding of an object of research through breaking a stereotype about it or including it in a new research context.

3. functions as a system of power relations based on social and political antipodes (binary positions) that serve as the means to construct a political reality.

I am going to focus on implementing the research goal through the use of various approaches (structural, functional, world-system, institutional) and various sociological and political concepts, including critical analysis, the concept of symbolic power as the power to produce, parameterization and factor analysis, and comparative analysis.

A Conceptual Framework and the Political Foundations of Sovereignty

Modern vectors in the study of sovereignty can be identified in three key areas: the legal (regulatory) approach, the sociopolitical approach, and an approach based on the theory of international relations (Krasner 2001: 1). My work adopts the sociopolitical approach, analyzing both the body of critical work on sovereignty and other leading approaches to understanding sovereignty as a system of power and power relations.

The first attempt at conceptualizing sovereignty is associated with the French political philosopher Jean Bodin, who in his work *On Sovereignty: Six Books of the Commonwealth* defined sovereignty as "absolute and perpetual power vested in a commonwealth" (Bodin 2009: 24). Bodin desacralizes political reality, which earlier was focused on religion and the church as key forms of worldview (ideology) and governance (organization). On the one hand, politics replaces theology; and therefore, divine power, or *auctoritas*, which previously was granted only to the pope, is now extrapolated to belong to the ruler (sovereign) of the state.

On the other hand, the ruler is above political processes within the framework of political reality, which frees the ruler from the legal regulation of the social system. That is, the ruler is simultaneously within the boundaries of the political reality of the state and is not within the boundaries of the law and the laws of the state. It should be understood that the ruler cannot obey "other" laws, commands, or will that come from outside the political system in which the ruler functions. That is, sovereignty is an exclusively internal, immanent property of the political system.

Jean Bodin outlines several important characteristics of power. First, the actions of sovereignty extend to the entire society (population) and the territory of the state, thereby becoming a form of public policy in which political decisions are (re)made and the social structure of power functions. Second, sovereign power must be constant, uninterrupted, and integral, submerging other possible power structures potentially on a par with or above itself. In Bodin's conceptualization of sovereignty one more property of sovereignty is revealed — permanence. Third, the goal of sovereignty is the common good, which comes from internal factors (factors connected to home affairs and home policy). Fourth, sovereign power should be desacralized, that is, separated from religion (as an ideology) meaningfully and from the church (as an organization) formally.

An important clarification that Bodin brings to the study of sovereignty concerns the definition of sovereignty, first of all as power, public or private, but also power as a method of governance through a system of control. If for Bodin sovereignty is a permanent and continuous power, then Carl Schmitt points to the fact that sovereignty defines itself through extraordinary emergencies that go beyond the "normal" existence of the state (Schmitt 2005: 20–24). For Schmitt, sovereignty has a casual nature that manifests informally, not systemically. Any difficult situation that cannot be explained, let alone resolved with the help of legal regulation, is a priori a matter not of power but of sovereignty — as an "emergency" power (Schmitt 2004).

Moreover, sovereignty is unregulated power that exists simultaneously with constitutional, lawful power. Constitutional power regulates and codifies normal situations that are the natural state of a political system or social relations. Sovereignty acts in the field of extraordinary circumstances; therefore, sovereignty is an extraordinary power that cannot be regulated in advance. Sovereignty is a kind of permanent power that is not produced from anything but exists in politics itself as a mechanism of management through political decision-making. Sovereignty is "real political power" (Schmitt [1932] 1996: 30-34) that ensures the sovereign order of political organization; it becomes especially relevant in those situations where the question is about the survival of the political system itself, which is under threat of destruction.

The sovereign, according to Schmitt, is a delimiter that points to "enemies," draws the boundaries between "normal" and "emergency" situations, and also directly and absolutely ensures the survival and reproducibility of the political system. The sovereign is the subject of political relations and political reality at the same time (Schmitt 2005). Certainly, the central element of Schmitt's theory is "political will" as a special instrumental quality of a sovereign. The sovereign is above the constitutional field, but acts within the framework of a specific political system. Thus, by acting outside the normative-legal field, the sovereign is able to impose his or her own political order, which in the future will acquire the features of a legal, constitutional, and legitimate one.

Criticism of and opposition to Carl Schmitt's perspective on sovereignty is provided by the French philosopher Michel Foucault, who points out that "sovereignty and discipline, legislation, the right of sovereignty and disciplinary mechanics are in fact the two things that constitute the general mechanisms of power in our society" (Foucault 2003: 39). Foucault designates several important epistemological positions: first, the subject of sovereignty cannot be single and exclusive within the political system; rather, we should be speaking about a plurality of subjects, or at least about the binary opposition "subject to subject." Second, sovereign power does not come "from above," according to the will of a sovereign-ruler, but "from below" as the fear of subordinates before the ruler (sovereign); therefore, it is necessary to highlight a certain plurality of powers, which in total should constitute the unity of political power. Third, sovereign power is based not on the law as a structure for normalizing and codifying the social space of the population but on a certain fundamental legitimacy that is the ground for all laws (ibid.: 44).

According to Foucault, sovereign power is in opposition to disciplinary power, but it can also have a set of disciplinary mechanisms to implement the reproduction of itself. Chiefly, this arises from the arrangement of the infrastructure for control, supervision, and observation — in aggregate, the expansive nature of biopower, or "power over the body." Sovereign power is a system of governance that has regulatory and political dimensions (Foucault 2009: 53-55). The normative aspect of sovereign power presupposes quite legal and legitimate mechanisms of "inclusion" and "exclusion" of various structural units from public administration while the political aspect of sovereign power is a legitimate, but beyond normative, way of resolving the situation that puts the political system in a situation of hopelessness, "a dead end."

Of most important concern here is the radical rejection of the law as a universal system of order that ensures the safety of the population within the boundaries of a specific territory. To resolve this stalemate which goes beyond the normative and transforms into the political Foucault suggests distinguishing between two regimes of power: sovereign law and disciplinary mechanisms. If sovereign law is a derivative of sovereign power and is aimed at controlling territory, then disciplinary power, through a certain set of mechanisms, controls the population:

> From the nineteenth century until the present day, we have then in modern societies, on the one hand, a legislation, a discourse, and an organization of public right articulated around the principle of the sovereignty of the social body and the delegation of individual sovereignty to the State; and we also have a tight grid of disciplinary coercions that actually guarantees the cohesion of that social body. (Ibid.: 37)

That is, sovereignty is transformed from social power into a constitutive property of political (state) power through management, communication, and control. Sovereignty is determined by its normative and legal nature (its legal component), while in sociopolitical discourse, sovereignty is transformed into an ideological construct, which, in my opinion, is aimed at legitimizing the practices of constructing the sociopolitical reality of the population of a particular state. Sovereignty exhausted itself meaningfully when it ceased to perform the functions of control over land and resources during the creation of the modern state. Disciplinary power is guided by a person and by social relations in the era of rationalization of the state as a system.

Taking into account the conceptual positions outlined above, I suggest considering *sovereignty as a system of (re)production and legitimation of political decisions within a specific political system (open or closed), focused exclusively on the internal "agenda" (requests, demands, proposals) of the population*. A sovereign system both hinders and resists both pressure and influence from outside. Sovereignty draws visible or invisible borders that distinguish "friends" from "enemies;" that is, it opposes two different systems of government, two different forms of internal political order.

Sovereignty should be understood as a tool for legitimizing the political system by other political systems; that is, "sovereignty differentiates the state ontologically and ethically from other forms of political life, and furnishes us simultaneously with the conditions for knowing the state as such" (Bartelson 1995: 189). Sovereignty is also interpreted as an internal property of the political system: the ability to adopt and legitimate political decisions and to use legitimate violence as a means of building the infrastructure of power relations, which is consolidated around the mechanisms of discipline and control.

On the one hand, sovereignty presupposes the normative and legitimate consolidation of the spatial organization of the population through the creation and maintenance of a security system and the functionality of a sociopolitical order, using control instruments (violence, domination, coercion, discipline, communication). On the other hand, sovereignty (re)creates the social reality of the political life of the population by: (1) constructing collective identities (through the prism of opposition, inclusion and exclusion, restriction); (2) creating an extensive infrastructure for managing a variety of objects of power; (3) bringing society to order from a multitude into a certain political whole, unity; and (4) constituting and legitimizing political power.

Does an Empire Construct Sovereignty or Does Sovereignty Construct an Empire?

Even though the conceptualization of sovereignty took place in the 16th century and was associated primarily with royal power and the feudal system of organizing the population within a limited territory, we can observe a ramified system of sovereign power, through the presence of signs of sovereignty, even in ancient Rome. The Roman Empire illustrates many of the systemic and functional features that formed the basis for the modern forms of (self)organization of the population. Sovereignty also existed in the structure of power relations not so much in the Roman Republic as in the Roman Empire. The first emperor, Octavian Augustus, consolidated the maximum amount of power in his hands, becoming a single subject of power relations (Hinsley 1986: 41–43). Such sovereignty could be designated "absolute," using the terminology proposed by Gottfried Leibniz (1988).

In analyzing the political structure of the Holy Roman Empire, however, Leibniz denied the existence of absolute sovereignty, giving scientific preference to a multitude of relative sovereignties, which are immanent, extend to a specific territory, may be influenced from outside, but at the same time constantly interact with each other. With respect to sovereign relations in the Roman Empire, we can identify several features:

1. The right to change political reality and lead political changes belongs to a single subject of power relations.
2. A single subject of power relations exercises direct control over the movement of capital, goods, people, and services in the territorial space of the imperial system.
3. A single subject of power relations is able to manage the system both in a peaceful period, when the paths and opportunities for the development of the system are predetermined, and in a period of uncertainty, when the system is engulfed in crisis.

It is during such systemic crises that exclusivity and a certain absoluteness of sovereignty are manifested, when the central government becomes not just power over the law, but also power capable of changing laws, political decisions, "rules of the game," and political reality, and of getting an opportunity beyond actions. We suggest speaking less about the absoluteness of the system (about its infinity, perfection, or unconditionality) and more about its autonomy and autarky (its focus on itself). This idea is developed further later in the chapter when the analysis turns to determining the degree of strength of sovereignty.

For absolute sovereignty, a characteristic feature is its personification, that is, its identification with a specific subject of power relations — with the ruler. Absolute sovereignty is not just above the law, that is, it is not just outside the normative legal system it also produces the normative reality itself, constructs it through a personified control system. Consequently, with absolute sovereignty, the system becomes autarky (focused on itself and ensuring its own security) and autocracy, in which power relations are monopolized and subsequently subjectively reproduced. Under these circumstances of uncertainty, absolute sovereignty is the embodiment of some (un)natural state of society, while sovereignty, according to Giorgio Agamben,

> ... presents itself as an incorporation of the state of nature in society, or, if one prefers, as a state of indistinction between nature and culture, between violence and law, and this very indistinction constitutes specifically sovereign violence. The state of nature is therefore not truly external to nomos but rather contains its virtuality. (Agamben 1998: 35)

The Roman Empire was a huge and multi-level political organization that required a certain system of government, being not just a set of territories but many political forms of organization of the population. The multifunctional Latin word *imperium* means control, power, limitation possessed by the subject of power relations. "Imperium" was received by the governors of the emperor, proconsuls or propraetors who ruled over a limited territory, realizing there the model of power relations that they projected from the center, Rome. Consequently, the provincial leaders controlled the movement of capital, goods, people, and services, and directed political changes, but could not change political reality itself.

Thus, the provincial leaders themselves became the subjects of power relations, which functioned in the system of a single subject of power relations, but at the same time they created their own "system within the system" (a subsystem of the system). In other words, within the framework of the absolute sovereignty of the entire Roman Empire, the type of sovereignty operated and reproduced what we may call *relative sovereignty*, following the logic of Leibniz.

A multitude of relative sovereignties constituted a hierarchy of power relations that provided control over the existing order. Moreover, it was precisely this set of relative sovereignties that legitimized absolute sovereignty; that is, the periphery legitimized the center's right to govern itself. In this case, sovereignty is the refusal of the regions to challenge the center (central power), as well as the refusal of any state to interfere in the internal affairs of any other state (Wallerstein 2004: 97).

In empires, which are both complex and multilevel systems of government, the problem of sovereignty was solved by identifying the object of political power – the individual as a structural component of the population. At the same time, an empire should be understood not only and not so much as a political form of organizing space but as a form of a sociopolitical order with an extensive infrastructure of control over the constant (re)production of this very order.

The empire always claims to be complete, to create its own imperial world, into which all the social and political structures of the periphery are integrated. However, the degree of integration can be different, and it depends on the institutional, structural, and functional capabilities first of all of the periphery itself, as well as on its willingness to integrate into the imperial system of order.

If we apply the conceptual and discursive practices of modern science to studying the empire, then the empire is a supranational entity within which imperial sovereignty operates and, in the system of imperial sovereignty, a subsystem of sovereignty of the periphery can operate. Claiming completeness, empires resolved the issue of sovereign power by identifying the population with the empire through either (1) *practices of citizenship* (citizen of the Roman Empire, citizen of the Soviet Union) or (2) *practices of subjectness* (subjects of the ruler in the British, Russian, or Ottoman Empires).

The peripheral constituents of an empire (principalities, kingdoms, provinces, and other political forms of organization) are part of the (re)production of imperial sovereignty. That is, we have a situation in which the emperor is a sovereign interacting with the entire system through the development of a certain sum of relations (decisions, actions, communications, structures, symbols and signs), which are accepted by the system as "their own," separated from "aliens' ones."

In this case, sovereignty acts as a property of the social system to order chaos, (re)producing the existing imperial order. However, owing to the territorial extent of the empire and its structural and functional complexity, the emerging situations of chaos or uncertainty (the so-called "bifurcation points" in political science) extrapolate the mechanisms of sovereignty to their "local" ruler, that is, to the one who is "here and now" managing the periphery and making decisions. In this understanding, the practice of "colonial administration" or "local government of colonies" is manifested when the king or emperor is formally a sovereign, and nominally these functions are (re)performed by the "colonial manager" who has a system of control; instruments of violence, discipline, and domination; and the ability to influence the construction of collective identities at his or her disposal.

Charles Tilly points to the fact that the colonization of new territories by the British, Dutch, and French focused on "giving their merchants permission to organize colonial rule" (Tilly 1992: 92). However, a certain clarification is in order: in addition to merchants, other structures of social power were also involved,[3] primarily missionaries, who formed the ideological basis of the imperial order, and the military, which functioned as an instrument for maintaining order, ensuring security, and protecting the territory

---

[3] By structures of social power, I mean what Michael Mann writes about in *Sources of Social Power*, where he points out the existence of four fundamental social types of power: commercial (merchant), military (guards, army), religious-ideological (priests), and political (ruler).

of the colony from external interference (McNeill 1963; Mann 1986). These power structures organized new territories, extrapolating the practices and methods of governing the center to the empire (in this case, the metropolis).

As a consequence, there is a process in which the empire institutionalizes the structures of sovereignty, creating, for example, the British, French or Dutch East India Company.[4] The development of new territories on the one hand turns the empire into a discrete management system, forcing it to seek new forms of management of the sociopolitical order. On the other hand, it transforms its system into a supraterritorial and multilevel one, forcing a consideration of sovereignty not just as a system but as a mechanism with the ability to reproduce and legitimize political decisions, where internal factors determine not only the interests of the center but also the needs of the periphery, though to a lesser extent.

Neoliberalism as a Projection of the "Imperial" Character of Sovereignty: The Degree of Strength, and Ways of Functioning

No matter how paradoxical it may sound, the modern neoliberal system of government that was formed during the 20th century is a projection of the colonial (imperial) system of government that was formed in the 16th to 18th centuries. In my opinion, neoliberalism is an attempt to legitimize the (post)imperial order in modern times by institutionalizing the structures of sovereignty: international and local associations (organizations or blocs), transnational corporations, and military-political alliances. As Giovanni Arrighi pointed out:

> Moreover, constraints and restrictions on state sovereignty came to be embodied in parastatal organizations—most notably, the UN and the Bretton

---

[4] The East India Company, which was created as a trade organization, evolved over time into a political structure with its own fleet and army, a bureaucratic management system, and territorial possessions; but, most important, it possessed sovereignty as a way of implementing decisions.

Woods organizations — which for the first time in the modern era institutionalized the idea of world government. (Arrighi 1994: 75)

Institutionalization, primarily of the network structures of sovereignty, is the process of creating a supranational level of government with dominant centers and (semi)peripheries lying within the sphere of the center's influence.

During the course of the collapse of empires, the creation of independent national states, and the process of decolonization that took place in the 19th and 20th centuries, sovereignty began to be associated with the independence of domestic politics (the political system) from external influence (other political systems). If we take the *state of modernity* (as a rational, secularized, and disciplining state) as an axiom of the existence of the modern state, then it is necessary to stipulate possible ways to evaluate the strength of sovereignty, that is, possible ways to evaluate the functioning of sovereignty.

We suggest distinguishing three degrees of strength of sovereignty, depending on the set of specific parameters: weak, medium and strong (see table 1). These degrees of strength of sovereignty are more characteristic of open political systems, in which sovereignty itself is relative to many other sovereignties or the same sovereignty both within the internal political system and beyond. On the one hand, in the modern world, the dominant form is an open political system, but recently conditions have been created for a "rollback from openness" and autonomy of the system.[5]

On the other hand, a closed political system is a "project" of the 20th century, associated primarily with the undemocratic regime characteristics of the political system.[6] In the case of a closed

---

5 A striking example of the autonomy of the political system is the policy of the US during the presidency of Donald Trump, when the US began either to withdraw from international platforms or to question their consistency and functionality. It also raises the question of the viability of the liberal democratic order not only in the US but also in other countries, for example in Western Europe.

6 In this case, the regime must be viewed as the state of the political system in a specific period, what we call the "here and now." Until the 20th century, a closed political system as such did not exist, if we do not take into account Japan in the period of Sakoku (isolation). In the case of Japan, the matter

political system, we are speaking about the autonomy of sovereignty, which, as a rule, is strong in terms of the degree of strength, and also tends to absoluteness (returning to Leibniz's idea of absolute sovereignty).

Table 1. Sovereignty's degree of strength: Structure and functions

Sovereignty Parameters	Weak	Medium	Strong
Power hierarchy	Weak hierarchy	Medium hierarchy	Strong hierarchy
Direction of the organization of power relations	From below	Consensus	From above
Type of bureaucracy	No bureaucracy	Client-oriented	Professional
Institutional design of the political system	Leaderism	Monarchy	Parliamentarism
Regulatory system	Custom / Morality	Morality / Law	Law / Politics
Social solidarity[7]	Mechanic (formal)	Organic (according to interests)	Societal (value)
Social structure[8]	Layers / Columns[9]	Classes / Strata	Estates / Guilds, Trusts

With **weak sovereignty**, the hierarchical structure of power relations is weak and rather formal. Such a hierarchy is volatile and unstable, depending on the internal or external social, military, or cultural environment. A weak hierarchy is characterized by a mismatch between elites and a blur in the clear planning of interactions between different social structures. Such a mechanism arises

---

concerns not so much the closedness of the system from other systems as it does isolation, that is, a sufficiently large restriction of Japan's ties and communication with other forms of political organization.

7   We consider social solidarity from the position of Emile Durkheim, adding to it an additional type societal.
8   The social structure in this case has a variable character since it is influenced by the openness or closedness of the political system, vertical or horizontal structures of sociopolitical relations, and the ways of (self)organization of the population.
9   We use the "Columns" category in the sense Arend Lijphart used it in his analysis of multiconstituent societies and in the theory of consocial democracy.

during political or social crises and is of a short-term nature. Because it is unstable and weak accordingly, it seeks to strengthen power hierarchies in any form. Weak sovereignty rests on organization "from below"; that is, the power of the sovereign is directly proportional to the desire of the population to obey, and also depends on the belief of the population in its ruler and the fear of subordinates before the ruler.

With weak sovereignty, there is no bureaucracy as such; its functions are performed by groups of persons close to the ruler who function according to a system of informal relations. Therefore, the structure of power relations is patrimonial, and also includes the practices of nepotism and crony capitalism. The political system itself is close to leaderism as a way of institutionalizing social relations. Leaderism presupposes the presence of a charismatic ruler — a leader who is both a catalyst for political reality and a coordinator of political processes.

Therefore, the normative system with weak sovereignty functions through the prism of customs and morality. A custom is a historically established norm that relies on literal performance; that is, it does not require individual or collective interpretation. The custom is not universal and the same for everyone; it may be different for different social groups, and the degree of its implementation will also differ. Morality precedes law; accordingly, the normative system tries to systematize norms in such a way that they are the same for everyone in terms of the degree of fulfillment and the degree of punishment for nonfulfillment. Morality goes beyond the everyday life in which the individual finds him- or herself and his or her social boundaries.

Social solidarity (Durkheim 1969: 37–43) as a way of legitimizing collective identity is mechanical, that is, formal. It is based on the underdevelopment and similarity of the constituent models of society. Inherent in mechanical solidarity is the use of violence and repressive mechanisms to support social structuring. With mechanical solidarity, an individual blends into a team, which the individual directly depends on. The social solidarity of a team depends on the level of interaction among its members, as well as on cooperation between socioeconomic functions reflecting the normative space of such a team. Mechanical solidarity is characterized by repressive sanctions, a similarity in sociocultural structures and norms, and a poorly developed infrastructure of social ties and social mobility.

The social structure is represented by the variation of layers/columns where the "filter" for the transition from one layer to another is the presence of certain resources and capabilities (financial, administrative, military, power, relatives). This structure is typical, for example, of some countries in Africa and the Middle East (Libya, Syria, Somalia, Democratic Republic of Congo, Zambia), where formally these political organizations are states, but nominally they are divided into many (self)organized groups (military formations, rebels, paramilitary groups that control a certain territory and the movement of capital, goods, and people on it).

With **medium sovereignty**, a medium hierarchy of power functions that is based on at least a two-level system of relations. The level of organization of the hierarchy depends on the level of organization of the political system and the society itself. As a rule, medium sovereignty is represented by the practices of populism, clientelism, and elitism in how the distribution of power is structured and in the formation of power inequalities. With respect to clientelism, there is an indirect interaction between the patron and the client whereby the latter directly depends on the former. Clients are loyal and devoted to the patron or to the person interested in obtaining both social prestige and socioeconomic benefits.

Consequently, during the functioning of the medium hierarchy, there is a consensus direction in the organization of power relations, whereby not only subjects of political power but also objects are allowed to develop and make a political decision. In this context, consensus is a way of coordinating the actions of the authorities that, in one way or another, depends on the relationship between the ruler, the bureaucracy, and the population. Bureaucracy, on the other hand, is client-oriented and its functions are aimed at identifying the needs and desires of the population for more flexible management and to prevent crises in the political system. On the one hand, the patron has broad social ties, power or economic resources on the other, the patron needs "his or her own people" in the appropriate areas of implementing the power policy and supporting the legitimacy of the existing system of government.

Institutional design with medium sovereignty is formalized as a monarchy, which cannot always be only and exclusively hereditary. The monarchical structure presupposes the creation of a vertical of power relations, a ramified infrastructure of power, as well as a differentiation of society — a normatively fixed social stratification of the population. The social structure is represented by classes and strata; the latter, in turn, are characterized by (1) the unification of people into a community on a nominal basis — property, blood, ethnos, language; and (2) the construction of a hierarchical model of interaction and relationships.

Classes, as Pierre Bourdieu defines them, are a set of agents that occupy an initial position (at the same time, they exist in specific conditions, and are subject to these conditions and circumstances); have similar dispositions, interests, and capital and produce similar social practices and positions (Bourdieu 1985: 726–727). A social class is a set of objective and subjective factors having in common the acceptance of the (re)production of the social order, a normative value system, and a "class consciousness." Class consciousness, in turn, is the construction of social reality, an ideology manifesting as a set of social practices, norms, values, and identification of oneself in the social and political system.

With **strong sovereignty**, a strong power hierarchy also functions, which is best represented in a meaningful way in corporatism and its structural varieties (bureaucratic, oligarchic, societal, economic, others). With strong sovereignty, we are speaking about the degree of integration of the elites into the political system, as well as their (in)direct participation in the development of political decisions and (re)production of the network structure of power. According to the logic of corporatism, the structural units of society are not separate individuals but social groups that have the best chance at being on the receiving end of the redistribution of power, capital, prestige, and social benefits. The power structure, as a system reproducing sovereign relations, is formed "from above," creating a ramified configuration of power: (1) as a relationship between subjects and objects, (2) as a struggle for the possession of power resources, and (3) as control over the organization of social space.

The production of mechanisms to legitimize power, the maintenance of a system of universal control, and the reproduction of the existing political order all require a professional bureaucracy that is rational, systemic, and multifunctional (Weber [1921] 1978; Merton 1968). Thus, the power hierarchy in strong sovereignty performs a management function that is, sovereignty in this case should be considered as the management and organization of social structures in the context of the political system. Therefore, the normative system is based on law as a process of codification, systematization, and universalization of existing norms in conjunction with politics as an instrument of the conscious regulation of society, social structures, social processes, and sociopolitical relations.

The social structure is also determined variably, through the prism of estates (when certain "filters" are evident, which slow down social mobility and fix the social distance between communities, groups, and individuals); the social structure may also take the form of guild trusts (when an impenetrable system is created that regulates social distance, forms hierarchical structures of interactions, and monopolizes the very right to power). Guild trusts also have their own specificities, depending on their content:

1. *economic character* — the dominance of the economy; for example, US transnational corporations, chaebols in South Korea, zaibatsus in Japan;
2. *political nature* — political parties, elites, and leaders; politics seen as a field of struggle and the redistribution of power;
3. *professional (consensus) character* — a combination of economic and political, when the economy is seen as a way to achieve political goals and politics is understood and accepted as an instrument of reproduction and satisfaction of social needs.

The degrees of strength of sovereignty, as was noted earlier, function in open and closed political systems, where open systems are characterized by relative sovereignty, (co)related to other relative sovereignty. In a closed system, the relativity of sovereignty is impossible, since any closed political system tends to autonomization, autarky, and, as a possible option, isolation. Therefore, in closed political systems (see figure 1), sovereignty is autonomous, one of the properties of which can be absoluteness, and strong in terms of power at the same time.

Figure 1. Sovereignty's degree of strength on a scale of relative to absolute

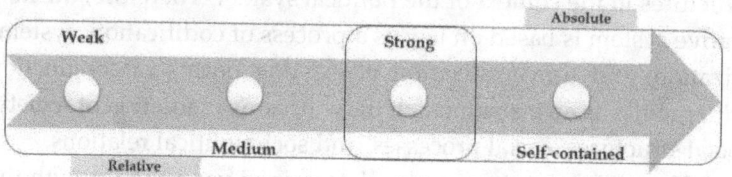

In other words, in open political systems, sovereignty is relative to a number of other relative sovereignties, which either line up in a hierarchy (vertical structure of sovereign power) or function with each other in equal conditions (horizontal structure of sovereign power) (see figure 2). Moreover, sovereignty is relative in relation to the very political system in which it functions. This type of sovereignty, as a rule, is permanent: it is a system of power relations that is (re)produced within the boundaries of a particular political system. Relative sovereignty presupposes the intervention of concomitant factors in the very process of producing sovereignty also, relative sovereignty can be influenced by social or political conjuncture, so it cannot be autonomous (tending to absoluteness).

Figure 2. Sovereignty in the context of political systems

Political System

Open	Closed

Sovereignty

Relative	Self-contained

Condition of Sovereignty

Permanent	Immanent

In closed political systems,[10] it is the autonomous (with development into absolute) sovereignty that functions; that is, the political system is in a constant state of tension and a state of emergency. The functionality of such a system is ensured through control over the social reality of the population, the use of physical violence, a system of disciplinary mechanisms, and the exercise of a power that stands above the law and constitutes both the laws themselves and the normative space. In such a system, law is perceived not as a way to codify the social order but as an instrument of direct subordination. In closed political systems, autonomous sovereignty proceeds from the quality of power (control over the system of violence) and the number of followers (the apparatus of the system of violence).

Sovereigntism as a "New" Political Reality: Factor Analysis

From the point of view of international law, sovereignty has been transformed into an attribute of a state independent of outside influence. However, the process of globalization that is taking place in our time calls into question the existence of sovereignty. Globalization presupposes, if you look at its substantive part, at least three

---

10 Examples of closed political systems are the Democratic People's Republic of Korea, Saudi Arabia, Iran, Turkmenistan, Tajikistan, Cuba, and Myanmar.

main aspects: universalism (as a system of universal norms, laws, and rules), codification (as ordering, first of all, the system of power relations and control systems), and unification (as a method of managing diversity with their further reduction to a single model).

In this perspective, we get at least two discursive directions: first, sovereignty as a system of power relations, and second, sovereignty as an attribute of the state, independent of outside influence. In such a consideration of sovereignty, the question arises about the study of sovereigntism as "politicized sovereignty." Modern researchers view sovereigntism either as a derivative of populism, particularism, and nationalism (Howell & Moe 2020; Kimball 2020; Sharma 2020) or as a mechanism for influencing communities about the internal politics of the state (Strang 1996; Rensmann 2016; Beetz & Rossi 2017; Agnew 2019).

In our opinion, for a more comprehensive and systematic analysis, it is necessary to separate sovereigntism as a *political movement* that claims to ideologically justify itself (here taking the form of political parties or organizations, e.g., French Action, France Arise, Popular Republican Union in France, New Force, Brothers of Italy, in Italy, Falange Española de las JONS, and Vox, in Spain) from sovereigntism as a set of *practices*, that is, immanent, discrete events or actions of a sociopolitical nature (rallies, protests, revolutions, uprisings) aimed at delegitimizing sovereign power or at deconstructing political reality itself.

So, if "sovereigntism [is] the belief in the uncontested primacy of national-level politics and the call to recover at this precise level (institutionally as well as territorially) power that has slipped away to more distant and diffuse layers of governance" (Kallis 2018: 299), then sovereigntism is adjacent to or conjoined with such social and political phenomena as particularism, separatism, nationalism, and populism. Sovereigntism is a natural reaction to the processes of globalization and universalization taking place in the modern world. Therefore, sovereigntism must be considered a completely natural reaction, a response to globalization, when the processes of integration and universalization "undermine" the ability of the authorities to focus exclusively on internal factors when making political decisions.

In order to conceptualize sovereigntism as a political phenomenon, we suggest analyzing the factors of the emergence and implementation of sovereignty, which are largely associated with the crisis of sovereignty itself as a system of power relations, on the one hand, and with the crisis in the system of internal government on the other. We distinguish the following factors: (1) the crisis of collective identity, (2) "universalization of the universal," (3) a clash of ideologies, (4) the crisis of the legitimacy of power and the system of universal control, (5) populism and particularism as instruments of sovereignty, (6) autonomization of sovereignty in open systems, and (7) the crisis of sovereignty as a discursive field.

The crisis of collective identity. Sovereignty, as was said earlier, presupposes the development of a certain collective identity, which constitutes a binary position in relation to the external environment. In other words, sovereignty appeals to society as a whole, the "friends" of the political system, which organizes them and protects them from "enemies" from outside. This "we or they" opposition is necessary to legitimize the system of power relations, as well as to create disciplinary mechanisms for managing the political system.

> It has been the source of greatest preoccupation and contention when conditions have been producing rapid changes in the scope of government or in the nature of society or in both. It has been resisted or reviled—it could not be overlooked—when conditions, by producing a close integration between society and government or else by producing a gap between society and government, have inclined men to assume that government and community are identical. (Hinsley 1986: 2)

Sovereigntism, on the other hand, demonstrates and constructs a completely different matrix of social actions. In connection with splits in collective identity, sovereignty raises the question of the opposition "we or they" inside the political system, and not outside it, when sovereignty and sovereign power itself become "enemies" and the split social structures and communities become "friends." The paradox of this situation is that sovereigntists, on the contrary, are trying to revive the collective identity as a "national whole," pointing out the inconsistency of the authorities, and their inability to maintain political order or the integrity of the entire system. This happens because any sovereign power should be a single whole, and the processes of globalization differentiate and fragment it. In this case, "national identity is never a finished product; it is always in the process of being constructed and reconstructed" (Doty 1996: 123).

A vivid example of such opposition is the migration crisis in the EU in 2015–2019, when, on the one hand, the EU member states refused to comply with the decisions of the supranational authorities, such as the European Commission, and on the other, nationalist social structures within individual countries refused to follow the decisions of both national and supranational authorities. In this situation, a discourse of migrants and refugees as enemies of the citizens of European states came into being (Pew Research Center 2016), when origin, religion, and language were named as key factors in the formation of both the national and collective identity of the EU member states. That is, sovereigntism actualizes issues related to fundamentalism as a political reaction to key factors: origin (place, status, position), language of communication (methods and forms of communication), and faith (religion, ideology).

Collective identity presupposes not just the social construction of the real dispositions of social groups, but also the political rationale and political legality of such an identity. With the collapse of the Soviet Union, a situation has developed when the collective identity in the form of the "Soviet citizen or person" nomination remains quite strong, but at the same time the collective identity of the population of already independent states is being constructed and constituted. As a rule, political regimes use nationalism to substantiate a "new collective identity," that is, there is an attachment to a specific nation that lives in a specific territory. In this context, it is interesting to parallel such processes with the ideas of Pierre Bourdieu regarding the symbolic struggle in various social fields (Bourdieu 1989).

In the context of the post-Soviet space, two spatial levels can be distinguished: the *macro* level (post-imperial space) and the *micro* level (independent states). Symbolic struggle is a process of exchanging social dispositions and redistributing social capital, which occurs as a deconstruction of the social and the political. The creation of a collective identity is a way of constructing new symbols of power relations, within which there are immanent and permanent variables, for example, the legitimation of power, a sense of belonging to a particular social group, social and political reflection, political dispositions of social groups. At the same time, it is important to reproduce the practices of opposition (inversion practices) when there are "we" and "they," "ours" and "others," that is, the construction of a certain "image of the enemy" or threat from the outside.

In (semi)closed political systems in the post-Soviet space, collective identity is perceived as a tool for the sovereignty of power, that is, for establishing control over the population in social, political, cultural or economic contexts (Abashin 2012). I have already indicated earlier (see Figure 1) that absolute sovereignty is possible either in an imperial political system or in an autonomous (closed) political system, which implies the creation of a kind of binary system of center-peripheral relations. Changes in the configurations of power require a change in the ways of legitimizing the same power, therefore, independent states in the post-Soviet space needed to reinvent the nation, offering their own vision of both history and politics. Therefore, the necessary basis for such a process appears in the form of a political theology of nationalism, for example, "Ruhnama" (is a book written by Saparmurat Niyazov, the President of Turkmenistan).

On the other hand, one can see the construction of collective identity through the prism of geopolitical orientations, as in the case of Lithuania, Latvia and Estonia (member states of the European Union) and with Ukraine, Moldova, Georgia (as those who wish to become member states of the European Union). Geopolitical orientation presupposes the extrapolation of symbolic power to the territory of the state, when a certain symbolic space with specific political or economic nominations arises. For example, acceptance or rejection of European culture and values, codification of social space, taking into account the specifics of the EU, universalization of the political system (modernization, democratization, reforms, etc.).

"**Universalization of the universal.**" The *state of modernity*, which is the dominant form of political organization in our time, presupposes the universalization of its own space, that is, the optimization of the mechanisms and tools for managing territory, population, and security. A sovereign state presupposes the universalization of the political system, the codification of the social and political space for more flexible and optimal management. However, globalization also implies the universalization and unification of many political and social structures.[11] In this regard, a problematic situation arises when processes overlap, namely a "universalization of the universal." Integration into the global space undermines the legitimacy of the very political order of the state as it indicates the imperfection of its universal norms, the imperfection of its universality. The globalization of the supranational level establishes the preconditions for the deligitimization of the sovereign power at the state level.

However, in our opinion, there is also a reverse process, which we can call the "paradox of universalization." It lies in the fact that the universalization of one's own political system in the context of the institutional design of the state does not lead to the optimization of this system but to its expansion. For example, political reforms in Ukraine over the past five years can be called an example of such a "paradox of universalization": the judicial reform, the anticorruption reform, the economic reform — all of them are aimed at creating new institutions within the political system (e.g., National Anti-Corruption Bureau of Ukraine, High Anti-Corruption Court of Ukraine, Specialized Anti-Corruption Prosecutor's Office). That is, the nature of the "paradox of universalization" lies not in the optimization of the political system as a mechanism for articulating power relations but in how political power itself is deconstructed, when viewed through the prism of governance and political decision-making. Therefore, sovereigntism in this context can be

---

11 As exemplified in the creation of a personal identification system, and common databases on internal security issues, the opening of borders, and the adoption of resolutions, memoranda, and decisions of international associations (the UN, IMF, World Bank, NATO, and others).

viewed as attempts to develop mechanisms to optimize the political system as a result of, for example, an emerging political crisis. That is, sovereigntism becomes a reaction not so much to the paradox of universalization as to the inability of institutions to effectively and optimally interact within one system.

The universalization of the states of the post-Soviet space takes place in the context of both globalization processes and the internal political ideological state of the system. On the one hand, such states need economic integration into the global economic system, what Immanuel Wallerstein called the world-economy. On the other hand, it is necessary to maintain the legitimacy of one's own power, which, as a rule, relies on charisma, the authority of a political leader, neo-patrimonial practices (Fisun 2012) and the principles of fundamentalism (ideological justification of power). Therefore, in this context, I propose to comprehend the principle of "universalization of the universal" from the position of understanding the power proposed by Michel de Certeau.

De Certeau suggests that power consists of two main categories (Certeau 2011): *strategies* (institutions and structures of power) and *tactics* (free individual space in the environment, which is determined by strategies). Strategies are a vision (not always ideological) of a political system, while tactics are a set of social practices of the population (social groups). Strategies and tactics are in a certain balance, the violation of which entails the emergence of bifurcation processes, for example, "color revolutions" in Georgia (Rose Revolution, 2003), Kyrgyzstan (Tulip Revolution, 2005), Ukraine (Maidan 2004, 2013-2014). Here I mean that any political system depends on foreign policy or economic conditions, therefore there are only two options (1) either to oppose it, (2) or to accept it: *from above* (when the political elite makes changes) and *from below* (social groups or the general population).

For example, in the case of Russia, Kazakhstan, Belarus, Turkmenistan, such changes were partially carried out from above, since it was necessary to build an integral political system in which the political and regime characteristics prevented the emergence of opposition to the current government. In the case of Georgia, Ukraine or the Baltic countries — from below (what can be described as the teleological potential of social groups), that is, the inability of the political elite to make changes. Universalization is not limited to specific economic processes (integration, unification, modernization), it is a set of mechanisms for the codification of social and political space. Universalization presupposes not just integrity, but the unity, for example, of subjects and objects of power, the political elite and other social groups, and the population as a whole.

Clash of ideologies. Another important factor in the emergence of sovereigntism is the clash of ideologies, and specifically the clash of constructed sociopolitical realities. The triumph of neoliberal ideology at the end of the 20th century is gradually fading, giving way to other forms of ideology, such as nationalism, fundamentalism, and traditionalism. A vivid confirmation of this development is the situation in Hong Kong (China), where a crisis of the management system arose associated with a clash of two ideologies the ideology of the PRC itself, which can be described as modernized traditionalism, and the ideology of Hong Kong, which can be described, primarily in economic terms as neoliberalism. Another example is the post-Soviet space during the period in which the former republics of the USSR gained their independence and the ideology of socialism (regulating) collided with the ideology of Western neoliberalism (regulated). The third example is Iran during the 1979 Islamic Revolution when Islamic fundamentalism and the liberal order clashed in the course of an unsuccessful attempt to Westernize the state ("universalization of the universal").

The clash of ideologies implies not only different social realities but also a different set of values, as well as ways of understanding reality (Dapiran 2020; Loong-Yu 2020). In the political, economic, and cultural spheres of society different ideologies can manifest through the construction of reality, forms of awareness of reality, and in different social practices or rituals, values, attitudes, or norms of behavior. The clash of ideologies takes place in one of the social fields, affecting different aspects of social life. The purpose of such a clash is either to oust one of the ideologies or to try to consolidate the conflicting ideologies.

The clash of ideologies is especially relevant in the context of the post-Soviet space. Here one should take into account two ontological bases of ideology: (1) as a social phenomenon (e.g. in the context of Karl Marx, Antonio Gramsci, Louis Althusser, György Lukács) and (2) as a political phenomenon (liberalism, conservatism, socialism and their branches). In most states in the post-Soviet space, authoritarianism dominates, which creates conditions for the autonomization of the political system. A (semi)closed political system with neo-patrimonial power relations and the reproduction of a system of universal control over the security of power, population and territory requires a specific ideology—not just a form of consciousness, but a way to legitimize the political regime (a specific state of the political system at a specific time).

As a rule, there are several directions for building such an ideology. The first is *nationalism*, which can be described as "the spontaneous distillation of a complex intersection of discrete or imaginary events, not as a result of social evolution" (Anderson 1983). Nations are always constructed, therefore nationalism acts as an ideological rationale, the pretentiousness of which is characterized by the constitution of the uniqueness of the nation in the context of historical evolution. In the case of the post-Soviet space, nationalism is characterized by stable social practices of sacralization of the head of state, his identification with the nation, autarkism of the political system, mythologization of power, nation and state (see Kudaibergenova 2020). For example, Turkmenbashy (head of the Turkmen in Turkmen) Saparmurat Niyazov or Arkadag (patron in Turkmen) Gurbanguly Berdimuhamedow in Turkmenistan, Elbasy (leader of the nation in Kazakh) Nursultan Nazarbayev in Kazakhstan, Peshvoyi leader Millat (In Tajik) Emomali Rahmon in Tajikistan, Yurtboshi (head of the country in Uzbek) Islam Karimov in Uzbekistan.

The second is *fundamentalism*, which is a political reaction to those processes that take place both inside and outside the political system. Fundamentalism can be thought of as the absolutization and universalization of power or a policy that does not want to change, that is, opposes revisionism. For example, fundamentalism in Russia (presidency of Vladimir Putin), in Azerbaijan (presidency of Ilham Aliyev), in Belarus (presidency of Alexander Lukashenko). At the same time, one should not designate fundamentalism as an exclusively religious phenomenon, as is customary in a number of methodological approaches. Here it is necessary to go from the opposite direction. Religion is a projection of ideology, the form of the consciousness of the world and the reality in which the individual is. Therefore, fundamentalism is a set of norms that regulate the ideological component of political power.

The crisis of the legitimacy of power and the system of universal control. The state has the legal right to use legitimate violence—this is Max Weber's classic definition, which outlines the state of modern states as political systems. Therefore, just as "on the level of economic policy, a state is considered sovereign when it has control over policy and decision-making mechanisms related to monetary and fiscal policy" (Maris 2019: 230), a political state is sovereign when it controls the reproduction of the political order, the mechanisms of legitimizing political decisions, and ensures the security of the population. Representatives of sovereigntism very often become catalysts for social movements (protests, revolutions, and so on). Quite often they resort to the use of violence against the authorities (police, prosecutor's office, army, national guard), which is illegitimate and illegal, that is, outside the law, but within the boundaries of legal regulation.

If sovereignty presupposes a system of power relations that is based on the use of legitimate violence and disciplinary mechanisms to maintain order, then sovereignty shows the inability to use violence, independently resorting to violence. In addition, the practices of sovereignty show the inability of liberal democratic states to maintain order without using violence (e.g., the protests after the death of George Floyd in the US, the Yellow Vest Movement and Standing at Night in France). From the point of view of sovereignty, such violence is usually physical. From the point of view of the state, it can take the form of both physical violence and different forms of sanctions, exclusion, displacement, and the deprivation of rights or freedom.

Another aspect of the current state of sovereignty is the loss of control over the territory and, above all, the borders of the state. The sovereignty of the state, and the power within this state, are determined by the ability to control the movement of goods, capital, and services, that is, to exert control over movement and distance. Failure to ensure traffic control or border control leads to the so-called illegal socioeconomic processes, including arms and human trafficking, drug trafficking, smuggling, and terrorism. To this list, in the 21st century, control over information and the internet is added, both of which can become quite real catalysts both for changing political reality and for the emergence of social movements.[12] Given the modern processes of globalization (integration, universalization and codification), open political systems tend to the autonomy of their own sovereignty, giving preference to solving internal problems to the detriment of international ones.

For example, in November 2020, an internal political conflict broke out in Ethiopia between the federal government and local authorities in the Tigray region, where regional general elections were held despite the federal government's ban because of the COVID-19 pandemic. The federal government had to send in an army to stabilize the situation. Thus, we see the process of delegitimation of federal power by the regional elites, and this can be viewed as a practice of sovereignty—an attempt to define the boundaries of power and to redistribute power at the same time. Another example is the military coup in Mali that took place on August 18, 2020, in response to the political crisis and mass protests over the resignation of the country's president, Ibrahim Boubacar Keïta. It is also necessary to mention the military coup in Myanmar that took place on February 1, 2021, and became a catalyst for sociopolitical protests, as a result of which an institutional and political crisis arose, at the center of which is the question of the possession of power and the ability to dispose of it.

Any modern state, as a political organization of the population, is a system of universal control over the population, mechanisms for organizing the population and a system of power relations. Control over the population can be varied: administrative,

---

12 An example, Is the "Arab Spring" of 2011–2015 the active phase of the uprisings when the social networks Facebook and Twitter became the main instruments of social movements in North Africa and the Middle East. They helped protestors maintain communication, and coordinate their actions in an attempt to bring order to the resulting sociopolitical chaos.

legal, political, economic. In any case, control is instrumental in nature and it can be both legal and quite radical, including such practices as discipline, punishment, torture (Foucault 1977). Continuing the ideas of Jeremiah Bentham, Michel Foucault points to the modern possibilities of creating a panopticon — a prison, which is a central tower with an overseer and the ability to observe the entire prison from one point. In the case of authoritarian regimes that exist in the post-Soviet space, the panopticon is the most successful metaphor, since it makes it possible to represent the level of control that is reproduced by the structures of political power.

Authoritarian power in Central Asia (Turkmenistan, Kazakhstan, Tajikistan) or in Russia, Azerbaijan, Belarus is ambiguous, since it combines charisma and carnivalization, monopolization of power structures, neo-patrimonial practices, privatization of the political system by a specific socio-political group. Therefore, control for such power is not just an instrument of legitimation, but a set of mechanisms to prevent the emergence of bifurcation processes. It is important that for such political regimes control is used not only in relation to the population, but also in relation to the territory, for example, control over the movement of goods, services, people, capital. Therefore, control is carried out as a system of methods and strategies with the help of which the individual constructs his behavior with those social, political and ideological norms, attitudes, prescriptions that are imposed on him by the power structures.

In the information age, when there is a movement of information and Internet technologies are actively developing, establishing control over the Internet is one of the ways to sovereign power. For example, in the annual rating of Internet freedom from Freedom House, the post-Soviet countries are characterized by the introduction of so-called cyber sovereignty, that is, regulated control over information flows. These states include Uzbekistan, Turkmenistan, Kazakhstan, Russia, Belarus, Tajikistan and Azerbaijan (Freedom House 2020). In Russia, for example, control over the Internet involves an inverse division into friends of the political regime and enemies of the political regime, which in turn is a way to cleanse the political system of unwanted subjects that constitute a threat

(Byford, Doak & Hutchings 2020). Another example is control over the movement of citizens both within the state and outside the state. In Turkmenistan, there are informal practices when families are used as hostages—a guarantee that a person who left the territory of the state for various reasons will return.

Populism and particularism as instruments of sovereigntism. Another feature of the current state of social relations is populism (considered as the leveling of established power relations) and particularism (considered as the desire to legitimize individual interests to the detriment of national or supranational interests). Populism plays the role of a catalyst for political relations that is based on antipodes—opposition within the political system, and the construction of the image of an external or internal enemy. Particularism, on the other hand, produces the interests of communities, individual social structures, as urgent, necessary, and relevant. Donald Trump's 2016 electoral victory, Brexit, Hong Kong's 2014 "Umbrella Revolution", Zelensky's victory in the presidential elections in Ukraine, the victory in the parliamentary elections in Italy, and Italy's "Five Star Movement" are all examples of the use of both populism and particularism that can and should be considered in the context of the practice of sovereignty.

Also, in addition to particularism, one of the trends of our time is particularity as manifested in the transfer of certain state functions to private companies, communities, or structures (e.g., outsourcing practices). This, in turn, leads to the fragmentation of sovereignty into many smaller sovereignties in the field of economic and trade relations, the imposition of law and order, the conduct of military or armed operations, and the provision of social, cultural or other services. The legitimacy of sovereignty with particularity depends on the state's degree of control over the private sector and on the strength of the state's influence over outsourcing companies.

At this point, a slightly more detailed discussion of populism versus sovereignty is warranted. Researchers have noted that "populism emerges and gains traction when political entrepreneurs with strong leadership qualities explore already existing identity conflicts" (Stankov 2021). This is an internal contradiction of power itself, which political scientists consider, among other things, to be the field of struggle for the possession of political power and power resources (recalling the ancient Greek understanding of politics as a struggle). In our opinion, populism is not so much an ideology as an instrument or a way to achieve a fairly rapid buildup of electoral support for a particular politician or political party, with a subsequent redistribution of power relations.

The Argentine political scientist Ernesto Laclau defines populism as an emancipatory social force through which social or political groups that are marginal in their behavior challenge dominant power structures (Laclau 2005). To some extent, we agree with his thesis, since populism opens up opportunities for nonsystemic structures to become part of the political system, having enlisted the support of voters. However, the definition of populism in terms of emancipation (and this is a characteristic thesis for representatives of post-Marxism) confronts us with a dilemma concerning both the role of the state in the life of society and the mechanisms of inclusion and exclusion.

Emancipation presupposes liberation followed by equality, while populism, in our opinion, appeals to the creation of a certain sociopolitical field in which the practice of excluding social or political groups from the process of producing politics will be reproduced. In other words, populism is viewed through the prism of ideology and hegemony. However, we propose to follow the research logic of Paris Aslanidis and shift the emphasis from the ideological aspect to the discursive one (Aslanidis 2016), to consider *populism as a discourse, that is, methods of political communication with the obligatory construction of an unstable and differentiated discursive field in which the mechanisms of inclusion or exclusion are reproduced.* One should not call populism a discursive frame, since a frame denotes a more or less stable structure of the individual's representations of social reality with obligatory reflection. Populism is, first of all, a communication of emotions that ignores rational ways of justifying positions, beliefs, norms or values.

It is in the discursive context that populism can be viewed as an additional tool or method for the reproduction of sovereigntism. Why can't they be identified with each other? Here it is appropriate to outline our assumptions on this matter. First, we view populism as a discourse with the subsequent creation of a discursive field, and sovereigntism as a political movement and political practices. Second, populism is focused on the internal space of state policy, while sovereigntism is opposed to the external space of state policy (though it does not exclude the redistribution of power within the political system). Third, populism, as a rule, has a carnival character or is presented as a certain political performance. That is, it is stylized for certain sociopolitical circumstances (see articles on populism as a political style by Moffitt & Tormey 2014 and Sengul 2019), while sovereigntism is a societal phenomenon in which questions of community, collectivity, solidarity, and the achievement of specific goals turn out to be dominant.

Fourth, populism sooner or later becomes personified. More precisely, it acquires a leader (Geiselberger 2017: 50–53) who strives to institutionalize the discursive field of populism by being elected president or deputy, and dominates his or her own party in parliament establishing control over government institutions. Sovereigntism, on the other hand, is a rather collective and poorly personified phenomenon in which the place of leadership is taken by the glorification and mythologization of specific groups or individuals. Two examples are the women who challenged the riot police during the protests in Belarus in July–August 2020 and students who protested against the arrest of Alexey Navalny in Russia and were later expelled from state universities in January 2021. Other examples include the "Nebesna sotnia" ("Heavenly Hundred"), those individuals killed during the 2014 Ukrainian revolution, and the "QAnon shaman," who was among those who stormed the US Capitol on January 6, 2021.

Therefore, integrating populism as a discourse and sovereigntism as a practice or movement in the context of neoliberalism (which we may take as a set of doctrines, ideas, and directions without a clearly expressed ideology), we will itemize those opportunistic features that affect both categories. Populism directly depends on a sociopolitical or economic crisis; that is, the emergence of populism is possible in the context of an immediate crisis of the sociopolitical system, for example the global economic crisis of 2008 (Slobodian 2018: 25) and the subsequent chain reaction in political, social, cultural, and other spheres. Sovereigntism also depends on crisis, but with one important difference: sovereigntism is a point of bifurcation, that is, a critical state of the system that causes uncertainty. Thus, populism is a derivative of the crisis, while sovereigntism is primary in relation to the crisis. Sovereigntism can both provoke a crisis (the storming of the US Capitol, a coup d'état in Myanmar), and legitimize a crisis that has already begun (the protests in several countries against the COVID-19 restrictions).

The study of populism in the context of neoliberalism takes place from the standpoint of opposing the neoliberal order to the authoritarian one (see Ivanou 2019; Edelman 2020; Diamond 2021). Researchers tend to assume that in most cases populism is used by leaders either in authoritarian political systems Belarus, Turkey, China, Cambodia or in countries where populism has become a catalyst for system authorization, for example, the US during the presidency of Donald Trump, Hungary during the premiership of Viktor Orban, and Poland during the presidency of Andrzej Duda. That is, populism is opposed not so much to neoliberalism as to liberal democracy. Because neoliberalism is more associated with economic policy, therefore, the political aspects of neoliberalism in the context of populist practices remain outside the field of political researchers. In addition, David Cayla points out that the roots of populism are to be found in the contradictions between democratic ideals and values citizens making political decisions through representative democracy; and neoliberal governance mechanisms in which competition and the market arbitrate social events (Cayla 2021).

The situation is different with sovereigntism. On the one hand, it can contribute to the autonomization of the political system with a further strengthening of authoritarian practices, that is, a "tightening the screws" by the current political elite (as in the case of the protests in Belarus 2020, the "Umbrella Revolution" in Hong Kong 2014, the attempted coup d'état in Turkey in 2016). On the other hand, sovereigntism can contribute to the undermining of the political situation, and the deconstruction of state policy, primarily by weakening the mechanisms for making political decisions and determining access to government institutions. In this regard, sovereigntism is a more flexible mechanism for deconstructing globalization, since the internal political system, claiming the universality of its own order, is opposed to external structures that also claim the universality of their own political order. The political order should be seen as a way of organizing the population and territory within the boundaries of the state.

Populism in the context of the post-Soviet space is an important opportunistic tool for (re)production of power. Naturally, populism is largely a discourse, as I pointed out earlier, however, populism is also the ability of a particular social group or political subject to designate the contours of power relations. Populism is used as an opportunity to control the flow of information between a political leader, power structures and the population; as the need for communication; as an ideological component of political power. Populism should not be viewed solely as an independent practice or phenomenon; rather, populism is one of the components of political power (March 2017).

So, populism, as mentioned earlier, creates a discursive field with its own stable boundaries, structures and content. Using populism, political power creates a discursive field as a designation, first of all, of a specific political ideology. Here it is necessary to outline an important research point. The goal of any ideology, as a social phenomenon or as a political teleology, is to construct a new social reality, which offers new substantiations of the existing social order (for example, the special role and exclusivity of the Turkmen people, Russia as a global leader and superpower, Belarus as an "island of stability and order," Kazakhstan as Central Asian Singapore). Consequently, populism is used as a tool for the reproduction of ideology, as the ability to substantiate this ideology.

However, in the case of the political regimes of the post-Soviet space, populism is used primarily as an instrument of power (the dominance of political capital in the interpretation of Pierre Bourdieu). Any political power is based on strength combined with authority, influence, prestige, which may be at a low level in the system of political communication. Authoritarian authorities seek to prevent doubts about their own strength, since their power rests precisely on strength. The force can take on various configurations—police, army, regulation, administrative resources. However, power must always regulate the political dispositions of the various participants in the symbolic struggle. In a sense, power is an extraordinary right or monopoly to produce rules to regulate public discourse.

Autonomization of sovereignty in open systems. The absolute sovereign shows him or herself only in extraordinary situations—in emergencies and situations of uncertainty and instability. The relative sovereignty that is characteristic of open political systems has been rendered incapacitated by the COVID-19 pandemic. Therefore, the governments and leaderships of many countries followed the principle of tightening the system of universal control, and optimizing the legal system. The pandemic, however, showed two important aspects of the modern political organization of the population: first, the crisis of power as a way of communicating between the elites and the population, and second, the state of emergency as a mechanism to legitimize extraordinary actions attendant on possessing political power.

In this sense, sovereignty reveals itself as the ability of the state to solve nonlinear, uncertain, emergency situations through resorting to particularism and populism, on the one hand, and using the apparatus of violence and disciplinary mechanisms on the other (Žižek 2020). The ability of the state is also associated with the growth of authoritarian methods of government,[13] that is, with limiting democracy to resolve an emergency or with applying international law as a tool for autonomizing the political system (Ginsburg 2020). At the same time, the practice of sovereigntism (which produced protests against quarantine measures, and featured certain political decisions of the state and the inability of the state to respond to a changing social reality) appears to us to be a

---

13   Such methods include restricting the movement of the population, restricting democratic rights and freedoms, the use of violence, and a strengthening of the disciplinary mechanisms for the reproduction of political order during a pandemic (as seen in Spain, Italy, France, and Great Britain). On the other hand, such restrictions may be a natural reaction of the political system to social movements challenging the practices of sovereigntism (through rallies, protests, uprisings), such as in the US, Russia, and Belarus.

mechanism for the deconstruction of sovereign power. It is characterized by the presence of a binary opposition within the state and a dynamically (re)produced inversion (replacement of the main concept with an antipode, a diametrical other).

The crisis of sovereignty as a discursive field. Sovereignty derived from a special type of power relations; the power itself was transformed into an attribute of the state from the point of view of normative legal interpretation. In the sociopolitical field, sovereignty is a discursive unit, that is, something that is resorted to in situations of instability, bifurcation, or emergency. In this sense, sovereignty as a discursive field that presupposes institutionalization, the presence of a theoretical framework, the maintenance of boundaries, and the reproduction of universal communication systems, deactualizes itself.

Sovereigntism, on the other hand, becomes a mechanism for deconstructing or refuting sovereign power, constituted by a social movement (practices) that tries to change political reality. Discourse is an external space where a network of set positions, nominations, structures, and groups is placed. The object, on getting into the discourse field, starts experiencing pressure, coercion, and enforcement as a result of the need to follow the set logic. One of the important specificities of a discourse field is constructing the space in which the subjects interact with their predecessors retranslating their normative and value positions. In other words, in the discourse field interaction is an "exclusive" type of social practices (Foucault [1966] 2002: 129–132).

Sovereigntism as an Instrument of Power in the Context of the Post-Soviet Space

As I mentioned earlier, in the case of an empire, a situation arises in which there is absolute sovereignty (the power of the empire, the center) and relative to absolute sovereignty (power relations in the periphery). After the collapse of the Soviet Union, a kind of political vacuum formed, during which the processes of building independent states began. On the one hand, absolute sovereignty lost its meaning as the empire collapsed. On the other hand, the process (political practices) of the reproduction of absolute sovereignty began in new political systems—independent states. As representatives of the world-systems analysis and modernization theories note, the process of "privatization of states" has begun in the post-Soviet space either in full (Uzbekistan, Tajikistan, Kyrgyzstan, Turkmenistan, Azerbaijan), or locally (for example, Ukraine). This refers to the size of the territory in which new power structures were created, for example, neo-patrimonial (Fisun 2012) or authoritarian. If the territory was relatively small and the population was also small, then the most favorable conditions were created for the "privatization" of the state and the creation of an autonomous and autarkic political system.

In the context of both authoritarian political practices in particular, and authoritarianism in general, sovereignty in the post-Soviet space designated its coordinates as power (1) over life, (2) over the body, and as (3) an emergency state of the political system. The latter concerns, for example, the events in Belarus, which are connected with the incident "Ryanair Flight 4978," when the plane of an international airline was forcibly landed. Extraordinary sovereignty manifests itself precisely in such situations, since it is intended to show the power of power, its ability to respond to any threats, as well as the presence of symbolic capital and resources. This event characterizes not only the authoritarian political power in Belarus (see retrospective analysis in Hancock 2006), but also the entire authoritarian power in general in the post-Soviet space. Such power is able to use any tools in order to provide for itself a stable and safe environment for reproduction.

For the states of the post-Soviet space, sovereignty is, first of all, borders, that is, power in a specific territory. This interpretation is typical for most post-Soviet states, except for Russia. In the case of Russia, as a modern empire and the successor to the empires of the past (the Soviet Union and the Russian Empire), sovereignty is power over space, that is, disregard for borders and territories. The ideological rationale for such foreign policy behavior (tactical component or geopolitical ambitions) is the concept of "sovereign democracy,"[14] about which, in particular, Richard Sakwa (2012) writes. The principle of sovereign democracy presupposes not only extreme independence from the foreign policy space, but also geopolitical claims to the post-Soviet space as a whole.

Sovereignty is used by political structures as a kind of claim to power, to the possession of power and the redistribution of power. I have already indicated in the previous parts of the chapter that sovereignty can acquire either (1) the character of politicized sovereignty, or (2) be a set of political practices for the deconstruction of sovereignty. In the case of social movements that have taken place over the past 30 years in the post-Soviet space ("color revolutions" in Georgia and Kyrgyzstan, Maidan in Ukraine, protests in Russia, Belarus, Uzbekistan and others), we are dealing with sovereignty as an attempt to deconstruct power structures (delegitimation of political power and political regime). In the case of Russia, Belarus, Kazakhstan and Turkmenistan, we are dealing with sovereignty as a politicized sovereignty, that is, the creation of an emergency power condition in a specifically limited area.

Another important aspect of sovereignty is the continuation of the reproduction of the center-peripheral model of political relations in the context of the post-imperial space. Russia, as the former center of the empire, is constructing a new imperial image taking into account globalization processes. In this case, sovereignty is an instrument of the Russian government not so much to restore the Soviet Union in a new configuration, but to create a system of control over the post-Soviet space. If for most of the independent states that arose after the collapse of the USSR, sovereignty is territory and power over this territory, then for Russia sovereignty is space and power in space and over space. Consequently, any processes of sovereignization that occur within this space are a threat to the center of this space — Russia. Therefore, it uses the practices of sovereignty

---

14   Sovereign democracy is a political concept invented by the Deputy Head of the Presidential Administration of Russia Vladislav Surkov in 2005-2006. Sovereign democracy presupposes a kind of political life in Russian society, when political decisions are made and controlled by the nation in order to achieve material wealth, freedoms and social justice.

as a mechanism for deconstructing the political system of independent states so that they remain in the orbit of Russian influence, and also be part of post-imperial sovereignty (for example, the war in the East of Ukraine, the war with Georgia, the conflicts in Transnistria).

In other words, in the context of the post-Soviet space, sovereignty is a way to demonstrate strength for a specific political elite. At the same time, power is both an internal political component (administrative and power apparatus, repressive policy, discipline and control, the authority and prestige of power structures, a centralized power apparatus) and a foreign policy component (a way of reproducing the binary position "friend — foe" to maintain the legitimacy of power specific political elite). At the same time, sovereignty is extremely close to such phenomena as populism, universalism and neo-patrimonialism. In the case of populism, which is used as a discursive filling of the practices of sovereignty, it also contributes to the creation of a stable discursive field of power structures. That is, a special or exclusive (unique) political language is being developed, which contributes to the establishment of regulated communication between (1) the central government and the population, (2) the central government and local government, (3) the central government of one state and the central government of another state.

However, perhaps, the main feature of sovereignty in the post-Soviet space is its strong attachment to nationalism (national question, national state, nation as a political category). In the case of the authoritarian states of the post-Soviet space, the category of nation is monopolized by the power elites to create a regulated and constituted configuration of the political order. A nation is a political construct, and nationalism is a set of mechanisms for the reproduction of such political constructs. Therefore, the very power of such states, which is based on political constructs, and therefore is itself a political construct, uses sovereignty as a justification for the social and political reality that was created by political elites. Moreover, in the case of relatively democratic states of the post-Soviet space, the category of nation is a bifurcation, that is, an unstable metamorphosis of political power, which very often comes into conflict with the nation.

Conclusion

Over the past few years, sovereigntism has been evolving from a local phenomenon to being part of the global mainstream as it is actively taken up by both the populations of different countries and the political elites of these countries. The factors itemized above that contribute to the spread of sovereigntism show us one key tendency: sovereigntism is the antipode not so much of sovereignty itself but of the neoliberal order in the context of globalization. If sovereignty is an established system, then sovereigntism either remains a political movement or manifests in social practices, namely, in the practices of sovereigntism aimed at deconstructing or refuting sovereignty.

The factor tendencies that we observe today reveal sovereigntism as a way of autonomizing the political system. Such autonomization presupposes:

1. localization in political decision-making, that is, an orientation toward internal requests and needs;
2. transformation of the regime characteristics of the political system, that is, a departure from liberal-democratic values toward the principles and practices of autarkism and authoritarianism; and
3. an increase in the functionality of the universal control system through the increased use of violence, and mechanisms of disciplinary power.

In addition, the practice of sovereigntism can lead to a shift in the degree of strength of sovereignty from weak to strong ("tightening the screws") or from strong to weak (creating a horizontal set of sovereignties, a weak hierarchy or social mobility, a lack of bureaucracy, the dominance of norms or customs).

Also, the practices of sovereigntism show similar tendencies with the schisms in political and social systems proposed by Seymour Lipset and Stein Rokkan (1967). They analyzed the factors that determined social splits in historical perspective, as well as the main binary positions between which these splits occurred: center–periphery, state–church, city–village, owners–workers. If we analyze the events mentioned at the beginning of this chapter (the growing dynamics of social movements) we see the existing dichotomy, when the periphery fights against the center for the sovereignty of its power and for the right to possess this power.

Another example of dichotomy is a political polarization between city and village regarding the support of one or another political elite. Dichotomy also exists when the church (and in a broader sense religion) claims sovereignty and legitimacy in the system of state sovereignty. It also exists when norms and rules (rituals, practices, ideologies) of different cultures collide and the social principles of fundamentalism become more acute, and when different ideologies construct the social reality of a particular individual, as opposed to a collective identity (i.e., the individualization of society, the existence of many communities).

Also, by distinguishing between sovereigntism and populism, we showed that these two phenomena are not identical. Populism is a discourse that creates its own discursive field and strives for institutionalization. Sovereigntism, on the other hand, is the practice and movement within which the articulation of populism can take place. In other words, populism is used as a tool to focus on the practices of sovereigntism, which, in turn, do not always need populism. Still, both sovereigntism and populism can become the reason for the autonomy of the political system, its transition to a state of semiclosure or closedness, which is happening, for example, with the political systems of Bulgaria, Poland, or Hungary.

In this context, authoritarian populism is used as a means of legitimizing power, while sovereigntism can be used as a means to achieve specific goals. The examples of Poland and Hungary, as well as the US, Myanmar, Belarus, and other countries show that sovereigntism is an instrument of the majority, that is, of the population, while populism is an instrument of a minority, that is, of the power itself and its structures. Consequently, we can assume that sovereigntism at this stage of its development is "politicized sovereignty," that is, a way of identifying and fixing crises in the system, primarily crises of domestic political and legitimate, sovereign power. Practitioners of sovereigntism decompose sovereignty as an integral system into constructs, within the boundaries of which there is a struggle both for power itself and for its redistribution.

In connection with the increase in the participatory practices of the population of different states, sovereigntism is being transformed into an egalitarian (open for everyone, or at least for the majority) way of exercising power as a public policy, of developing and making political decisions, of making power accessible. Sovereignty in its turn remains an elite form of politics, when political elites act as limited holders of sovereign power. Finally, it is necessary to ask the question. *Will sovereigntism become a real policy, or will it remain a way of expressing the unstable and unpredictable "will of the people" aimed at delegitimating the established system of power?*

Bibliography

Abashin, Sergei. (2012). Nation-construction in Post-Soviet Central Asia. In *Soviet and Post-Soviet Identities*, Bassin, M. & Kelly, C. (eds). Cambridge: Cambridge University Press,150–168.

Agamben, Giorgio. (1998). *Homo Sacer: Sovereign Power and Bare Life*. Palo Alto: Stanford University Press.

Agnew, John. (2017). *Globalization and Sovereignty: Beyond the Territorial Trap*. Lanham, MD: Rowman & Littlefield Publishers.

Agnew, John. (2019). Taking back control? The myth of territorial sovereignty and the Brexit fiasco. *Territory, Politics, Governance* 8(2): 259–272.

Anderson, Benedict. (1983). *Imagined Communities: Reflections on the Origin and Spread of Nationalism*. London: Verso.

Arrighi, Giovanni. (1994). *The Long Twentieth Century: Money, Power and the Origins of Our Times*. London: Verso.

Aslanidis, Paris. (2016). Is Populism an Ideology? A Refutation and a New Perspective. *Political Studies* 64(1): 88–104.

Baldassari, Marco, Castelli, Emanuele, Truffelli, Matteo & Vezzani, Giovanni. (2020). *Anti-Europeanism*. Berlin: Springer International Publishing.

Bartelson, Jens. (1995). *A genealogy of sovereignty*. Cambridge studies in international relations. Cambridge: Cambridge University Press.

Beetz, Jan & Rossi, Enzo. (2017). The EU's democratic deficit in a realist key: multilateral governance, popular sovereignty and critical responsiveness. *Transnational Legal Theory* 8(1): 22–41.

Bille, Franck. (2020). *Voluminous States: Sovereignty, Materiality, and the Territorial Imagination.* Durham: Duke University Press.

Bodin, Jean. ([1992] 2009). *On Sovereignty: Six Books of the Commonwealth.* Scotts Valley: CreateSpace Independent Publishing Platform.

Bourdieu, Pierre. (1985). The Social Space and the Genesis of Groups. *Theory and Society* 14(6): 723–744.

Bourdieu, Pierre. (1989). Social Space and Symbolic Power. *Sociological Theory* 7(1): 14–25.

Bourke, Richard, & Skinner, Quentin. (2017). *Popular Sovereignty in Historical Perspective.* Cambridge: Cambridge University Press.

Byford, Andy & Doak, Connor & Hutchings, Stephen. (2020). *Transnational Russian Studies.* Liverpool: Liverpool University Press.

Cayla, David. (2021). *Populism and Neoliberalism.* New York: Routledge.

CEIP. (2021). Global Protest Tracker. *Carnegie Endowment for International Peace (CEIP)*, n.d., https://carnegieendowment.org/publications/interactive/protest-tracker (accessed February 13, 2021).

Certeau, Michel. (2011). *Practice of Everyday Life.* Berkeley, CA: University of California Press.

Craig, Dylan. (2019). *Sovereignty, War, and the Global State.* London: Palgrave Macmillan.

Damiani, Marco. (2020). *Populist Radical Left Parties in Western Europe: Equality and Sovereignty.* London: Routledge.

Dapiran, Antony. (2020). *City on Fire: The Fight for Hong Kong.* Melbourne: Scribe Publications.

Diamond, Larry. (2021). Democratic regression in comparative perspective: scope, methods, and causes. *Democratization* 28(1): 22–42.

Doty, Roxanne. (1996). Sovereignty and the nation: constructing the boundaries of national identity. *Cambridge studies in international relations*, Biersteker, Thomas & Weber, Cynthia (eds). Cambridge: Cambridge University Press, 121–147.

Durkheim, Emile. ([1893] 1969). *The Division of Labor in Society*, trans. G. Simpson. New York: Free Press.

Edelman, Marc. (2020). From "populist moment" to authoritarian era: challenges, dangers, possibilities. *The Journal of Peasant Studies* 47(7): 1418–1444.

Fisun, Oleksandr. (2012). Rethinking post-Soviet politics from a neopatrimonial perspective. *Demokratizatsiya The Journal of Post-Soviet Democratization* 20(2): 87–96.

Foucault, Michael. (2009). *Security, Territory, Population: Lectures at the Collège de France, 1977–78*. London: Picador.

Foucault, Michel. ([1966] 2002). *The Order of Things: An Archaeology of the Human Sciences*. London, New York: Routledge.

Foucault, Michel. (1977). *Discipline and Punish: The Birth of the Prison*. New York: Pantheon Books.

Foucault, Michel. (2003). *Society Must Be Defended: Lectures at the College de France, 1975–76*. London: Picador.

Freedom House. (2020). Freedom on the Net 2020: The Pandemic's Digital Shadow. *Freedom House*, October, https://freedomhouse.org/sites/default/files/2020-10/10122020_FOTN2020_Complete_Report_FINAL.pdf (accessed 25 June 2021).

Geiselberger, Heinrich. (2017). *The Great Regression*. London: Polity Press.

Ginsburg, Tom. (2020). How Authoritarians Use International Law. *Journal of Democracy* 31(4): 44–58.

Hancock, Kathleen. (2006). The Semi-Sovereign State: Belarus and the Russian Neo-Empire. *Foreign Policy Analysis* 2(2): 117-136.

Herzog, Don. (2020). *Sovereignty, RIP*. New Haven: Yale University Press.

Hinsley, Harry. (1986). *Sovereignty*. Cambridge: Cambridge University Press.

Howell, William & Moe, Terry. (2020). *Presidents, Populism, and the Crisis of Democracy*. Chicago: University of Chicago Press.

Ivanou, Aleh. (2019). Authoritarian populism in rural Belarus: distinction, commonalities, and projected finale. *The Journal of Peasant Studies* (46)3: 586–605.

Kallis, Aristotle. (2018). Populism, sovereigntism, and the unlikely re-emergence of the territorial nation-state. *Fudan Journal of the Humanities and Social Sciences* 11(3): 285–302.

Kimball, Roger. (2020). *Who Rules? Sovereignty, Nationalism, and the Fate of Freedom in the Twenty-First Century*. New York: Encounter Books.

Krasner, Stephen. (2001). *Problematic Sovereignty: Contested Rules and Political Possibilities*. New York: Columbia University Press.

Kudaibergenova, Diana. (2020). *Toward Nationalizing Regimes: Conceptualizing Power and Identity in the Post-Soviet Realm*. Pittsburgh: University of Pittsburgh Press.

Laclau, Ernesto. (2005). *On populist reason*. London: Verso.

Leibniz, Gottfried. (1988). *Political writings*. New York: Cambridge University Press.

Lipset, Seymour & Rokkan, Stein. (1967). *Party Systems and Voter Alignments: Cross-national Perspectives*. New York: Free Press.

Loong-Yu, Au. (2020). *Hong Kong in Revolt: The Protest Movement and the Future of China*. London: Pluto Press.

Mann, Michael. (1986). *The Sources of Social Power: Volume 1, A History of Power from the Beginning to AD 1760*. Cambridge: Cambridge University Press.

March, Luke. (2017). Populism in the Post-Soviet States. In *The Oxford Handbook of Populism*, Kaltwasser, Cristóbal & Taggart, Paul & Ochoa Espejo, Paulina & Ostiguy, Pierre (eds). Oxford: Oxford University Press, 276–297.

Maris, Georgios. (2019). National Sovereignty, European Integration and Domination in the Eurozone. *European Review* 28(2): 225–237.

McNeill, William. (1963). *The Rise of the West: A History of the Human Community*. Chicago: University of Chicago Press.

Merton, Robert. (1968). *Social Theory and Social Structure*. New York: Free Press.

Mitchell, William & Fazi, Thomas. (2017). *Reclaiming the State: A Progressive Vision of Sovereignty for a Post-Neoliberal World*. London: Pluto Press.

Moffitt, Benjamin & Tormey, Simon. (2014). Rethinking populism: Politics, mediatization and political style. *Political Studies* 62(2): 381–397.

Pew Research Center. (2016). Europeans Fear Wave of Refugees Will Mean More Terrorism, Fewer Jobs. By Richard Wike, Bruce Stokes & Katie Simmons. *Pew Research Center*, July 11, https://www.pewresearch.org/global/wp-content/uploads/sites/2/2016/07/Pew-Research-Center-EU-Refugees-and-National-Identity-Report-FINAL-July-11-2016.pdf (accessed November 30, 2020).

Rensmann, Lars. (2016). National Sovereigntism and Global Constitutionalism: An Adornian Cosmopolitan Critique. *Critical Horizons* 17(1): 24–39.

Sakwa, Richard. (2012). Sovereignty and Democracy: Constructions and Contradictions in Russia and Beyond. *Region* 1(1): 3–27.

Schmitt, Carl. ([1932] 1996). *The Concept of the Political*. Chicago: University of Chicago Press.

Schmitt, Carl. (2004). *Legality and Legitimacy*. Durham: Duke University Press.

Schmitt, Carl. (2005). *Political Theology: Four Chapters on the Concept of Sovereignty*. Chicago: University of Chicago Press.

Scholte, Jan. (2020). After Liberal Global Democracy: New Methodology for New Praxis. *Fudan Journal of the Humanities and Social Sciences* 13(1): 67–92.

Sengul, Kurt. (2019). Populism, democracy, political style and post-truth: issues for communication research. *Communication Research and Practice* 5(1): 88–101.

Sharma, Nandita. (2020). *Home Rule: National Sovereignty and the Separation of Natives and Migrants*. Durham: Duke University Press.

Slobodian, Quinn. (2018). *Globalists: The end of empire and the birth of neoliberalism*. Cambridge, MA: Harvard University Press.

Stankov, Petar. (2021). *The political economy of populism: An Introduction*. Abingdon, Oxon; New York: Routledge.

Stilz, Anna. (2019). *Territorial sovereignty: A philosophical exploration*. Oxford: Oxford University Press.

Strang, David. (1996). Contested sovereignty: the social construction of colonial imperialism. *Cambridge studies in international relations*. Eds. Thomas Biersteker & Cynthia Weber. Cambridge: Cambridge University Press, 22–49.

Tilly, Charles. (1992). *Coercion, capital and European states, A.D. 990–1992*. Hoboken: Wiley-Blackwell.

Wallerstein, Immanuel. (2004). *World-systems analysis: An introduction*. Durham: Duke University Press.

Waltermann, Antonia. (2019). *Reconstructing sovereignty*. Berlin: Springer.

Weber, Max. ([1921] 1978). *Economy and Society: An Outline of Interpretive Sociology*. Berkeley: University of California Press.

Žižek, Slavoj. (2020). *Pandemic! COVID-19 Shakes the World*. New York: OR Books.

8 Sovereignty as a Contested Concept
The Cases of Trumpism and Putinism

Mikhail Minakov

In 2021, in connection with the COVID-19 pandemic and the associated socioeconomic crisis, the existing political contradictions sharpened in global, regional, national, and subnational contexts. The sources of these contradictions, however, are predominantly to be found in the prepandemic era: in the exodus of America from international politics and its abrupt "return" in 2021, in a certain declared "Westlessness", in the manifest disappearance of common, West-supported rules, in the growing role of non-Western states and economies in shaping the global agenda, and in the many other changes that our "full world" lived through in the immediate past decade.[1]

One of several core contradictions that have escalated in 2020 is the sharpened contest for the understanding of sovereignty. On the one hand, sovereignty is interpreted as state sovereignty, an underlying legal and political principle guiding processes inside and among states for several centuries until the post-World War II period (Kelsen 1920; Schmitt [1922] 1985; Reisman 1990). And this interpretation sparks anew the conflict with the other meanings of sovereignty. Specifically, it tries to undermine an understanding of sovereignty as an undeniable quality of a person as defined by

---

1   Here I refer to several concepts that critically differentiate our era from the previous periods of modernity. "Westlessness" is a process whereby the world "is becoming less Western" and the West itself is "getting less Western, less rule-based, less value-oriented" and may become less Western, too (see: Westlessness 2020: 6; Beyond Westlessness 2021). "Full world" denotes the relatively recent situation in which humanity has lived since the mid-20th century where no more "empty space" is available for growth and every action in every national sector influences other sectors in other nations (see: Weizsäcker & Wijkman 2018: 9ff). Both concepts describe the profound change in the global cultural and political situation in which "sovereignty" becomes a freshly contested concept, with potentially far-reaching consequences for the international order.

transnational human rights treaties and acknowledged by sovereign states (Brand 1994; Cohen 2004; Benhabib 2016). Since the end of World War II, these two meaningful conceptualizations of sovereignty have been drawing closer together, and with the third wave of democratization and the dissolution of the *socialist camp*, they began changing fundamental practices in politics, human development, state-building, and international relations (Huntington 1993; Benhabib 2016; Brunkert et al. 2018).

However, in our times and in our full world, the conjunction of two major meanings of sovereignty is under attack by powerful ideological groups that deny the second meaning and reinterpret the first in a very specific way. These political groups came to power in old and new democracies and autocracies and acquired the label of "new sovereigntists". They have already had a strong ideological impact on the policies of Brazil, Hungary, Poland, Russia, the US, and the UK, which may further change the nature of international relations and the quality of democracy around the world.

In this article I analyze the reinterpretation of the concept of sovereignty by today's sovereigntists. For my analysis I use two cases—Trumpism and Putinism—in which the sovereigntist ideology was well articulated and had a strong impact on foreign and domestic policies. In my analysis I try to answer the question, what is new and what is borrowed in the sovereigntist understanding of sovereignty, a core ideologeme of this movement? In the course of the analysis I will test my hypothesis that the sovereigntist interpretation of sovereignty is only partially a political reaction to the widespread practice of sovereignty that balances human rights and state supremacy; what is more important, sovereigntism offers a new worldview that not only denies rights and liberties to the individual but also promotes a new conservative understanding of world, state, government, people, human person, and their hierarchy.

Accordingly, this article is divided into five parts. In the first part I show how the imagery of sovereignty has changed over the past several centuries and how the alterations affected state-building and international relations. In the second part I describe the sovereigntist turn in understanding sovereignty in general terms to establish the context for further analysis. In the third part I analyze the Trumpian imagery of sovereignty, a (hopefully) short-lived sovereigntist turn in an "old democracy". The next section is dedicated to the sovereigntist turn in Putin's Russia and its impact on Russian political culture and the country's constitutional system. In the conclusion I summarize the answer to my key question and review my hypothesis.

Conceptual and Historical Contexts

The sovereigntist turn is an ideologically driven political process that Is taking place in many countries around the world, affecting equally both old and new democracies and old and new autocracies. This turn changes the post–World War II understanding of sovereignty, and thus of a state, of international politics, and of law. Sovereigntism is the political ideology that drives it. Sovereigntism as such is not a new ideology; it was actually a logic of political action, legal judgment, and international relations since Jean Bodin's and Thomas Hobbes's theories of sovereignty and the state-building practice stemming from the Peace of Westphalia (Hobbes [1651] 1980; Holmes 1988; Bodin [1586] 1992). And between 16th century and today, the concept of sovereignty has evolved over the course of a long history that saw its meaning contested among at least five interpretations. In her conceptual history of sovereignty, Raia Porokhovnik (2013) writes that by the mid-20th century, four major forms of sovereignty could be identified. First, sovereignty was understood as an absolute, indivisible power (a view held by Bodin, Hobbes, and to some extent Spinoza and Kant). Second, sovereignty was perceived as the location of supreme and final authority at the top of a pyramid of discrete lower powers (as proposed by Locke and his followers). Third, sovereignty was applied as a common term to denote two distinct authorities, supreme lawmaking authority and the legitimate power to rule, that limited each other's scope and endowed the *people*, not the ruler, with sovereignty (the liberal tradition). Fourth, sovereignty was treated as the coexistence of internal sovereignty (which granted a monopoly on the use of legitimate force within a specific territory) and external sovereignty (which granted external war- and peacemaking powers) (Prokhovnik 2013: 5–8). The fifth interpretation—sovereignty as the supremacy of a human person (both a citizen and an alien), acknowledged by states—became intellectually and practically influential since the mid-20th century (Benhabib 2004).

These five interpretations of sovereignty were imagined and practiced differently in various periods of modern political history, but sovereignty always remained important as a legal and political concept. The synthesis of different, often conflicting elements of this concept was achieved through the force of the social imagination. Human participation in socioeconomic and political processes is possible owing to the combination of direct personal experience, individual and group judgment, and complex conscious processes that produce certain views, beliefs, and ideologemes. This production is the activity of the social imagination, and its result is social imagery. As such, imagination is a cognitive operation carried out on an unreal thing or situation, where all rational categories are applied to the possible object of sensation which is not actually present at the given time; imagination unites aspects of fantasy, virtuality, and possibility in cognition and action (Ricoeur 1994; Cocking 2005; Bottici 2014; Glaveanu 2018). The synthetic and productive force of imagination also transcends the individual–collective dichotomy (Adams 2004; Zittoun & Cerchia 2013). The physical, semiotic, individual, collective, and other aspects of reality come together owing to the creative force of the human imagination, which makes, among other things, the political realm a space of human creativity, of the application of collectively shared ideas to reality and its change (Berger & Luckman 1956; Schutz & Luckman 1960; Castoriadis 1987; Taylor 1989; Honnet 1995). Accordingly, in this paper I treat the concept of sovereignty as the product of a long process that transformed individual and collective practices and understandings of state, citizen, and relations between states and citizens, which in turn created today's social reality with its unequal distribution of wealth and power in the world-system and attempts to rectify such an inequality.

Initially, the imagery of sovereignty manifested as a "commitment to territoriality, national politics ... and resistance to comity or international law" (Koh 2005: 52). For several centuries, the political order within and among nations was based on an understanding of political sovereignty as the principle of the undisputed supremacy of norms, values, and interests within the confines of a territory controlled by the government of some sovereign state. In the course of this history the sovereign has been reconsidered: first it was a traditional monarch, then it was an absolute monarch in a regular state with an emerging bureaucracy, then it was the regular nation-state with a systemic bureaucracy (Tilly 1994; Du Gay 2005). This last idea of a sovereign was a universally accepted norm up until the existential crisis of World War II (Schrijver 1999; Biersteker 2002).

Despite its universal acceptance, this imagery of sovereignty was constantly in conflict with itself. What is the source and who is the bearer of such sovereignty? The clash for sovereign status was being conducted among a "prince" (which soon became an absolute monarch), a state (which turned into a bureaucratic political machine in metropolises and into colonial administrations in the boundless imperial networks around the world), and a nation (which oscillated between a δῆμος, a political community of citizens, and an ὄχλος, a crowd, masses) — all these conflicting imaginaries of sovereignty were constantly undermining the stability of a state and relations in the world-system. By the 20th century this internally incongruous understanding of sovereignty had differentiated into the above-mentioned five meanings of sovereignty. And these conceptual differences materialized in practical conflicts within and among contemporary nations and jurisdictions, manifesting in loss of the old universally accepted imagery of the sovereign.

After the shock of World War I, the most influential states — those that survived the war and those that came into existence because of it — did their best to create a less contradictory world by developing some common understanding of sovereignty. The contradictory content of different sovereignties called for legal solutions and political action. Among other ends, the League of Nations was supposed to be a mechanism for resolving conflicting sovereignties (Stone 2000; Anghie 2001). The Montevideo Convention on the Rights and Duties of States (enacted in 1933) represented an attempt to reinforce the old imaginary melding state sovereignty and people sovereignty into one concept right before World War II — a barren effort that did not keep the world from global total war (Österud 1997; Grant 1998).

The conceptual contradictions of sovereignty were visible not only in the governmental practices of the decaying colonial states and the unstable nationalist states. They were also evident in the debates among legal scholars and political philosophers of the interwar period. World War II and the political history of the early 20th century showed that states, through their establishments and for their sovereign purposes, could engage in criminal acts (total war, genocide, purges) that contradicted another image, the state as a super-institution based in the idea of justice (Ackerman 1980; Emlyn-Jones & Preddy 2013). In this ideological context, states as sovereigns couldn't be judged and punished. Thus the founding idea of a state — justice — was put into question. How can justice and sovereignty coexist?

In 1922, Carl Schmitt offered the following definition of a sovereign: "Sovereign is he who decides on the exception" and who decides on "the distinction between friend and enemy" (Schmitt [1922] 1985: 5; Schmitt 1996: 12). Schmitt criticized the liberal democracy with its commitment to legal limits on the political authority, which, in his interpretation, meant that the constitutional-democratic state was incapable of being sovereign. In a way, he expressed the most radical view on the supremacy of sovereignty over justice, a view supported by other theorists (e. g., Jellinek 1905). In this statement Schmitt offered a universalist maxim of power-based sovereignty: whoever is in government has the legitimacy to make any exceptional decision and to divide humanity into two categories — those who are *us*, and the rest, who are *enemies*. This image of sovereignty in many ways continued Bodin's and Hobbes's logic of sovereignty as the possession of exceptional power in an isolated state-controlled territory, and it prescribed sovereignty to be of a particularistic nature, with no space for international law or obligations.

At around the same time, Hans Kelsen famously argued that every legal system is a hierarchy of norms based on a fundamental norm of the system. According to such logic, if there are conflicting norms in a system of justice, the conflict can be resolved through recourse to a higher norm. In a sovereign state, the fundamental norms are in the state's constitution. However, international law can become a higher norm for national legal systems, which makes the entire idea of a sovereign system unsatisfactory (Kelsen 1920: 320-321). Thus the principles of justice and sovereignty were seen as incompatible as well, which forced political actors to assign primacy to only one of the principles. To continue with this logic, if justice is a universal value on which political communities are grounded, then it should be formulated as a principle in an international law that could resolve conflicting norms of sovereign nations. The two principles were seen as incompatible, and this difference indeed became among the key ideological factors that drove nations into the catastrophe of World War II.

The reconstruction of the world after the new experience of unprecedented state-guided violence during World War II and after required a reimagining of sovereignty that would not contradict justice—both within and outside the nation—and would not undermine the existence of humanity (Deák et al. 2000; Krasner 2005: 71ff.; Judt 2006: 12ff.). This reimagination of sovereignty was indeed an ambiguous process in the condition of globalization leading to the "full world", in which political systems, jurisdictions, economies, ecological systems, and humanity as a biological species were unable to remain isolated in national territories (Weizsäcker & Wijkman 2018: 10ff.; Schwab & Malleret 2020). On one side, a sovereign state as such was thought to be part of the problem. To lessen the risks a sovereign state produces for peace and life on the planet, the United Nations organization was established as an all-embracing platform for interstate conflict prevention, resolution, and management (Peck 1996). On another side, after World War II most colonies were emancipated from subjection to national sovereignty (Strang 1990; Asprenger 2018). So some new postcolonial polities were keen to practice the outdated, particularistic imagery of sovereignty. On a third side, the sovereignty of the state was more and more outweighed by the increasing sovereignty of the human person and the growing role of human rights within and among states—an imaginary that was providing a new approach to understanding sovereignty (Rudolph 2005; Levy & Sznaider 2006; Benhabib 2018). Altogether, a new, universalist—that is, applicable to all societies around the globe—imaginary of sovereignty was developed as the unity of national and personal sovereignty.

With the introduction and ratification of the Universal *Declaration of Human Rights in 1948*, the new universalist imaginary of sovereignty acquired a serious legal tool to become a widespread practice. But it took another four decades for the practice to became reality. First, the stability of this universal unity needed a strong argumentation. One of those who offered such an argument was John Rawls. Rawls (1999: 577) offered "democratic citizenship in a constitutional democracy" as a solution to the contradictory nature of a state and personal sovereignty. He implied that states were to base themselves on recognition of human personal sovereignty and the superiority of international legal norms, which would transform a Leviathan into democratic "cooperative venture(s) for mutual advantage" (Rawls 1971: 84). In this way, the citizens of a democratic state would become the "owners" or shareholders of the republic in the form of a territorial association. In this state, individuals would be the "sovereigns", with the ultimate authority to decide on state matters. This theory may seem idealistic, but it indeed describes the imaginary that guided the post-World War II legal and political development of the Western core polities (Bell 2000; Benhabib 2016).

Second, this development was constantly undermined by the logic of the Cold War: as a result of the fight against "global communism", Western governments had a security argument to rule, with limited respect for civil rights. The lasting Cold War state of emergency opened Western authorities to the temptation to use the Schmittian understanding of sovereignty in their own countries (despite limitations imposed by their own constitutions) and in their ally states (Latham 2011: 2, 5; Gustafson 2007: 13ff.).

Third, the socialist camp and parts of the economically developing world were opposed to the new universalist imaginary of sovereignty. Global socialism, despite its many varieties, from Brezhnev's and *Deng Xiaoping's* opportunism to Castro's and Pol Pot's radicalism, cherished the imagery of world social revolution. In this framework, sovereignty was not connected with a state: if a state is to be a machine to administer production (Marx 1845), it needs neither political nor legal sovereignty. The peoples of the world were expected to be freed from the accumulation of capital and from capitalism's superstructure, including the dominance of the political machine. The practices of socialist states in the post–World War II period, however, were based on etatism, state corporate capitalism, and an administrative economy (Yakovlev 2010; Krasnobel'mov 2013; Resnick & Wolff 2013). And the international politics of the USSR and China were based on the spread of a socialist anticolonial revolution and the socialist model of state-building. By 1984 the network of states "developing by the socialist path" had reached its historical zenith, and the networks of states oriented toward either Moscow or Beijing included almost half of existing states, which were national states with "limited sovereignty" and different degrees of dependency on one of the core socialist states, enjoyed growing access to social benefits, and had extremely low respect for human rights and civil liberties (Wallerstein 1984; Jayatilleka 2014; Alles & Badie 2016: 11; Verhoeven 2020). In this network of states, constitutional democracy and a human person's rights were close to nonexistent (Osakwe 1981; Kartashkin 1991; Balboni & Danisi 2020). The USSR and China themselves were governed not by a public government but by the party at every level and in every sphere of decision-making, which made the ruling bodies of the party a peculiar sovereign (Shapiro 1965; Schubert 2008; Friedgut 2014). State sovereignty was rather a bargaining point between the Communist Party of the USSR (which de jure was not part of the state) and the pro-communist parties in the countries of Eastern Europe and the global south, which could lead either to cases similar to Angola's or Afghanistan's civil wars, with permanent interference from external actors, or to communist isolationism, such as in Ceausescu's Romania or Hoxha's Albania. The "affirmative action empire" of the USSR (Martin 2001) saw a sovereign in the party leadership, which paid lip service to some level of sovereignty in the working class/people (which could have some identity/*natsionalnost'*), but this was definitely not state sovereignty. In the overarching Marxist political imaginary, sovereignty — in any of its political or legal forms — was simply not among the key issues.[2]

It was the end of Cold War that provided a new universalist imaginary of sovereignty with the chance to become one of the leading practices in politics, state-building, and international relations. One of the results of the end of the global conflict between the capitalist and the socialist camps was an opportunity to build a more just and cooperative system of international relations. Seyla Benhabib describes this perspective as follows:

> [W]e have entered a phase in the evolution of global civil society which is characterized by the rise of *cosmopolitan* norms of justice. (Benhabib 2016: 113)

With the dissolution of the socialist bloc, for several decades this global civil society and states coexisted in a system of nonconflicting double norms. On the one hand, international law was organized around treaty obligations recognized by sovereign states as part of their own national legislation. On the other hand, the norms of international law indeed became cosmopolitan when individuals — whether as citizens or just as human beings — were treated as subjects endowed with universally acknowledged rights, which no state could deny them, even if at times these rights might be regarded as contradictory to the interests of a government. The fact is that after 1948, the new sovereignty imaginary — and all related political, legal, security, and other practices — more and more saw states through a liberal lens. When the emergency argument of Cold War times ceased to undermine it, a state was a recognized sovereign only if it could fulfill its human rights obligations and adhere to the prohibition of crimes against humanity (Grimm 2015:

---

2 Which does not exclude the importance of nonpolitical sovereignty. On this, please read Yurchak (2015).

89–92; Benhabib 2016: 113–14). And the expectations of global populations concerning their governments and their freedoms were in accord with it (Inglehart & Welzel 2005: 5–7).

The 21st century opened in a globalized world where sovereignty was largely understood and practiced in the unity of a state's and a human person's balanced rights, with the strong involvement of international obligations. The universality of liberally understood democracy and a state's obligation to serve its citizens were at the heart of the international order that had emerged. However, already in the first decade of the 21st century a number of crises — the wars in Iraq and Afghanistan, the global financial crisis of 2008–2009, the Russo-Georgian war — showed the limits of the practical application of the new imagery of sovereignty and laid the groundwork for the future sovereigntist turn.

The Sovereigntist Turn

As I discussed earlier, the social imagination is a source of great power for transforming reality. The interconnection of personal and collective will, creativity, and action can change the materiality of social, legal, and political systems (Bottici 2014: 17ff.; Etkind & Minakov 2020: 10ff.). However, the cosmopolitan sovereignty was quickly contested by political philosophers and legal thinkers, as well as by politicians and civic activists from different camps. For example, Michael Walzer and Samuel Moyn have argued that cosmopolitan sovereignty had little impact on practices in national legal and political systems in most countries of the world; this means that the imagery was deficient, it did not extend to social practice (Walzer 2004; Moyn 2010). Jean Cohen has argued that, to grant social and political justice, the human rights regime must be balanced with the principle of self-determination, which in turn implies the coexistence of global cosmopolitanism and national sovereigntism (Cohen 2012). Or thinkers like Thomas Nagel insisted that cosmopolitan sovereignty is a regime founded on the contractual commitments of sovereign states, which could rightfully be withdrawn by such states; that is, the cosmopolitan imagery depends on the sovereigntist imagery (Nagel 2005). To each of these arguments equally strong counterarguments have been posed by other thinkers (e.g., Seyla Benhabib, Jürgen Habermas, Wolfgang Merkel), but the mere discussion was enough to weaken the influence of the cosmopolitan imagination (Fine & Smith 2003; Benhabib 2011a, 2011b, 2016; De Wilde 2019).

Simultaneously, the growth of inter- and transnational systems of norms globally and regionally provoked resistance from those political actors who valued the sovereignty of states more than the rule of law and human rights. For example, despite the cautionary pace of European integration, the Maastricht Treaty (1992) and the Treaty of Lisbon (2007) provoked strong movements against further integration in old and new member states (Schimmelfennig 2019; Rozenberg 2020). As Rozenberg demonstrates, these sovereigntist movements arose simultaneously on both the left and the right, had a very vaguely defined ideology, and reused for their purposes the old continental ideologies such as "nationalism, Gaullism, traditionalism, and republicanism" (Rozenberg 2020: 166).

If from inside the nations, the emerging sovereigntist turn relied on long-established ideologies and varied tremendously from place to place, when viewed from the outside, from an international perspective, the sovereigntist movements of the 21st century have taken three major forms. Analyzing cases of sovereigntist movements from all the nations of the world, Delphine Alles and Bertrand Badie divided them into three categories: archeo-sovereigntism, conservative sovereigntism, and neo-sovereigntism (Alles & Badie 2016: 12). In a nutshell, the first was a reaction to unfair globalist practices and called for a return to the order existing before World War II or earlier; the second aimed at preserving the interstate order without further integration and situated the Westphalian vision at the center of its imagery; and the third responded to the binary cosmopolitan sovereignty with demands to promote norms protecting the independence of each existing state, to grant equality between and among states, and to contain core states in their attempts to influence other nations (Alles & Badie 2016: 16–18). In that last perspective, the sovereigntist turn was guided by the need for a conservative reinvention of justice, which would be provided by the sovereign state, not by some international institutions with unclear legitimacy.

Both approaches, of Rozenberg and of Alles & Badie, define contemporary sovereigntism from within and without mainly as a reaction to the full world and its global political, economic, and legal order that emerged at the beginning of the 21st century. But this provides only part of the answer as to the sources of the sovereigntist turn. Still to be addressed is the *positive* guiding ideas of these sovereigntist movements.

In my opinion, contemporary sovereigntism—in its different forms and categories—is based on the reinterpretation of sovereignty in such a way that it would let the power elites of certain states adapt the political system and economy to the conditions of the full world, where political egoism and legal particularism are, in a longer-term perspective, suicidal. Thus the sovereigntist turn is only partially of a reactionary nature; it is also a conservative form of ideological creativity that attempts to find new forms of particularism that would permit a political community to resist the global challenges without losing its politically and legally understood state sovereignty. And certainly a human person's sovereignty, with its individual and minority rights regime, was to be dismantled as a danger to the political community.

My hypothesis is supported by an analysis of two cases of sovereigntism that, despite their different contexts, have in common a merger of the reactive response to globalization—namely, a desire to return to the pre-World War II or earlier order—and the conservative ideological creativity that would situation sovereignty with the individual nation, not subject to supranational agreements or organizations. These cases concern the interpretation of sovereignty by Donald Trump and his supporters, and the interpretation of sovereignty by sovereigntists from Vladimir Putin's entourage.

The Trumpist Interpretation of Sovereignty

Unlike Marxism or liberalism, Trumpism as a political ideology lacks a fundamental body of texts that would supply a basis for analysis. For that reason, those who analyze Donald Trump's ideological and political views must rely on mediated speeches, bits of quoted conversations, and short posts on social media (Brock 2016: 16ff.; Mollan & Geesin 2020: 407ff.). This is probably its peculiarity: the Trumpist ideology should be spoken, it should avoid firm definitions, and it should rely on the active participation of supporters in interpreting short statements or posts. The term "sovereignty" and its derivatives, for example, in the mass of these statements and posts is quite rare (my search in the archive of the Twitter account "President Trump 45 Archived" found only seven mentions of the term or its derivatives, and all are mainly emotional in their use). And before Trump became president, as Mollan and Geesin, who studied media materials with the participation of Donald Trump before his political career took off, argue, he was reluctant to discuss international politics (and issues such as sovereignty) (Mollan & Geesin 2020). This mediated and undefined use of terms in Trumpism probably stems from the specific subculture of the tea party movement, with its irrational polemics and its own mass media networks (DiMaggio 2011; Street & DiMaggio 2015).

The link between Donald Trump and the tea party movement was mainly provided by Stephen K. Bannon, a person important to the electoral victory of Donald Trump in 2016 and the ideological framework of his presidency, at least in its initial phase. First of all, Trumpism borrows from the tea party worldview an understanding of sovereignty in the context of the denial of the full world condition and the transnational character of many security, legal, social, and ecological problems. Instead, the sovereignty issue was very important for tea party ideologues. Already in a speech at a tea party gathering in New York in 2010, Bannon placed the primacy of the interests of "the people" at the core of his sovereignty concept:

> This accumulated debt at all levels of our society poses an immediate existential threat to America . . . Now unlike the manufactured crises of global warming and healthcare, this is a true crisis. This crisis threatens the very sovereignty of our country. (Bannon 2010)

Later the idea of sovereignty was developed in Bannon's famous Vatican speech (2016). Here sovereignty was demonstrated to be the central issue for the solution of the global crisis of capitalism. According to Bannon, to cope with the current crisis of capitalism, which is ruining the lives of erstwhile middle-class citizens (or *the people*), it is necessary to downplay, dilute, or ignore the influence of transnational organizations (the Davos World Economic Forum, the EU) and federal governments (e.g., of the US) that cannot respect political communities of working people at a state level:

> Look, we believe—strongly—that there is a global tea party movement... The central thing that binds that all together is a center-right populist movement of really the middle class, the working men and women in the world who are just tired of being dictated to by what we call the party of Davos. (Bannon 2016)

In this context, Bannon offers a remedy: sovereignty and nationalism that would ensure the functionality of freedoms for the middle class (or the *majority* as *the people*):

> I think that people, particularly in certain countries, want to see the sovereignty for their country, they want to see nationalism for their country. They don't believe in this kind of pan-European Union or they don't believe in the centralized government in the United States. They'd rather see more of a states-based entity that the founders originally set up where freedoms were controlled at the local level. (Bannon 2016)

And this "nationalist sovereignty" becomes a particularistic maxim with universalist aspiration:

> I happen to think that the individual sovereignty of a country is a good thing and a strong thing. I think strong countries and strong nationalist movements in countries make strong neighbors, and that is really the building blocks that built Western Europe and the United States, and I think it's what can see us forward. (Bannon 2016)

In this way, the tea party ideology raised the issue of sovereignty as a key element that would later be adopted by Trumpism.

It is also important to note that the term *people* applies to a specifically defined political community of citizens. Bannon is not an ethnonationalist, he is an "inclusive nationalist" who looks at "the center" or "the majority" of society. This societal center is the Judeo-Christian relative majority that "invites people of different backgrounds to unite under a common 'American' sense of self" and "dissolves minority identities—leading to the emphasis on 'color-blindness' of 'all lives matter' and opposition to affirmative action" (Guilford & Sonnad 2017). By inventing such "people" as the real sovereign, Bannon gains the ideological ground to deny the sovereignty aspirations of human persons, minorities, and humanity as represented in the form of transnational institutions or the liberal globalist imagery. This ideologeme also provided the ground to prohibit immigration: "On a March 2016 episode, Bannon said that restoring sovereignty meant reducing immigration. In his radio shows, he criticized the federal H-1B visa programs that permit U.S. companies to fill technical positions with workers from overseas" (Sellers & Fahrenthold 2017).

Another important influence on the Trumpian understanding of sovereignty was John R. Bolton, former US ambassador to the UN and former US national security adviser. In Bolton's worldview, the post-World War II order was constantly undermined by the leftist, anti-American activity of the UN and other inter- or transnational institutions (Bolton 1997). Long before joining President Trump's administration, Bolton was an ardent critic of international law (see, e.g.: Bolton 2000). And in the Trump administration, as Aaron Ettinger argues, Bolton was the most important figure promoting a sovereigntist vision of sovereignty:

> Bolton's line of thinking is most consistent with the emergence of sovereignty as the conceptual anchor of Trump's foreign policy... [H]e objects to international institutions on the grounds that they are unconstitutional and violate the principles of popular sovereignty in the US—a position characteristic of the 'new sovereigntism'. (Ettinger 2020: 4)

With these sources of understanding sovereignty, this concept became central to the foreign policy strategy of President Trump (Patrick 2018: 76ff.; Ettinger 2020: 10-11). The ideological impact of Trumpism on US domestic policy was realized in repressions against migrants and in growing conflicts with US minorities (Gonzales 2017; Morris 2019). The same impact on foreign policy meant reduced US participation in global issues and NATO, withdrawal from the Paris climate agreement, and growing conflict with UN (McGee 2017; Thompson 2017). And the ideological background of these processes was partially connected with the sovereignty ideologeme.

In his public statements in the highest international arenas, President Trump constantly referred to sovereignty. For example, unlike in the statements of other US presidents at the UN General Assembly in the 21st century, Trump used that term quite often: ten times in a 2018 speech and five times in a 2019 speech (Trump 2018; Trump 2019). Here are some typical statements in which sovereignty shows its strategic role for the US leader:

> I honor the right of every nation in this room to pursue its own customs, beliefs, and traditions. The United States will not tell you how to live or work or worship. We only ask that you honor our sovereignty in return. (Trump 2018)
> We will never surrender America's sovereignty to an unelected, unaccountable, global bureaucracy. (Trump 2018)
> Around the world, responsible nations must defend against threats to sovereignty not just from global governance, but also from other, new forms of coercion and domination. (Trump 2018)
> The United States is also working with partners in Latin America to confront threats to sovereignty from uncontrolled migration. (Trump 2018)
> Liberty is only preserved, sovereignty is only secured, democracy is only sustained, greatness is only realized, by the will and devotion of patriots. In their spirit is found the strength to resist oppression, the inspiration to forge legacy, the goodwill to seek friendship, and the bravery to reach for peace. Love of our nations makes the world better for all nations. (Trump 2019)

In these statements, sovereignty is stressed as a core undiscussed ideologeme linked to the (patriotic) people, to tradition, and to the state that is elected by and cares about them.

In the vast literature analyzing the Trumpist ideology, it is stressed that sovereignty is among several key ideas of Donald Trump and his supporters. After reviewing this literature, Aaron Ettinger (2020: 11–12) concluded that Trump's view on sovereignty had three dimensions:

1. World order and international peace can rest only on "self-regarding sovereign states looking after themselves, as opposed to a world of interdependent and integrated countries".

2. "[S]overeignty [is] the duty of government to take care of the needs" [of the people].
3. Sovereignty was "the banner" of his party's campaign against other US parties and groups (Ettinger 2020: 11).

This understanding of sovereignty was in fact Donald Trump's and his supporters' creative reinterpretation of sovereignty in US domestic and foreign policy discourse in 2016-2020. This reinterpretation denies the long evolution of liberal politics and constitutional practice in the US, the realities of the full world, and the practiced complex notions of sovereignty in international relations and law in the 21st century. Instead, in this populist ideological framework the status of the sovereign — the people — is ascribed to the relative majority of the population the government should serve and whose interests the state should defend. The interests and identities of other parts of the population, especially minorities, may be subjugated to the supremacy of the sovereign. The demands for equality between the majority and minorities, or for recognition of the international mechanisms defending individual rights or the common interests of humankind, constitute a threat to the sovereignty of *the people*. These ideological posits are examples of populist ideologemes of a particularistic kind: they deny the universality of human persons' sovereignty and the common, shared interests of all the human population of the world. In the Trumpian imaginary, the world is a place of peoples (with their traditional cultures and the states founded by them) who live together but share a minimum of rules necessary to provide for a peaceful coexistence, a place of trade based on the exclusive interests of the peoples, and a place where the principle of noninterference in national political systems and jurisdictions is observed. Altogether, this worldview is spread through mediated images or short posts that avoid definiteness, contradict logic, and have no other reference than the imagination of certain groups of believers.

The Putinist Interpretation of Sovereignty

Unlike Trumpism, Putinist sovereigntism has been influencing Russia's domestic and foreign policy for about fifteen years and has a solid textual basis. As an ideology and a set of relevant policies, it started in the last years of Vladimir Putin's second presidential term (2004–2008), influenced the decisions of the following Medvedev administration, and has continued during Putin's third and fourth terms in office, right into the present.

In 2007, in his final address to the Federal Assembly before temporarily leaving office, Vladimir Putin showed himself to be a politician with an established conservative ideology — something that he lacked in the early 2000s. In this lengthy speech he mentioned sovereignty only three times, but every time it is part of the key ideological message that — seen in retrospective — explains Putin's evolution through reelection in 2012, the aggression against Ukraine beginning in 2014, support for the "Russian Spring" ideology, and the recent constitutional amendments that give him many more years to run for the presidency. In the speech, first, Putin links "national wealth" (which includes morality, language, cultural values, the memory of the forefathers, and history) to the "unity and sovereignty of the country" (Putin 2007a). Second, he cites Dmitrii Likhachev's conservative statement that "state sovereignty is also defined by cultural criteria", which means the unity of different ethnic groups in one united people of Russia with an assembly of cultures in one state tradition. And third, state sovereignty is meaningful only if a government cares about its people and defends their economic and security interests (Putin 2007a). This speech was made as part of Putin's legacy to his successor and in the wake of the end of an "antiterrorist operation" in Chechnia.

Two months before, Vladimir Putin had delivered his famous speech at the Munich Security Conference in which he criticized the decline of national sovereignty in the "unipolar world":

> However, what is a unipolar world? However one might embellish this term, at the end of the day it refers to one type of situation, namely one centre of authority, one centre of force, one centre of decision-making. It is world in which there is one master, one sovereign. And at the end of the day

this is pernicious not only for all those within this system, but also for the sovereign itself because it destroys itself from within. And this certainly has nothing in common with democracy. (Putin 2007b)

He also criticized the international organizations he considered to be serving the interest of the core threat of a unipolar world, the OSCE, and NATO. However, he supported the "truly universal" character of the UN and nuclear disarmament treaties (ibid.).

Both 2007 speeches were actually signaling the start of an era of "sovereign democracy" (Okara 2007: 9). This term in Russian ideological use was introduced by Vladislav Surkov in 2006 in a lecture that later was published as an article in Russian and English (Surkov 2009). Here Surkov, a young presidential aide and emerging ideologue, stipulated the following understanding of sovereign democracy:

> The supreme independent (sovereign) power of the people (democracy) is charged with satisfying these aspirations and requirements on all levels of civic activity—from the individual to the national... Here, in Russia, democracy faces major challenges. It must test upon itself and turn to its advantage the might of globalization; overcome shadow institutions that block its progress—corruption, criminality, the market in counterfeits and disinformation; withstand the reactionary attacks of isolationism and oligarchy. It must create a new society, a new economy, a new army, a new faith. It must demonstrate that freedom and justice can and ought to be thought and discussed in Russia. (Surkov 2009: 8)

As a sovereign democracy, Russia is seen as among the same sovereign democratic states that together constitute the world:

> These ideas are rooted in the conception of a just world order as a community of free communities (sovereign democracies) that cooperate and compete on the basis of rational rules. And they therefore presuppose the liberalization of international relations and the demonopolization of the global economy. For this reason, of course, they irritate the planetary strongmen and monopolists. (Surkov 2009: 9)

The people that has its dignity in sovereignty must respect others' and its own supremacy. That posture is also appropriate when some groups want international integration, as in the EU. For the isolationist imagery, these groups (NGOs) urging the supranational integration of discrete nations are not truly representative of the people since they are driven by other, nonsovereign interests:

> Certain devotees of commercial philosophy working in specialized 'noncommercial' and 'nongovernmental' organizations write that in our age of integration and interdependence it is foolish to cling to sovereignty. Among the governments that sponsor such writings, however, it will be hard to find a single one willing to eliminate its own national legislation, economy, armed forces, and itself. (Surkov 2009: 12)

Basically, these ideas are evident in Putin's speeches I quoted from earlier. So basically, 2006–2007 was a period of formation of Putinist sovereigntism aimed at state sovereignty in the name of the people and government's service to that people in socioeconomic and security terms. Among the security tasks is the defense of the people's sovereignty from the Western core and those individuals and groups that want to promulgate this core's illegitimate interests on the sovereign soil of Russia.

Later, this sovereigntist vision was tested in 2008, in the Russo-Georgian War, and in 2014, in Ukraine. At first glance, the "sovereign democracy" doctrine would appear to make the Russian Federation's actions illegitimate in both cases. However, according to the sovereigntist ideology, in both cases the sovereignty of the Georgian and Ukrainian peoples was not respected, essentially on the ground that it did not exist: these peoples, in Putin's sovereigntist vision, had lost their sovereignty in a "color revolution" and through attempts at European and Euro-Atlantic integration, acts by which national states were reordered to align with the Western core and lost their sovereignty.[3] Here the sovereigntist ideology shows that the supremacy of sovereignty is recognized only if "the people" stays isolated and avoids integratory policies.

Fifteen years after the first announcement of sovereign democracy, it is evident that many of the initial sovereigntist ideologemes

---

3   On this, see Vladimir Putin's statements on color revolutions (Putin 2014) and war with Ukraine (BBC Ukraina 2014); data from the Surkov emails hacked in 2016 (Panfilov 2016); Surkov's own public speech (Ria Novosti 2018); and witnesses speaking on Surkov's role in the Donbas war (Deutsche Welle 2017).

have become guidelines for the domestic and foreign policymaking in Russia. In President Putin's recent speech at Davos, one can see the same criticism of international law that violates people's sovereignty and of the Western core that does not respect political multilateralism (Putin 2021). Much stronger, however, were his statements in the spirit of social conservatism, notably the emphasis on caring for a population struggling with the pandemic and the associated economic crisis, on the need to support family values and privacy, and on the need to inspire demographic growth and a return to social cooperation based on traditions (Putin 2021). These statements were made by a ruler who was successfully reelected in 2018 in nonfree and noncompetitive elections, who introduced draconian control over civil organizations through "foreign agent" legislation in 2017–2020, and who amended his country's constitution in accordance with his sovereigntist program in 2020 (OSCE ODIHR 2018; Tysiachniouk et al. 2018; European Parliament 2020; Kazun & Semykina 2020).

Probably the most visible influence of sovereigntism on Russia can be seen in the constitutional amendments of 2020. The sovereigntist constitutional amendments included the following stipulations:

1. Recognition of international obligations only if they "do not contradict the constitution of the Russian Federation" (Article 79). Here the Putinist program managed to sever the constitutional grounds for the impact of the cosmopolitan part of the concept of sovereignty. De iure, the Russian state can now be exempt from all previously ratified international human rights and civil liberties agreements that provided Russian citizens with the same sovereignty as the citizens of other nation-signatories to these agreements.

2. Prohibition of foreign citizenship or a foreign residence permit for public servants of higher categories (Articles 77 and 78). In sovereigntist logic, the ownership of foreign assets, such as an apartment, makes public officials vulnerable to foreign influence on decision-making, which in turn makes Russia less able to serve its people and thus less sovereign.
3. A ban on foreign citizenship for Russia's president and the requirement of 25 years of permanent residence in Russia prior to the election (Article 81). This also is connected with the sovereigntist strategy to promote those politicians that have minimal firsthand experience with living in other societies and dealing with other cultures.
4. References to a "thousand-year-long history", "remembering the ancestors, their ideals and faith in God", and "defense of historical truth" (Articles 67, 2-3). All these statements are connected with the people's sovereignty ideologeme where *the people* is essentialized through its historical rootedness (or the Surkovian "depth") in Russian soil, in synthesized "local multiethnic" tradition, in traditional confessions, and in specific Eurasian genetics.
5. Provision for "the balance between civil rights and obligations, of social partnership, and of economic, political, and social solidarity" (Article 71) (Zakon 2020; Venice Commission 2020). This amendment reflects the idea that the sovereign people is at the center of relations between public and private organizations, so that solidarity gains a social conservative overtone.

Altogether these amendments have finalized the rewriting of the Russian constitution as a text based on sovereigntist legal-political imagery, which strictly differs from the liberal imagery of the constitution of 1993.[4] Instead of imagining the future, today's power elites in Russia orient their political imagery toward the past, which

---

[4] For more on liberal-modernist imaginary of the post-Soviet constitutions of Russia and other countries, see Minakov (2018: 237ff.).

is defined in sociogenetic, traditionalist, and populist terms. Despite its surface conservatism, this ideology must create new and reinterpret old ideologemes in order to accommodate Russia's ideological, cultural, social, lingual, and religious diversity. So the unifying terms of "multiethnic" (*mnogonatsional'naia*) tradition and people require that elites and other social groups reinterpret this multiethnicity in their own way. This sovereigntist imagery demands the participation of both the rulers and the ruled in producing the meanings of such ideological posits.

This Russian sovereigntist creativity can be seen in several sovereigntist circles that in different times were close to Vladimir Putin and his immediate entourage. I should mention first of all Vladislav Surkov's opinion paper, "The loneliness of the half-breed". Here Surkov, who at the time of writing it was losing his political influence and moving toward the margins of active politics in Russia, analyzed the direction of Russia's "post-Crimean"[5] development. According to him, Russia had launched itself on a trajectory of isolating itself from the rest of the world:

> Beyond 2014 there lies an indefinitely long period, Era [20]14+, in which we are destined to a hundred years (or possibly two hundred or three hundred) of geopolitical loneliness. (Surkov 2018)

In lengthy pessimistic lines he lists several waves of Russian Westernization that never served the good of the Russian people. For example, the most recent, post-Soviet Westernization was a mistake:

> We agreed to shrink. We began to worship Hayek as fiercely as we had worshiped Marx. We slashed the demographic, industrial and military potential by half. We turned our backs on the other Soviet republics and were about to say good-bye to the autonomies. . . . But even a downsized and humble Russia proved unable to negotiate the turn towards the West. Lastly, a decision was made to do away with downscaling and downsizing and, what is

---

5   This term is widely used in the social sciences to describe Russian politics and society after the annexation of Crimea and its consequences for Russia's political culture and regime, its international position, and relations with neighboring nations (see: Shlapentokh 2014; Fabrykant & Magun 2019).

more, to come out with a declaration of rights. The events of 2014 were unavoidable. (Surkov 2018)

This "decision to... come out with a declaration of rights" also shows how the Putinists understand laws and rights: as rightfully belonging to the people, not the individual, and to the majority (defined by local tradition), not to minorities (who by defending their identity undermine the majority's sovereignty).

Another important part of the sovereigntist imagery is a specific genetics. Surkov stipulates Russia's cultural specificity as a "Western-Eastern half-breed nation" with a "double-headed statehood, hybrid mentality, intercontinental territory and bipolar history", and offers the only viable solution for its development in the contemporary full world: a long strategic "geopolitical loneliness". This loneliness is required for Russia to cease "mixing" with Others and to reidentify itself, ideologically and genetically. Understanding the impossibility of such loneliness in the full world, Surkov is forced to look for a "creative solution": Russia is supposed to participate in international politics and trade, and should focus not on "abroad" but deep inside itself, in its "depth", from where "a slowly traveling message from deep space has just begun to reach our ears" (Surkov 2018).

Another failed Putin ideologue, Aleksander Dugin, came up with a new sovereigntist manifesto-like document that reacted to two recent ideological events. In the first event, Klaus Schwab published a report promoting the "Great Reset" idea, which calls for a "more inclusive, more equitable and more respectful of Mother Nature" economy (Schwab & Malleret 2020). The second event was Putin's social-conservative address in Davos (Putin 2021), to which Dugin responded in an online conversation.

In his text, Dugin declares Schwab's idea to be a new liberal attempt at a "takeover of humanity's imagination" that would lead to a global economy without the use of oil and its products, and to "greener" development (Dugin 2021). Dugin's reading of Schwab's reset idea immediately discloses the sovereigntist imagery. First, he immediately stipulates that through the use of mass media and social networks, liberal globalists are to trying to impose laws that would (1) "glorify" minorities ("gender, sexual, ethnic, biological") and (2) "demonize" national states. Second, the concepts promoted by the Club of Rome (sustainable development in a full world) means decreasing Earth's human population. Third, the decarbonized economy is designed to hit the economies of Russia, the Arab countries, and some Latin American countries; thus the new economic plan means a strike against countries opposed to the liberal international order with its cosmopolitan understanding of sovereignty. Dugin's fourth claim Is that the liberal globalists promote digitalization as a means of seeking total control over human populations through AI, robotization, and genetic mutations. And finally, the natural environment, according to the new globalist plan, is to become another form of capital itself (Dugin 2021).

Altogether, Aleksandr Dugin interprets Schwab's Great Reset proposal as paving the way to "a triumph of liberal ideology in its highest stage, the stage of globalization", which "dooms" humankind to be liberated. To resist this kind of future, Dugin offers instead a "Great Awakening" plan, which, in his opinion, was prepared by the supporters of Donald Trump. The Great Awakening means understanding the threat that liberal globalists pose to all people who disagree with liberal principles and the principles of cosmopolitan sovereignty:

> 'The Great Awakening' is the insight that modern liberalism in the stage of globalization has become a real dictatorship, has become a totalitarian ideology that denies — like any other totalitarianism — the right to have any point of view different from the dominant one. (Dugin 2021)

The manifesto ends with the description of today's world as the scene of an approaching war between globalists and their liberal supporters in each nation-state, on one side, against those who, like Putin, support "the people's" sovereignty, on the other side.

The Putinist understanding of sovereignty has both reactionary and creative elements that, unlike in the Trumpist case, have had an impact on Russia's domestic and foreign policy for about fifteen years, at least since 2006. President Putin's endless reign has resulted in the wide spreading of sovereigntist beliefs that have affected not only Russia's political institutions but also its political culture. This profound influence can be seen both in the constitutional amendments themselves and in the popular support for these changes,[6] or in the sovereigntist imagery of the Russian mainstream creative class.[7] The Putinist interpretation of sovereignty describes the world as a battlefield—ideological, political, and economic—between sovereign peoples and their states, on one side, and transnational institutions with their neoliberal and cosmopolitan ideologies undermining sovereignty and even the ontological foundations for the life of the peoples on the other side. In such a context, human rights and civil liberties are either marginal issues or a source of threat for the majority and its culture, identity, and genetics. Minorities are seen either as the traditional ones, which have their place in the hierarchy of the "multiethnic Russian people", or as nontraditional ones (organized around civic, gender, sexual, social, religious, or other identities), which constitute a threat to the sovereignty of the people and its state. Any demand for equality of minorities with the majority should be seen through the lens of the supreme interest of the people. The interests of collectives bigger or smaller than the people (humanity, the individual, civic organizations, a minority group) can be regarded as legitimate only if they agree with the people's interests. Altogether, the Putinist worldview is a mainstream political religion, adherence to which opens up a political career or the status of a legitimate citizen. Alternative ideologies, including those that promote ideas about cosmopolitan sovereignty, are marginalized and characterized as either foreign or promoted by "foreign agents".

Conclusion

Today's political and ideological processes take place in such a globalized world that domestic and external events are increasingly

---

6   According to official data, 68% of Russian registered voters participated in the referendum on the constitutional amendments in 2020; almost 78% of voters supported the amendments, and only 21% of them abstained (please see data of the Central Voters Commission at http://www.cikrf.ru/).

7   This can be seen, for example, in the recent debates around the so-called "Bogomolov Manifesto" (Bogomolov 2021; Novaya Gazeta 2021), or in the analysis of the ideological background to recent Russian film-making (2020).

less distinguishable. This interconnectedness of political plans inspires different ideological camps to compete in redefining the key concepts that serve as a foundation for both the global order and the national order at the same time. Among these key concepts is sovereignty. Above I briefly described the history of this concept's development through five different definitions that in the post–World War II and post–Cold War period has ended with the imaginary of sovereignty in the form of a unity of national and personal sovereignty that promoted cosmopolitan norms of justice in each national jurisdiction. This unity was partially based on the liberal idea of the self-determination of the individual, who has the inalienable right to decide (even arbitrarily and irrationally) about his or her body (including abortion or euthanasia), property, lifetime, participation in collective life, and so forth. At the same time, this unity was enabled by states' approval of these universal norms as part of their own laws and obligations. The unity so achieved provided political, social, and economic actors with new opportunities for development. However, the unity itself and this development had their contradictions and drawbacks, which became the targets of criticism from different ideological groups, one of which is the new sovereigntists.

The contemporary sovereigntists vary greatly from country to country, region to region. But their common feature is a specific interpretation of the concept of sovereignty. I analyzed this specificity using two examples, Trumpism and Putinism. The first ideology gripped the strongest old democracy on the planet, though just for four years (2017–2020). The second ideology has guided Russia's development from a partially free state in 2000 to an achieved autocracy in 2021.

The Trumpist ideology ascribes sovereignty to the people, an imagined entity that has the qualities of working people, the majority, Judeo-Christian tradition, peacefulness, and readiness to include those who do not Insist on their minority identity. Such a people is the owner of a state—the state as part of the US as a country and of the federal government. International institutions or minorities that create obligations for the US are seen as hostile to the sovereign. This ideology avoids clear universalist definitions of sovereignty and the sovereign, and relies on blurred statements on social networks, visual materials, and permanent rediscussion in communities of supporters.

The Putinist ideology ascribes sovereignty to the people, an imagined collective that has the qualities of a multinational people united by a long history of living together, of majority, of traditional religion (Orthodox Christian or traditional Islam), and of a readiness to include those who neither stipulate their minority identity nor intend integration with the global core. Such a people is the object of care by the state. With the recent constitutional amendments, the state has become a monopolist in providing wealth and security to the people and a coordinator of other public and private organizations for the common good of the majority. Putinism is much more widespread among elites and the general population than Trumpism is. It is also better described in legal norms and publicized lengthy texts written by the ideologues. Alternative views and their spread exist under the control of the state and thus far do not constitute a threat to the ruling sovereigntist.

The sovereigntists of the old democracy and the new autocracy alike seem to share a distrust in international organizations and treaties that support the personal sovereignty of an individual human. However, Putinism treats the UN as a useful tool to inform other nations about the Russian government's policies, while for Trumpism, the UN is a dangerous organization that challenges the sovereignty of the American people. A certain level of distrust can also be witnessed vis-à-vis NATO and the EU, although for different reasons. For Trumpists, transnational organizations can be tolerated as long as they do not undermine the exclusive interests of the people, the sovereign of the world's core state. Conversely, Putinists are much more oriented toward isolation from international organizations; after several violations of international law against neighboring sovereign nations and imposed sanctions, the outside world is seen as a source of existential risk for the people and its historical traditions.

Both sovereigntist movements are hostile to human personal sovereignty, to minority rights, and to the universal norms of cosmopolitan justice. "Justice" stems from what is right for the collective imagined as a majority. Whatever undermines the supremacy of the majority is unjust. Thus the liberal concept of sovereignty that has also become part of national juridicality is seen as unjust and cannot be practiced by a government loyal to its people.

Trumpism and Putinism represent two cases of the sovereigntist turn in different political, economic, cultural, and geopolitical contexts. They share the core vision of sovereignty as a quality that belongs to the people, which is an imagined majority whose specific qualities are traditional for each country. The role of the state in general is viewed as that of a caretaker of the people's interests; however, the level of etatist paternalism is much stronger in the Russian case. Both movements imply exceptionalism and isolationism, but again, Putinism is much more radical on both these counts.

With the above analysis and conclusions in hand, I can now answer the key question of this paper. Both cases of sovereigntist ideology react negatively to the challenges and responsibilities the full world demands from contemporary states and their citizens. Sovereigntist exceptionalism and isolationism are of a reactionary nature and reuse a traditional, pre-World War II understanding of sovereignty. However, in both cases the sovereigntist imagery demands the creation of a new understanding of the people, human and individual rights, minorities, post-World War II international organizations, and transnational challenges such as ecological erosion. In that respect, contemporary sovereigntism is an example of a conservative creativity that invents new identities (Judeo-Christianity, traditional religions), new temporalities (of those honest working peoples who are undermined by minorities and globalists; of the deep people; of strategic loneliness), and new functions for the state (which are less political or legal and more oriented toward the security of the majority and its biological and cultural reproduction). From that perspective, human rights, minority rights, planetary transnational issues, and the institutions that are responsible for keeping these issues on the international political agenda are seen as illegitimate and dangerous for the sovereign peoples and their polities. Thus it is logical to conclude that contemporary sovereigntism offers a worldview that denies the cosmopolitan norms of justice and stipulates that the world is a space of coexisting sovereign peoples and their states, on one side, and, on the other side, global transnational groups that try to achieve global supremacy, subdue the peoples, and pervert the traditional understanding of man and woman, human being, family, and religion through cosmopolitan values and technologies.

Bibliography

Ackerman, Bruce. (1980). *Social justice in the liberal state.* New Haven: Yale University Press.

Adams, Jacqueline. (2004). The Imagination and Social Life. *Qualitative Sociology* 27(3): 277-297.

Alles, Delphine, Badie, Bertrand. (2016). Sovereigntism in the International System: From Change to Split. *European Review of International Studies* 3(2): 5-19.

Anderson, John. (2016). Religion, state and 'sovereign democracy' in Putin's Russia. *Journal of Religious and Political Practice* 2(2): 249-266.

Anghie, Antony. (2001). Colonialism and the birth of international institutions: Sovereignty, economy, and the mandate system of the League of Nations. *New York University Journal of International Law* 34: 513-529.

Ansprenger, Franz. (2018). *The dissolution of the colonial empires.* London: Routledge.

Balboni, Marco, Danisi, Carmelo. (2020). Reframing Human Rights in Russia and China: How National Identity and National Interests Shape Relations with, and the Implementation of, International Law. In *Rekindling the Strong State in Russia and China.* Eds. Stefano Bianchini, Antonio Fiori. Leiden: Brill, 61-78.

Bannon, Stephen K. (2010). Bannon at Tea Party, New York City. *Quazcam Yutube page,* April 18, https://www.youtube.com/watch?v=Jf_Yj5X xUE0&t=535s (accessed March 10, 2021).

Bannon, Stephen K. (2016) Remarks of Stephen Bannon at a Conference at the Vatican. *The American Catholic,* November 16, https://the-americ an-catholic.com/2016/11/18/remarks-of-stephen-bannon-at-a-conf erence-at-the-vatican/ (accessed March 10, 2021).

BBC Ukraina. (2014). Piat' gromkikh zayavlienii Putina ob Ukraine [from Rus.: Five loud statements of Putin on Ukraine]. *BBC Ukraina,* November 10, https://www.bbc.com/ukrainian/ukraine_in_russian/ 2014/11/141110_ru_s_putin_on_history_ukraine (accessed March 10, 2021).

Bell, Daniel A. (2000). *East meets west: Human rights and democracy in East Asia*. Princeton: Princeton University Press.

Benhabib, Seyla. (2004). *The Rights of Others. Aliens, Residents and Citizens*. Cambridge: Cambridge University Press.

Benhabib, Seyla. (2011a). Claiming Rights across Borders. International Human Rights and Democratic Sovereignty. In *Dignity in Adversity. Human Rights in Troubled Times*. Cambridge: Polity Press, 117–137.

Benhabib, Seyla. 2011b. Twilight of Sovereignty or the Emergence of Cosmopolitan Norms? Rethinking Citizenship in Volatile Times. In *Dignity in Adversity. Human Rights in Troubled Times*. Cambridge: Polity Press, 94–117.

Benhabib, Seyla. (2016). The new sovereigntism and transnational law: Legal utopianism, democratic scepticism and statist realism. *Global Constitutionalism* 5(1): 109–144.

Berger, Peter, Luckman, Thomas. (1956). *The social construction of knowledge*. New York: Doubleday.

Beyond Westlessness. (2021). Beyond Westlessness: Report from the MSC Special Edition 2021. *Munich Security Conference*, February 2021, https://securityconference.org/en/news/full/beyond-westlessness-a-report-from-the-msc-special-edition-2021/ (accessed March 10, 2021).

Biersteker, Thomas J. (2002). State, sovereignty and territory. *Handbook of international relations*. Eds. W. Carlsnaes, T. Risse, B. A. Simmons. New York: Sage, 157–176.

Bodin, Jean. (1992[1586]). *Bodin: On Sovereignty*. Cambridge: Cambridge University Press.

Bogomolov, Konstantin. (2021). Pokhishchenie Evropy 2.0 [from Rus.: The Abduction of Europe]. *Novaya Gazeta*, February 10, https://novayagazeta.ru/articles/2021/02/10/89120-pohischenie-evropy-2-0 (accessed March 10, 2021).

Bolton, John. (1997). The Creation, Fall, Rise, and Fall of the United Nations. *Delusions of Grandeur: The United Nations and Global Intervention*. Ed. T. G. Carpenter. Washington, DC: Cato Institute, 45–59.

Bolton, John. (2000). Is there really law in international affairs. *Transnational Law and Contemporary Problems* 10: 1–12.

Bottici, Chiara (2014). *Imaginal politics: images beyond imagination and the imaginary*. New York: Columbia University Press.

Brand, Ronald A. (1994). External sovereignty and international law. *Fordham International Law Journal* 18: 1685–1699.

Brock, M. (2016). Fantastic Mr President: The hyperrealities of Putin and Trump. *Euro Crisis in the Press*, LSE Blog, September 9, https://blogs.lse.ac.uk/eurocrisispress/2016/09/09/fantastic-mr-president-the-hyperrealities-of-putin-and-trump/ (accessed March 10, 2021).

Brunkert, Lennart, Kruse, Stefan, Welzel, Christian. (2018). A tale of culture-bound regime evolution: the centennial democratic trend and its recent reversal. *Democratization*, DOI: 10.1080/13510347.2018.1542430.

Castoriadis, Cornelius. (1987). *The imaginary institution of society*. Cambridge, MA: Polity.

Cocking, John. (2005). *Imagination: A study in the history of ideas*. London: Routledge.

Cohen, Jean L. (2004). Whose sovereignty? Empire versus international law. *Ethics and International Affairs* 18(3): 1–24.

Cohen, Jean L. (2012). *Globalization and Sovereignty: Rethinking Legality, Legitimacy and Constitutionalism*. Cambridge: Cambridge University Press.

De Wilde, Pieter, Koopmans, Rafael, Merkel, Wolfgang, Zürn, Marcus. (Eds.). (2019). *The struggle over borders: Cosmopolitanism and communitarianism*. Cambridge: Cambridge University Press.

Deák, Istvan, Gross, Jan T., Judt, Tony. (2000). *The politics of retribution in Europe: World War II and its aftermath*. Princeton: Princeton University Press.

Deutsche Welle. (2017). Ex-lidery separatistov rasskazali Reuters o roli Surkova v konflikte v Donbasse [from Rus.: Ex-leaders of the separatists told Reuters on Surkov's role in the Donbas conflict]. *Deutsche Welle*, May 11, https://www.dw.com/ru/%D1%8D%D0%BA%D1%81-%D0%BB%D0%B8%D0%B4%D0%B5%D1%80%D1%8B-%D1%81%D0%B5%D0%BF%D0%B0%D1%80%D0%B0%D1%82%D0%B8%D1%81%D1%82%D0%BE%D0%B2-%D1%80%D0%B0%D1%81%D1%81%D0%BA%D0%B0%D0%B7%D0%B0%D0%BB%D0%B8-reuters-%D0%BE-%D1%80%D0%BE%D0%BB%D0%B8-%D1%81%D1%83%D1%80%D0%BA%D0%BE%D0%B2%D0%B0-%D0%B2-%D0%BA%D0%BE%D0%BD%D1%84%D0%BB%D0%B8%D0%BA%D1%82%D0%B5-%D0%B2-%D0%B4%D0%BE%D0%BD%D0%B1%D0%B0%D1%81%D1%81%D0%B5/a-38800675 (accessed March 10, 2021).

DiMaggio, Angelo. (2011). *The rise of the Tea Party: Political discontent and corporate media in the age of Obama*. New York: New York University Press.

Du Gay, Peter. (2005). Bureaucracy and liberty: State, authority, and freedom. *The values of bureaucracy*. Ed. P. Du Gay. Oxford: Oxford University Press, 41–62.

Dugin, Aleksandr. (2021). Bolshaia Perezagruzka i Velikoie Probuzhdenie [from Rus.: Big Reset and Great Awakening]. *Ria Novosti*, February 15, https://ria.ru/20210215/perezagruzka-1597564983.html?fbclid= IwAR1m-HzHPOcoA8YUVjiUX0Lo_fQ6_RzTZINFq9KTMEuOVkZ 2ZaqPKAgBRlo (accessed March 10, 2021).

Emlyn-Jones, Clair J., Preddy, William. (Eds.). (2013). *Plato: Republic* (Vol. 1). Cambridge, MA: Harvard University Press.

Etkind, Alexander, Minakov, Mikhail. (2020). Post-Soviet Ideological Creativity. *Ideology after Union*. Eds. A. Etkind, M. Minakov. Stuttgart: ibidem, 9–18.

Ettinger, Aaron. (2020). Principled realism and populist sovereignty in Trump's foreign policy. *Cambridge Review of International Affairs* 33(3): 410–431.

European Parliament. (2020). Constitutional and political change in Russia. *European Parliament official website*, February, https://www.europarl.europa.eu/RegData/etudes/ATAG/2020/646168/EPRS_ATA(2020)646168_EN.pdf (accessed March 10, 2021).

Fabrykant, Marharyta, Magun, Vladimir. (2019). Dynamics of National Pride Attitudes in Post-Soviet Russia, 1996–2015. *Nationalities Papers* 47(1): 20–37.

Fine, Ronald, Smith, William. (2003). Jürgen Habermas's theory of cosmopolitanism. *Constellations* 10(4): 469–487.

Friedgut, Theodore H. (2014). *Political Participation in the USSR*. Princeton: Princeton University Press.

Glaveanu, Vlad Petre. (2018). Perspectival Collective Futures: Creativity and Imagination in Society. In *Imagining Collective Futures. Perspectives from Social, Cultural and Political Psychology*. Eds. C. De Saint-Laurent, S. Obradović, K. R. Carriere. London: Palgrave Macmillan, 83–106.

Gonzales, Alfonso. (2017). Trumpism, authoritarian neoliberalism, and subaltern Latina/o politics. *Aztlán: A Journal of Chicano Studies* 42(2): 147–164.

Grant, Thomas D. (1998). Defining statehood: The Montevideo Convention and its discontents. *Columbia Journal of Transnational Law* 37: 403–426.

Gudkov, Lev. (2011). The Nature of "Putinism". *Russian Social Science Review* 52(6): 21–47.

Guilford, Gwynn, Sonnad, Nikhil. (2017). What Steve Bannon really wants. *Quartz*, February 3, https://qz.com/898134/what-steve-bannon-really-wants/ (accessed March 10, 2021).

Gustafson, Krisian. (2007). *Hostile Intent: US Covert Operations in Chile, 1964–1974*. Washington, DC: Potomac Books.

Heller, Patrik, Evans, Peter. (2010). Taking Tilly south: Durable inequalities, democratic contestation, and citizenship in the Southern Metropolis. *Theory and Society* 39(3-4): 433-450.

Hobbes, Thomas. (1980[1651]). *Leviathan*. Oxford: Oxford University Press.

Holmes, Stephen. (1988). Jean Bodin: The paradox of sovereignty and the privatization of religion. *NOMOS: American Society for Political and Legal Philosophy* 30: 5-22.

Honneth, Axel. (1995). *The Struggle for Recognition: The Moral Grammar of Social Conflict*. Cambridge, MA: Polity.

Inglehart, Ronald, Welzel, Christian. (2005). *Modernization, cultural change, and democracy: The human development sequence*. Cambridge: Cambridge University Press.

Isaev, Egor. (2020). The militarization of the past in Russian popular historical films. In *Ideology after Union. Political Doctrines, Discourses, and Debates in Post-Soviet Societies*. Eds. A. Etkind, M. Minakov. Stuttgart: ibidem, 237-250.

Jayatilleka, Dayan. (2014). *The Fall of Global Socialism: A Counter-Narrative from the South*. Basingstoke: Palgrave Macmillan.

Jellinek, Georg. (1905). Allgemeine Staatslehre [from German: General Theory of State]. Berlin: Stahl.

Judt, Tony. (2006). *Postwar: A history of Europe since 1945*. London: Penguin.

Kartashkin, V. A. (1991). Human Rights and the Emergence of the State of the Rule of Law in the USSR. *Emory Law Journal* 40: 889-901.

Kazun, Anastasia, Semykina, Kseniia. (2020). Presidential elections 2018: the struggle of Putin and Navalny for a media agenda. *Problems of Post-Communism* 67(6): 455-466.

Kelsen, Hans. (1920). Das Problem der Souveränität und die Theorie des Völ-kerrechts [from German: The Problem of Sovereignty and the Theory of International law]. Berlin.

Kelsen, Hans. (1959). Sovereignty and international law. *Georgia University Law Journal* 48: 627-638.

Krasner, Stephen D. (2005). Building democracy after conflict: The case for shared sovereignty. *Journal of Democracy* 16(1): 69-83.

Krasnobel'mov, Anatolii. (2013). Gosudarstvennyj kapitalizm: istoki vozniknovenia i vyzov sovremennoj ekonomike [from Rus.: State Capitalism: Sources, Emergence, and Challenges for Contemporary Economy]. *Social'no-ekonomicheskie iavlenia i processy* 7(53): 17-23.

Latham, Michael E. (2011). *The right kind of revolution: Modernization, development, and US foreign policy from the Cold War to the present*. Ithaka, NY: Cornell University Press.

Levy, David, Sznaider, Noah. (2006). Sovereignty transformed: a sociology of human rights. *The British journal of sociology* 57(4): 657–676.

Luk'ianova, Ekaterina. (2009). Zakon v postsovetskoj Rossii: problemy adekvatnosti vospriiatiia i ispol'zovaniia [from Rus.: Law in the Post-Soviet Russia: Problems of Understanding and Use]. *Gosudarstvo i parvo* 8: 62–71.

Maritain, Jean. (1950). The concept of sovereignty. *The American Political Science Review* 44(2): 343–357.

Martin, Terry D. (2001). *The affirmative action empire: nations and nationalism in the Soviet Union, 1923–1939*. Ithaka, NY: Cornell University Press.

Marx, Karl. (1845). The German Ideology. *Marxist Internet Archive*, n.d., https://www.marxists.org/archive/marx/works/1845/german-ideology/ch01a.htm#a4 (accessed March 10, 2021).

McAdam, Doug, Tarrow, Sidney, Tilly, Charles. (2009). Comparative perspectives on contentious politics. *Comparative politics: Rationality, culture, and structure*. Eds. M. I. Lichbach, A. S. Zuckerman. Cambridge: Cambridge University Press, 260–290.

McGee, Kyle. (2017). *Heathen Earth: Trumpism and political ecology*. Santa Barbara: punctum books.

Minakov, Mikhail. (2018). Demodernization in Post-Soviet Eastern Europe. *Demodernization: A Future in the Past*. Eds. Y. Rabkin, M. Minakov. Stuttgart: ibidem Verlag, 237–256.

Miullerson, Roman. (2020). Kak liberalizm vstupil v konflikt s demokratiej [from Rus.: How liberalism entered in conflict with democracy]. *Rossiia v global'noj politike* 18(5): 43–59.

Mollan, Simon, Geesin, Beverly. (2020). Donald Trump and Trumpism: Leadership, ideology and narrative of the business executive turned politician. *Organization* 27(3): 405–418.

Morris, Edwin K. (2019). Inversion, paradox, and liberal disintegration: Towards a conceptual framework of Trumpism. *New Political Science* 41(1): 17–35.

Moyn, Samuel. (2010). *The Last Utopia: Human Rights in History*. Cambridge: Cambridge University Press.

Nagel, Thomas. (2005). The Problem of Global Justice. *Philosophy and Public Affairs* 33(2): 113–47.

Novaya Gazeta. (2021). "Ok Boomer" Otkrytoie pismo Konstantinu Bogomolovu [from Rus.: Ok Boomer: an open letter to Konstantin Bogomolov]. Novaya Gazeta, February 15, https://novayagazeta.ru/articles/2021/02/13/89202-ok-bumer (accessed March 10, 2021).

Okara, Andrei. (2007). Sovereign democracy: a new Russian idea or a PR project? *Russia in Global Affairs* 5(3): 8–20.

Osakwe, Christopher. (1981). Soviet Human Rights Law under the USSR Constitution of 1977: Theories, Realities and Trends. *Tulane Law Review* 56: 249–263.

OSCE ODIHR. (2018). Russian Federation, Presidential Election, 18 March 2018: Final Report. *OSCE Office for Democratic Institutions and Human Rights*, June 6, https://www.osce.org/odihr/elections/383577 (accessed March 10, 2021).

Österud, Öyvind. (1997). The narrow gate: entry to the club of sovereign states. *Review of International Studies* 23(2): 167–184.

Panfilov, Oleg. (2016). Gruzia izuchaet tainy Surkova [from Rus.: Georgia studies the Surkov secrets]. *Krym.Realii*, October 31, https://ru.krymr.com/a/28083806.html (accessed March 10, 2021).

Parker, David. (1989). Sovereignty, absolutism and the function of the law in seventeenth-century France. *Past & Present* 122: 36–74.

Patrick, Stewart. (2017). Trump and world order. *Foreign Affairs* 2(96): 52–57.

Peck, Connie. (1996). *The United Nations as a dispute settlement system: improving mechanisms for the prevention and resolution of conflict*. Berlin: Springer.

Prokhovnik, Raia. (2013). *Sovereignty: History and theory*. Luton: Andrews UK Limited.

Putin, Vladimir. (2007a). Poslanie Federal'nomu Sobraniiu Rossijskoj Federacii Prezidenta Rossii [from Rus.: Presidential Address to the Federal Assembly of Russian Federation]. *Rossijskaia gazeta*, April 27, https:// rg.ru/2007/04/27/poslanie.html (accessed March 10, 2021).

Putin, Vladimir. (2007b). Speech and the Following Discussion at the Munich Conference on Security Policy. *President of Russia website*, February 10, http://en.kremlin.ru/events/president/transcripts/24034 (accessed March 10, 2021).

Putin, Vladimir. (2014). Putin: "tsvetnyie revoliutsii" v riade stran—eto urok dlia Rossii [from Rus.: Putin: "Color Revolutions" in some countries are a lesson for Russia]. *Ria Novosti*, November 20, https://ria.ru/20141120/1034329699.html (accessed March 10, 2021).

Putin, Vladimir. (2021). Special Address by Vladimir Putin at Davos Forum. *World Economic Forum website*, January 27, https://www.weforum.org/events/the-davos-agenda-2021/sessions/special-address-by-vladimir-putin-president-of-the-russian-federation (accessed March 10, 2021).

Rawls, John. (1971). *A Theory of Justice*. Cambridge, MS: Harvard University Press.

Rawls, John. (1999). The Idea of Public Reason Revisited. In J. Ralws, Collected Papers. London: Harvard University Press, 573–615.

Reisman, W. Michael. (1990). Sovereignty and human rights in contemporary international law. *The American Journal of International Law* 84(4): 866–876.

Resnick, Steven A., Wolff, Richard D. (2013). *Class theory and history: Capitalism and communism in the USSR*. London: Routledge.

Ria Novosti. (2018). Surkov nazval priznanie Yuahnoi Osetii spravedlivym shagom [from Rus.: Surkov has called the South Ossetia's recognition as a just move]. *Ria Novosti*, March 3, https://ria.ru/20180826/1527248931.html (accessed March 10, 2021).

Ricoeur, Paul. (1994). Imagination in discourse and action. In *Rethinking imagination: Culture and creativity*. Eds. John F. Robinson and Gillian Robinson. London: Routledge, 118–135.

Rozenberg, Olivier. (2020). The Sovereigntist: An Ephemeral Role. In *The French Parliament and the European Union*. New York: Palgrave Macmillan, 165–191.

Rudolph, Christopher. (2005). Sovereignty and territorial borders in a global age. *International studies review* 7(1): 1–20.

Schapiro, Leonard. (1965). *The government and politics of the Soviet Union*. New York: Hutchinson.

Schimmelfennig, Frank. (2019). Getting around no: how governments react to negative EU referendums. *Journal of European Public Policy* 26(7): 1056–1074.

Schmitt, Carl. (1985 [1922]). *Political theology: Four Chapters on the Concept of Sovereignty*. Boston: MIT Press.

Schmitt, Carl. (1996). *The Concept of the Political*. Chicago: University of Chicago Press.

Schrijver, Nico. (1999). The changing nature of state sovereignty. *British Year Book of International Law* 70(1): 65–98.

Schubert, Gunter. (2008). One-party rule and the question of legitimacy in contemporary China: Preliminary thoughts on setting up a new research agenda. *Journal of Contemporary China* 17(54): 191–204.

Schutz, Alfred, Luckman, Thomas. (1960). *The Structures of the Life-World*. London: Heinemann.

Schwab, Klaus, Malleret, Thierry. (2020). COVID-19: The Great Reset. In *World Economic Forum*, November, https://thepowershift.ca/wp-content/uploads/2020/11/COVID-19_-The-Great-Reset.pdf (accessed March 10, 2021).

Sellers, Frances S., Fahrenthold, David A. (2017). 'Why even let 'em in?' Understanding Bannon's worldview and the policies that follow. *Washington Post*, January 31, https://www.washingtonpost.com/politics/bannon-explained-his-worldview-well-before-it-became-official-us-policy/2017/01/31/2f4102ac-e7ca-11e6-80c2-30e57e57e05d_story.html?utm_term=.026e83bb66ad (accessed March 10, 2021).

Shlapentokh, Dmitriy. (2014). Implementation of an ideological paradigm: Early Duginian eurasianism and Russia's post-Crimean discourse. *Contemporary security policy* 35(3): 380–399.

Stone, David R. (2000). Imperialism and Sovereignty: The League of Nations' Drive to Control the Global Arms Trade. *Journal of contemporary history* 35(2): 213–230.

Strang, David. (1990). From dependency to sovereignty: An event history analysis of decolonization 1870-1987. *American Sociological Review* 55(6): 846–860.

Street, Paul, DiMaggio, Anthony R. (2015). *Crashing the Tea Party: Mass Media and the Campaign to Remake American Politics.* New York: Routledge.

Surkov, Vladimir. (2018). The loneliness of the half-breed. *Russia in Global Affairs* 28 https://eng.globalaffairs.ru/articles/the-loneliness-of-the-half-breed/ (accessed March 10, 2021).

Surkov, Vladimir. (2009). Nationalization of the future: Paragraphs pro sovereign democracy. *Russian studies in philosophy* 47(4): 8–21.

Taylor, Brian D. (2018). *The code of Putinism.* Oxford: Oxford University Press.

Taylor, Charles. (1989). *Sources of the Self. The Making of Modern Identity.* Cambridge: Cambridge University Press.

Thompson, Jack. (2017). Understanding Trumpism: the New President's Foreign Policy. *SIRIUS-Zeitschrift für Strategische Analysen* 1(2): 1–6.

Tilly, Charles. (1994). States and nationalism in Europe 1492-1992. *Theory and society* 23(1): 131–146.

Trump, Donald. (2018). Remarks by President Trump to the 73rd session of the United Nations General Assembly. *US Embassy in Uruguay*, September 25, https://uy.usembassy.gov/remarks-by-president-trump-to-the-73rd-session-of-the-united-nations-general-assembly/ (accessed March 10, 2021).

Trump, Donald. (2019). Remarks by President Trump to the 74th session of the United Nations General Assembly. *US Embassy in Mali*, September 24, https://ml.usembassy.gov/remarks-by-president-trump-to-the-74th-session-of-the-united-nations-general-assembly/ (accessed March 10, 2021).

Tysiachniouk, Maria, Tulaeva, Svetlana, Henry, Laura A. (2018). Civil society under the law 'on foreign agents': NGO strategies and network transformation. *Europe-Asia Studies* 70(4): 615–637.

Venice Commission. (2020). Opinion on draft amendments to the Constitution (as signed by the President of the Russian Federation on 14 March 2020). *The Venice Commission*, 18 June, https://www.venice.coe.int/webforms/documents/?pdf=CDL-AD(2020)009-e&fbclid=IwAR1JO8IojBv-7uxOyz9s14a-WK6mMVaGYrPTR1oHN-PGPp24WqO4UCusTRw (accessed March 10, 2021).

Verhoeven, Harry. (2020). What is to be done? Rethinking socialism (s) and socialist legacies in a postcolonial world. *Third World Quarterly* doi: 10.1080/01436597.2020.1867528, 1-16.

Von Weizsäcker, Ernst U., Wijkman, Anders. (2018). *Come on!* Berlin: Springer.

Wallerstein, Immanuel. (1984). *The politics of the world-economy: The states, the movements and the civilizations.* Cambridge: Cambridge University Press.

Wallerstein, Immanuel. (1991). World system versus world-systems: A critique. *Critique of Anthropology* 11(2): 189–194.

Walzer, Michael. (2004). Governing the Globe. In *Arguing About War*. New Haven, CT: Yale University Press, 171–191.

Westlessness. (2020) Westlessness. Munich Security Report—2020. *Munich Security Conference*, February 2020, https://securityconference.org/assets/user_upload/MunichSecurityReport2020.pdf (accessed March 10, 2021).

Yakovlev, Aleksandr. (2010). Gosudarstvennyj kapitalizm, korrupcia i effektivnost' gosapparata. *Obshchestvennye nauki i sovremennost'* 4: 18–25.

Yurchak, Aleksey. (2015). Bodies of Lenin: The hidden science of communist sovereignty. *Representations* 129(1): 116–157.

Zakon. (2020). Zakon "O popravke k Konstitucii Rossijskoj Federacii" [from Rus.: On Amendments for the Constitution of Russian Federation]. *Duma official website*, March 14, http://duma.gov.ru/news/48045/ (accessed Jul 10, 2021).

Zanko, Tigran. (2020). Constitutional Amendments 2020: Influence on Federal Executive Branch. *Public administration issues* 3: 7–22.

Ziegler, Charles E. (2012). Conceptualizing sovereignty in Russian foreign policy: Realist and constructivist perspectives. *International Politics* 49(4): 400–417.

Zittoun, Tania, Cerchia, Frederik. (2013). Imagination as expansion of experience. *Integrative Psychology and Behavioral Sciences* 47: 305–324.

9 Implementing International Human Rights Law
Recent Sovereigntist and Nationalist Trends

Gulnara Shaikhutdinova

"New Sovereigntism" as a phenomenon and a concept introduced in the social science literature at the beginning of the 21st century aggravated the debate over the relationship between international and national law. Increasingly, contemporary nations have been committing to a territorial stance, prioritizing their exclusive political and economic interests, and confronting international law. Sovereigntism as an ideology and a policy is a dominant trend in the present-day relation between the international legal order and the domestic legal order in a number of states. States embrace sovereigntism to highlight their policies of resisting international law and to justify derogations from their international obligations. The EU has exhibited what can be called "sovereigntist behavior"[1] or "nationalism"[2] by putting its order before the international order, especially in the sphere of human rights.

The present chapter touches on one of the aspects of sovereigntism — its reflection in domestic constitutional law and judicial practice with respect to human rights protection. The sphere of human rights is my focus since it forms the arena of *erga omnes* ("toward all") norms of international law, being understood as the obligations of states owed to "the international community as a whole" (Fragmentation 2006: 196).

---

1   The term "sovereigntist order" is used with a certain degree of analogy, since the EU is not a sovereign state. However, comparable practices allow reference to the example of the EU in order to demonstrate the processes of sovereigntization in a wider sense.
2   As Juliane Kokott, German advocate general at the EU's Court of Justice, and Christoph Sobotta, legal secretary (*référendaire*) In Kokott's chambers, put it after the *Kadi* case (see: Grand Chamber 2008).

In a famous obiter dictum, the International Court of Justice in the 1970 case concerning Barcelona Traction, Light and Power Company, a Canadian company operating utilities in Barcelona, stated:

> [O]bligations erga omnes ... derive, for example, in contemporary international law, from the outlawing of acts of aggression, and of genocide, as also from the principles and rules concerning the basic rights of the human person, including protection from slavery and racial discrimination. (International Court of Justice 1970: 32)

Examples of the sovereigntist behavior of the subjects of international law appear from time to time (Alles & Badie 2016), and these examples unfolded well before the respective concept, sovereigntism, was introduced into broad circulation in the scientific discourse. During the last decade, sovereigntism has strengthened, especially in the sphere of human rights protection. Among other states, Germany, Italy, the UK, and Russia put the provisions of their respective constitutions above the Council of Europe conventional order and claimed that, in certain circumstances, they could derogate from executing the judgments of the European Court of Human Rights (ECtHR) in Strasbourg. This legal view is based on a presumption (and ideology) of the superiority of a nation-state's interests vis-à-vis universal norms, a posture that undermines the authority of international law, and is supported by the respective countries' practices. Constitutional courts (or supreme courts) exercise the prerogative of declaring a nation's position in regard to the possibility of carrying out the ECtHR judgments. William Pomeranz makes the general case in discussing the specific case of Russia:

> By its very mandate, the ECtHR intrudes on the national sovereignty of its members, and Russia is by no means unique among member states in reacting to what it perceives as direct interference in domestic affairs. This inherent tension will not go away any time soon, especially in light of Russia's poor human rights record. (Pomeranz 2011: 21)

The ECtHR held that the Russian legal system provides lower human rights protection than the ECHR does in matters concerning discriminatory treatment based on sexual orientation and the right to a fair trial and freedom of assembly[3] in comparison with the equal or higher human rights protections afforded by the legal systems of Germany, Italy, and the UK.

These four legal systems were selected for analysis because they reflect liberal (Germany and Italy) and radical (the UK and Russia) approaches. Moreover, these approaches are easily discernible in the respective national legislation and judicial practice in each country. Last but not least, these countries have a statistical record of pending ECtHR judgments (Ministry of Justice 2014: 61–63). Finally, analysis of the practices of the EU contributes to a holistic picture since the tendency toward nationalism can be identified from EU policies regarding human rights protections, which border those of a sovereigntist, especially the practices of the Court of Justice of the European Union.

Germany

The Bundesverfassungsgericht (BVerfG), or German Federal Constitutional Court, was the first among the higher national courts of Council of Europe member states to formulate its position in regard to the limits of implementing the decisions of the ECtHR. Its case law may lead to the nonexecution of international judgments.

The BVerfG in an order dated October 14, 2004, voted unanimously to apply the well-known counterlimits theory as developed in the *Solange* case to the relationship between the German Federal Constitution and the European Convention on Human Rights (and, more generally, international law). In the first part of the decision, "[T]he ECHR is equalized to any other statutory norm ... [I]n the German legal order, the Convention, since it is given force by an ordinary federal statute, gets the same rank as the ordinary ratification norm" (Dal Monte & Fontanelli 2008: 29).

The court stated that in national law, the ECHR is subordinate to Germany's Basic Law (the German Federal Constitution). However, the provisions of the Basic Law are to be interpreted in a manner that is open to international law. At the level of constitutional

---

3 See, for example, cases adjudicated by the ECHR (2017, 2010, 2015).

law, the text of the European Convention and the case law of the ECtHR function as interpretation aids to determine the contents and scope of fundamental rights and of rule-of-law principles of the Basic Law. The possibility of interpreting the Basic Law in a manner open to international law ends when it no longer appears justifiable according to the recognized methods of interpretation of statutes and of the German Constitution (Bundesverfassungsgericht 2011).

When no "adapting" interpretation is possible, there is an unresolvable conflict between the domestic source and the conventional one. Such a conflict occurs when the statutory norm, as interpreted in light of the ECHR, counters the substance of a fundamental constitutional right: the statutory domestic norm – as construed following the German Constitution's directions – must then prevail over the international obligation (Dal Monte & Fontanelli 2008: 917).

Italy

The Italian Constitutional Court has a duty to examine whether the provision of the ECHR as interpreted by the Strasbourg Court is compatible with the Constitution of Italy, if a national court raises before it a question of compatibility of a domestic provision with ECtHR case law (Judgments Nos. 348 and 349, 2007). The Italian Constitution Court held that international law may not be used to set aside Italy's constitutional law and that the Constitutional Court "must always aim to establish a reasonable balance between the duties flowing from international law obligations, as imposed by Article 117(1) of the [Italian] Constitution, and the safeguarding of the constitutionally protected interests contained in other articles of the [Italian] Constitution" (Corte Costituzionale 2007a).

The Constitutional Court reaffirmed its position regarding the place of the ECHR in the hierarchy of the Italian legal system in its Decision 349 of 2007. As far as the provisions of the ECHR are concerned, in the absence of a specific constitutional provision, and in light of its internal ratification by ordinary legislation, the ECHR acquires the same status and hence is not classified as constitutional legislation (Corte Costituzionale 2007b; Judgments No. 388 [1999], 315 [1990], 188 [1980]; and Order No. 464 [2005]).

The ECHR, as interpreted by the Strasbourg Court, does not acquire the force of constitutional law and is not immune to assessments by the Italian Constitutional Court of its constitutional legitimacy. It is precisely because the provisions in question supplement a constitutional principle, while always retaining a lower status, that it is necessary that they respect the Italian Constitution. Since the ECHR is given the force of law through an act of ordinary law in the Italian order, that will be the place in the system of sources occupied by its norms, next to other Italian statute laws: chiefly, this means that the European Convention is subordinate to Italy's constitution (Dal Monte & Fontanelli 2008: 67).

The Strasbourg Court stressed that no limitation on national sovereignty can be identified in favor of the specific treaty provisions in question (Judgment No. 188 [1980]). It should also be emphasized that fundamental rights cannot be considered a "field" in relation to which it is possible for the state to relinquish its sovereign powers beyond the granting of jurisdiction limited to the interpretation of the convention (Corte Costituzionale 2007b; Judgment No. 349).

The Court recognizes that in accordance with Article 32(1) of the ECHR, the ECtHR is charged with interpreting the provisions of the convention. The international law obligations undertaken by Italy in signing and ratifying the ECHR include the duty to bring its own legislation in line with the convention, that is, in line with the meaning attributed by the court specifically charged with its interpretation and application. The ECtHR took all relevant ECtHR case law under consideration, since "[ECHR] law lives in the interpretation given by the ECtHR on it" and because the constitutionality test's object is to view the norm as the product of an interpretation activity, rather than just the provision in itself (Dal Monte & Fontanelli 2008: 898).

The UK

A somewhat extreme position is held by the UK. The UK Supreme Court has said it might decline to follow Strasbourg jurisprudence if it contradicts the fundamental principles or fundamental substantive or procedural aspects of UK law.

The UK Supreme Court, in answering the question, "Should the Supreme Court follow Strasbourg case law?," pointed out that, under section 2(1) of the Human Rights Act, it is obliged only to "take into account" any judgment or decision of the ECtHR when determining a question that has arisen in connection with a convention right (Supreme Court 2013).

The UK Supreme Court held that the requirement to "take into account" Strasbourg jurisprudence would normally result in the domestic court applying principles that were clearly established by the Strasbourg Court. There would, however, be rare occasions on which the domestic court would have concerns as to whether a decision of the Strasbourg Court sufficiently appreciated or accommodated particular aspects of the UK domestic process. In such circumstances, the domestic court may decline to follow the Strasbourg decision, giving reasons for adopting this course. This is likely to give the Strasbourg Court the opportunity to reconsider the particular aspect of the decision that is at issue, so that there takes place what may prove to be a valuable dialogue between the domestic court and the Strasbourg Court (Supreme Court 2013).

> This court is not bound to follow every decision of the European court. Not only would it be impractical to do so: it would sometimes be inappropriate, as it would destroy the ability of the court to engage in the constructive dialogue with the European court which is of value to the development of Convention law ... Of course, we should usually follow a clear and constant line of decisions by the European court ... But we are not actually bound to do so or (in theory, at least) to follow a decision of the Grand Chamber ... Where, however, there is a clear and constant line of decisions whose effect is not inconsistent with some fundamental substantive or procedural aspect of our law, and whose reasoning does not appear to overlook or misunderstand some argument or point of principle, we consider that it would be wrong for this court not to follow that line. (Supreme Court 2010)
> The Court states, however, that there are limits to this process, particularly where the matter has been already to a Grand Chamber once or, even more ... It would have then to involve some truly fundamental principle

of. . . [the UK domestic] law or some most egregious oversight or misunderstanding before it could be appropriate . . . to contemplate an outright refusal to follow Strasbourg authority at the Grand Chamber level. (Supreme Court 2013)

The English Court of Appeal has in the past disagreed with the decisions of the ECtHR; the case of *Vinter and Others v. the United Kingdom* (ECHR 2013) can serve as an example. *Vinter* is one in a series of ECtHR's rulings on whether so-called "life sentences" — imprisonment for an indefinite term — are compatible with the European Convention or constitute inhuman or degrading treatment under Article 3. The Court of Appeal concluded that the UK system met the Article 3 criteria (Court of Appeal 2014).

It "clarified" the operation of the Home Secretary's statutory power of compassionate release, describing it as having a "wide meaning" beyond its literal (and non-binding) wording, allowing (and requiring) the evaluation of penological grounds for incarceration. (Graham 2018: 9)

Russian Federation

The Constitutional Court of the Russia Federation has provided vast legal analysis as to the grounds of implementation and interpretation of the judgments of interstate bodies in the national legal system.

The Constitution of the Russian Federation establishes that human rights and fundamental freedoms are recognized and guaranteed in the Russian Federation in accordance with generally recognized principles and norms of international law (Article 17, part 1). International treaties of the Russian Federation form an integral part of its legal system, and if an international treaty of the Russian Federation establishes rules other than those provided by law, then the rules of the international treaty are applied (Article 15, part 4) (KS RF 2012).

It follows from the above legal provisions that the Russian Federation has no right to evade implementing in good faith international treaties that have entered into force and to which it is a party. The Russian Federation, possessing the state sovereignty (Preamble; Article 3, part 1; Article 4, part 1, of the Constitution of the Russian Federation), is an independent and equal participant in interstate communication and, at the same time, declaring itself a democratic legal rule-of-law state (Article 1, part 1 of the Constitution of the Russian Federation), must follow the obligations voluntarily assumed under international agreements, which is confirmed by the provisions of the Vienna Convention on the Law of Treaties.

The Russian Federation has ratified the ECHR and thus has recognized it as an integral part of its legal system. The Russian Federation has recognized the jurisdiction of the ECtHR by virtue of Article 46 of the convention, ipso facto and without a special agreement, binding on the interpretation and application of the provisions of the convention and its protocols in cases of their alleged violation by the Russian Federation.

Russia, as a member of the world community, in which universally recognized principles and norms of international law operate, concludes international treaties and participates in interstate organizations, transferring to them a part of its powers (Preamble; Article 1, part 1; Article 15, part 4; Article 17, part 1; Article 79 of the Constitution of the Russian Federation), which, however, does not mean it renounces state sovereignty.

However, the Russian Constitutional Court admits that Russia may, as an exception, deviate from the fulfillment of international obligations imposed on it when such a deviation is the only possible way to avoid violation of the fundamental principles and norms of the Constitution of the Russian Federation (KS RF 2015).

The Constitutional Court of the Russian Federation in its ruling concerning the execution of the ECtHR's judgment in the case of *Anchugov and Gladkov v. Russia* states that the Russian constitutional order is not subordinate to the ECHR system (KS RF 2016).

The Constitutional Court further points out that the ECHR, as an international treaty to which the Russian Federation is a signatory, has greater legal force in the law enforcement process than a federal law, but not equal and not greater than the legal force of the Constitution of the Russian Federation (KS RF 2016). The place of the ECHR in the hierarchy of the Russian legal system is below the Federal Constitution but higher than ordinary federal law.

The Constitutional Court found it impossible to execute the ECtHR's judgment in the case of *Anchugov and Gladkov* since it contradicted the imperative prohibition enshrined in the Constitution of the Russian Federation, which has supremacy and the highest legal force in the Russian legal system.

The Constitutional Court asserts that "the interaction of the European conventional and the Russian constitutional legal orders is impossible in the conditions of subordination, insofar as only a dialogue between different legal systems is a basis for the proper balance" (KS RF 2016).

Examining the possibility of executing the judgment of the ECtHR in the case of *OAO Neftyanaya Kompaniya Yukos v. Russia*, the Constitutional Court of the Russian Federation in its judgment of January 19, 2017, stated that a judgment of the ECtHR cannot be considered binding on the Russian Federation if the specific provision of the ECHR on which this judgment is based, as a result of an interpretation carried out in violation of the general rule of interpretation of treaties, in its meaning enters into a contradiction with the provisions of the Constitution of the Russian Federation, which are grounded in the international public order and form the national public order, primarily related to the rights and freedoms of a person and a citizen and to the foundations of the constitutional system of Russia (KS RF 2017).

The recent amendments to the Russian Federal Constitution, adopted by a nationwide vote held on June 25 to July 1, 2020, are in line with the decisions of the Russian Constitutional Court of 2016 and 2017, which expressed the opinion that a judgment of the ECtHR cannot be regarded as binding for execution by the Russian Federation "if its interpretation comes into conflict with the provisions of the Constitution of the Russian Federation" (KS RF 2016).

Article 15(4) of the Federal Constitution, which declares the universally-recognized norms of international law and international treaties of the Russian Federation a component part of its legal system, was not changed. This article also determines that if an international treaty of the Russian Federation establishes rules other than those envisaged by law, the rules of the international treaty shall be applied. Amendments were made to Article 79:

> Decisions of interstate bodies adopted on the basis of the provisions of international treaties of the Russian Federation in their interpretation, contrary to the Constitution of the Russian Federation, are not subject to execution in the Russian Federation.

It is presumed that not the international treaties of the Russian Federation but the decisions of interstate bodies adopted on the basis of such treaties shall not be subject to enforcement if construed contrary to the Russian Federal Constitution. Moreover, Article 125(4) of the Russian Constitution was amended to state that the Constitutional Court of the Russian Federation resolves the issue on the possibility of executing such decisions and the decisions of foreign or international courts in case they contradict the foundations of public order of the Russian Federation.

European Union

The Court of Justice of the European Union in the judgment in *Kadi* focuses on the interplay between the provisions of international law and EU law. The Court of Justice states that if international law contravenes the basic values of the EU, especially in the sphere of human rights protection, the EU law provisions should prevail (Grand Chamber 2008). Therefore, the EU may not be able to fully implement UN Security Council resolutions that are in conflict with fundamental human rights obligations flowing not only from the EU legal order and the European Convention but also from the UN Charter itself. Although the Court of Justice's focus is on the implementation of Security Council resolutions by the EU and the European Community, rather than on the validity of the international norms as such, the consequence of this exercise could very well be that any implementation of a Security Council resolution could entail the violation of fundamental EU rights. In this concrete case, the Court of Justice annulled the contested acts. Rather than taking the formal hierarchical relationship between UN law and EU law as the basis for establishing an immunity from jurisdiction of the Security Council, the Court of Justice chose to look at this hierarchy in more substantive terms. Security Council resolutions remain "untouchable," but the acts by which the EU implements the resolutions are not, and are subject to the fundamental rights and constitutional principles that form the basis of the EU's legal order (Grand Chamber 2008).

Analysis of the cases before the EU Court of Justice shows that the judgments of the court depend on whether the issue of human rights protection is at stake. As examples, in *Intertanko*, the court did not give priority to international law since no individual rights or obligations were affected. By contrast, in *Kadi*, where the rights of individuals were affected, the court underlined "domestic" constitutional principles.

Well before *Kadi*, in the famous case of *Flaminio Costa v. ENEL*, decided in 1964, the European Court of Justice established the primacy of EU law (then European Community law) over the laws of EU member states. At the same time, the court underlined the separate character and the special and original nature of the European Community law:

> [The Treaty instituting the E.E.C. has created its own order . . . by creating a Community of unlimited duration, having its own institutions, its own personality and its own capacity in law, . . . the member-States, albeit within limited spheres, have restricted their sovereign rights and created a body of law applicable both to their nationals and to themselves. . . .
> [T]he law stemming from the treaty, an independent source of law, . . . because of its special and original nature. (EuroLex 1964)

The International Law Commission in its report *Fragmentation of International Law: Difficulties Arising from the Diversification and Expansion of International Law* describes the European law/EU law as a "self-contained (special) regime." Among others, the European law/EU law is often identified as "special" in the sense that the rules of general international law are assumed to be modified or even excluded in its administration (UN GA 2006: 68).

As we see, in *Kadi* the EU Court of Justice took another step, based on *Costa*, and declared the EU legal order separate not only from the legal orders of its member-states but also from the international legal order. After *Kadi*, the court's dual approach was described as unfaithful to its traditional fidelity to public international law and inserting itself in the tradition of nationalism (Kokott & Sobotta 2012: 1015).

The above examples can be regarded as sovereigntism and nationalism leading to the fragmentation of international law, whereas regional and national legal regimes may be contradictory to universally adopted principles and norms. Fragmentation and diversification account for the development and expansion of international law in response to the demands of a pluralistic world. At the same time, fragmentation may occasionally create conflicts between rules and regimes in a way that might undermine their effective implementation (UN GA 2006).

The UK and Russia exhibit a radical attitude in comparison with Germany and Italy. In the UK, despite ratification of the ECHR, the decisions of the ECtHR are considered acts "to be taken into account," but create no obligation. The Russian Federation has constitutionalized the conditions for nonexecution of judgments of the ECtHR since the enforcement of decisions of international organizations in which Russia participates (such as the judgments of the ECtHR) often poses allegedly "serious" problems (Opinion of the Venice Commission 2020: 12). The respective positions of the constitutional courts of Germany and Italy are liberal, leaning toward consensus and dialogue (i.e., the principle of openness toward international law — *Völkerrechtsoffenheit* and *Völkerrechtsfreundlichkeit* — of the German legal system). The comparative analysis of the place of the ECHR in the hierarchy of domestic legal systems shows that in Germany and Italy, the European Convention has the same legal rank as an ordinary law, while in Russia it occupies a place higher than ordinary (federal) law but lower than the Federal Constitution.

The EU is not backing down from its commitments to human rights, but it has created the relatively autonomous internal system of human rights protection, thus fragmenting and behaving as "a self-contained regime," which can come into contradiction with the universal legal order.

The examples provided in this chapter show how the principle of sovereign equality of states, one of the ten main principles of contemporary international law, recognized by the UN Charter, has transformed into its antipode, exaggerating its essence to the point of meaninglessness. It is not merely heightened sovereignization.

State sovereignty has never ever been understood in a way contemporary sovereigntists choose to understand it. The very meaning of state sovereignty is highly diversified; different concepts of state sovereignty are operationalized in different contexts. Moreover, "the sovereignty principle is less and less considered as a rule" (Alles & Badie 2016: 19). Neo-sovereigntism can be described by way of six specific features: self-affirmation, self-protection, a new mutualism, an assertion of antihierarchy, protest, and flexible norms. Sovereignty is thus more a protest than it is the basis of real institutions, and is used by the neo-sovereigntists in the battle against the institutionalized hierarchy (Alles & Badie 2016: 16, 19).

As an independent exercise of internal and external affairs, state sovereignty always and necessarily correlates with the sovereignty of other states, subjects of international law. The international legal maxim *Par in parem non habet imperim*, "Equals have no sovereignty over each other," has been proved by the judiciary in many states. The classic definition from *The Parlement Belge* case recalls "a consequence of the absolute independence of every sovereign authority, and of the international comity which induces every sovereign state to respect the independence and dignity of every other sovereign state" (Parlement Belge 1880: 214–215).

This indispensable correlation, the vital importance of coexisting with other sovereignties, requires a state to take into account the presence and the legitimate rights of other states and other subjects of international law in its behavior.

As a result, a certain degree of self-restraint of state sovereignty takes place. Each state possesses its "personal space," and no other state has a right to infringe on it; however, in behalf of mutual interest and cooperation, and with a certain degree of proportionality, states limit their personal space in order to coexist in the community of states.

There is a clear distinction between state sovereignty and sovereigntism. State sovereignty respects other sovereignties, has the ability to be flexible and to shrink, and is capable of managing its own scope, if international relations so demand, while sovereigntism, being an extreme form, ignores or denies other sovereignties and the rights inherent in a sovereignty.

Sovereigntism has a direct impact on international law, international relations, and the international system as a whole. The role and authority of the general legal regulator in the international system — international law — is undermined by states demonstrating the possibility to derogate from the previously agreed-upon rules and, claiming their own singularity, allow such derogation for themselves, while not recognizing the right to such derogations for other states. The collapse of the international system is evident if the majority of states behave in such a way. For the time being, international law has proved able to cope with the situation. The vast majority of states are respectful of international law, keeping the whole system from failure.

The reasoning *in abstracto* is important for the analysis of the functioning of the European Convention's system of human rights protection as specified in the ECHR and protocols to it. The ECtHR found that failure to comply with its decisions amounted to a violation of the ECHR and, in a wide sense, an undermining of the whole system of Council of Europe human rights protection. The Committee of Ministers stressed that speedy and efficient execution of judgments is essential for the credibility and efficacy of the ECHR as a constitutional instrument of European public order, on which the democratic stability of the continent depends.

The constitutional courts of Italy, Germany, and Russia and the Supreme Court of the UK have declared that in their respective legal systems, the European Convention acquires the same status as ordinary legislation or higher, but is not equal to that of the constitutions of these states. And therefore, when the ECtHR's judgment and the constitutional provisions come In conflict, a state can derogate from executing its obligations under the European Convention. It is equally the same when the ECtHR's judgment is based on the interpretation of the ECHR by the ECtHR in a way contrary to a state's constitution. In other words, the states do not dispute the meaning of the provision of the ECHR, but find its interpretation by the ECtHR incompatible with their constitutions. The question is whether a state is bound by the ECtHR's interpretation. There is no doubt that a state is bound by international treaties it has duly ratified, including the ECHR. Is a state also bound by the *consequent* interpretation of ECHR in the decisions of the ECtHR, and therefore obliged to execute such decisions?

The jurisdiction of the ECtHR is determined by Article 32 of the ECHR, which states:

> 1. The jurisdiction of the Court shall extend to all matters concerning the interpretation and application of the Convention and the Protocols thereto. (CoE 1950)

The ECtHR is the only body granted the privilege to interpret the provisions of the ECHR. If a party to the convention accepts the jurisdiction of the ECtHR, it is also bound by the ECtHR's interpretation of the convention.

The very essence of international legal norms is that they are the result of a coherence of wills of different states in order to achieve their common interests, sometimes at the expense of a part of their state sovereignty. State sovereignty envisages that a state is free to enter (or not to enter) into an international agreement, because by doing so a state sacrifices a part of its sovereignty. And so do other states. International law is able to exist because of the mutual restriction of sovereignty by the subjects of international law, especially states. For the smooth operation of the international legal system, domestic law should be in conformity with international law; so, prior to taking an obligation under international law, a state should revise its national legislation in order to reveal collisions with international norms and put it in accordance with them. Of course, this situation is somewhat ideal.

In terms of the interrelation of international law and domestic law it is obvious that when a state recognizes its obligations under an international treaty — that is, when expresses its *opinio juris* — the domestic law should be brought into conformity with provisions of a relevant treaty.

The 1969 Vienna Convention on the Law of Treaties in Article 27 declares:

> A party may not invoke the provisions of its internal law as justification for its failure to perform a treaty. (United Nations 1969)

However, the problem of a state's noncompliance with the fundamental principle of international law — *Pacta sunt servanda* ("Every treaty in force is binding upon the parties to it"), in this case connected with the ECHR — and the possible answers are not so straightforward. At the heart of the problem is not only the issue of interplay (and/or precedence) of international and domestic law but also the problem of application and interpretation of international treaties in good faith.

The Vienna Convention on the Law of Treaties of 1969 in Article 31(1) states:

> A treaty shall be interpreted in good faith in accordance with the ordinary meaning to be given to the terms of the treaty in their context and in the light of its object and purpose. (United Nations 1969)

The aim of interpretation of an international treaty is the clarification of the content of the negotiated wills of states-parties to a treaty. Therefore, any interpretation given should take into account these agreed-to wills, not just the will of a single party. An interpretation in good faith would not add to or diminish the rights or obligations of states-parties under a treaty.

If interpretation is not in good faith, it does add to or diminish the rights or obligations of states, thus changing the treaty provisions already agreed upon, including the object and purpose of the treaty. Therefore, what is in question is not the treaty, consent to which was given at the time of its ratification. Otherwise, could a state derogate from its obligations under this "new" treaty, which is actually found in the instrument of its interpretation?

According to Article 32 of the ECHR, the states-parties a priori accept that any future interpretation of the ECHR by the ECtHR will be in good faith. Bearing in mind the collective character of ECHR, the result of an accumulated joint will of the states-parties, we can assume that every state-party has a right to participate in defining the content and scope of this will, that is, in interpreting the rights and obligations of the states-parties to the ECHR. The right to interpret the European Convention vested in the ECtHR should imply a dialogue between the court and the states, because it was the states that created this court of their own volition.

Moreover, the ECHR and the protocols to it are international treaties, and they can be renegotiated by the states-parties any time.

Sovereigntism and nationalism lead to a system of international law whereby there is no unity; and this is accompanied by the emergence of specialized and (relatively) autonomous rules or rule-complexes, legal institutions, and spheres of legal practice (UN GA 2006: 11). This situation in turn leads to the diversification of the meaning of state sovereignty and a blurring of the concept of state sovereignty. Implementation of the vague principle of sovereign equality is a serious obstacle to the proper functioning of international system.

The phenomenon of a fragmented international system discourages efforts to protect human rights as the highest value. The examples of Germany, Italy, the UK, Russia, and the EU show how human rights are endangered or suffer depending on the level of human rights protection. At the same time, the trend toward sovereigntism and nationalism reveals the problems that exist in the sphere of international human rights protection, especially in the Council of Europe Human Rights system; It lays bare the weak link in an otherwise relatively successful and sustainable mechanism. Any system is a living organism; by the same token, the ECHR is a living instrument. Dialogue and openness of the actors in the international system who create the system itself and vest their rights in its bodies are the most valuable way, and the only possible way, to overcome the challenges to contemporary international law.

Bibliography

Alles, Delphine and Badie, Bertrand. (2016). Soverigntism in the international system: from change to split. *European Review of International Studies* 3(2): 5–19.

Barnhoorn, L. A. N. M. and Wellens, Karel (eds.). (1995). *Diversity in Secondary Rules and the Unity of International Law*. The Hague: Nijhof.

Belgium v. Spain. (1970). *Case concerning the Barcelona Traction, Light and Power Company, Limited (Belgium v. Spain) (Second Phase)*. I.C.J. Reports, 1970.

Bundesverfassungsgericht. (2011). Headnotes to the judgment of the Second Senate of 4 May 2011. *Bundesverfassungsgericht*, 2 BvR 2365/09, paras. 1-178, https://www.bundesverfassungsgericht.de/SharedDocs/Entscheidungen/EN/2011/05/rs20110504_2bvr236509en.html (accessed November 21, 2020).

CoE. (1950). Convention for the Protection of Human Rights and Fundamental Freedoms. *Council of Europe (CoE)*, n. d., https://www.echr.coe.int/documents/convention_eng.pdf (accessed March 29, 2021).

Corte Costituzionale. (2007a). Judgment No. 348 Year 2007. *Corte Costituzionale*, July 3, https://www.cortecostituzionale.it/actionScheda Pronuncia.do?anno=2007&numero=348 (accessed November 29, 2020).

Corte Costituzionale. (2007b). Judgment No. 349 Year 2007. *Corte Costituzionale*, October 22, https://www.cortecostituzionale.it/documenti/download/doc/recent_judgments/S349_2007_Eng.pdf (accessed November 29, 2020).

Cour Internationale de Justice. (1970). Case concerning the Barcelona Traction, Light and Power Company, Limited. *Cour Internationale de Justice*, February 5, https://www.icj-cij.org/public/files/case-related/50/050-19700205-JUD-01-00-EN.pdf (accessed March 29, 2021).

Court of Appeal. (2014). McLoughlin Regina - and - Lee William Newell Appeal. *Court of Appeal*, January 24, https://www.judiciary.uk/wp-content/uploads/JCO/Documents/Judgments/r-v-mcloughlin-and-r-v-newell.pdf (accessed March 11, 2021).

Dal Monte, Francesca Biondi and Fontanelli, Filippo. (2008). The Decisions No. 348 and 349/2007 of the Italian Constitutional Court: The Efficacy of the European Convention in the Italian Legal System. *German Law Journal* 9(7): 889–931.

Dupuy, Pierre Marie. (2002). L'unité de l'ordre juridique internationale. Cours général de droit international public. *Recueil des Cours* 297. Leiden: Martinus Nijhoff Publishers.

ECHR. (2010). Case of Sakhnovskiy v. Russia. *European Court of Human Rights*, November 2, https://hudoc.echr.coe.int/fre#{%22itemid%22:[%22001-101568%22]} (accessed 11 March 2021).

ECHR. (2013). Case of Vinter and Others v. the United Kingdom. *European Court of Human Rights*, July 9, https://hudoc.echr.coe.int/fre#{%22itemid%22:[%22001-122664%22]} (accessed 29 March 2021).

ECHR. (2015). Case of Navalnyy and Yashin v. Russia – 2015. *European Court of Human Rights*, n.d., https://hudoc.echr.coe.int/rus#_ftnref3 (accessed March 11, 2021).

ECHR. (2017). Case of Bayev and Others v. Russia. *European Court of Human Rights*, June 20, https://www.doev.de/wp-content/uploads/2017/Leitsaetze/19/E_0561.pdf (accessed March 11, 2021).

EuroLex. (1964). Case of Flaminio Costa v. ENEL. *EuroLex*, n.d., https://eur-lex.europa.eu/legal-content/EN/TXT/PDF/?uri=CELEX:61964CJ0006&from=EN) (accessed March 11, 2021).

Fisher-Lescano, Andreas and Teubner, Günther. (2004). Regime-Collisions: The Vain Search for Legal Unity in the Fragmentation of Global Law. *Michigan Journal of International Law* 25(4): 999–1046.

Govaere, Ihge, and Garben, Sacha. (Eds.). (2019). *The interface between EU and international law: contemporary reflections.* New York: Bloomsbury Publishing.

Graham, Lewis. (2018). From Vinter to Hutchinson and Back Again? *The Story of Life Imprisonment Cases in the European Court of Human Rights*, n.d., https://core.ac.uk/download/pdf/189162901.pdf (accessed March 11, 2021).

Grand Chamber. (2008). Judgment of the Court (Grand Chamber) of 3 September 2008. Yassin Abdullah Kadi and Al Barakaat International Foundation v Council of the European Union and Commission of the European Communities. *Grand Chamber*, September 3, https://eur-lex.europa.eu/legal-content/EN/TXT/PDF/?uri=CELEX:62005CJ0402&from=EN (accessed November 12, 2020).

Kokott, Juliane and Sobotta, Christoph. (2012). The Kadi Case – Constitutional Core Values and International Law – Finding the Balance? *The European Journal of International Law* 23: 1015–1024.

Konsultant Plus. (1993). The Constitution of the Russian Federation (adopted by popular vote on 12.12.1993 with amendments approved during the all-Russian vote on 01.07.2020). *Konsultant Plus*, December 12, http://www.consultant.ru/document/cons_doc_LAW_28399/ (accessed March 11, 2021).

Koskenniemi, Martti and Leino, Päivi. (2002). Fragmentation of International Law. Postmodern Anxieties? *Leiden Journal of International Law* 15: 553–579.

KS RF. (2012). Postanovleniye Konstitutsionnogo Suda RF (KS RF) ot 27.03.2012 N 8-P "Po delu o proverke konstitutsionnosti punkta 1 stat'i 23 Federal'nogo zakona "O mezhdunarodnykh dogovorakh Rossiyskoy Federatsii" v svyazi s zhaloboy grazhdanina I.D. Ushakova" [from Rus.: Resolution of the Constitutional Court of the Russian Federation of 27.03.2012 N 8-P "In the case of checking the constitutionality of paragraph 1 of Article 23 of the Federal Law" On International Treaties of the Russian Federation "in connection with the complaint of the citizen I.D. Ushakov"]. *Sobraniye zakonodatel'stva RF*,

09.04.2012, N 15, st. 1810 [from Rus.: Collection of laws of the Russian Federation, 09.04.2012, N 15, art. 1810].

KS RF. (2015). Postanovleniye Konstitutsionnogo Suda RF ot 14.07.2015 N 21-P [from Rus.: Resolution of the Constitutional Court of the Russian Federation of 14.07.2015 N 21-P]. *Sobraniye zakonodatel'stva RF*, 27.07.2015, N 30, st. 4658, para. 2.2. [from Rus.: Collection of laws of the Russian Federation, 27.07.2015, N 30, art. 4658, para. 2.2.].

KS RF. (2016). Postanovleniye Konstitutsionnogo Suda RF ot 19.04.2016 N 12-P "Po delu o razreshenii voprosa o vozmozhnosti ispolneniya v sootvetstvii s Konstitutsiyey Rossiyskoy Federatsii postanovleniya Yevropeyskogo Suda po pravam cheloveka ot 4 iyulya 2013 goda po delu "Anchugov i Gladkov protiv Rossii" v svyazi s zaprosom Ministerstva yustitsii Rossiyskoy Federatsii" [from Rus.: Resolution of the Constitutional Court of the Russian Federation of 19.04.2016 N 12-P "In the case of resolving the issue of the possibility of execution in accordance with the Constitution of the Russian Federation of the judgment of the European Court of Human Rights of July 4, 2013 in the case "Anchugov and Gladkov v. Russia" in connection with by the request of the Ministry of Justice of the Russian Federation"]. *Sobraniye zakonodatel'stva RF*, n.d., https://legalacts.ru/doc/postanovlenie-konstitutsionnogo-suda-rf-ot-19042016-n/ (accessed November 21, 2020).

KS RF. (2017). Postanovleniye Konstitutsionnogo Suda RF ot 19.01.2017 N 1-P [from Rus.: Resolution of the Constitutional Court of the Russian Federation of 19.01.2017 N 1-P]. *Sobraniye zakonodatel'stva RF*, n.d., https://legalacts.ru/sud/postanovlenie-konstitutsionnogo-suda-rf-ot-19012017-n-1-p/ (accessed 11 November 2020).

Ministry of Justice. (2014). Report to the Joint Committee on Human Rights on the Government response to human rights judgments 2012-13. *Ministry of Justice*, December (61–63), https://assets.publishing.service.gov.uk/government/uploads/system/uploads/attachment_data/file/389272/responding-to-human-rights-judgments-2013-2014.pdf (accessed March 11, 2021).

Molnár, Támas. (2021). *The Interplay between the EU's Return Acquis and International Law*. London: Edward Elgar Publishing.

Parlement Belge. (1880). Public Vessel—Exemption from Arrest—Trading by Public Vessel. *The Parlement Belge—Court of Appeal*, February 27. https://www.uniset.ca/other/css/5PD197.html (accessed November 11, 2020).

Pomeranz, William. (2011). Uneasy Partners: Russia and the European Court of Human Rights. *Corte Interamericana de Derechos Humanos*, n.d., https://www.corteidh.or.cr/tablas/r29628.pdf (accessed March 11, 2021).

Supreme Court. (2010). Manchester City Council v Pinnock, UKSC 45. *The Supreme Court*, November 3, https://www.supremecourt.uk/cases/docs/uksc-2009-0180-judgment.pdf (accessed November 11, 2020).

Supreme Court. (2012). Judgment R (on the application of Chester) (Appellant) v Secretary of State for Justice (Respondent). McGeoch (AP) (Appellant) v The Lord President of the Council and another (Respondents) (Scotland). *The Supreme Court*, October 16, https://www.supremecourt.uk/cases/uksc-2012-0151.html (accessed November 11, 2020).

Supreme Court. (2013). R v Secretary of State for Justice, UKSC 63. *The Supreme Court*, October 16, https://www.supremecourt.uk/cases/docs/uksc-2012-0151-judgment.pdf (accessed March 29, 2021).

UN GA. (2006). Fragmentation of international law: difficulties arising from the diversification and expansion of international law. Report of the Study Group of the International Law Commission. *UN General Assembly (UN GA)*, July 18, https://legal.un.org/ilc/documentation/english/a_cn4_l702.pdf (accessed November 29, 2020).

United Nations. (1969). Vienna Convention on the Law of Treaties. *United Nations legal documents collections*, n. d., https://legal.un.org/ilc/texts/instruments/english/conventions/1_1_1969.pdf (accessed March 11, 2021).

Venice Commission. (2020). Russian Federation - Opinion on draft amendments to the Constitution (as signed by the President of the Russian Federation on 14 March 2020) related to the execution in the Russian Federation of decisions by the European Court of Human Rights, adopted by the Venice Commission on 18 June 2020 by a written procedure replacing the 123rd Plenary Session. *The Venice Commission website*, March 14, https://www.venice.coe.int/webforms/documents/?pdf=CDL-AD(2020)009-e (accessed March 11, 2021).

Wellens, Karel and Huesa Vinaixa, Rosario (eds.). (2006). *L'influence des sources sur l'unité et la fragmentation du droit international*. Brussels: Bruylant.

Ziegler, Katja. (2016). *The Relationship between EU Law and International Law. In book: A Companion to European Union Law and International Law*. London: Wiley-Blackwell.

Zimmermann, Andreas and Hoffmann, Reiner. (2006). *Unity and Diversity of International Law*. Berlin: Duncker & Humblot.

10 The Evolution of Sovereignty
From Nation State to Human Person

Yurii Mielkov

The problem of political sovereigntism and a general illiberalism in today's world could appear as a paradox under the ongoing processes of economic and cultural globalization, and especially because the collapse of the socialist bloc at the end of the 1980s, followed by a wave of liberalization in the newly independent states of Eastern Europe, led to proclamations about "the end of history" (Fukuyama 1989), with Western-style liberal democracy now seemingly commonly accepted as the world political standard. At the same time, in the 1990s there appeared several works by more realistically inclined researchers arguing, on the contrary, about for "the end of democracy" in one or another way, the result of both unilateral Westernization under the banner of globalization and growing global inequality (Guéhenno 1993; Lasch 1995; Ohmae 1995; Crouch 2004).

The recent turns of events that led to similar pessimistic evaluations and made even liberal scholars start talking about the crisis of liberalism are thus in no way surprising as even in the 1980s and 1990s the main drive against the internationalist socialist ideology of the now seemingly obscure age of modernity was indeed quite nationalist, populist, and right wing in its nature. As Tom Junes recently wrote, the contemporary European Illiberalism is but a legacy of 1989:

> In fact, the nationalist turn in Eastern Europe was fueled by the late socialist regimes which had resorted to nationalism as a substitute for increasingly hollowed-out Marxist-Leninist phraseology. In light of that, the fledgling opposition movements that contested these regimes resorted to patriotic rhetoric and the abundant use of national flags. Understandable as it was at the time for many participants, it masked some uglier nationalist and nativist undercurrents that were present in Eastern Europe's "civil society." (Junes 2019)

Among other researchers who have investigated the contemporary political illiberalism from a position of pessimism we should mention Igor Štiks, who analyzed such events as the COVID-19 pandemic and Brexit and came to the following macabre conclusion:

> The vultures of souverenism, nationalism and neo-fascism are there and have already convinced large groups of European citizens, including moderate ones, that the world is basically a jungle in which only your—national—community could protect you. (Štiks 2020)

Still, in my opinion, it would be incorrect to consider the trend toward sovereigntism solely in the light of its political illiberalism. The main aim of this chapter is to analyze the current sovereigntist trends within the broader scope of the process of the development of democracy and sovereignty using the dialectical method. The latter implies considering the subject of study not only as a process rather than a given static state of affairs but also within the scope of the principle of "unity in plurality," as opposed to thinking in binary oppositions.

In fact, the populist sovereigntist and nationalist agenda could well be presented as a kind of logical reaction to the noted ultraliberal ideas of "the end of history," the monopolizing trend of a Pax Americana that metaphysically tries to reduce the plurality of world cultural, political, ethnic, and similar phenomena to a single entity, thus viewing the complex processes of globalization as the simple and unilateral process of Westernization. At the same time, the growing recognition of global problems, including ecological disaster, climate change, and the aggravation of problems caused by social demographics, demonstrates the need for a corresponding global subject able to solve those problems while still not losing the concrete level of action (as exemplified by the well-known slogan, "Think globally, act locally"). In fact, the contradiction of the universal and the particular could well serve as a starting point for further social development—and for philosophical consideration of the current world situation with respect to not only politics but morality as well.

The Dialectic of the Universal and the Particular

In ethics, the opposition of *morality* and *ethos* could be posed as a reflection of the contradiction between the universal and the particular. Half a century ago, the English researcher Abraham Edel articulated two qualitatively different types of morality: the first answers the question "What will our conscience say?" while the second is more concerned with "What will help to preserve our community?" (Edel 1963). In this regard, the conscience, speaking in the language of the universal categorical imperative (e.g., "Do not steal"), could well collide with the empirical recognition of the allegedly existing customs in a particular society ("everyone steals", "everyone takes (gives) bribes", etc.) — and would not always emerge the winner from such clashes. In practice, that's the moral collision experienced by the former socialist bloc in its later years, with the "hollowed-out Marxist-Leninist phraseology" noted above: a proclaimed moral obligation (with its universality and internationalism) was outdone in practice by everyday actions performed in accordance with totally different maxims. As a result, post-Soviet society quickly experienced a complete demoralization — it could even be said that in this case, a particular ethos has replaced universal morality, has usurped its place — with the marginal ethos of right-wing nationalist groups claiming the space of the missing moral guidelines while obviously lacking their universality.

On the other hand, the contradiction of public morality is not reduced to the designated opposition of deontological (imperative) and factual (custom-based) hypostases of social morality. This contradiction manifests itself in other forms as well: as a universal phenomenon, morality has an intrinsic value and a goal in itself — while the ethos is just a way to achieve a calm life and a stable society, "to preserve our community," and so forth. The problem, in fact, is not that the goals of the ethos — stability, peace, preserving the community — are "bad" or immoral in comparison with other, categorical imperatives but that they have little in common with such a phenomenon as morality, and the reduction of universal morality to particular goals narrows the horizon of the human *Weltanschauung* and makes the means take the place of the ends.

Morality concerns itself with what is good and what is bad — separate from a specific context, of course: otherwise the good could be called "good" in a completely different way (e.g., "profitable" — which always benefits something or someone). Even if in the latter case it is a good goal that is meant, such as the preservation of a stable human community, this goal is still external to the conscience of each human person. Actually, the main question that makes it possible to judge the degree of perfection of social morality is the question of *who is the subject* of a moral obligation: my human conscience or an external entity, which is in fact my own conscience but alienated from me, the ability to make moral judgments having been taken from me and granted to this or that institution, be it an ethnos, a state, or a nation?

Moral particularism is thus a kind of relativism as it affirms that the goals of such an institution take precedence over universal morality. As Nicholas Rescher rightly points out:

> The fatal flaw of such radical relativism lies in its failure to distinguish sufficiently clearly between *matters of custom and social approval* on the one hand and *matters of principle and moral propriety* on the other. (Rescher 1997: 145)

In other words, we are talking about the inability to separate ethos from morality, particular customs from universal norms — or, more generally, *primary values* from *secondary values*, goals from means, ideology from ideals.

I would argue that it is precisely the presence of purpose and value in a human's personal moral consciousness that enables the value dimension of a community in which the person lives, and not vice versa: the universal is the precondition for the particular. A striking example would be science and its values: based on objectivity and strict universalism, science defies any partisanship ("Objectivity precludes particularism," as explained by Robert Merton ([1942] 1973: 270)). Any attempts to build a kind of "national science," such as Hitler's attempts in Germany in the 1930s or Stalin's attempts in the USSR in the late 1940s, have resulted in failure. Still, an interesting example from the history of natural science is the little-known work of the French physicist Pierre Duhem, published in the midst of World War I under the provocative title *German Science*. Based on Pascal's idea of "*l'esprit de finesse*" (as opposed to *l'esprit de géométrie*, particular to math), Duhem more or less objectively examined the influence of the German national character on the features of German science and concluded that the shortcomings of "the German mind" were actually a continuation of its good qualities, such as methodicalness and scrupulousness. A German, he wrote, possesses little ability to come up with new ideas, but is quite capable of combining and developing other people's inventions, as a result of excessive development of *l'esprit de géométrie*, which suppresses common sense (*bon sens*) and prevents it from developing into the intuitive spirit of sophistication (*l'esprit de finesse*) (Duhem 1915: 42–43). Duhem described the latter as a specific feature of the French mind, as opposed to the German tendency toward mathematical deduction.

How should a modern researcher of science treat this work of the famous physicist today? How should it be evaluated by, for example, a historian or a philosopher of science? The simplest option would be to forget it as a small and forgivable weakness of a great physicist expressed under very specific historical conditions and the corresponding apogee of anti-German nationalist hysteria in France. However, it would be unwise not to recognize some point in Duhem's musings on assessing the dependence of scientific activity (which is of a universal nature) on national (and not just personal or situational) psychology and particular national traditional values. After all, no one can deny that the German nation possesses rather strong traditions of mental discipline—of course, neglecting any possible accusation as to whether that leads us to consider the Germans (or any other nation) to be more (or less) "valuable" for science (and in general). I should add that it is the second, more profound approach to the evaluation of the noted work by Pierre Duhem and the very subject of its study that seems to be more appropriate today. It is no coincidence that this book, which has been purposefully excluded from many bibliographies of the French physicist for almost a hundred years, was recently published for the first time in English translation. I think that this position indeed corresponds to the hierarchical understanding of the values of culture in general and science in particular.

The point is that any "national features," however fruitful they may be for the development of science, are useless without the subordination of those features to the universal goal of science itself, which lies (generally speaking) in the search for the truth without any borders and without any particular interest ("disinterestedness"). In fact, that would be true not only for science but for any other global enterprise of humanity, not excluding the social and the political spheres, where the contradiction of the universal and the particular could be traced no less convincingly. Thus it is not surprising that Henri Bergson grounds his idea of "open" and "closed" societies in the idea of "open" and "closed" morality. The open society (*société ouverte*) means here something different from a similar idea developed later by Karl Popper and other thinkers, who insisted on the antitraditionalism and antifundamentalism of an open rational society: according to Bergson, a "closed" society is one that includes some people and excludes others, while an "open" society "is deemed in principle to embrace all humanity" (Bergson 1935: 230). If a closed community is based on instinct and is a static entity devoid of development, then an open one is based on morals and ideas of progress. And although the French philosopher was thinking in binary categories here, it is obvious that his concept is more meaningful and fully meets the current problems of constituting a democratic world community. Actually, only a "particularist" community can be a closed one, to the degree that it puts its particular party values above the universal values of humanity. It is precisely what we witness in today's world, with its nationalist and sovereigntist trends, and what Jürgen Habermas back in 1962 described as *"Refeudalisierung der Öffentlichkeit,"* or refeudalization of the public sphere (Habermas 1990: 90).

According to the German philosopher, the process of such refeudalization consists in private interests acquiring direct political functions: large corporations begin to gradually control the public sphere (primarily through the media) and the nation-state itself. The latter, in turn, becomes an increasingly active player in the private sphere, blurring the boundaries between private and public and turning citizens into consumers. Anyway, the main idea is that the essence of the social sphere, as Habermas rightly demonstrates, lies in its universality—and as soon as some social groups are excluded from it, it is not that the social sphere becomes less complete or less adequate. It simply ceases to exist at all.

Actually, that's where the fundamental distinction between the dialectical and the metaphysical approach comes into view: different values, positions, opinions should no longer be considered just as binary oppositions, either/or. Openness, pluralism, tolerance—all these positive qualities can exist only in the presence of a certain value background. Tolerance is not the same as indifference, and pluralism does not coincide with postmodernist relativism. In politics, or rather in the philosophy of politics, that would relate to the dialectical understanding of democracy as a process of the gradual development of its subject from the particular to the universal.

Subjectness of Democracy and Sovereignty

Democracy in its liberal and Westminster model was in fact that ground on which "the end of history" conceptions were formulated in the 1980s, which in turn was one of the main reasons for the later nationalist and sovereigntist trends to appear as unexpected and discouraging phenomena. However, the Westminster model is actually just a one-sided and abstract understanding of democracy that does not suit the circumstances of the 21st century. Classical democracy as the supremacy of the people, the sovereignty of the people, whereby the people are construed as the source and bearer of state political power—such a formulation could indeed have served as an effective guideline and as an ideal of social and political organization in times of absolutism, during the period in history when usual reality was the dominance of a sole monarch or a narrow circle of persons who held power as a birthright. At that time, the dominance of the people—not of a single person or of an exclusive estate—was a progressive and revolutionary slogan. But today such an approach to understanding and defining democracy turns out to be too abstract—that is, it is insufficiently clear to serve as a lodestar in the semidarkness of the political life of our society. The supremacy of the demos does not really mean the fullness of people's power. Democracy, according to this distinction in notions I propose (see: Mielkov, Tolstoukhov & Parapan 2016), is literally not so much "people's power" as it is "people's supremacy." Under the formal supremacy of the people (in all historical varieties of the latter term, even in its broadest understanding), social administration and governance could still be a monopolized property belonging to one person or even to several narrow social groups. In this sense, one can even talk about the existence of, say, a "democracy-monarchy" or a "democracy-oligarchy": in the first case, a formal supremacy of the people is realized under "the guidance" of one single person (an excellent example of such a "democratic monarchy" is the Soviet Union under Stalin or, say, Juan Perón's Argentina); the second case represents an elite-based form of social and state government organization (being, by the way, a much more frequent phenomenon, as exemplified by most contemporary representative democracies).

If we talk about power as supremacy, we should remember that already by the end of the 20th century in most countries of the world, an understanding of the source of supremacy as different from "all the people" was historical: even most authentic dictators and oligarchs preferred to be called and to govern "in the name of the people." But If one takes into account the actual and the potential development of democracy, the concretization of democracy in respect to different forms of administration under the declared supremacy of the people, it is easy to conclude that both democracy-monarchy and democracy-oligarchy are not proper democracies in the full and precise meaning of the word, as there is a nonpopular power of administrators hiding behind a curtain of the people's supremacy.

That is, I would argue that in the course of the development of human civilization, sovereignty and power gradually make their way from the top of the political pyramid to the bottom of it, from monarchy to grassroots democracy. The power of everyone in today's vision of democracy means the moral sovereignty and social power of *each* person who is able to do something within the field of his or her own competence. That's what could be called the power of authority limited by a sphere of corresponding knowledge and abilities. The sovereign, the supervisor, is not the one who is older, richer, or more famous, and not the one who holds a higher formal post, and not even the one who has been elected by voters, but the one who exceeds others in concrete ability, who knows his or her current sphere of activity best of all. As an old Ukrainian proverb goes: "The landlord is not the one who walks the land but the one who plows it."

Such an approach to democracy allows us to talk about democratic progress not only in terms of the workplace and grassroots democracy but also in the global sphere of political power. It is in politics that the current understanding of power as supremacy over other people is being replaced by the comprehension of power as an ability, in C. B. Macpherson's words, to develop one's own personality under the conditions of a society that overcomes the situation of alienation:

> As soon as democracy is seen as a kind of society, not merely a mechanism of choosing and authorizing governments, the egalitarian principle inherent in democracy requires not only "one man, one vote" but also "one man, one equal effective right to live as fully humanly as he may wish." (Macpherson 1973: 51)

If previously the development of one human personality (that of a leader or an autocrat) could be achieved only through and at the expense of suppressing the others, the majorities, then democracy now could only mean *universal equal development* — and not just a universal and equal right to choose who exactly should develop himself or herself in this society at the expense of the others. Could such a way of social organization be really achieved? I think the answer is yes, because human persons have now reached that stage of their development that helps them recognize the injustice and imperfection of the historically available state of social life, even if that recognition expresses itself only through a traditionalist opposition to electoral democracy in the current crisis of liberalism and the growing illiberal sovereigntism. I would argue that both those trends do not reflect the needs of the current situation and the growing competence of each human person that would no longer need to alienate its sovereignty, its right to govern one's own life either to one single monarch or to a handful of elected elite members. In the course of democracy development, in place of a socially differentiated society there arises an "aristocracy of everyone," in Benjamin Barber's apt turn of a phrase (Barber 1992).

For justice's sake, it should be stressed that the major problem of the globalizing world is not the nation-state dying out but the nation-state losing its *exclusive status* as the arena of realization of a democratic way of social organization in particular and its political life in general. As the famous social thinker and founder of communitarism Amitai Etzioni said, "The world is returning to a pre-Westphalia stage" (Etzioni 2004: 138). In other words, medieval Germany divided into numerous semi- and quasi-independent principalities is a much more adequate and attractive image for the 21st century than one single, uniform, great "German Reich" of the 19th and 20th centuries. According to the classical approach to understanding the history of human civilization, a weak and scattered state is an indication of the historical failure of the German nation, and the processes of centralization and unification—in Germany as well as in other countries—have been almost unambiguously evaluated as progressive, as indicia of modernization and the further development of civilization. However, if we were to try to evaluate that problem from the position of the human person rather than that of GDP and political dominance, we would then have to ask ourselves: what period in history (of Germany, e.g.) would we like to live in and would we choose today as an example to be imitated—a handful of mediocre independent states, a number of small principalities and free cities, say, in the 16th to 18th centuries that enriched the world culture with its greatest names in literature, music, philosophy, and science, or the superpower, totalitarian, soldered-by-iron-and-blood state machine of the German Empire before World War I or World War II that brought death and suffering to millions of people outside and inside the empire? The answer is obvious.

Moreover, according to the champion of the "many civilizations" approach to human history Samuel Huntington, the age similar to pre-Westphalia is already here: if in 1920 there was one world and in 1960 there were three of them (i.e., the Western world, the first world; the second world, comprising the socialist countries; and a third world of economically underdeveloped or nonaligned countries), then since the 1990s there are about ten such worlds on our planet.

> We are witnessing the end of the progressive era dominated by Western ideologies and are moving into an era in which multiple and diverse civilizations will interact, compete, coexist, and accommodate each other. (Huntington 1996: 95)

We should not fear that such a state of affairs and proliferation of sovereignty would mean a retreat for democracy, its metamorphosis into just one of many ways of social existence, on a level with the authoritarianism that is more traditional for non-Western civilization. On the contrary: I think that authoritarianism cloaks itself in "authoritarian democracy" as a result of non-Western countries having imposed on them the Westminster type of representative democracy that is ineffective for their conditions. The answer to such inefficiency (which manifests in more detail in such unpleasant phenomena as corruption of government officials and the general alienation of the state from the life of human persons) is the development of authoritarian democracy in the 20th century, when a non-Western person who has little sympathy for (and little comprehension of) complicated and remote state structures and institutes prefers to delegate a share of his or her rights not to depersonalized political parties but to a concrete "father of the fatherland" (or "mother of the motherland," for female populist politicians thrive as well) whom he or she could trust (or rather, whom he or she supposes he or she could trust). The way out of that impasse can only be the further development of democracy as a democracy of the human person.

It is most important to stress here that the problem is not that sovereignty in general, and particularly sovereignty as the center of political life and the focus of the space for communal discourse and decision-making process, is being relocated from the national to the global level (or, alternatively, to a local level) but that there is a process of *decentralization* of social space and the political sphere taking place in the contemporary world. The said process does manifest in different illiberal kinds of nationalism as well, but it is in no way limited to such forms as, on the one hand, it should not actually deny the universality of human values (instead, it opposes existing trends to present such values as only those of Western and liberal origins), and on the other hand, decentralization falls to the subnational level as well, enabling the development of democracy as the actual sovereignty and power of everybody, so that each person is endowed with the power or ability to make decisions and to govern his or her own life, while "the people" are considered to be constituted by the humankind population, with no national or other exceptions, taken as a socially and personally advanced demos.

Unity and Plurality in World Politics and Human Identity

From this point of view, the institutionalization of a nation-state under present conditions hampers rather than promotes the development of democratic processes in society. Nations have been and are created by violence, by inner colonization—by reducing the diversity of ethnic groups, cultures, dialects, and subnational identities of the people living on the territory of a state to a common denominator. It is almost impossible to create a nation-state out of a multiethnic community by democratic means.

And currently, *literally all communities are plural and multicultural* (Holovatyi 2014; Mielkov 2017), and their plurality—as well as the proliferation of identities, manifested by the personalities they consist of—is increasing as they follow the course of their cultural and civilizational development. As for the scenario of the creation of a polynational state, one that would be more democratic and more adequate to the circumstances of the global world, it is seldom being realized in fact. Thus, as shown by Juan Linz and Alfred Stepan, out of the number of "new nations" created after the Russian czarist and the Habsburgs' Austro-Hungarian empires dissolved after World War I in 1917–1918, the only country to follow the path of democracy in the 20th century without yielding to the temptation of authoritarianism and totalitarianism was Finland—because only that country at the dawn of its independence managed to restrain the elements of ethnic nationalism. In particular, Swedish was given the status of second state language, though only 5% of the population spoke that language and though Swedish colonization of the past centuries was still alive in the Finnish national memory (Linz & Stepan 1996: 17–37).

Unfortunately, the temptation of authoritarianism and totalitarianism is quite evident not only in the fate of the nation-states created in the ruins of the empires that perished in the course of World War I but also in that of the newly independent states that arose as a result of the Cold War. However, the situation is somewhat different now owing to the increasing proliferation of human identities. The very right of "the people" to self-determination and to the creation of their own national state supposes, so to speak, a one-dimensional identity—the thing that in the 20th century gradually ceases to exist. Such unidimensional abstraction is actually a by-product of the previous historical age when the will of the nation could be embodied in a single person. "*L'etat, c'est moi*," as Louis XIV is famously said to have confessed, was the simplest and clearest way to formulate this idea. And now, when no single person, be it a president or a prime minister, has the right to affirm a national identity and national sovereignty in such a convenient way, a state cannot be reduced to a single ethnic group, culture, language, or dialect. In other words, the common will can no longer be either personified or represented: each human person can represent his or her own interests by himself or herself only, as such a unique combination of interests, identities, and cultural and biological traits could be possessed by no one else, even if that other someone might prove to be more able or competent in any *one* of those spheres of activity and fields of identification.

At first, for newly independent states, gaining sovereignty from a foreign (alien) political and cultural center often leads to the literal reproduction of the former centrism in the liberated land, if on a smaller scale. For example, as the sociologist Igor Bestuzhev-Lada has observed, each part of the dissolved Soviet Union became "a Soviet Union in miniature," a proud little empire that treated any "separatism" in a similarly jealous way as the USSR did, just on a lesser scale (Bestuzhev-Lada 1998: 199).

Democratization processes are processes of the development of human personality, when it obtains new forms, ways, and levels of identification—and that's why such processes are incompatible with the unification of culture, with the imposition of one single identity and sovereignty. Hewing to obsolete binary oppositions ("us" and "them"), such ideological movements strictly discriminate people of a different race, sex, ethnos, and so forth by not allowing the political discourse to be interpolated by any other human qualities. That feature of any abstract identity and a self-contained sovereignty can be well demonstrated using the example of *nationalism*, which is rather historical now in Western countries but still presents a threat to social stability in Eastern Europe. The Croatian writer Slavenka Drakulić (who lives in Sweden today) describes how things felt in the 1990s in the following striking way:

> Being Croat has become my destiny... I am defined by my nationality, and by it alone.... Along with millions of other Croats, I was pinned to the wall of nationhood.... That is what the war is doing to us, reducing us to one dimension: the Nation. The trouble with this nationhood, however, is that whereas before, I was defined by my education, my job, my ideas, my character—and, yes, my nationality too—now I feel stripped of all that. I am nobody because I am not a person any more. I am one of 4.5 million Croats.... I am not in a position to choose any longer. Nor, I think, is anyone else.... One doesn't have to succumb voluntarily to this ideology of the nation—one is sucked into it. So right now, in the new state of Croatia, no one is allowed not to be a Croat. (Drakulić 1993: 50–52)

In 2020, a similar opinion was expressed by Igor Štiks, who compared the new European unity with the old situation in Yugoslavia:

> [T]he EU seemed like a future that was stolen from us. A combination of all the good things Yugoslavia had (supra-national, multi-lingual, multi-religious, diverse), but more prosperous and, in contrast to the criminal chauvinist regimes that proliferated on the corpse of Yugoslavia, committed to the basic rule of law. While we disintegrated in a bloodshed, Europe was uniting itself; whilst Belgrade became a nationalist shadow of its former cosmopolitan self and whilst the spectacular Croatian coast had been deserted. (Štiks 2020)

One might think that the one and only state identity is just being replaced by other identities, also artificial. Thus Anthony Smith, who favors nationalism, argues that the "European identity" that has become so popular recently could not substitute for natural national identities, which are the only real ground for human social life (Smith 1995). However, I could argue that a "European identity" is in no way more artificial than a "French" or "German" identity—those national identities were in turn created in a more or less violent way at the expense of eliminating the more natural identities of the Burgundians and the Languedociens, or by subordinating the Franconians and the Bavarians to one Prussian dialect and Prussian police state organization. It is understood, of course, that at the beginning of the 21st century, European identity is not being created by such means—it is just found to be more suitable *on a global level*, where the more natural identities of neighborhood and township are just irrelevant, as they are too remote from the problems discussed. And that means that the European identity does not deny a French or a German identity—on the contrary, it is possible on their ground only, manifesting itself and becoming actual in other contexts and in other times. That's what Habermas means when he states:

> European identity this way already could not mean anything else but unity in national diversity; by the way, German federalism after the defeat of Prussia and reconciliation between confessions proposes not the worst model for that. (Habermas 2006: 228)

In my opinion, Europe as a single organic formation is an example of what takes shape in the social space succeeding the depleted nation-state. *National* is but one of many levels and contexts for constituting identity and social space; it as an important level but not an exclusive one, not even in purely political matters. The notion of "the people" is always broader than the notion of nations, and not only because it includes representatives of different nations and ethnic groups, cultures, and races but also because the identity of each person cannot be reduced to national identity, although it is augmented by the latter. There is no tragedy in the fact that both human personality and democracy as a way of social organization outgrow the national stage of determination in their development. The death of national democracy is not to be feared as it signifies the birth of a new, more concrete and more complete form of democratic society.

It could be argued that Brexit and influential illiberal and nationalist movements in Eastern Europe (and not only there) contradict that optimistic opinion about the future of the world. However, I would repeat that the noted phenomena are a reaction not to actual globalization and democratization but to their geopolitical distortion, to globalization conducted as a linear unification effort instead of constituting a dialectical "union in plurality". Absolute particularism and nationalism have no future in the global world not because of some political power of the unification-based kind, be it the US or the EU, but because of the ongoing development of human personalities and the proliferation of their identities, which can no longer be easily reduced to one single identity, either of an ethnic, national, or ideological nature. Besides, explicit *national* sovereignty is no longer possible in today's global world owing to the inability of national leaders to actually defy, say, the currency exchange rate (some possible exceptions, such as North Korea, only confirm that rule). And, more important, human persons, even considered as abstract citizens, are no longer the masses of the modern age possessing a single common identity.

As shown by Jean Baudrillard, the people, the class, the proletariat is no more — there are only the masses remaining: the nameless, barely sensible, "silent" majority. The silent majority does not have representatives, asserts Baudrillard — representation pays the price for its former supremacy. "The masses" are no longer entities that can be characterized, as once they were, as a class of people. Submerged in their silence, they are no longer subjects (first of all, they are not the subject of history), and therefore they remain outside the sphere of articulated speech (Baudrillard 1982: 22–28). That view could sound as pessimistic, but only if we relied on the former modern understanding of masses as the subject of history and the subject of democracy. Masses exit the stage of history, to be replaced by separate human personalities.

That is, the agenda of sovereigntism and nationalism is rather an archaism professed by certain politicians pursuing their own particular goals. As the Polish sociologist Jadwiga Staniszkis has observed, there is a seemingly strange discrepancy between the enthusiastic elites who dream and talk about some national renaissance and the pragmatically oriented "people's masses" who are already starting to understand the lessons of globalization and mind their own business while not being really interested in the phantasmagorical discourse of today's national state, particularly post-communist Poland (Staniszkis 2006: 9–10).

In fact, Aleksandr Zinovyev similarly noted at the beginning of our century that the only alternative to adapting to the injustices of the outer world is to build one's own "small autonomous society, that correspond[s] to my ideal" (Zinovyev 2002: 16). Some could call it escapism and political absenteeism; I think that it is the conscious rejection of old and abstract political alienation in favor of concrete personal development.

Conclusion

The topic of human sovereignty is a vast one for philosophical consideration, and the problem of the correlation of the universal and the particular in morality, social activity, and politics, to say nothing of the development of human personality, is a complex undertaking replete with contradictions. Still, I will try to summarize the ideas and arguments expressed in this chapter in the following way. The current processes of globalization and democratization are multilayer processes that lawfully combine the trends toward the unification of humanity and the constitution of humankind as the global subject of activity with the trends toward decentralization and the proliferation of human identities. But those trends are opposite and contradictory only on the face of it: decentralization means not that the center of political life and decision-making is relocating from the national level to the global one or vice versa but that the center could now be literally everywhere.

Both human personality and democracy as a way of social organization outgrow the national stage of constitution in their development, but the unilateral unification of the world according to the liberal agenda of "the end of history" is no less violent and compulsory than the illiberal nationalist attempts to stop the natural unification and globalization processes (the latter being the reaction to the former). Almost all communities are plural and multicultural today, and their plurality, along with the proliferation of identities of the human personalities they consist of, increases as they follow the course of their cultural development. The structure of the identities in question takes the form of a complex hierarchy similar to the hierarchy of values, whereby the universal serves as the ground enabling the particular. Any attempt to assert a moral particularism is relativist and doomed to failure in a world of multitudes and complexity, even if it could be seen as a threat to the liberal unification trend. The identities of human personalities can no longer be easily reduced to one single identity, either of ethnic, national, or ideological nature, and thus the sovereigntism is but a sign of the sovereignty shifting from just the national level to a plurality of levels, from global to regional to national (as the most traditional but no longer exclusive one) and to communal and finally to personal. Each human person can now have the chance to become sovereign, to be the subject of social power and moral obligation, the subject of politics and the subject of democracy—that is, under the New Enlightenment, to have the courage to use one's own reason.

Bibliography

Barber, Benjamin. (1992). *An aristocracy of everyone: the politics of education and the future of America*. New York: Ballantine Books.

Baudrillard, Jean. (1982). *À l'ombre des majorités silencieuses, ou, La fin du social, suivi de, L'extase du socialisme*. Paris: Denoel/Gonthier.

Bergson, Henri. (1935). *The Two Sources of Morality and Religion*. London: MacMillan and Co.

Bestuzhev-Lada, Igor Vasilyevich. (1998). *Alternativnaya Tsivilizatsiya* [From Rus.: *Alternative civilization*]. Moscow: Humanitarian publishing center VLADOS.

Crouch, Colin. (2004). *Post-Democracy*. Cambridge: Polity Press.

Drakulić, Slavenka. (1993). *The Balkan Express: Fragments from the Other Side of War*. New York: W. W. Norton & Co.

Duhem, Pierre. (1915). *La Science Allemande*. Paris: Librairie Scientifique A. Hermann et Fils.

Edel, Abraham. (1963). *Method in Ethical Theory*. London: Routledge & Kegan Paul.

Etzioni, Amitai. (2004). *From Empire to Community: A New Approach to International Relations*. New York: Palgrave Macmillan.

Fukuyama, Francis. (1989). The End of History? In *The National Interest* 16: 3–18.

Guéhenno, Jean-Marie. (1993). *La Fin de la Démocratie*. Paris: Flammarion.

Habermas, Jürgen. (1990). *Strukturwandel der Öffentlichkeit: Untersuchungen zu einer Kategorie der bürgerlichen Gesellschaft*. Frankfurt a. M.: Suhrkamp.

Habermas, Jürgen. (2006). *Zaluchennya inshoho: Studiyi z politychnoyi teoriyi* [From Ukr.: The inclusion of the Other. Studies in political theory]. Lviv: Astrolabia.

Huntington, Samuel. (1996). *The clash of civilizations and the remaking of world order*. New York: Simon & Schuster.

Holovatyi, Mykola Fedorovich. (2014). Multiculturalism as a means of nations and countries interethnic unity achieving, In *Economic Annals-XXI* 11–12: 15–18.

Junes, Tom. (2019). Illiberalism in eastern Europe is a legacy of 1989. *Open Democracy*, November 20, https://www.opendemocracy.net/en/can-europe-make-it/illiberalism-eastern-europe-legacy-1989/ (accessed 18 June 2021).

Lasch, Christopher. (1995). *The Revolt of the Elites and the Betrayal of Democracy*. New York: Norton.

Linz, Juan J. & Stepan, Alfred. (1996). *Problems of democratic transition and consolidation: Southern Europe, South Africa, and post-communist Europe*. Baltimore; London: The Johns Hopkins University Press.

Macpherson, Crowford Brough. (1973). *Democratic theory: essays in retrieval*. Oxford: Clarendon Press.

Merton, Robert. ([1942]1973). The Normative Structure of Science, In: Merton, R. *The Sociology of Science. Theoretical and Empirical Investigations*. Chicago; London, 267–278.

Mielkov, Iurii, Tolstoukhov, Anatoliy, Parapan, Iryna. (2016). *The Many-Faced Democracy*. Saarbrücken: Lambert Academic Publishing.

Mielkov, Iurii. (2017). **Human Personality in the Complex World: Pluralism of Identities and the Problem of World-Attitude.** *Likarska Sprava* 1144(7): 168–174.

Ohmae, Kenichi. (1995). *The End of the Nation State: The Rise of Regional Economies.* New York: Free Press.

Rescher, Nicholas. (1997). *Objectivity: the Obligations of Impersonal Reason.* Notre Dame, Indiana; London.

Smith, Anthony. (1995). *Nations and Nationalism in a Global Era.* Cambridge, MA: Polity Press.

Staniszkis, Jadwiga. (2006). Revolutionäre Eliten, pragmatische Massen: Der Pyrrhussieg der polnischen Populisten. *Osteuropa* 11/12: 7–12.

Štiks, Igor. (2020). A Europe Too Far: The Myth of European Unification. *ROAR Magazine*, Iss. 10, https://roarmag.org/magazine/a-europe-too-far-the-myth-of-european-unification/ (accessed 18 June 2021).

Zinovyev, Aleksandr Aleksandrovich. (2002). Formula Zhizni [From Rus.: The Formula of Life]. *Fenomen Zinovyeva – 80* [From Rus.: *The Phenomenon of Zinovyev – 80*]. Moscow: Sovremennyie tetradi, 2002, 13–18.

On the Authors

Petra Colmorgen works as a foreign policy advisor to the Governing Mayor of Berlin. Previously she worked as an award-winning journalist for several TV and radio stations, as well as an Executive for renowned media enterprises in Germany and Russia. More recently she has been a Consultant for the Brussels based "European Endowment for Democracy". Petra holds a bachelor's degree in economics and a master's degree in European Studies. Her academic work focuses on questions of sovereignty and agency within the post-Soviet space, with special emphasis on Russian, Turkish and EU foreign policy.

Augusto Dala Costa is a triple master in political science from the University of Glasgow, University of Tartu and Ilia State University, specialized in memory and history and Caucasian studies. He is a history graduate from the University of Paraná and Portuguese letters and literature student at the same university. He is currently a writer and proofreader as well as a contributor to the political news website Lossi 36.

Oleksandr Fisun, Dr. Hab., is a Professor of Political Science at V.N. Karazin Kharkiv National University. His primary research interests are comparative politics and democratic theory. He has held visiting fellowships at the Woodrow Wilson Center's Kennan Institute, the Centre for European, Russian, and Eurasian Studies at the University of Toronto, Aleksanteri Institute at the University of Helsinki, the Netherlands Institute for Advanced Study in Amsterdam, and the Polish Institute of Advanced Studies in Warsaw. He has published "Demokratiia, neopatrimonializm i global'nye transformatsii [Democracy, Neopatrimonialism, and Global Transformations]" (Kharkiv, 2006), as well as numerous book chapters and articles on comparative democratization, neopatrimonialism, regime change in post-Soviet Eurasia, and Ukrainian politics.

Ivan Gomza, PhD, is an Associate Professor of Political Science and currently Head of Public Policy and Governance Department at Kyiv School of Economics. His scholarly interests comprise democratization, authoritarian regimes, nationalism, contentious politics, and good governance. He authored two books (the most recent title is *The Republic of Decadent Days: Ideology of French Integral Nationalism in the Third Republic*, 2021) and articles on Ukrainian nationalism, democratization, and social movements. Ivan is a member of PONARS Eurasia. He also sits on *Communist and Post-Communist Studies* journal editorial board. In addition, Ivan teaches six academic courses at Kyiv School of Economics and Kyiv-Mohyla Academy.

Roman Horbyk is a postdoctoral researcher with Södertörn University, Sweden. He is primarily a media scholar studying fake news and viral disinformation, mediatization of warfare, and journalism in the political context, while also working interdisciplinarily in the fields of Soviet history, postcolonial theory, sociolinguistics, and history of ideas. He is the author of over 30 published studies as well as the monograph *Mediated Europes: Discourse and Power in Ukraine, Russia and Poland during Euromaidan* (2017).

Nadiia Koval is a foreign and security policy analyst, currently heading Research and Analytics at the Ukrainian Institute, and a lecturer in European integration in Kyiv School of Economics. Previously she occupied different positions in Foreign Policy Council "Ukrainian Prism," Diplomatic Academy of Ukraine, National Institute for Strategic Studies and the Ukrainian Institute for the Future. She is a member of the International Studies Association and specializes in European Studies; Ukrainian foreign policy; Ukrainian-Polish relations; French, Greek and Polish policies towards Ukraine and Ukraine crisis. She also has a deep research interest in the development of international relations studies in Ukraine.

Natalia Kudriavtseva is a professor in the Department of Translation and Slavic Philology at Kryvyi Rih State Pedagogical University, Ukraine. She holds a PhD in Social Philosophy, and her habilitation thesis is in Linguistics and Translation Studies. Her research interests lie within the fields of sociolinguistics, linguistic anthropology and theory of translation. She focuses on language ideologies and identities with a special reference to Ukraine, the country she has researched most extensively. In particular, her work explores how language is held up as an instrument of Ukraine's independent nation-building, including the realisation of this ideology in the toponymic cityscape. In 2020, she co-edited a special issue of the *Ideology and Politics Journal* devoted to renaming and place name politics in post-Soviet states. She is also a Fulbright-Kennan Program alumna (2009) and a Cambridge Colleges Hospitality Scheme grantee (2013).

Yurii Mielkov, Dr. Hab., Ph. D. in philosophy, is a senior research fellow at the Institute of Higher Education, National Academy of Pedagogical Sciences of Ukraine, and a philosopher and a scholar working in the areas of philosophy of science and humanities, philosophy of education, and philosophy of democracy. He is the author or co-author of four books, and the author of numerous articles on philosophy and methodology of the contemporary science, philosophy of politics, and higher education. Yurii has over twenty years of experience in research and teaching.

Mikhail (Mykhailo) Minakov, Dr. Hab., is a senior advisor at the Wilson Center's Kennan Institute and a philosopher and a scholar working in the areas of political philosophy, social theory, development, and history of modernity. He is the author of six books, co-author of five books, and of numerous articles in philosophy, political analysis, history, and policy studies. Mikhail has over twenty years of experience in research and teaching in Ukraine, Germany, Italy, Switzerland, and United States. He is the editor-in-chief of the peer-reviewed journal *Ideology and Politics Journal*, of the *Kennan Focus Ukraine* blog, and of the philosophical web portal *Koinè*.

Yana Prymachenko is senior researcher in the Institute of history of Ukraine, National Academy of Sciences of Ukraine. Her research interests cover the OUN-UPA problem and the history of World

War II in the memory culture of modern Ukraine and Russian Federation. She is a co-author of 10 non-fiction books dedicated to the history of Ukraine, among which is «*The War and the Myth: The Unknown Second World War*» (2018). Her current research focuses on the concept of «Russkyi mir» as well as the instrumentalization of the history of World War II in memory politics in Eastern Europe.

Gulnara Shaikhutdinova is a professor at the Chamber of International and European Law of the Faculty of Law of Kazan (Volga Region) Federal University. Holding her LL.M from Northwestern University (Chicago, IL) and a Doctor of International Law from Kazan University she is working in the areas of public international law, European law, human rights and constitutional law. She is the author of seven books, co-author of 15 books and textbooks, and of numerous articles in international law, European law, international human rights and federalism. Gulnara has devoted ten years to the Russian civil service and over twenty years to research and teaching in Russia, The Netherlands, Italy, Finland, and United States. She was awarded the title of the Woman of the Year 2021 in the nomination of the Woman-Scholar at KFU.

Nataliya Vinnykova, Dr. Hab., Professor, working in the Department of Political Science of V.N. Karazin Kharkiv National University in Ukraine. She is an author of numerous research publications, including several books. She focuses her research on issues of political decision-making, global governance, transformation of governance under the non-state actor involvement in policy-making.

Yuliya Yurchuk is a Senior Lecturer of History at Umeå University, Sweden. She specializes in memory studies, history of religion, and the study of nationalism in East European countries. She is the author of the book *Reordering of Meaningful Worlds: Memory of the Organization of Ukrainian Nationalists and the Ukrainian Insurgent Army in Post-Soviet Ukraine* (Acta 2014). Her articles have appeared in *Memory Studies, Nationalities Papers, Europe-Asia Studies, Nordisk Østforum, Baltic Worlds, Ukraina Moderna*.

Ruslan Zaporozhchenko, MA in Political Science, is a PhD student of the department of Political Science, School of Philosophy, V.N. Karazin Kharkiv National University. Studies the political forms of organizing space in the context of contemporary globalization processes. The junior researcher of international scientific projects ARDU (Accommodation of Regional Diversity in Ukraine) and FUSILLI (Fostering the Urban Food System Transformation through Innovative Living Labs Implementation). The author of articles on the analytical and world-system analysis of empires and modern states, sovereignty and ideology, power and structures of hegemony, global governance and international affairs.

Index

Abkhazia 17, 61, 64, 66, 71, 74, 77, 78, 79, 81, 82, 83, 84, 160, 163, 165, 166, 171
Adjara 17, 70, 71, 74, 77, 83
Anchugov and Gladkov 328, 329, 340
Anchugov and Gladkov case 328, 329, 340
Area studies 18, 92, 95, 100, 101, 106, 116, 117, 118, 119, 120, 121, 130
authority 7, 14, 99, 146, 186, 216, 225, 257, 267, 272, 283, 286, 288, 299, 313, 322, 327, 333, 334, 351
autocracy 63, 308, 309
Azaryahu, Maoz 27, 29, 52, 141, 143, 144, 173, 174
Bannon, Stephen K. 294, 295, 311, 314, 319
Barber, Benjamin 352, 360
Barcelona Traction case 322, 337, 338
Baudrillard, Jean 358, 360
Belarus, Belraussian 86, 91, 178, 179, 186, 187, 194, 198, 199, 201, 257, 259, 262, 265, 266, 267, 268, 270, 271, 274, 277, 363
Benhabib, Seyla 282, 284, 288, 290, 291, 292, 312
Bergson, Henri 348, 360
Bestuzhev-Lada, Igor 355, 360
Bodaveli, Elene 142, 145, 147, 152, 170, 174

Bolton, John R. 296, 312
Brzeziński, Zbigniew 106, 107, 133
Chelidze, Zurab 142, 148, 149, 151, 155, 156, 157, 158, 161, 162, 163, 164, 165, 166, 174
cityscape 5, 19, 27, 28, 50, 141, 142, 143, 145, 147, 149, 151, 158, 169, 170, 173, 365
civil society 94, 217, 290, 320, 343
conservatism, conservative 11, 56, 72, 73, 75, 81, 259, 282, 292, 293, 299, 302, 303, 304, 305, 310
cosmopolitanism, cosmopolitan 21, 22, 147, 170, 198, 232, 278, 290, 291, 292, 302, 306, 307, 308, 309, 310, 312, 313, 314, 356
cultural memory 141, 149, 172, 181, 182, 183
decentralization 353, 359
decommunization 5, 17, 27, 28, 30, 31, 34, 36, 44, 45, 48, 50, 51, 53, 54

democracy, democratization 20, 21, 22, 59, 60, 65, 67, 75, 78, 79, 81, 82, 83, 84, 106, 117, 133, 175, 206, 207, 218, 227, 228, 229, 245, 255, 266, 268, 271, 276, 277, 278, 279, 282, 283, 286, 288, 289, 291, 297, 300, 301, 308, 309, 311, 312, 313, 315, 316, 319, 343, 344, 349, 350, 351, 353, 354, 356, 357, 358, 359, 360, 361, 363, 364

Drakulić, Slavenka 356, 361

Drozdzewski, Danielle 141, 144, 147, 148, 174

Dugin, Aleksander 305, 306, 314

Duhem, Pierre 347, 361

Edel, Abraham 345, 361

Educational reforms 96

empire 38, 63, 68, 71, 75, 156, 165, 174, 189, 231, 239, 240, 241, 242, 243, 269, 270, 271, 277, 279, 290, 313, 316, 352, 355, 361

entangled history 180

ethos 21, 345, 346

Etzioni, Amitai 352, 361

European Union, EU 21, 56, 59, 60, 62, 64, 74, 75, 76, 80, 82, 83, 132, 215, 221, 222, 223, 232, 254, 255, 276, 278, 295, 300, 309, 318, 321, 323, 330, 331, 332, 337, 339, 340, 341, 356, 358, 363

Fisun, Oleksander 5, 20, 205, 206, 219, 221, 226, 227, 257, 270, 277, 363

fragmentation 21, 213, 216, 221, 224, 233, 263, 321, 331, 332, 339, 341

Fukuyama 106, 107, 134, 343, 361

Gal, Susan 31, 41, 48, 53

Gamsakhurdia, Zviad 19, 146, 153, 164, 165, 171, 172

Georgia, Georgian 5, 17, 18, 40, 55, 56, 57, 58, 59, 60, 61, 62, 63, 64, 65, 66, 67, 68, 69, 70, 71, 72, 73, 74, 75, 76, 77, 78, 79, 80, 81, 82, 83, 84, 141, 142, 145, 146, 147, 148, 149, 150, 152, 153, 154, 156, 158, 159, 160, 161, 162, 163, 164, 165, 166, 167, 169, 171,172, 173, 174, 175, 255, 257, 271, 272, 291, 301, 315, 317

Georgian foreign policy 59, 78, 80, 82, 84

Gleckman, Harris 227

globalism, globality 20

Gnatiuk, Oleksiy 29, 30, 32, 33, 39, 46, 52

good faith 327, 336

grassroots democracy 350, 351

Habermas, Jürgen 292, 314, 348, 349, 357, 361

historical myth 19, 191, 192

historical propaganda 201

INDEX 371

history 5, 11, 14, 18, 19, 22, 27, 28, 33, 40, 41, 42, 43, 44, 47, 48, 49, 50, 51, 55, 90, 91, 92, 99, 101, 102, 103, 107, 108, 117, 129, 135, 136, 137, 142, 143, 144, 150, 155, 166, 170, 172, 173, 174, 175, 177, 178, 179, 181, 182, 183, 184, 185, 186, 187, 188,189, 190, 191, 192, 193, 194, 195, 196, 197, 198, 199, 200, 201, 225, 255, 278, 283, 284, 285, 286, 299, 303, 305, 308, 309, 311, 313, 315, 316, 317, 318, 319, 343, 344, 346, 349, 352, 358, 360, 361, 363, 364, 365, 366

Hjarvard, Stig 179, 180, 197

Hoskins, Andrew 182, 183, 185, 191, 194, 197

human personality 351, 356, 357, 359

human sovereignty 359

Huntington, Samuel 106, 107, 135, 282, 352, 353, 361

identity 5, 16, 17, 19, 28, 30, 31, 32, 33, 36, 37, 40, 41, 44, 45, 46, 48, 51, 52, 53, 54, 55, 56, 57, 58, 59, 60, 61, 64, 65, 67, 68, 69, 71, 72, 74, 75, 76, 77, 78, 79, 80, 81, 82, 84, 94, 106, 133, 138, 141, 142, 143, 144, 145, 147, 152, 160, 170, 172, 173, 174, 175, 181, 209, 246, 253, 254, 255, 263, 274, 276, 277, 278, 290, 305, 307, 308, 309, 311, 319, 354, 355, 356, 357, 358, 360

ideology 5, 12, 15, 16, 17, 21, 22, 23, 25, 27, 30, 32, 49, 51, 52, 55, 63, 79, 82, 93, 136, 141, 142, 145, 152, 156, 158, 164, 167, 174, 227, 233, 234, 235, 248, 254, 258, 259, 260, 264, 265, 267, 275, 282, 283, 292, 293, 295, 297, 299, 301, 304, 306, 308, 309, 310, 314, 315, 316, 321, 322, 343, 346, 356, 364, 365, 367

imagery 8, 12, 15, 282, 285, 288, 289, 291, 303, 305, 307, 310

imagination 8, 9, 10, 11, 12, 13, 14, 21, 22, 23, 24, 276, 284, 292, 298, 305, 311, 312, 313, 314, 318, 320

international law 21, 96, 113, 119, 121, 124, 251, 268, 285, 287, 290, 296, 302, 309, 312, 313, 315, 318, 321, 322, 323, 324, 325, 327, 328, 329, 330, 331, 332, 333, 334, 335, 336, 337, 339, 341, 366

International Relations (IR) 5, 18, 79, 85, 86, 87, 88, 89, 90, 91, 92, 93, 94, 95, 96, 97, 98, 99, 101, 102, 103, 104, 105, 106, 107, 108, 109, 110, 111, 112, 113, 114, 115, 116, 117, 118, 119, 121, 122, 123, 124, 125, 127, 128, 129, 130, 131, 132, 133, 134, 135, 136, 137, 138, 139, 140, 361

IR paradigms 18, 96, 111

Irvine, Judith T. 31, 41, 48, 53

Junes, Tom 343, 361

Kadi case 321

Kelsen, Hans 281, 287, 315

Kissinger, Henry 106, 107, 123

language ideology 17, 31, 41, 53, 54
legal order, domestic 321
legal order, international 21, 321, 331
legal order, of EU 293, 323, 329, 330, 331, 332
legitimacy 16, 21, 146, 205, 207, 208, 209, 213, 214, 216, 218, 219, 222, 225, 228, 233, 236, 248, 253, 256, 257, 260, 263, 272, 274, 278, 286, 313, 318
liberalism, liberal 13, 65, 69, 75, 110, 113, 124, 130, 232, 233, 244, 258, 259, 260, 266, 273, 279, 283, 286, 290, 293, 296, 298, 303, 305, 306, 308, 310, 311, 316, 323, 332, 343, 349, 351, 354, 360
Light, Duncan 27, 28, 30, 53, 54, 91, 92, 136, 322, 337, 338
Likbez 19, 178, 185, 188, 189, 190, 191, 192, 193, 199, 201
linguistic landscape 27, 52
Lithuania 178, 179, 186, 187, 194, 196, 255
mediatization of history 178, 179, 182, 186, 189, 192, 193, 194, 195
memory, cultural 8, 11, 14, 19, 27, 42, 43, 49, 54, 141, 143, 144, 147, 149, 170, 171, 172, 173, 174, 175, 178, 181, 182, 183, 185, 186, 188, 189, 192, 193, 194, 195, 197, 199, 299, 355, 363, 366
Merton, Robert 249, 278, 346, 361

Minakov, Mikhail 5, 6, 7, 15, 22, 220, 223, 224, 227, 281, 291, 303, 314, 315, 316, 365
minority 51, 71, 72, 75, 77, 96, 125, 193, 274, 293, 296, 307, 308, 309, 310
moral particularism 21, 346, 360
morality 73, 75, 245, 246, 344, 345, 346, 360
morality and ethos 345
multistakeholder governance 216, 217, 218, 220
mythbuster 190
nationalism, nationalist 6, 20, 21, 67, 72, 79, 146, 178, 181, 188, 191, 195, 197, 200, 232, 233, 252, 254, 255, 258, 259, 272, 275, 277, 286, 292, 295, 316, 319, 321, 323, 331, 332, 337, 343, 344, 345, 347, 348, 349, 354, 355, 356, 357, 358, 359, 360, 362, 364, 366
nationality, natsional'nost', natsional'nist' 10, 34, 110, 170, 356
neoliberalism, neoliberal 226, 243, 258, 265, 266, 273, 276, 278, 279, 307, 314
oligarchic rule 220, 226
open society 348
Orthodoxy 17, 55, 56, 67, 68, 71, 73, 74, 75, 77, 162
othering 17, 56, 57, 58, 62, 63, 64, 65, 68, 69, 71, 72, 73, 76, 77, 79
Parlement Belge case 333
Pavlenko, Aneta 29, 31, 54
philosophy of democracy 365

place name 17, 19, 27, 28, 29, 30, 31, 32, 34, 36, 39, 40, 41, 42, 44, 45, 46, 47, 48, 49, 50, 51, 52, 142, 147, 148, 175, 365

Poland 85, 95, 107, 121, 129, 133, 148, 178, 179, 184, 185, 190, 194, 196, 266, 274, 282, 359, 364

Popper, Karl 348

populism 20, 233, 247, 252, 253, 263, 264, 265, 266, 267, 268, 272, 274, 275, 276, 277, 278, 279

power 10, 11, 12, 14, 16, 19, 20, 52, 57, 60, 61, 62, 64, 68, 73, 80, 81, 82, 86, 94, 96, 98, 100, 102, 117, 118, 123, 127, 128, 129, 134, 140, 141, 142, 144, 167, 169, 171, 173, 178, 194, 205, 206, 207, 213, 214, 215, 218, 221, 222, 224, 225, 229, 231, 232, 233, 234, 235, 236, 237, 238, 239, 240, 241, 242, 245, 246, 247, 248, 249, 250, 251, 252, 253, 255, 256, 257, 258, 259, 260, 261, 262, 263, 264, 265, 267, 268, 269, 270, 271, 272, 273, 274, 275, 276, 277, 278, 282, 283, 284, 286, 291, 293, 300, 303, 322, 327, 337, 338, 349, 350, 351, 354, 358, 360, 364, 367

prosthetic memory 179, 181, 182, 186, 193, 194

Putin, Vladimir 73, 259, 283, 293, 299, 300, 301, 302, 304, 305, 306, 311, 313, 315, 317

Putinism 6, 21, 281, 282, 308, 309, 310, 314, 319

realism 18, 92, 95, 110, 113, 115, 123, 130, 135, 312, 314

renaming 5, 17, 18, 27, 28, 29, 30, 32, 34, 36, 39, 40, 42, 43, 44, 45, 46, 48, 49, 50, 51, 52, 53, 54, 63, 141, 142, 145, 148, 149, 150, 151, 152, 153, 154, 155, 156, 157, 161, 164, 165, 167, 168, 169, 173, 365

representation, political 208, 211, 212, 226

Rescher, Nicholas 346, 362

rights, civil rights 6, 21, 54, 66, 75, 78, 81, 84, 119, 210, 219, 232, 260, 268, 282, 286, 288, 289, 290, 291, 293, 298, 303, 305, 309, 310, 311, 312, 315, 316, 317, 321, 322, 323, 324, 325, 326, 329, 330, 331, 332, 333, 334, 336, 337, 338, 339, 340, 341, 353, 366

rights, human rights 20, 21, 76, 84, 130, 282, 288, 289, 290, 291, 292, 302, 307, 310, 312, 316, 318, 321, 322, 323, 327, 330, 331, 332, 334, 337, 340, 366

Russia, Russian 16, 17, 19, 21, 29, 32, 33, 35, 38, 42, 48, 49, 50, 52, 55, 56, 57, 58, 61, 62, 63, 64, 65, 66, 68, 70, 71, 72, 73, 74, 75, 77, 78, 79, 80, 81, 82, 83, 84, 85, 86, 87, 92, 94, 105, 107, 109, 115, 118, 119, 120, 124, 128, 129, 130, 136, 138, 139, 140, 145, 148, 156, 158, 162, 165, 166, 170, 174, 185, 188, 189, 190, 191, 194, 197, 201, 220, 221, 222, 223, 224, 225, 226, 229, 231, 242, 257, 259, 262, 265, 267, 268, 270, 271, 276, 277, 278, 282, 283, 299, 300, 301, 302, 303, 304, 305, 306, 307, 308, 309, 310, 311, 314, 315, 316, 317, 319, 320, 322, 323, 327, 328, 329, 330, 332, 334, 337, 338, 339, 340, 341, 354, 363, 364, 366

Saakashvili, Mikheil 19, 60, 61, 62, 65, 67, 70, 77, 78, 146, 165, 166, 171

Schmitt, Carl 235, 236, 278, 281, 286, 318

shared history 172, 179, 181, 186, 191, 195

Smith, Anthony 95, 139, 140, 292, 314, 357, 362

social imagination 13, 14, 284, 291

social space 231, 236, 249, 255, 353, 357

South Caucasus 77, 81, 82, 83

South Ossetia 17, 61, 64, 66, 71, 77, 79, 82, 83, 84, 171, 318

sovereigntism 5, 6, 19, 20, 203, 231, 233, 251, 252, 253, 254, 256, 258, 260, 263, 264, 265, 266, 268, 269, 273, 274, 275, 277, 278, 282, 283, 291, 292, 293, 296, 299, 301, 302, 310, 311, 312, 321, 322, 332, 333, 334, 337, 343, 344, 351, 359, 360

sovereignty 6, 20, 21, 77, 124, 141, 169, 172, 205, 206, 207, 208, 213, 214, 215, 219, 220, 221, 222, 223, 224, 225, 226, 227, 228, 231, 232, 233, 234, 235, 236, 237, 238, 239, 240, 241, 242, 243, 244, 245, 246, 247, 248, 249, 250, 251, 252, 253, 255, 260, 261, 262, 263, 268, 269, 270, 271, 272, 273, 274, 275, 276, 277, 278, 279, 281, 282, 283, 284, 285, 286, 287, 288, 289, 290, 291, 292, 293, 294, 295, 296, 297, 298, 299, 300, 301, 302, 303, 305, 306, 308, 309, 310, 311, 312, 313, 314, 315, 316, 317, 318, 319, 320, 322, 325, 327, 328, 333, 335, 337, 343, 344, 349, 350, 352, 353, 355, 356, 358, 360, 363, 367

Soviet, Soviet Union 5, 7, 14, 15, 16, 17, 18, 19, 20, 21, 22, 28, 33, 35, 37, 38, 39, 40, 41, 43, 44, 45, 46, 47, 48, 51, 57, 60, 61, 63, 65, 66, 68, 69, 71, 75, 78, 79, 80, 81, 82, 83, 86, 91, 92, 93, 94, 97, 99, 102, 111, 113, 115, 118, 119, 120, 123, 128, 129, 136, 138, 140, 141, 143, 145, 146, 147, 148, 149, 151, 152, 153, 154, 155, 156, 157, 160, 162, 163, 164, 167, 169, 170, 171, 173, 174, 175, 179, 188, 191, 192, 196, 197, 198, 199, 203, 207, 217, 219, 221, 224, 226, 227, 241, 254, 255, 257, 258, 259, 262, 267, 269, 270, 271, 272, 275, 277, 278, 303, 304, 314, 315, 316, 317, 318, 345, 350, 355, 363, 364, 365, 366

Staniszkis, Jadwiga 359, 362

state, modern state 6, 13, 14, 17, 20, 23, 30, 33, 35, 38, 44, 49, 51, 53, 54, 56, 59, 60, 62, 64, 65, 68, 70, 74, 75, 84, 86, 90, 91, 92, 93, 94, 95, 106, 111, 113, 115, 117, 120, 123, 124, 125, 126, 128, 131, 132, 133, 136, 146, 160, 185, 186, 187, 188, 189, 190, 193, 194, 196, 205, 206, 207, 208, 209, 212, 213, 214, 215, 216, 217, 218, 219, 220, 222, 223, 224, 225, 226, 227, 231, 232, 233, 234, 235, 237, 238, 240, 241, 243, 244, 251, 252, 255, 256, 257, 258, 259, 260, 261, 263, 264, 265, 266, 268, 269, 270, 272, 274, 276, 277, 278, 281, 282, 283, 284, 285, 286, 287, 288, 289, 290, 291, 292, 293, 295, 297, 298, 299, 301, 302, 306, 307, 308, 309, 310, 311, 312, 313, 315, 318, 321, 322, 325, 327, 328, 330, 333, 334, 335, 336, 337, 341, 343, 344, 346, 348, 349, 351, 352, 353, 354, 355, 356, 357, 359, 362, 363, 366, 367

Štiks, Igor 344, 356, 362

StopFake 194

subjectness 242, 349

supremacy 20, 21, 282, 284, 285, 286, 298, 300, 301, 310, 311, 329, 349, 350, 351, 358

Surkov, Vladislav 271, 300, 301, 304, 305, 313, 317, 318, 319

Tbilisi 5, 18, 63, 69, 73, 75, 78, 79, 81, 83, 84, 141, 142, 145, 146, 147, 148, 149, 151, 152, 153, 154, 155, 156, 158, 168, 169, 170, 172, 173, 174, 175

toponymic ideology 48, 51
toponymy 5, 28, 30, 39, 40, 41, 42, 46, 47, 51, 54, 141, 142, 143, 144, 145, 148, 149, 150, 151, 152, 153, 154, 155, 157, 158, 165, 166, 170, 171, 174, 175
tradition, traditional 18, 34, 63, 70, 72, 98, 99, 108, 129, 144, 146, 180, 193, 194, 209, 211, 212, 216, 217, 283, 285, 297, 298, 299, 303, 304, 305, 307, 308, 309, 310, 331, 347, 353, 360
TRIP survey 88, 101, 105, 108, 115, 119
Trump, Donald 231, 244, 263, 266, 293, 294, 296, 297, 298, 306, 313, 314, 316, 317, 319
Trumpism 6, 21, 281, 282, 293, 294, 295, 296, 299, 308, 309, 310, 314, 316, 319
Turkey 17, 55, 56, 57, 58, 68, 69, 70, 71, 73, 74, 77, 78, 79, 80, 82, 84, 117, 266

Ukraine, Ukrainian 5, 16, 17, 18, 19, 20, 22, 27, 28, 30, 31, 32, 33, 35, 36, 37, 38, 40, 42, 43, 44, 45, 46, 47, 48, 49, 50, 51, 52, 53, 54, 78, 82, 83, 85, 86, 87, 88, 89, 90, 91, 93, 94, 95, 96, 97, 98, 99, 100, 101, 102, 103, 104, 105, 106, 107, 108, 109, 110, 111, 112, 113, 114, 115, 116, 118, 119, 120, 121, 123, 124, 125, 126, 127, 128, 129, 130, 131, 132, 133, 135, 136, 137, 138, 139, 163, 178, 179, 184, 185, 186, 187, 188, 189, 190, 191, 192, 193, 194, 196, 197, 198, 199, 200, 201, 207, 211, 219, 220, 221, 222, 223, 224, 225, 226, 227, 228, 229, 255, 256, 257, 263, 265, 270, 271, 272, 299, 301, 311, 351, 363, 364, 365, 366, 367
Ukrainian IR community 86, 87, 90, 97, 100, 103, 105, 106, 108, 110, 112, 119, 120, 124, 127, 129, 130
United States of America, USA 85, 117, 221, 222
urban toponymy 27, 50
value 62, 72, 110, 212, 248, 269, 287, 326, 345, 346, 349
Venice Commission 303, 320, 332, 341
Wedel, Janine 217, 218, 229
Westernization 18, 59, 64, 74, 86, 91, 94, 95, 97, 128, 131, 304, 343, 344
Westernness 17, 56, 59, 60, 63, 64, 67, 74, 75, 77
Westlessness 281, 312, 320
Zinovyev, Aleksandr 359, 362

SOVIET AND POST-SOVIET POLITICS AND SOCIETY
Edited by Dr. Andreas Umland | ISSN 1614-3515

1 Андреас Умланд (ред.) | Воплощение Европейской конвенции по правам человека в России. Философские, юридические и эмпирические исследования | ISBN 3-89821-387-0

2 Christian Wipperfürth | Russland – ein vertrauenswürdiger Partner? Grundlagen, Hintergründe und Praxis gegenwärtiger russischer Außenpolitik | Mit einem Vorwort von Heinz Timmermann | ISBN 3-89821-401-X

3 Manja Hussner | Die Übernahme internationalen Rechts in die russische und deutsche Rechtsordnung. Eine vergleichende Analyse zur Völkerrechtsfreundlichkeit der Verfassungen der Russländischen Föderation und der Bundesrepublik Deutschland | Mit einem Vorwort von Rainer Arnold | ISBN 3-89821-438-9

4 Matthew Tejada | Bulgaria's Democratic Consolidation and the Kozloduy Nuclear Power Plant (KNPP). The Unattainability of Closure | With a foreword by Richard J. Crampton | ISBN 3-89821-439-7

5 Марк Григорьевич Меерович | Квадратные метры, определяющие сознание. Государственная жилищная политика в СССР. 1921 – 1941 гг | ISBN 3-89821-474-5

6 Andrei P. Tsygankov, Pavel A. Tsygankov (Eds.) | New Directions in Russian International Studies | ISBN 3-89821-422-2

7 Марк Григорьевич Меерович | Как власть народ к труду приучала. Жилище в СССР – средство управления людьми. 1917 – 1941 гг. | С предисловием Елены Осокиной | ISBN 3-89821-495-8

8 David J. Galbreath | Nation-Building and Minority Politics in Post-Socialist States. Interests, Influence and Identities in Estonia and Latvia | With a foreword by David J. Smith | ISBN 3-89821-467-2

9 Алексей Юрьевич Безугольный | Народы Кавказа в Вооруженных силах СССР в годы Великой Отечественной войны 1941-1945 гг. | С предисловием Николая Бугая | ISBN 3-89821-475-3

10 Вячеслав Лихачев и Владимир Прибыловский (ред.) | Русское Национальное Единство, 1990-2000. В 2-х томах | ISBN 3-89821-523-7

11 Николай Бугай (ред.) | Народы стран Балтии в условиях сталинизма (1940-е – 1950-е годы). Документированная история | ISBN 3-89821-525-3

12 Ingmar Bredies (Hrsg.) | Zur Anatomie der Orange Revolution in der Ukraine. Wechsel des Elitenregimes oder Triumph des Parlamentarismus? | ISBN 3-89821-524-5

13 Anastasia V. Mitrofanova | The Politicization of Russian Orthodoxy. Actors and Ideas | With a foreword by William C. Gay | ISBN 3-89821-481-8

14 Nathan D. Larson | Alexander Solzhenitsyn and the Russo-Jewish Question | ISBN 3-89821-483-4

15 Guido Houben | Kulturpolitik und Ethnizität. Staatliche Kunstförderung im Russland der neunziger Jahre | Mit einem Vorwort von Gert Weisskirchen | ISBN 3-89821-542-3

16 Leonid Luks | Der russische „Sonderweg"? Aufsätze zur neuesten Geschichte Russlands im europäischen Kontext | ISBN 3-89821-496-6

17 Евгений Мороз | История «Мёртвой воды» – от страшной сказки к большой политике. Политическое неоязычество в постсоветской России | ISBN 3-89821-551-2

18 Александр Верховский и Галина Кожевникова (ред.) | Этническая и религиозная интолерантность в российских СМИ. Результаты мониторинга 2001-2004 гг. | ISBN 3-89821-569-5

19 Christian Ganzer | Sowjetisches Erbe und ukrainische Nation. Das Museum der Geschichte des Zaporoger Kosakentums auf der Insel Chortycja | Mit einem Vorwort von Frank Golczewski | ISBN 3-89821-504-0

20 Эльза-Баир Гучинова | Помнить нельзя забыть. Антропология депортационной травмы калмыков | С предисловием Кэролайн Хамфри | ISBN 3-89821-506-7

21 Юлия Лидерман | Мотивы «проверки» и «испытания» в постсоветской культуре. Советское прошлое в российском кинематографе 1990-х годов | С предисловием Евгения Марголита | ISBN 3-89821-511-3

22 Tanya Lokshina, Ray Thomas, Mary Mayer (Eds.) | The Imposition of a Fake Political Settlement in the Northern Caucasus. The 2003 Chechen Presidential Election | ISBN 3-89821-436-2

23 Timothy McCajor Hall, Rosie Read (Eds.) | Changes in the Heart of Europe. Recent Ethnographies of Czechs, Slovaks, Roma, and Sorbs | With an afterword by Zdeněk Salzmann | ISBN 3-89821-606-3

24 Christian Autengruber | Die politischen Parteien in Bulgarien und Rumänien. Eine vergleichende Analyse seit Beginn der 90er Jahre | Mit einem Vorwort von Dorothée de Nève | ISBN 3-89821-476-1

25 Annette Freyberg-Inan with Radu Cristescu | The Ghosts in Our Classrooms, or: John Dewey Meets Ceauşescu. The Promise and the Failures of Civic Education in Romania | ISBN 3-89821-416-8

26 John B. Dunlop | The 2002 Dubrovka and 2004 Beslan Hostage Crises. A Critique of Russian Counter-Terrorism | With a foreword by Donald N. Jensen | ISBN 3-89821-608-X

27 Peter Koller | Das touristische Potenzial von Kam''janec'–Podil's'kyj. Eine fremdenverkehrsgeographische Untersuchung der Zukunftsperspektiven und Maßnahmenplanung zur Destinationsentwicklung des „ukrainischen Rothenburg" | Mit einem Vorwort von Kristiane Klemm | ISBN 3-89821-640-3

28 Françoise Daucé, Elisabeth Sieca-Kozlowski (Eds.) | Dedovshchina in the Post-Soviet Military. Hazing of Russian Army Conscripts in a Comparative Perspective | With a foreword by Dale Herspring | ISBN 3-89821-616-0

29 Florian Strasser | Zivilgesellschaftliche Einflüsse auf die Orange Revolution. Die gewaltlose Massenbewegung und die ukrainische Wahlkrise 2004 | Mit einem Vorwort von Egbert Jahn | ISBN 3-89821-648-9

30 Rebecca S. Katz | The Georgian Regime Crisis of 2003-2004. A Case Study in Post-Soviet Media Representation of Politics, Crime and Corruption | ISBN 3-89821-413-3

31 Vladimir Kantor | Willkür oder Freiheit. Beiträge zur russischen Geschichtsphilosophie | Ediert von Dagmar Herrmann sowie mit einem Vorwort versehen von Leonid Luks | ISBN 3-89821-589-X

32 Laura A. Victoir | The Russian Land Estate Today. A Case Study of Cultural Politics in Post-Soviet Russia | With a foreword by Priscilla Roosevelt | ISBN 3-89821-426-5

33 Ivan Katchanovski | Cleft Countries. Regional Political Divisions and Cultures in Post-Soviet Ukraine and Moldova | With a foreword by Francis Fukuyama | ISBN 3-89821-558-X

34 Florian Mühlfried | Postsowjetische Feiern. Das Georgische Bankett im Wandel | Mit einem Vorwort von Kevin Tuite | ISBN 3-89821-601-2

35 Roger Griffin, Werner Loh, Andreas Umland (Eds.) | Fascism Past and Present, West and East. An International Debate on Concepts and Cases in the Comparative Study of the Extreme Right | With an afterword by Walter Laqueur | ISBN 3-89821-674-8

36 Sebastian Schlegel | Der „Weiße Archipel". Sowjetische Atomstädte 1945-1991 | Mit einem Geleitwort von Thomas Bohn | ISBN 3-89821-679-9

37 Vyacheslav Likhachev | Political Anti-Semitism in Post-Soviet Russia. Actors and Ideas in 1991-2003 | Edited and translated from Russian by Eugene Veklerov | ISBN 3-89821-529-6

38 Josette Baer (Ed.) | Preparing Liberty in Central Europe. Political Texts from the Spring of Nations 1848 to the Spring of Prague 1968 | With a foreword by Zdeněk V. David | ISBN 3-89821-546-6

39 Михаил Лукьянов | Российский консерватизм и реформа, 1907-1914 | С предисловием Марка Д. Стейнберга | ISBN 3-89821-503-2

40 Nicola Melloni | Market Without Economy. The 1998 Russian Financial Crisis | With a foreword by Eiji Furukawa | ISBN 3-89821-407-9

41 Dmitrij Chmelnizki | Die Architektur Stalins | Bd. 1: Studien zu Ideologie und Stil | Bd. 2: Bilddokumentation | Mit einem Vorwort von Bruno Flierl | ISBN 3-89821-515-6

42 Katja Yafimava | Post-Soviet Russian-Belarussian Relationships. The Role of Gas Transit Pipelines | With a foreword by Jonathan P. Stern | ISBN 3-89821-655-1

43 Boris Chavkin | Verflechtungen der deutschen und russischen Zeitgeschichte. Aufsätze und Archivfunde zu den Beziehungen Deutschlands und der Sowjetunion von 1917 bis 1991 | Ediert von Markus Edlinger sowie mit einem Vorwort versehen von Leonid Luks | ISBN 3-89821-756-6

44 Anastasija Grynenko in Zusammenarbeit mit Claudia Dathe | Die Terminologie des Gerichtswesens der Ukraine und Deutschlands im Vergleich. Eine übersetzungswissenschaftliche Analyse juristischer Fachbegriffe im Deutschen, Ukrainischen und Russischen | Mit einem Vorwort von Ulrich Hartmann | ISBN 3-89821-691-8

45 Anton Burkov | The Impact of the European Convention on Human Rights on Russian Law. Legislation and Application in 1996-2006 | With a foreword by Françoise Hampson | ISBN 978-3-89821-639-5

46 Stina Torjesen, Indra Overland (Eds.) | International Election Observers in Post-Soviet Azerbaijan. Geopolitical Pawns or Agents of Change? | ISBN 978-3-89821-743-9

47 Taras Kuzio | Ukraine – Crimea – Russia. Triangle of Conflict | ISBN 978-3-89821-761-3

48 Claudia Šabić | „Ich erinnere mich nicht, aber L'viv!" Zur Funktion kultureller Faktoren für die Institutionalisierung und Entwicklung einer ukrainischen Region | Mit einem Vorwort von Melanie Tatur | ISBN 978-3-89821-752-1

49 *Marlies Bilz* | Tatarstan in der Transformation. Nationaler Diskurs und Politische Praxis 1988-1994 | Mit einem Vorwort von Frank Golczewski | ISBN 978-3-89821-722-4

50 *Марлен Ларюэль (ред.)* | Современные интерпретации русского национализма | ISBN 978-3-89821-795-8

51 *Sonja Schüler* | Die ethnische Dimension der Armut. Roma im postsozialistischen Rumänien | Mit einem Vorwort von Anton Sterbling | ISBN 978-3-89821-776-7

52 *Галина Кожевникова* | Радикальный национализм в России и противодействие ему. Сборник докладов Центра «Сова» за 2004-2007 гг. | С предисловием Александра Верховского | ISBN 978-3-89821-721-7

53 *Галина Кожевникова и Владимир Прибыловский* | Российская власть в биографиях I. Высшие должностные лица РФ в 2004 г. | ISBN 978-3-89821-796-5

54 *Галина Кожевникова и Владимир Прибыловский* | Российская власть в биографиях II. Члены Правительства РФ в 2004 г. | ISBN 978-3-89821-797-2

55 *Галина Кожевникова и Владимир Прибыловский* | Российская власть в биографиях III. Руководители федеральных служб и агентств РФ в 2004 г.| ISBN 978-3-89821-798-9

56 *Ileana Petroniu* | Privatisierung in Transformationsökonomien. Determinanten der Restrukturierungs-Bereitschaft am Beispiel Polens, Rumäniens und der Ukraine | Mit einem Vorwort von Rainer W. Schäfer | ISBN 978-3-89821-790-3

57 *Christian Wipperfürth* | Russland und seine GUS-Nachbarn. Hintergründe, aktuelle Entwicklungen und Konflikte in einer ressourcenreichen Region| ISBN 978-3-89821-801-6

58 *Togzhan Kassenova* | From Antagonism to Partnership. The Uneasy Path of the U.S.-Russian Cooperative Threat Reduction | With a foreword by Christoph Bluth | ISBN 978-3-89821-707-1

59 *Alexander Höllwerth* | Das sakrale eurasische Imperium des Aleksandr Dugin. Eine Diskursanalyse zum postsowjetischen russischen Rechtsextremismus | Mit einem Vorwort von Dirk Uffelmann | ISBN 978-3-89821-813-9

60 *Олег Рябов* | «Россия-Матушка». Национализм, гендер и война в России XX века | С предисловием Елены Гощило | ISBN 978-3-89821-487-2

61 *Ivan Maistrenko* | Borot'bism. A Chapter in the History of the Ukrainian Revolution | With a new Introduction by Chris Ford | Translated by George S. N. Luckyj with the assistance of Ivan L. Rudnytsky | Second, Revised and Expanded Edition ISBN 978-3-8382-1107-7

62 *Maryna Romanets* | Anamorphosic Texts and Reconfigured Visions. Improvised Traditions in Contemporary Ukrainian and Irish Literature | ISBN 978-3-89821-576-3

63 *Paul D'Anieri and Taras Kuzio (Eds.)* | Aspects of the Orange Revolution I. Democratization and Elections in Post-Communist Ukraine | ISBN 978-3-89821-698-2

64 *Bohdan Harasymiw in collaboration with Oleh S. Ilnytzkyj (Eds.)* | Aspects of the Orange Revolution II. Information and Manipulation Strategies in the 2004 Ukrainian Presidential Elections | ISBN 978-3-89821-699-9

65 *Ingmar Bredies, Andreas Umland and Valentin Yakushik (Eds.)* | Aspects of the Orange Revolution III. The Context and Dynamics of the 2004 Ukrainian Presidential Elections | ISBN 978-3-89821-803-0

66 *Ingmar Bredies, Andreas Umland and Valentin Yakushik (Eds.)* | Aspects of the Orange Revolution IV. Foreign Assistance and Civic Action in the 2004 Ukrainian Presidential Elections | ISBN 978-3-89821-808-5

67 *Ingmar Bredies, Andreas Umland and Valentin Yakushik (Eds.)* | Aspects of the Orange Revolution V. Institutional Observation Reports on the 2004 Ukrainian Presidential Elections | ISBN 978-3-89821-809-2

68 *Taras Kuzio (Ed.)* | Aspects of the Orange Revolution VI. Post-Communist Democratic Revolutions in Comparative Perspective | ISBN 978-3-89821-820-7

69 *Tim Bohse* | Autoritarismus statt Selbstverwaltung. Die Transformation der kommunalen Politik in der Stadt Kaliningrad 1990-2005 | Mit einem Geleitwort von Stefan Troebst | ISBN 978-3-89821-782-8

70 *David Rupp* | Die Rußländische Föderation und die russischsprachige Minderheit in Lettland. Eine Fallstudie zur Anwaltspolitik Moskaus gegenüber den russophonen Minderheiten im „Nahen Ausland" von 1991 bis 2002 | Mit einem Vorwort von Helmut Wagner | ISBN 978-3-89821-778-1

71 *Taras Kuzio* | Theoretical and Comparative Perspectives on Nationalism. New Directions in Cross-Cultural and Post-Communist Studies | With a foreword by Paul Robert Magocsi | ISBN 978-3-89821-815-3

72 *Christine Teichmann* | Die Hochschultransformation im heutigen Osteuropa. Kontinuität und Wandel bei der Entwicklung des postkommunistischen Universitätswesens | Mit einem Vorwort von Oskar Anweiler | ISBN 978-3-89821-842-9

73 *Julia Kusznir* | Der politische Einfluss von Wirtschaftseliten in russischen Regionen. Eine Analyse am Beispiel der Erdöl- und Erdgasindustrie, 1992-2005 | Mit einem Vorwort von Wolfgang Eichwede | ISBN 978-3-89821-821-4

74 *Alena Vysotskaya* | Russland, Belarus und die EU-Osterweiterung. Zur Minderheitenfrage und zum Problem der Freizügigkeit des Personenverkehrs | Mit einem Vorwort von Katlijn Malfliet | ISBN 978-3-89821-822-1

75 *Heiko Pleines (Hrsg.)* | Corporate Governance in post-sozialistischen Volkswirtschaften | ISBN 978-3-89821-766-8

76 *Stefan Ihrig* | Wer sind die Moldawier? Rumänismus versus Moldowanismus in Historiographie und Schulbüchern der Republik Moldova, 1991-2006 | Mit einem Vorwort von Holm Sundhaussen | ISBN 978-3-89821-466-7

77 *Galina Kozhevnikova in collaboration with Alexander Verkhovsky and Eugene Veklerov* | Ultra-Nationalism and Hate Crimes in Contemporary Russia. The 2004-2006 Annual Reports of Moscow's SOVA Center | With a foreword by Stephen D. Shenfield | ISBN 978-3-89821-868-9

78 *Florian Küchler* | The Role of the European Union in Moldova's Transnistria Conflict | With a foreword by Christopher Hill | ISBN 978-3-89821-850-4

79 *Bernd Rechel* | The Long Way Back to Europe. Minority Protection in Bulgaria | With a foreword by Richard Crampton | ISBN 978-3-89821-863-4

80 *Peter W. Rodgers* | Nation, Region and History in Post-Communist Transitions. Identity Politics in Ukraine, 1991-2006 | With a foreword by Vera Tolz | ISBN 978-3-89821-903-7

81 *Stephanie Solywoda* | The Life and Work of Semen L. Frank. A Study of Russian Religious Philosophy | With a foreword by Philip Walters | ISBN 978-3-89821-457-5

82 *Vera Sokolova* | Cultural Politics of Ethnicity. Discourses on Roma in Communist Czechoslovakia | ISBN 978-3-89821-864-1

83 *Natalya Shevchik Ketenci* | Kazakhstani Enterprises in Transition. The Role of Historical Regional Development in Kazakhstan's Post-Soviet Economic Transformation | ISBN 978-3-89821-831-3

84 *Martin Malek, Anna Schor-Tschudnowskaja (Hgg.)* | Europa im Tschetschenienkrieg. Zwischen politischer Ohnmacht und Gleichgültigkeit | Mit einem Vorwort von Lipchan Basajewa | ISBN 978-3-89821-676-0

85 *Stefan Meister* | Das postsowjetische Universitätswesen zwischen nationalem und internationalem Wandel. Die Entwicklung der regionalen Hochschule in Russland als Gradmesser der Systemtransformation | Mit einem Vorwort von Joan DeBardeleben | ISBN 978-3-89821-891-7

86 *Konstantin Sheiko in collaboration with Stephen Brown* | Nationalist Imaginings of the Russian Past. Anatolii Fomenko and the Rise of Alternative History in Post-Communist Russia | With a foreword by Donald Ostrowski | ISBN 978-3-89821-915-0

87 *Sabine Jenni* | Wie stark ist das „Einige Russland"? Zur Parteibindung der Eliten und zum Wahlerfolg der Machtpartei im Dezember 2007 | Mit einem Vorwort von Klaus Armingeon | ISBN 978-3-89821-961-7

88 *Thomas Borén* | Meeting-Places of Transformation. Urban Identity, Spatial Representations and Local Politics in Post-Soviet St Petersburg | ISBN 978-3-89821-739-2

89 *Aygul Ashirova* | Stalinismus und Stalin-Kult in Zentralasien. Turkmenistan 1924-1953 | Mit einem Vorwort von Leonid Luks | ISBN 978-3-89821-987-7

90 *Leonid Luks* | Freiheit oder imperiale Größe? Essays zu einem russischen Dilemma | ISBN 978-3-8382-0011-8

91 *Christopher Gilley* | The 'Change of Signposts' in the Ukrainian Emigration. A Contribution to the History of Sovietophilism in the 1920s | With a foreword by Frank Golczewski | ISBN 978-3-89821-965-5

92 *Philipp Casula, Jeronim Perovic (Eds.)* | Identities and Politics During the Putin Presidency. The Discursive Foundations of Russia's Stability | With a foreword by Heiko Haumann | ISBN 978-3-8382-0015-6

93 *Marcel Viëtor* | Europa und die Frage nach seinen Grenzen im Osten. Zur Konstruktion ‚europäischer Identität' in Geschichte und Gegenwart | Mit einem Vorwort von Albrecht Lehmann | ISBN 978-3-8382-0045-3

94 *Ben Hellman, Andrei Rogachevskii* | Filming the Unfilmable. Casper Wrede's 'One Day in the Life of Ivan Denisovich' | Second, Revised and Expanded Edition | ISBN 978-3-8382-0044-6

95 *Eva Fuchslocher* | Vaterland, Sprache, Glaube. Orthodoxie und Nationenbildung am Beispiel Georgiens | Mit einem Vorwort von Christina von Braun | ISBN 978-3-89821-884-9

96 *Vladimir Kantor* | Das Westlertum und der Weg Russlands. Zur Entwicklung der russischen Literatur und Philosophie | Ediert von Dagmar Herrmann | Mit einem Beitrag von Nikolaus Lobkowicz | ISBN 978-3-8382-0102-3

97 *Kamran Musayev* | Die postsowjetische Transformation im Baltikum und Südkaukasus. Eine vergleichende Untersuchung der politischen Entwicklung Lettlands und Aserbaidschans 1985-2009 | Mit einem Vorwort von Leonid Luks | Ediert von Sandro Henschel | ISBN 978-3-8382-0103-0

98 *Tatiana Zhurzhenko* | Borderlands into Bordered Lands. Geopolitics of Identity in Post-Soviet Ukraine | With a foreword by Dieter Segert | ISBN 978-3-8382-0042-2

99 *Кирилл Галушко, Лидия Смола (ред.)* | Пределы падения – варианты украинского будущего. Аналитико-прогностические исследования | ISBN 978-3-8382-0148-1

100 *Michael Minkenberg (Ed.)* | Historical Legacies and the Radical Right in Post-Cold War Central and Eastern Europe | With an afterword by Sabrina P. Ramet | ISBN 978-3-8382-0124-5

101 *David-Emil Wickström* | Rocking St. Petersburg. Transcultural Flows and Identity Politics in the St. Petersburg Popular Music Scene | With a foreword by Yngvar B. Steinholt | Second, Revised and Expanded Edition | ISBN 978-3-8382-0100-9

102 *Eva Zabka* | Eine neue „Zeit der Wirren"? Der spät- und postsowjetische Systemwandel 1985-2000 im Spiegel russischer gesellschaftspolitischer Diskurse | Mit einem Vorwort von Margareta Mommsen | ISBN 978-3-8382-0161-0

103 *Ulrike Ziemer* | Ethnic Belonging, Gender and Cultural Practices. Youth Identitites in Contemporary Russia | With a foreword by Anoop Nayak | ISBN 978-3-8382-0152-8

104 *Ksenia Chepikova* | ‚Einiges Russland' - eine zweite KPdSU? Aspekte der Identitätskonstruktion einer postsowjetischen „Partei der Macht" | Mit einem Vorwort von Torsten Oppelland | ISBN 978-3-8382-0311-9

105 *Леонид Люкс* | Западничество или евразийство? Демократия или идеократия? Сборник статей об исторических дилеммах России | С предисловием Владимира Кантора | ISBN 978-3-8382-0211-2

106 *Anna Dost* | Das russische Verfassungsrecht auf dem Weg zum Föderalismus und zurück. Zum Konflikt von Rechtsnormen und -wirklichkeit in der Russländischen Föderation von 1991 bis 2009 | Mit einem Vorwort von Alexander Blankenagel | ISBN 978-3-8382-0292-1

107 *Philipp Herzog* | Sozialistische Völkerfreundschaft, nationaler Widerstand oder harmloser Zeitvertreib? Zur politischen Funktion der Volkskunst im sowjetischen Estland | Mit einem Vorwort von Andreas Kappeler | ISBN 978-3-8382-0216-7

108 *Marlène Laruelle (Ed.)* | Russian Nationalism, Foreign Policy, and Identity Debates in Putin's Russia. New Ideological Patterns after the Orange Revolution | ISBN 978-3-8382-0325-6

109 *Michail Logvinov* | Russlands Kampf gegen den internationalen Terrorismus. Eine kritische Bestandsaufnahme des Bekämpfungsansatzes | Mit einem Geleitwort von Hans-Henning Schröder und einem Vorwort von Eckhard Jesse | ISBN 978-3-8382-0329-4

110 *John B. Dunlop* | The Moscow Bombings of September 1999. Examinations of Russian Terrorist Attacks at the Onset of Vladimir Putin's Rule | Second, Revised and Expanded Edition | ISBN 978-3-8382-0388-1

111 *Андрей А. Ковалёв* | Свидетельство из-за кулис российской политики I. Можно ли делать добро из зла? (Воспоминания и размышления о последних советских и первых постсоветских годах) | With a foreword by Peter Reddaway | ISBN 978-3-8382-0302-7

112 *Андрей А. Ковалёв* | Свидетельство из-за кулис российской политики II. Угроза для себя и окружающих (Наблюдения и предостережения относительно происходящего после 2000 г.) | ISBN 978-3-8382-0303-4

113 *Bernd Kappenberg* | Zeichen setzen für Europa. Der Gebrauch europäischer lateinischer Sonderzeichen in der deutschen Öffentlichkeit | Mit einem Vorwort von Peter Schlobinski | ISBN 978-3-89821-749-1

114 *Ivo Mijnssen* | The Quest for an Ideal Youth in Putin's Russia I. Back to Our Future! History, Modernity, and Patriotism according to Nashi, 2005-2013 | With a foreword by Jeronim Perović | Second, Revised and Expanded Edition | ISBN 978-3-8382-0368-3

115 *Jussi Lassila* | The Quest for an Ideal Youth in Putin's Russia II. The Search for Distinctive Conformism in the Political Communication of Nashi, 2005-2009 | With a foreword by Kirill Postoutenko | Second, Revised and Expanded Edition | ISBN 978-3-8382-0415-4

116 *Valerio Trabandt* | Neue Nachbarn, gute Nachbarschaft? Die EU als internationaler Akteur am Beispiel ihrer Demokratieförderung in Belarus und der Ukraine 2004-2009 | Mit einem Vorwort von Jutta Joachim | ISBN 978-3-8382-0437-6

117 *Fabian Pfeiffer* | Estlands Außen- und Sicherheitspolitik I. Der estnische Atlantizismus nach der wiedererlangten Unabhängigkeit 1991-2004 | Mit einem Vorwort von Helmut Hubel | ISBN 978-3-8382-0127-6

118 *Jana Podßuweit* | Estlands Außen- und Sicherheitspolitik II. Handlungsoptionen eines Kleinstaates im Rahmen seiner EU-Mitgliedschaft (2004-2008) | Mit einem Vorwort von Helmut Hubel | ISBN 978-3-8382-0440-6

119 *Karin Pointner* | Estlands Außen- und Sicherheitspolitik III. Eine gedächtnispolitische Analyse estnischer Entwicklungskooperation 2006-2010 | Mit einem Vorwort von Karin Liebhart | ISBN 978-3-8382-0435-7

120 *Ruslana Vovk* | Die Offenheit der ukrainischen Verfassung für das Völkerrecht und die europäische Integration | Mit einem Vorwort von Alexander Blankenagel | ISBN 978-3-8382-0481-9

121 *Mykhaylo Banakh* | Die Relevanz der Zivilgesellschaft bei den postkommunistischen Transformationsprozessen in mittel- und osteuropäischen Ländern. Das Beispiel der spät- und postsowjetischen Ukraine 1986-2009 | Mit einem Vorwort von Gerhard Simon | ISBN 978-3-8382-0499-4

122 *Michael Moser* | Language Policy and the Discourse on Languages in Ukraine under President Viktor Yanukovych (25 February 2010–28 October 2012) | ISBN 978-3-8382-0497-0 (Paperback edition) | ISBN 978-3-8382-0507-6 (Hardcover edition)

123 *Nicole Krome* | Russischer Netzwerkkapitalismus Restrukturierungsprozesse in der Russischen Föderation am Beispiel des Luftfahrtunternehmens „Aviastar" | Mit einem Vorwort von Petra Stykow | ISBN 978-3-8382-0534-2

124 *David R. Marples* | 'Our Glorious Past'. Lukashenka's Belarus and the Great Patriotic War | ISBN 978-3-8382-0574-8 (Paperback edition) | ISBN 978-3-8382-0675-2 (Hardcover edition)

125 *Ulf Walther* | Russlands „neuer Adel". Die Macht des Geheimdienstes von Gorbatschow bis Putin | Mit einem Vorwort von Hans-Georg Wieck | ISBN 978-3-8382-0584-7

126 *Simon Geissbühler (Hrsg.)* | Kiew – Revolution 3.0. Der Euromaidan 2013/14 und die Zukunftsperspektiven der Ukraine | ISBN 978-3-8382-0581-6 (Paperback edition) | ISBN 978-3-8382-0681-3 (Hardcover edition)

127 *Andrey Makarychev* | Russia and the EU in a Multipolar World. Discourses, Identities, Norms | With a foreword by Klaus Segbers | ISBN 978-3-8382-0629-5

128 *Roland Scharff* | Kasachstan als postsowjetischer Wohlfahrtsstaat. Die Transformation des sozialen Schutzsystems | Mit einem Vorwort von Joachim Ahrens | ISBN 978-3-8382-0622-6

129 *Katja Grupp* | Bild Lücke Deutschland. Kaliningrader Studierende sprechen über Deutschland | Mit einem Vorwort von Martin Schulz | ISBN 978-3-8382-0552-6

130 *Konstantin Sheiko, Stephen Brown* | History as Therapy. Alternative History and Nationalist Imaginings in Russia, 1991-2014 | ISBN 978-3-8382-0665-3

131 *Elisa Kriza* | Alexander Solzhenitsyn: Cold War Icon, Gulag Author, Russian Nationalist? A Study of the Western Reception of his Literary Writings, Historical Interpretations, and Political Ideas | With a foreword by Andrei Rogatchevski | ISBN 978-3-8382-0589-2 (Paperback edition) | ISBN 978-3-8382-0690-5 (Hardcover edition)

132 *Serghei Golunov* | The Elephant in the Room. Corruption and Cheating in Russian Universities | ISBN 978-3-8382-0570-0

133 *Manja Hussner, Rainer Arnold (Hgg.)* | Verfassungsgerichtsbarkeit in Zentralasien I. Sammlung von Verfassungstexten | ISBN 978-3-8382-0595-3

134 *Nikolay Mitrokhin* | Die „Russische Partei". Die Bewegung der russischen Nationalisten in der UdSSR 1953-1985 | Aus dem Russischen übertragen von einem Übersetzerteam unter der Leitung von Larisa Schippel | ISBN 978-3-8382-0024-8

135 *Manja Hussner, Rainer Arnold (Hgg.)* | Verfassungsgerichtsbarkeit in Zentralasien II. Sammlung von Verfassungstexten | ISBN 978-3-8382-0597-7

136 *Manfred Zeller* | Das sowjetische Fieber. Fußballfans im poststalinistischen Vielvölkerreich | Mit einem Vorwort von Nikolaus Katzer | ISBN 978-3-8382-0757-5

137 *Kristin Schreiter* | Stellung und Entwicklungspotential zivilgesellschaftlicher Gruppen in Russland. Menschenrechtsorganisationen im Vergleich | ISBN 978-3-8382-0673-8

138 *David R. Marples, Frederick V. Mills (Eds.)* | Ukraine's Euromaidan. Analyses of a Civil Revolution | ISBN 978-3-8382-0660-8

139 *Bernd Kappenberg* | Setting Signs for Europe. Why Diacritics Matter for European Integration | With a foreword by Peter Schlobinski | ISBN 978-3-8382-0663-9

140 *René Lenz* | Internationalisierung, Kooperation und Transfer. Externe bildungspolitische Akteure in der Russischen Föderation | Mit einem Vorwort von Frank Ettrich | ISBN 978-3-8382-0751-3

141 *Juri Plusnin, Yana Zausaeva, Natalia Zhidkevich, Artemy Pozanenko* | Wandering Workers. Mores, Behavior, Way of Life, and Political Status of Domestic Russian Labor Migrants | Translated by Julia Kazantseva | ISBN 978-3-8382-0653-0

142 *David J. Smith (Eds.)* | Latvia – A Work in Progress? 100 Years of State- and Nation-Building | ISBN 978-3-8382-0648-6

143 *Инна Чувычкина (ред.)* | Экспортные нефте- и газопроводы на постсоветском пространстве. Анализ трубопроводной политики в свете теории международных отношений | ISBN 978-3-8382-0822-0

144 *Johann Zajaczkowski* | Russland – eine pragmatische Großmacht? Eine rollentheoretische Untersuchung russischer Außenpolitik am Beispiel der Zusammenarbeit mit den USA nach 9/11 und des Georgienkrieges von 2008 | Mit einem Vorwort von Siegfried Schieder | ISBN 978-3-8382-0837-4

145 *Boris Popivanov* | Changing Images of the Left in Bulgaria. The Challenge of Post-Communism in the Early 21st Century | ISBN 978-3-8382-0667-7

146 *Lenka Krátká* | A History of the Czechoslovak Ocean Shipping Company 1948-1989. How a Small, Landlocked Country Ran Maritime Business During the Cold War | ISBN 978-3-8382-0666-0

147 *Alexander Sergunin* | Explaining Russian Foreign Policy Behavior. Theory and Practice | ISBN 978-3-8382-0752-0

148 *Darya Malyutina* | Migrant Friendships in a Super-Diverse City. Russian-Speakers and their Social Relationships in London in the 21st Century | With a foreword by Claire Dwyer | ISBN 978-3-8382-0652-3

149 *Alexander Sergunin, Valery Konyshev* | Russia in the Arctic. Hard or Soft Power? | ISBN 978-3-8382-0753-7

150 *John J. Maresca* | Helsinki Revisited. A Key U.S. Negotiator's Memoirs on the Development of the CSCE into the OSCE | With a foreword by Hafiz Pashayev | ISBN 978-3-8382-0852-7

151 *Jardar Østbø* | The New Third Rome. Readings of a Russian Nationalist Myth | With a foreword by Pål Kolstø | ISBN 978-3-8382-0870-1

152 *Simon Kordonsky* | Socio-Economic Foundations of the Russian Post-Soviet Regime. The Resource-Based Economy and Estate-Based Social Structure of Contemporary Russia | With a foreword by Svetlana Barsukova | ISBN 978-3-8382-0775-9

153 *Duncan Leitch* | Assisting Reform in Post-Communist Ukraine 2000–2012. The Illusions of Donors and the Disillusion of Beneficiaries | With a foreword by Kataryna Wolczuk | ISBN 978-3-8382-0844-2

154 *Abel Polese* | Limits of a Post-Soviet State. How Informality Replaces, Renegotiates, and Reshapes Governance in Contemporary Ukraine | With a foreword by Colin Williams | ISBN 978-3-8382-0845-9

155 *Mikhail Suslov (Ed.)* | Digital Orthodoxy in the Post-Soviet World. The Russian Orthodox Church and Web 2.0 | With a foreword by Father Cyril Hovorun | ISBN 978-3-8382-0871-8

156 *Leonid Luks* | Zwei „Sonderwege"? Russisch-deutsche Parallelen und Kontraste (1917-2014). Vergleichende Essays | ISBN 978-3-8382-0823-7

157 *Vladimir V. Karacharovskiy, Ovsey I. Shkaratan, Gordey A. Yastrebov* | Towards a New Russian Work Culture. Can Western Companies and Expatriates Change Russian Society? | With a foreword by Elena N. Danilova | Translated by Julia Kazantseva | ISBN 978-3-8382-0902-9

158 *Edmund Griffiths* | Aleksandr Prokhanov and Post-Soviet Esotericism | ISBN 978-3-8382-0903-6

159 *Timm Beichelt, Susann Worschech (Eds.)* | Transnational Ukraine? Networks and Ties that Influence(d) Contemporary Ukraine | ISBN 978-3-8382-0944-9

160 *Mieste Hotopp-Riecke* | Die Tataren der Krim zwischen Assimilation und Selbstbehauptung. Der Aufbau des krimtatarischen Bildungswesens nach Deportation und Heimkehr (1990-2005) | Mit einem Vorwort von Swetlana Czerwonnaja | ISBN 978-3-89821-940-2

161 *Olga Bertelsen (Ed.)* | Revolution and War in Contemporary Ukraine. The Challenge of Change | ISBN 978-3-8382-1016-2

162 *Natalya Ryabinska* | Ukraine's Post-Communist Mass Media. Between Capture and Commercialization | With a foreword by Marta Dyczok | ISBN 978-3-8382-1011-7

163 *Alexandra Cotofana, James M. Nyce (Eds.)* | Religion and Magic in Socialist and Post-Socialist Contexts. Historic and Ethnographic Case Studies of Orthodoxy, Heterodoxy, and Alternative Spirituality | With a foreword by Patrick L. Michelson | ISBN 978-3-8382-0989-0

164 *Nozima Akhrarkhodjaeva* | The Instrumentalisation of Mass Media in Electoral Authoritarian Regimes. Evidence from Russia's Presidential Election Campaigns of 2000 and 2008 | ISBN 978-3-8382-1013-1

165 *Yulia Krasheninnikova* | Informal Healthcare in Contemporary Russia. Sociographic Essays on the Post-Soviet Infrastructure for Alternative Healing Practices | ISBN 978-3-8382-0970-8

166 *Peter Kaiser* | Das Schachbrett der Macht. Die Handlungsspielräume eines sowjetischen Funktionärs unter Stalin am Beispiel des Generalsekretärs des Komsomol Aleksandr Kosarev (1929-1938) | Mit einem Vorwort von Dietmar Neutatz | ISBN 978-3-8382-1052-0

167 *Oksana Kim* | The Effects and Implications of Kazakhstan's Adoption of International Financial Reporting Standards. A Resource Dependence Perspective | With a foreword by Svetlana Vlady | ISBN 978-3-8382-0987-6

168 *Anna Sanina* | Patriotic Education in Contemporary Russia. Sociological Studies in the Making of the Post-Soviet Citizen | With a foreword by Anna Oldfield | ISBN 978-3-8382-0993-7

169 *Rudolf Wolters* | Spezialist in Sibirien Faksimile der 1933 erschienenen ersten Ausgabe | Mit einem Vorwort von Dmitrij Chmelnizki | ISBN 978-3-8382-0515-1

170 *Michal Vít, Magdalena M. Baran (Eds.)* | Transregional versus National Perspectives on Contemporary Central European History. Studies on the Building of Nation-States and Their Cooperation in the 20th and 21st Century | With a foreword by Petr Vágner | ISBN 978-3-8382-1015-5

171 *Philip Gamaghelyan* | Conflict Resolution Beyond the International Relations Paradigm. Evolving Designs as a Transformative Practice in Nagorno-Karabakh and Syria | With a foreword by Susan Allen | ISBN 978-3-8382-1057-5

172 *Maria Shagina* | Joining a Prestigious Club. Cooperation with Europarties and Its Impact on Party Development in Georgia, Moldova, and Ukraine 2004–2015 | With a foreword by Kataryna Wolczuk | ISBN 978-3-8382-1084-1

173 *Alexandra Cotofana, James M. Nyce (Eds.)* | Religion and Magic in Socialist and Post-Socialist Contexts II. Baltic, Eastern European, and Post-USSR Case Studies | With a foreword by Anita Stasulane | ISBN 978-3-8382-0990-6

174 *Barbara Kunz* | Kind Words, Cruise Missiles, and Everything in Between. The Use of Power Resources in U.S. Policies towards Poland, Ukraine, and Belarus 1989–2008 | With a foreword by William Hill | ISBN 978-3-8382-1065-0

175 *Eduard Klein* | Bildungskorruption in Russland und der Ukraine. Eine komparative Analyse der Performanz staatlicher Antikorruptionsmaßnahmen im Hochschulsektor am Beispiel universitärer Aufnahmeprüfungen | Mit einem Vorwort von Heiko Pleines | ISBN 978-3-8382-0995-1

176 *Markus Soldner* | Politischer Kapitalismus im postsowjetischen Russland. Die politische, wirtschaftliche und mediale Transformation in den 1990er Jahren | Mit einem Vorwort von Wolfgang Ismayr | ISBN 978-3-8382-1222-7

177 *Anton Oleinik* | Building Ukraine from Within. A Sociological, Institutional, and Economic Analysis of a Nation-State in the Making | ISBN 978-3-8382-1150-3

178 *Peter Rollberg, Marlene Laruelle (Eds.)* | Mass Media in the Post-Soviet World. Market Forces, State Actors, and Political Manipulation in the Informational Environment after Communism | ISBN 978-3-8382-1116-9

179 *Mikhail Minakov* | Development and Dystopia. Studies in Post-Soviet Ukraine and Eastern Europe | With a foreword by Alexander Etkind | ISBN 978-3-8382-1112-1

180 *Aijan Sharshenova* | The European Union's Democracy Promotion in Central Asia. A Study of Political Interests, Influence, and Development in Kazakhstan and Kyrgyzstan in 2007–2013 | With a foreword by Gordon Crawford | ISBN 978-3-8382-1151-0

181 *Andrey Makarychev, Alexandra Yatsyk (Eds.)* | Boris Nemtsov and Russian Politics. Power and Resistance | With a foreword by Zhanna Nemtsova | ISBN 978-3-8382-1122-0

182 *Sophie Falsini* | The Euromaidan's Effect on Civil Society. Why and How Ukrainian Social Capital Increased after the Revolution of Dignity | With a foreword by Susann Worschech | ISBN 978-3-8382-1131-2

183 *Valentyna Romanova, Andreas Umland (Eds.)* | Ukraine's Decentralization. Challenges and Implications of the Local Governance Reform after the Euromaidan Revolution | ISBN 978-3-8382-1162-6

184 *Leonid Luks* | A Fateful Triangle. Essays on Contemporary Russian, German and Polish History | ISBN 978-3-8382-1143-5

185 *John B. Dunlop* | The February 2015 Assassination of Boris Nemtsov and the Flawed Trial of his Alleged Killers. An Exploration of Russia's "Crime of the 21st Century" | ISBN 978-3-8382-1188-7

186 *Vasile Rotaru* | Russia, the EU, and the Eastern Partnership. Building Bridges or Digging Trenches? | ISBN 978-3-8382-1134-3

187 *Marina Lebedeva* | Russian Studies of International Relations. From the Soviet Past to the Post-Cold-War Present | With a foreword by Andrei P. Tsygankov | ISBN 978-3-8382-0851-0

188 *Tomasz Stępniewski, George Soroka (Eds.)* | Ukraine after Maidan. Revisiting Domestic and Regional Security | ISBN 978-3-8382-1075-9

189 *Petar Cholakov* | Ethnic Entrepreneurs Unmasked. Political Institutions and Ethnic Conflicts in Contemporary Bulgaria | ISBN 978-3-8382-1189-3

190 *A. Salem, G. Hazeldine, D. Morgan (Eds.)* | Higher Education in Post-Communist States. Comparative and Sociological Perspectives | ISBN 978-3-8382-1183-1

191 *Igor Torbakov* | After Empire. Nationalist Imagination and Symbolic Politics in Russia and Eurasia in the Twentieth and Twenty-First Century | With a foreword by Serhii Plokhy | ISBN 978-3-8382-1217-3

192 *Aleksandr Burakovskiy* | Jewish-Ukrainian Relations in Late and Post-Soviet Ukraine. Articles, Lectures and Essays from 1986 to 2016 | ISBN 978-3-8382-1210-4

193 *Natalia Shapovalova, Olga Burlyuk (Eds.)* | Civil Society in Post-Euromaidan Ukraine. From Revolution to Consolidation | With a foreword by Richard Youngs | ISBN 978-3-8382-1216-6

194 *Franz Preissler* | Positionsverteidigung, Imperialismus oder Irredentismus? Russland und die „Russischsprachigen", 1991–2015 | ISBN 978-3-8382-1262-3

195 *Marian Madeła* | Der Reformprozess in der Ukraine 2014-2017. Eine Fallstudie zur Reform der öffentlichen Verwaltung | Mit einem Vorwort von Martin Malek | ISBN 978-3-8382-1266-1

196 *Anke Giesen* | „Wie kann denn der Sieger ein Verbrecher sein?" Eine diskursanalytische Untersuchung der russlandweiten Debatte über Konzept und Verstaatlichungsprozess der Lagergedenkstätte „Perm'-36" im Ural | ISBN 978-3-8382-1284-5

197 *Alla Leukavets* | The Integration Policies of Belarus and Ukraine vis-à-vis the EU and Russia. A Comparative Case Study Through the Prism of a Two-Level Game Approach | ISBN 978-3-8382-1247-0

198 *Oksana Kim* | The Development and Challenges of Russian Corporate Governance I. The Roles and Functions of Boards of Directors | With a foreword by Sheila M. Puffer | ISBN 978-3-8382-1287-6

199 *Thomas D. Grant* | International Law and the Post-Soviet Space I. Essays on Chechnya and the Baltic States | With a foreword by Stephen M. Schwebel | ISBN 978-3-8382-1279-1

200 *Thomas D. Grant* | International Law and the Post-Soviet Space II. Essays on Ukraine, Intervention, and Non-Proliferation | ISBN 978-3-8382-1280-7

201 *Slavomír Michálek, Michal Štefansky* | The Age of Fear. The Cold War and Its Influence on Czechoslovakia 1945–1968 | ISBN 978-3-8382-1285-2

202 *Iulia-Sabina Joja* | Romania's Strategic Culture 1990–2014. Continuity and Change in a Post-Communist Country's Evolution of National Interests and Security Policies | With a foreword by Heiko Biehl | ISBN 978-3-8382-1286-9

203 *Andrei Rogatchevski, Yngvar B. Steinholt, Arve Hansen, David-Emil Wickström* | War of Songs. Popular Music and Recent Russia-Ukraine Relations | With a foreword by Artemy Troitsky | ISBN 978-3-8382-1173-2

204 *Maria Lipman (Ed.)* | Russian Voices on Post-Crimea Russia. An Almanac of Counterpoint Essays from 2015–2018 | ISBN 978-3-8382-1251-7

205 *Ksenia Maksimovtsova* | Language Conflicts in Contemporary Estonia, Latvia, and Ukraine. A Comparative Exploration of Discourses in Post-Soviet Russian-Language Digital Media | With a foreword by Ammon Cheskin | ISBN 978-3-8382-1282-1

206 *Michal Vít* | The EU's Impact on Identity Formation in East-Central Europe between 2004 and 2013. Perceptions of the Nation and Europe in Political Parties of the Czech Republic, Poland, and Slovakia | With a foreword by Andrea Pető | ISBN 978-3-8382-1275-3

207 *Per A. Rudling* | Tarnished Heroes. The Organization of Ukrainian Nationalists in the Memory Politics of Post-Soviet Ukraine | ISBN 978-3-8382-0999-9

208 *Kaja Gadowska, Peter Solomon (Eds.)* | Legal Change in Post-Communist States. Progress, Reversions, Explanations | ISBN 978-3-8382-1312-5

209 *Pawel Kowal, Georges Mink, Iwona Reichardt (Eds.)* | Three Revolutions: Mobilization and Change in Contemporary Ukraine I. Theoretical Aspects and Analyses on Religion, Memory, and Identity | ISBN 978-3-8382-1321-7

210 *Pawel Kowal, Georges Mink, Adam Reichardt, Iwona Reichardt (Eds.)* | Three Revolutions: Mobilization and Change in Contemporary Ukraine II. An Oral History of the Revolution on Granite, Orange Revolution, and Revolution of Dignity | ISBN 978-3-8382-1323-1

211 *Li Bennich-Björkman, Sergiy Kurbatov (Eds.)* | When the Future Came. The Collapse of the USSR and the Emergence of National Memory in Post-Soviet History Textbooks | ISBN 978-3-8382-1335-4

212 *Olga R. Gulina* | Migration as a (Geo-)Political Challenge in the Post-Soviet Space. Border Regimes, Policy Choices, Visa Agendas | With a foreword by Nils Muižnieks | ISBN 978-3-8382-1338-5

213 *Sanna Turoma, Kaarina Aitamurto, Slobodanka Vladiv-Glover (Eds.)* | Religion, Expression, and Patriotism in Russia. Essays on Post-Soviet Society and the State. ISBN 978-3-8382-1346-0

214 *Vasif Huseynov* | Geopolitical Rivalries in the "Common Neighborhood". Russia's Conflict with the West, Soft Power, and Neoclassical Realism | With a foreword by Nicholas Ross Smith | ISBN 978-3-8382-1277-7

215 *Mikhail Suslov* | Geopolitical Imagination. Ideology and Utopia in Post-Soviet Russia | With a foreword by Mark Bassin | ISBN 978-3-8382-1361-3

216 Alexander Etkind, Mikhail Minakov (Eds.) | Ideology after Union. Political Doctrines, Discourses, and Debates in Post-Soviet Societies | ISBN 978-3-8382-1388-0

217 Jakob Mischke, Oleksandr Zabirko (Hgg.) | Protestbewegungen im langen Schatten des Kreml. Aufbruch und Resignation in Russland und der Ukraine | ISBN 978-3-8382-0926-5

218 Oksana Huss | How Corruption and Anti-Corruption Policies Sustain Hybrid Regimes. Strategies of Political Domination under Ukraine's Presidents in 1994-2014 | With a foreword by Tobias Debiel and Andrea Gawrich | ISBN 978-3-8382-1430-6

219 Dmitry Travin, Vladimir Gel'man, Otar Marganiya | The Russian Path. Ideas, Interests, Institutions, Illusions | With a foreword by Vladimir Ryzhkov | ISBN 978-3-8382-1421-4

220 Gergana Dimova | Political Uncertainty. A Comparative Exploration | With a foreword by Todor Yalamov and Rumena Filipova | ISBN 978-3-8382-1385-9

221 Torben Waschke | Russland in Transition. Geopolitik zwischen Raum, Identität und Machtinteressen | Mit einem Vorwort von Andreas Dittmann | ISBN 978-3-8382-1480-1

222 Steven Jobbitt, Zsolt Bottlik, Marton Berki (Eds.) | Power and Identity in the Post-Soviet Realm. Geographies of Ethnicity and Nationality after 1991 | ISBN 978-3-8382-1399-6

223 Daria Buteiko | Erinnerungsort. Ort des Gedenkens, der Erholung oder der Einkehr? Kommunismus-Erinnerung am Beispiel der Gedenkstätte Berliner Mauer sowie des Soloveckij-Klosters und -Museumsparks | ISBN 978-3-8382-1367-5

224 Olga Bertelsen (Ed.) | Russian Active Measures. Yesterday, Today, Tomorrow | With a foreword by Jan Goldman | ISBN 978-3-8382-1529-7

225 David Mandel | "Optimizing" Higher Education in Russia. University Teachers and their Union "Universitetskaya solidarnost'" | ISBN 978-3-8382-1519-8

226 Mikhail Minakov, Gwendolyn Sasse, Daria Isachenko (Eds.) | Post-Soviet Secessionism. Nation-Building and State-Failure after Communism | ISBN 978-3-8382-1538-9

227 Jakob Hauter (Ed.) | Civil War? Interstate War? Hybrid War? Dimensions and Interpretations of the Donbas Conflict in 2014–2020 | With a foreword by Andrew Wilson | ISBN 978-3-8382-1383-5

228 Tima T. Moldogaziev, Gene A. Brewer, J. Edward Kellough (Eds.) | Public Policy and Politics in Georgia. Lessons from Post-Soviet Transition | With a foreword by Dan Durning | ISBN 978-3-8382-1535-8

229 Oxana Schmies (Ed.) | NATO's Enlargement and Russia. A Strategic Challenge in the Past and Future | With a foreword by Vladimir Kara-Murza | ISBN 978-3-8382-1478-8

230 Christopher Ford | Ukapisme – Une Gauche perdue. Le marxisme anti-colonial dans la révolution ukrainienne 1917-1925 | Avec une préface de Vincent Présumey | ISBN 978-3-8382-0899-2

231 Anna Kutkina | Between Lenin and Bandera. Decommunization and Multivocality in Post-Euromaidan Ukraine | With a foreword by Juri Mykkänen | ISBN 978-3-8382-1506-8

232 Lincoln E. Flake | Defending the Faith. The Russian Orthodox Church and the Demise of Religious Pluralism | With a foreword by Peter Martland | ISBN 978-3-8382-1378-1

233 Nikoloz Samkharadze | Russia's Recognition of the Independence of Abkhazia and South Ossetia. Analysis of a Deviant Case in Moscow's Foreign Policy | With a foreword by Neil MacFarlane | ISBN 978-3-8382-1414-6

234 Arve Hansen | Urban Protest. A Spatial Perspective on Kyiv, Minsk, and Moscow | With a foreword by Julie Wilhelmsen | ISBN 978-3-8382-1495-5

235 Eleonora Narvselius, Julie Fedor (Eds.) | Diversity in the East-Central European Borderlands. Memories, Cityscapes, People | ISBN 978-3-8382-1523-5

236 Regina Elsner | The Russian Orthodox Church and Modernity. A Historical and Theological Investigation into Eastern Christianity between Unity and Plurality | With a foreword by Mikhail Suslov | ISBN 978-3-8382-1568-6

237 Bo Petersson | The Putin Predicament. Problems of Legitimacy and Succession in Russia | With a foreword by J. Paul Goode | ISBN 978-3-8382-1050-6

238 Jonathan Otto Pohl | The Years of Great Silence. The Deportation, Special Settlement, and Mobilization into the Labor Army of Ethnic Germans in the USSR, 1941–1955 | ISBN 978-3-8382-1630-0

239 Mikhail Minakov (Ed.) | Inventing Majorities. Ideological Creativity in Post-Soviet Societies | ISBN 978-3-8382-1641-6

240 Robert M. Cutler | Soviet and Post-Soviet Foreign Policies I. East-South Relations and the Political Economy of the Communist Bloc, 1971–1991 | With a foreword by Roger E. Kanet | ISBN 978-3-8382-1654-6

241 *Izabella Agardi* | On the Verge of History. Life Stories of Rural Women from Serbia, Romania, and Hungary, 1920–2020 | With a foreword by Andrea Pető | ISBN 978-3-8382-1602-7

242 *Martin Malek, Sebastian Schäffer (Eds.)* | Ukraine in Central and Eastern Europe. Kyiv's Foreign Affairs and the International Relations of the Post-Communist Region | With a foreword by Pavlo Klimkin | ISBN 978-3-8382-1615-7

243 *Volodymyr Dubrovskyi, Kalman Mizsei, Mychailo Wynnyckyj (Eds.)* | Eight Years after the Revolution of Dignity. What Has Changed in Ukraine during 2013–2021? | With a foreword by Yaroslav Hrytsak | ISBN 978-3-8382-1560-0

244 *Rumena Filipova* | Constructing the Limits of Europe. Identity and Foreign Policy in Poland, Bulgaria, and Russia since 1989 | With forewords by Harald Wydra and Gergana Yankova-Dimova | ISBN 978-3-8382-1649-2

245 *Oleksandra Keudel* | How Patronal Networks Shape Opportunities for Local Citizen Participation in a Hybrid Regime. A Comparative Analysis of Five Cities in Ukraine | With a foreword by Sabine Kropp | ISBN 978-3-8382-1671-3

246 *Jan Claas Behrends, Thomas Lindenberger, Pavel Kolar (Eds.)* | Violence after Stalin. Institutions, Practices, and Everyday Life in the Soviet Bloc 1953–1989 | ISBN 978-3-8382-1637-9

247 *Leonid Luks* | Macht und Ohnmacht der Utopien Essays zur Geschichte Russlands im 20. und 21. Jahrhundert | ISBN 978-3-8382-1677-5

ibidem.eu